The
Story
of the
Noncommissioned
Officer Corps

The NCO, *Adam Glenday, 1990*

The Story of the Noncommissioned Officer Corps

The Backbone of the Army

David W. Hogan, Jr.
Arnold G. Fisch, Jr.
Robert K. Wright, Jr.

General Editors

Center of Military History
United States Army
Washington, D.C., 2010

U.S. Army Center of Military History

Brig. Gen. John S. Brown, Chief of Military History

Chief Historian
Chief, Histories Division
Editor in Chief

Jeffrey J. Clarke
Richard W. Stewart
John W. Elsberg

Library of Congress Cataloging-in-Publication Data

The story of the noncommissioned officer corps : the backbone of the Army / David W. Hogan, Jr., Arnold G. Fisch, Jr., Robert K. Wright, Jr., general editors.—Rev. ed.
    p. cm.
  Includes bibliographical references.
    1. United States. Army—Non-commissioned officers—History. I. Hogan, David W., 1958– II. Fisch, Arnold G. III. Wright, Robert K., 1946–

UB408.5.S76 2003
355.3'38—dc21

2003043520

Revised Edition—CMH Pub 70–38

For sale by the Superintendent of Documents, U.S. Government Printing Office
Internet: bookstore.gpo.gov Phone: toll free (866) 512-1800; DC area (202) 512-1800
Fax: (202) 512-2104 Mail: Stop IDCC, Washington, DC 20402-0001

ISBN 978-0-16-067868-4

FOREWORD

This volume originally appeared in 1989 as part of the U.S. Army's commemoration of The Year of the NCO. The purpose was to capture the history of the noncommissioned officer—a rich history that continues to evolve. Today's generation of NCOs and Soldiers is the Next Greatest Generation. With the fall of the Berlin Wall on 9 November 1989, the Cold War came to an end because of the model democratic government the Greatest Generation helped stand up after World War II in Germany. That model democratic society contributed to lowering the Iron Curtain and served as an example to countries that have since become democracies and members of the European Union. Fast forward to what our Next Greatest Generation is doing today in the Middle East, where they are cultivating democratic societies that in turn will serve as role models for their neighbors. Our Soldiers are answering the call to duty, giving freedom and stability to our world, just as the Greatest Generation did after World War II. Although our Army today is, in many respects, a very different force than the Army of 1989 or 1945, many things stay the same. Our Soldiers still serve the people of the United States and live the Army values. They embody the Soldier's creed and our warrior ethos, which states, "I will always place the mission first, I will never accept defeat, I will never quit, and I will never leave a fallen comrade."

Army NCOs trace their roots to the beginnings of American military history. They helped Washington preserve the Continental Army at Valley Forge, stood with Winfield Scott at Chippewa, and directed Zachary Taylor's guns at Palo Alto. They carried the nation's colors at Gettysburg and Vicksburg, fought yellow fever in Cuba with Walter Reed, and led Pershing's and Eisenhower's legions into Germany. Whether helping local populations build a village in Southeast Asia or teaching young Iraqi soldiers to conduct operations, American NCOs are leading from the front and are some of our nation's best ambassadors. Over time, through various changes in tactics and technology, Army NCOs have emerged as the Army's small-unit leaders, trainers, and guardians of standards.

Our NCO Corps is unrivaled by any Army in the world, envied by our allies, and feared by our enemies. Throughout the Army's history, the NCO has been a pivotal figure, but never more so than today with our spectrum of operations: full combat, tank-on-tank fighting, as during the invasion of Iraq; the guerilla/insurgency war ongoing in Iraq and Afghanistan; peacekeeping operations in Kosovo; and humanitarian support for survivors of the tsunami in Asia, hurricanes in the southeast, and fires in the southwest. Our Army must be ready for this broad range of operations in the years ahead. As NCOs embrace their ever-growing responsibilities in the twenty-first century, this volume will help them remember how they came to be the "backbone of our Army."

Washington, D.C.   KENNETH O. PRESTON
1 July 2005   Sergeant Major of the Army

PREFACE

Fourteen years have passed since Brig. Gen. William A. Stofft first published and prefaced *The Story of the Noncommissioned Officer Corps* in commemoration of the Year of the NCO. Since that time the book has proved extraordinarily popular as a source of inspiration and anecdote, as a repository of history and heritage, and as a compendium of documents, paintings, and photographs relevant to the contributions and experiences of our Noncommissioned Officer Corps. Indeed, it consistently numbers among the Center of Military History's "best sellers." This popularity and continuing utility make it even more appropriate that the Center of Military History update and republish *The Story of the Noncommissioned Officer Corps*, an updated and expanded edition that we are proud to release on the Army Birthday, 2003.

This new edition of *The Story of the Noncommissioned Officer Corps* preserves the format, attention to anecdote, and mixture of art and text that made the original so popular. We have added chapters on DESERT STORM, the Army during the 1990s, the Army in Afghanistan, and a new Epilogue to carry the story forward. We have also added a chapter on the critical role of NCOs to the success of the famous Lewis and Clark Expedition, an event whose Bicentennial Commemoration coincides with a 2003 publication date. We also have worked with text and supporting materials throughout the manuscript to assure its continuing correspondence to contemporary scholarship. We believe the new version will prove even more popular than the old.

The American noncommissioned officer is a timeless icon, representing the strength and resolution of the American people. With ample reason, we affectionately refer to them as "the backbone of the Army." We truly hope that you will enjoy and profit from this updated version of their inspiring story.

Washington, D.C.   JOHN S. BROWN
1 April 2003   Brigadier General, U.S. Army
                                                       Chief of Military History

Preface to the First Edition

The publication of *The Story of the Noncommissioned Officer Corps* culminates the Center of Military History's contribution to the Year of the NCO. The Secretary of the Army and the Chief of Staff directed this year-long consideration of the special responsibilities and accomplishments of the noncommissioned officer so that members of our Army might come to appreciate better the vital role they have played and continue to play in the defense of the nation.

For its part in this commemoration, the Center used its Army Artist Program to commission three enlisted artists to prepare eighteen paintings that depict American noncommissioned officers exercising their historic responsibilities in peace and war. These paintings, with detailed captions that explain the historical significance of the NCO's traditional roles as small unit leader, trainer, and guardian of Army standards, were recently published as a print set and are available through the Army's Publication Center.

The Center also published *Time-Honored Professionals*, a booklet describing the work of today's NCOs as part of a long tradition of military service. Aimed specifically at recent graduates of the Primary Leader Development Course, this illustrated essay describes the evolution of the NCO's duties through two hundred years of our nation's history.

Expanding on these preliminary efforts, *The Story of the Noncommissioned Officer Corps* attempts to place the corps in its wider historical context. The emergence of NCOs as recognized professionals, a development whose importance is being commemorated this year throughout the Army, is a stirring story of accomplishment, perseverance, and dedication to the highest military standards. As General Vuono says elsewhere in this volume, "The noncommissioned officer is the standard bearer of our Army." I believe that the aptness of his statement is amply demonstrated in the pages that follow.

We in the military history community are acutely aware of the need for a detailed, scholarly study of the American noncommissioned officer and look forward to seeing such a project launched in the near future. Meanwhile, I recommend these three projects to the members of the Total Army, especially to its company grade officers and noncommissioned officers, those most intimately involved in leading and training the men and women of the Army. Our goal, as expressed in these publications, is to foster a better understanding of the difficult tasks routinely assumed by the NCO and of the continuing need for excellent small unit leaders, trainers, and guardians of our Army's standards.

Washington, D.C.
13 June 1989

WILLIAM A. STOFFT
Brigadier General, U.S. Army
Chief of Military History

ACKNOWLEDGMENTS

Although only three names appear on the title page, this volume was very much a collaborative effort. Thirteen contributing historians wrote this book. Three Army specialists created the series of paintings that were the original basis for the essays in Part Two: Anita Y. Sonnie, Theresa L. Unger, and Manuel B. Ablaza; and one of CMH's own NCOs, Sfc. Marshall T. Williams, designed and drew the NCO insignia that enhance this volume as Appendix A.

We also wish to acknowledge the important contributions made by John W. Elsberg, Editor in Chief, who designed and directed the production of both versions of this book; Morris J. MacGregor, Jr., Acting Chief Historian at the time of the first edition; Albert E. Cowdrey, Acting Chief of the Histories Division at the time of the first edition, Richard W. Stewart, Chief of the Histories Division during the preparation of this revised edition, and Jeffrey J. Clarke, Chief Historian at the time of the revised edition, who served as exacting readers; Arthur S. Hardyman, Chief, Graphics Branch, who directed the selection and placement of the illustrations for the first edition; Beth F. MacKenzie, who as acting Chief of the Graphics Branch directed the selection and placement of the many additional illustrations for this edition; Linda M. Cajka, who designed the photographic essays and prepared the final layout for the first edition; Howell C. Brewer, Jr., who did the original photographic research; Teresa K. Jameson, who digitized the NCO insignia and designed and prepared the final layout for this edition; Julia Simon, Roger Wright, and Gene Snyder, who prepared the artwork for the revised edition; Bianka J. Adams and Erik B. Villard, who assisted with the preparation of the appendixes in the revised edition; Walter H. Bradford and David C. Cole, who helped with the revision of the section on grade insignia and the section on Army values; Catherine A. Heerin, Chief, Editorial Branch, who worked on both manuscripts; Barbara H. Gilbert, who edited the original manuscript into final shape; Diane M. Donovan, who edited this edition; James B. Knight and Mary L. Haynes, who provided stellar support in the CMH Library; and Shelby Stanton, Peter Harrington of the Anne K. Brown Collection, Marie Yates of the Defense Audiovisual Agency, M. Sgt. David N. Schad of the Office of the Sergeant Major of the Army, Leslie D. Jensen of the West Point Museum, the staff of *Soldiers* magazine, and the staff of the Special Collections Branch at the National Defense University Library, all of whom assisted in the search for pictures. Maj. Les A. Melnyk of the National Guard Bureau History Office and Edwin Larkin, Director of Public Affairs, General Services Administration, provided photos for the Leadership section.

Special thanks to Robert Bouilly, historian at the Sergeants Major Academy; Larry Arms, director of the Army Museum of the Noncommissioned Officer; Judy Bellafaire and Britta Granrud of the Women in Military Service for America Memorial Foundation; and Amy Hill of the U.S. Army Women's Museum for their input. The draft of this work was read and critiqued by Col. Robert A. Doughty, Head, Department of History, USMA; Roger A. Beaumont, Texas A&M University; and Maj. Christopher G. Clark, U.S. Army Sergeants Major Academy. We would also like to thank William

M. Hammond and Terrence J. Gough of the Histories Division, Terry Van Meter of the Museum Division, and Graham A. Cosmas of the Joint History Office for their support during the preparation of the revised edition; Sfc. Al Sanchez, PERSCOM, who reviewed the section on NCOES for the first edition, and Joanne M. Brignolo, Joycelyn M. Canery, Rae T. Panella, M. Dixon Robin, LaJuan R. Watson, and Wyvetra B. Yeldell, who provided careful assistance during the first edition's production process.

A list of those historians who contributed to the writing of this volume follows below. Each contributor assumes full responsibility for his part of this study, to include any errors of commission or omission.

Charles R. Anderson (M.A., Western Michigan University), a CMH historian, is the author of two personal accounts of the Vietnam War: *The Grunts* and *Vietnam: The Other War*. He wrote eight essays for this volume: "Ready for Patrol," "Ambulance Corps Proficiency," "Sustaining the Offensive," "A Hidden Resource," "Keeping the System Moving," "From Information to Intelligence," "War in a Maze," and "Training the Trainers."

Larry A. Ballard is a historian with the Center of Military History and the author of numerous articles on U.S. Army history, as well as *Battle of Ball's Bluff*. He served as an NCO with the Army in Vietnam and as a historian with the 116th Military History Detachment, Virginia Army National Guard. He contributed the essays "Guardians of Standards," "Laying the Gun," and "Dress on the Colors." He also compiled "Selected Documents" and the appendix on NCO sleeve insignia.

Brig. Gen. John S. Brown (Ph.D., Indiana University) has been the Chief of Military History, U.S. Army, since 1998. A graduate of West Point, he has commanded an armor unit at every company and field grade level, including an armored battalion during the Gulf War. He also authored *Draftee Division: The 88th Infantry Division in World War II*. For this volume, he wrote the essays "Hell Night on Objective NORFOLK" and "Expeditionary Operations."

Maj. Christopher G. Clark (M.A., Kearney State College) was a military historian serving as the chief of the Course Development Division at the U.S. Army Sergeants Major Academy. He contributed the appendix on Suggestions for Further Reading for the original edition.

Arnold G. Fisch, Jr. (Ph.D., Pennsylvania State University) authored *Military Government in the Ryukyu Islands, 1945–1950* and *The Department of the Army*. He coauthored the essay "Teamwork, Firepower, Responsibility." He also prepared the original versions of "The Evolution and Development of the NCO Corps Since 1775" and the appendix "A Gallery of Noncommissioned Officer Heroes."

Ernest F. Fisher, Jr. (Ph.D., University of Wisconsin) is the author of, among other works, *Cassino to the Alps*, in the U.S. Army in World War II series. He wrote the initial versions of "The Evolution of and Development of the NCO Corps Since 1775" and the appendix "A Gallery of Noncommissioned Officer Heroes."

David W. Hogan, Jr. (Ph.D., Duke University) is a historian at the Center of Military History. He authored *225 Years of Service: The U.S. Army, 1775–2000* and several books and articles. He updated "The Evolution and Development of the NCO Corps Since 1775," coauthored "Ambulance Corps Proficiency" and "Teamwork, Firepower, Responsibility," and served as the general editor for the rest of the updated volume.

Robert S. Rush (Ph.D., Ohio State University) is a retired command sergeant major and author of *Hell in the Huertgen Forest: The Ordeal of an American Combat Regiment*, as well as *The NCO Guide* and *The Enlisted Man's Guide*. Now a historian at the Center of

Military History, he wrote the essays "War Against Terror in the Mountains" and "The Future" and prepared the photograph section "Deployment."

Mark D. Sherry (Ph.D., Georgetown University) is assigned to the Center of Military History's Histories Division. His special area of interest is post–World War II national strategy. He contributed the essay "Give Me Ten."

Lt. Col. Adrian G. Traas, U.S. Army, Retired (M.A., Texas A&M University) served with Corps of Engineers units in Korea, Vietnam, Italy, and Virginia. He is currently preparing a volume on engineer operations for the U.S. Army in Vietnam series and has published *From the Golden Gate to Mexico City: The U.S. Army Topographical Engineers in the Mexican War, 1846–1848*. He wrote the essay "Into the Provinces."

Charles E. White (Ph.D., Duke University) is currently the historian for the Lewis and Clark Commemorative Office at the Center of Military History. He previously served as infantry branch historian and as command historian for the 21st Theater Army Area Command. He is the author of *The Enlightened Soldier: Scharnhorst and the Militarische Gesellschaft in Berlin, 1801–1805* and wrote the essay "Along the Frontier" for this volume.

Lt. Col. Joseph W. A. Whitehorne, U.S. Army, Retired (Ph.D., Pennsylvania State University) is the author of several books and articles and Associate Professor of History at Lord Fairfax College in Virginia. He contributed the essay "Checking Cartridge Boxes."

Robert K. Wright, Jr. (Ph.D., College of William and Mary), who served as a non-commissioned officer in Vietnam, authored *The Continental Army* and coauthored *Soldier-Statesmen of the Constitution*. He developed the format for the "Portraits of NCOs in Action" section of the book and wrote the essays "To Range the Woods" and "An Ordered and Disciplined Camp."

Washington, D.C.   DAVID W. HOGAN, JR.
1 April 2003   ARNOLD G. FISCH, JR.
                                                                   ROBERT K. WRIGHT, JR.

CONTENTS

Illustrations

The following illustrations appear between pages 233 and 253:

Leadership
The Skirmish Line
Storming of a British Redoubt
Soldiers on a Troopship
A First-Class Fighting Man
Full Study of Corporal, 15th New York Infantry
Antiaircraft Artillery Position along the Siegfried Line
A Patrol Returns to Fire Support Base in Vietnam
A Squad Deploys From an M113 Armored Personnel Carrier
An Instructor Demonstrating Counseling Skills
Drill Sergeant Giving Sign of Encouragement
Trainees under the Watchful Eye of Their Drill Sergeant
Medic Completing a Twelve-Mile Road March in Bosnia
Training
The First Muster, Salem, Massachusetts, 1637
Bayonet Drill at Fort Huachuca
Hands-on Instruction with the M60 Machine Gun
Hand-to-Hand Combat Training
The Jump Tower at Fort Benning
Steuben at Valley Forge
Give Me Ten!
A Tank Crew Training at Grafenwöhr, Germany
Scaling the Wall with a Little Help
Technical
Pathology Lab at Dewitt Army Hospital, Fort Belvoir, Virginia
A Women's Army Corps NCO Operating a Printing Press
Medic Stowing Equipment for a Training Mission
Harper's Sketch of a Civil War Regimental Aid Station
Signal Corps Radio Tractor and Crew in 1915
Refitting a Stryker Infantry Carrier Vehicle
Microwave Repair Specialist
Rearming an AH–1G Cobra
Standards
Basic Trainees and Drill Sergeant Marching to the Mess Hall
A First Lesson in the Art of War
The 9th Cavalry Stands for Inspection
Drill Sergeant Teaching Recruits How To Fold the National Colors
Sentinels From the Old Guard at the Tomb of the Unknowns
Three Breaks to the Ground, Ready, Go!

Illustrations courtesy of the following: *Frontispiece*, p. 2, Valley Forge Historical Society; pp. 2, 5 (*bottom*), 6, 9, 13, 17, 21, 22, 26, 35, 36, 42, 50, 53, 70, 78, 86, 102, 110, 113, 121, 126, 136, 144, 152, 160, 166, 168, 176, 178, 184, 187, 192, 195, 200, 203, 206, 212, 214, 216, 222, 240 (*bottom*), 247 (*bottom*), 249, 320, 324 (*bottom*), 338 (*bottom*), Army Art Collection; pp. 4 (*top*), 38, 62, 147, 171, 236, 237, 242 (*left*), 243 (*top*), 244 (*bottom left*), 248, *Soldiers* magazine; pp. 4 (*bottom*), 98, 102, 114, 130, 131, 140, National Museum of the United States Army; p. 5 (*top*), private collection; p. 10, New Britain Museum of Art; p. 11, Gilcrease Museum, Tulsa; pp. 14, 31, 234 (*bottom right*), 243 (*bottom*), 246 (*middle*), 322, Anne S. K. Brown Military Collection, Brown University Library; pp. 19, 118, 202, 323, 325 (*bottom*), Smithsonian Institution; p. 29, Fort Riley Regimental Museum; p. 34, U.S. Army Sergeants Major Academy; p. 44, Continental Insurance Company; p. 45, *Jane's*; pp. 52, 138, Library of Congress; p. 58, 67, Michael Haynes; pp. 72, 94, 238 (*top*), Painting by Don Troiani, *www.historicalartprints.com*; pp. 74, 240 (*middle*), 246 (*top*), Shelby Stanton; p. 80, Virginia National Guard; pp. 88, 234 (*top left*), 235 (*top left*), West Point Museum, U.S. Military Academy; p. 96, Yale University Art Gallery, Trumbull Collection; p. 104, Amon Carter Museum; p. 112, National Infantry Museum; p. 128, Rock Island Arsenal Museum; p. 129, DOD Joint Combat Camera Center; pp. 139, 155, Federation of American Scientists; p. 194, U.S. Army Transportation Museum; p. 220, Reuters/Jim Hollander; pp. 233, 250 (*bottom*), 252 (*top, middle right, bottom*), 253 (*bottom*), 340 (*top*), 345, Defense Visual Information Center; p. 234 (*top right*), The Library of Virginia; p. 239 (*bottom*), Pennsylvania Capitol Preservation Committee; pp. 242 (*right*), 341 (*top*), Army Women's Museum; p. 247 (*top*), Fort George G. Meade Museum; pp. 250 (*top left, right*), 251 (*top left, right*), 252 (*middle left*), 253 (*top*), 328, 329 (*top, bottom*), 330, 333 (*bottom*), 334 (*top*), 335 (*top*), 336, 337, National Archives; pp. 324 (*top*), 325 (*top*), 327, 335 (*bottom*), Moorland-Spingarn Research Center, Howard University; p. 326, Freedom Foundation at Valley Forge; p. 329 (*middle*), Mary Tordorevich; pp. 331 (*bottom*), 332 (*top*), Hall of Heroes (*www.homeofheroes.com*); p. 333 (*top*), Audie Murphy Research Foundation; p. 334 (*bottom*), Richard Summers; p. 338 (*top*), Congressional Medal of Honor Society; p. 340 (*bottom*), S. Sgt. David Bata; p. 344 (*bottom*), Camp Bondsteel Public Affairs Office. All other illustrations are from the Department of the Army.

Part One

The Evolution and Development of the NCO Corps

"The backbone of the Army is the noncommissioned [officer.]"

—*Rudyard Kipling, The 'Eathen, 1896*

"We are the finest Army in the world today. Let's keep it that way. We got here because we have the finest noncommissioned officers. And we have never satisfied ourselves with being just a little bit better than the next guy. Every day, insist on being the best and on getting better. Every day, train your soldiers and grow them into leaders. Every day, strengthen the ties that bind us together as warriors, officer and noncommissioned officer."

—*General Eric K. Shinseki, Army Chief of Staff, 2000*

The March to Valley Forge, December 19, 1777, *by William B. T. Trego*

THE
EVOLUTION
AND
DEVELOPMENT
OF THE
NCO CORPS

Colonial America adapted continental European and English traditions and practices to fit local circumstances. The colonists took the same approach when they formed military forces, including noncommissioned officers.

In continental Europe, noncommissioned officers appeared with the emergence of standing armies. Over time, European NCOs became administrative managers, drillmasters, and enforcers of camp discipline—the only authority figures in constant contact with the troops. A huge social distance existed between the aristocratic officer corps and the men—both NCOs and private soldiers. This social gap, combined with Old World military tactics, placed very strict limitations on the lives of noncommissioned officers. Even the battlefield allowed them little independence of action. NCOs merely browbeat the soldiers to stand fast in the line of battle despite horrific casualties.

In contrast to the standing armies of the European powers, the British settlers in colonial America brought with them a militia tradition dating back to the Anglo-Saxons. Every free, able-bodied adult male was expected to own arms and to be a part of the militia company of his local community. This local company quickly divided into squads, each with its own NCO, to share the burden of rotating guard duty. The militia of Jamestown, Virginia, for example, organized by squads as early as 1609. Such small units were well suited to counter Indian hit-and-run tactics and to operate in the heavily wooded country around the settlements, where larger units had no chance of chasing and catching raiders. Colonial NCOs thus enjoyed many more opportunities to exercise initiative. Militia units, led by qualified NCOs, combined into larg-

A drill sergeant works with his basic training platoon at Fort Jackson, S.C., 2001. Throughout our Army's history, NCOs have performed vital tasks as small-unit leaders, trainers, technical experts, and guardians of Army standards.

er formations for a specific campaign, helping British forces to defeat the French in Canada and to meet threats from the Spanish along the borders of South Carolina and Georgia.

Birth of an Army, 1775–1860

Militia units paved the way for the formation of the Continental Army. Immediately after the skirmishing at Lexington and Concord in April 1775, the New England colonies raised separate armies. In June 1775 the Continental Congress assumed responsibility for these troops, as well as others raised by New York, and formed a national force of ten (later thirteen) companies of "expert riflemen." Over the next two years the Continental Army expanded to include 110 regiments from all thirteen colonies and Canada.

Although tables of organization reflected patriot knowledge of British and European armies, variations in details showed local innovation. By 1776 a typical infantry regiment had a regimental staff and eight companies. Along with three field officers and six staff officers, the regimental staff included four staff NCOs: a sergeant major, a quartermaster sergeant, and two lead musicians (a drum major and a fife major). The two lead musicians trained the company fifers and drummers and were responsible for signal functions on the battlefield. In practice, these numbers varied considerably due to shortages of personnel, especially experienced NCOs.

Colonial companies, with their NCOs, also varied somewhat in size during the War of Independence. When at full strength a typical infantry company included four sergeants, four corporals, and two musicians (a fifer and drummer) among its ninety members. The four

Powder Horn *Powder horns were used to store powder for priming and charging firearms. They were used by local militia at the beginning of the Revolutionary War but were quickly replaced by cartridge boxes with the standardization of military uniforms and accoutrements. Powder horns continued to be used by NCOs into the first quarter of the nineteenth century to re-prime muskets in the event of a misfire. This powder horn belonged to Levi Gasset and was used at the Battle of Dorchester Heights during the siege of Boston, 1775.*

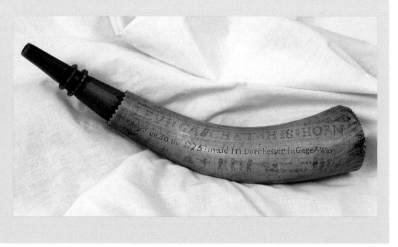

Detail from Arnold's March to Quebec, N. C. Wyeth. In September 1775 Col. Benedict Arnold and about 1,100 American soldiers began their march toward Quebec. Only about half of them survived the 350-mile, six-week journey.

Guilford Court House, H. Charles McBarron, c. 1975. During the Revolutionary War, the Continental Army relied on competent NCOs to match the British in actions like this one.

corporals and seventy-six privates constituted the "rank and file," those men who stood in the line of battle (ranks parallel to the line, files perpendicular) carrying muskets. The fifer and drummer, whom the Continental Army classified as NCOs, handled battlefield communications. For administrative purposes, each infantry company divided into four squads, consisting of a sergeant, a corporal, and nineteen privates. These men formed into two ranks of ten files each, with the corporal serving as the file closer

in the rear of the formation and the sergeant performing the same function on the flank.

Artillery and light dragoon (cavalry) regimental organizations were similar to the infantry regiment but made provision for spe-

Those Are Regulars, By God,
H. Charles McBarron, 1957.
This painting of the American
charge at Chippewa depicts
one of the Army's highlights,
a War of 1812 triumph that
solidified the NCO's role as
small-unit leader.

cialized ratings such as gunners, bombardiers, saddlers, and black-smiths. As specialists, these skilled individuals drew higher pay than privates. They did not, however, have the command responsibility of noncommissioned officers.

As with the European armies, the Continental NCO possessed a status little better than the privates he was supervising. Initially, sergeants received 48 shillings per month and corporals and musicians 44, compared to a private's pay of 40. From this amount, the Army deducted a portion for clothing; the soldier was expected to obtain his own arms and blankets. Over time, General George Washington was able to secure from Congress an additional dollar per month for sergeants major, quartermaster sergeants, and drum and fife majors. He also made provision for short swords as NCO side arms and for NCO quarters separate from those of privates.

In 1778 a Prussian volunteer, Baron Frederick Wilhelm von Steuben, arrived at Washington's camp at Valley Forge. Many historians have doubted Steuben's claim to the title "Baron" and to the aristocratic "von" in his name, but he did possess considerable military skills. Published at Washington's direction, Steuben's *Regulations for the Order and Discipline of the Troops of the United States* (1779), popularly known as the "Blue Book" because of the color of the first edition, established the principle that the noncommissioned officer was selected by and responsible to the company commander, subject to the battalion or regimental commander's approval. Unfortunately, this close connection with the parent unit became one of the factors hindering NCO professional development. Unlike commissioned officers, until World War II the noncommissioned officer was locked for his entire career into the one regiment that had accepted his enlistment. No NCO could transfer in grade from one regiment to another without the permission of the general-in-chief of the Army, a permission seldom sought or granted.

However, Steuben's *Regulations* did aid the NCO's evolving role as caretaker of soldiers. The Blue Book covered all aspects of infantry service and stressed NCO responsibilities for the care, discipline, and training of the men, both in garrison and in the field, areas that Steuben had found weak in the Continental Army. The regimental sergeant major served as the assistant to the regimental adjutant, maintaining rosters and handling issues concerning the interior management and discipline of the regiment. The quartermaster sergeant likewise assisted the regimental quartermaster and supervised the loading and transport of the regiment's baggage on the march. The first or senior sergeants of the companies enforced discipline, maintained the duty roster, and delivered the morning report to the company commander. They also kept company descriptive books that listed the name, age, height, place of birth, and prior occupation of every enlisted man in the unit. The Army maintained similar books into the first years of the twentieth century, when they were finally replaced by other documents describing the individual soldiers.

Steuben's *Regulations* also introduced a new emphasis on the noncommissioned officer's battlefield role, enhancing his status and further distinguishing him from his British counterpart. The NCO's traditional importance as a file closer was already well established in America. Because both the American and European armies generally fought standing in lines facing the enemy (linear tactics), the noncommissioned officers kept the long ranks steady to maintain volley-fire discipline. But the Americans' French-made muskets were more accurate than the British weapons. American NCOs consequently became responsible for aimed volley fire, while the British volleys remained untargeted. Other nations had light formations, such as rangers and jaegers, who used aimed fire, but this emphasis on aiming by the whole force, rather than merely pointing the musket in the general direction of the enemy, made Americans unique among the infantrymen of the day. To enable Americans to engage the British redcoats with cold steel, Steuben emphasized training in the use of the bayonet. The continentals also learned precision high-speed maneuvering and flexibility on the battlefield.

As in eighteenth-century continental Europe, training was the responsibility of officers, not NCOs, but Steuben's system did provide for training noncommissioned officers in leadership skills. Staff NCOs supported staff officers, and line NCOs backed up—and could take over for—line officers in combat. On the battlefield, the "covering sergeant" stood in the second rank immediately behind the company officer and was responsible for protecting him. The covering sergeant kept his bayonet fixed and carried his musket at shoulder arm. He did not fire in volleys, but reserved his fire until needed to defend his captain or lieutenant. One of the corporals assumed a similar guard function in protecting the junior officer (the ensign) who carried the colors, until the color sergeant later assumed that position with an expanded guard of corporals. NCOs thus became essential figures in the linear tactics that survived until after the Civil War, and their influence grew as the Army refined its tactics.

Although pay, education, and status of the NCO improved somewhat during the years between the Revolution and the Civil War, the changes were largely incremental. The Regular NCO was part of a small, frontier constabulary, isolated physically and mentally from a people who viewed the professional military as dregs too lazy to grasp the opportunities in civilian life. In volunteer units, the fact that soldiers elected their officers and NCOs often led to major problems with discipline. After years of living with a pay scale barely higher than that of common soldiers, the NCO experienced a jump in pay during the War of 1812, only to see it decline again with the war's end. For the average NCO, the amount of pay probably mattered less than the fact that, if he were stationed on a frontier outpost, it might be four to six months before he saw it. Professional education for NCOs was practically unknown beyond rudimentary on-the-job instruction by company commanders. Occasionally, NCOs in the artillery, engineers, medical department, and signal corps received more specialized training. From time to time, Army leaders like Maj. Gen. Anthony Wayne and Secretary of War Jefferson Davis took steps to raise the status of NCOs, making sure that they were treated with consideration and not berated in front of their men; Davis supported the commissioning of officers from those NCOs who could pass an exam. For selected line sergeants with eight years of service, the Army did, in 1832, create the rank of ordnance sergeant, a position that paid a sergeant an extra $5 per month to receive and preserve ordnance, arms, and other military stores of his assigned post.

Notwithstanding their comparatively low status, the NCOs played critical roles in the Army of the new nation. As the Army explored and established posts to protect the fur trade and emigrant routes in the lands beyond the Mississippi River, NCOs frequently found themselves on independent missions with a fair amount of discretion. They became highly proficient in small-unit tactics, the supply of small groups, marching and camping in the wilderness, patrols, and road and blockhouse construction, developing in the process a good deal of self-reliance, resilience, and capacity for improvisation. Farther east, NCOs accompanied officers on recruiting details. And when war broke out again with Britain in 1812, NCOs once more provided the glue that held together the linear formations of Chippewa, Lundy's Lane, and New Orleans.

In 1815 Brig. Gen. Winfield Scott published his *Rules and Regulations for the Field Exercise and Maneuvers of Infantry*, which replaced Steuben's earlier *Regulations*. Scott's book placed particular stress on the importance of swift movement from the column of march to linear formation on the battlefield. In executing this maneuver the color guard, led by the color sergeant, played the key role, maintaining the proper alignment and cadence that enabled the men to hold their ranks. The color sergeant, with his guard of from five to eight corporals, therefore became the focal point on which the men dressed, wheeled, and advanced into battle. This emergence of the color sergeant, who replaced the commissioned ensign in carrying the flag, clearly and significantly enhanced the noncommissioned officer's role in combat.

The brief, inconclusive War of 1812 (1812–1815) was followed by thirty years of relative peace. The NCO and the Army accompanied the wave of settlers crossing the continent, surveying the land, building roads and stockades, and garrisoning posts along the routes the pio-

Convent of Churubusco, *James Walker, c. 1947. During the Mexican War, an outnumbered American force gained victory by applying the concept of combined-arms operations. Infantry, artillery, and dragoon regiments had mastered the necessary skills of working together.*

neers followed. Duty was varied and sometimes dangerous, as NCOs led their men in missions that included enforcing treaties with the Great Plains Indians, protecting trading caravans, and blazing trails on the way to Oregon and the Mexican territories of California and Texas. But the NCOs were still small-unit leaders and disciplinarians only. The engineering and surveying technology of the peacetime Army was considered the business of officers who had learned it in the nation's first engineering school, the U.S. Military Academy at West Point.

The battles of the Mexican War (1846–1848) broadened the Army's experience. The American soldiers who campaigned south of the Rio Grande learned how to conduct successful amphibious landings at Vera Cruz, experienced street-to-street and house-to-house fighting in the battles of Monterrey and Mexico City, won the battle of Contreras after a surprise night march in the pouring rain, and demonstrated the uses of effective artillery—both siege mortars and "flying artillery"—at the battle of Palo Alto and elsewhere. Many NCOs learned skills they would soon need in a greater war, as did many of their officers, including Ulysses Grant and Robert E. Lee.

Victory over Mexico ushered in another decade of peace, at least with foreign nations. The whole southwestern United States had been conquered and annexed, and the immediate task was to explore, survey, and map the new regions. The Corps of Topographical Engineers took the lead: "Topogs" worked with the Mexican Boundary Commission, protected by an infantry and a cavalry company. The Gold Rush and the movement of settlers into Indian lands helped to bring on new battles with the tribes, and during the decade of the 1850s the Army recorded no fewer than twenty-two separate Indian "wars." But even while NCOs led their men across the vast spaces of the West, the United States was drifting toward war.

The Civil War and Its Aftermath

Neither the Regular Army nor the militia was prepared for the kind of fighting that developed during the Civil War. Some Regular

Skirmish in the Wilderness, *Winslow Homer, 1864. NCOs took on added leadership responsibilities as battlefield tactics changed during and after the Civil War.*

Army NCOs were veterans of the Mexican War, and others had gained experience against nomadic Indian tribes on the Great Plains; but the huge, massed battles of the Civil War were completely different. Most of the thousands of volunteers on both sides who hurried to enlist had no military experience at all. Even members of militia companies who had participated in musters had spent more time on ceremonial or social duties than on serious training. Once in the field, both Regular and volunteer units faced similar challenges and dangers, fighting on many battlefields. Over time, these ordeals in combat created a large cadre of experienced noncommissioned officers, but only at the cost of terrible losses.

With few exceptions, Regular Army noncommissioned officers remained loyal to the Union when the Civil War broke out. Many were foreign born: some were Canadians and Englishmen, but they included mostly Germans and Irish who had arrived in the United States through the cities of the eastern seaboard and had settled either in the North or the Midwest. They remained loyal to the Union at a time when about a third of the commissioned officers joined the Confederacy.

These men had to rely on the training manuals then in print. The most important when the war broke out were Maj. Gen. Winfield Scott's *Infantry Tactics*, first published in 1854, and Col. William J. Hardee's *Rifle and Light Infantry Tactics*, published in 1855. A third manual, Maj. Gen. Silas Casey's *U.S. Army Infantry Tactics for the Instructions, Exercises, and Maneuvers of the Soldier, a Company, a Line of Skirmishers, Battalion, Brigade, or Corps D'Armée*, appeared in 1862 and soon superseded the earlier books. (Changes in weaponry outdated Scott's Tactics, and Hardee defected to the Confederacy.)

All three books prescribed a similar role for the noncommissioned officers with some differences. Casey, like Scott, emphasized the color sergeant's role in controlling unit cadence and direction. Unlike Scott, however, Casey foresaw the heavy battlefield losses the war would bring, and his manual envisioned situations in which senior sergeants would have to take command of units on the spot when all the officers became casualties. He insisted, therefore, that all NCOs received training in giving commands.

During the Civil War both Regular and volunteer full-strength regiments consisted of ten companies, although the volunteer units varied considerably in other respects from state to state. The Regular regimental NCO staff consisted of a sergeant major, a quartermaster sergeant, a commissary sergeant, a hospital steward, and two musicians. Each company had 4 officers, 5 sergeants, 1 wagoner, and 64 to 82 corporals and privates.

A fundamental problem in the Civil War was that the linear tactics of the day were designed for men carrying smoothbore muskets. With soldiers now armed with rifled muskets, which had a much greater accuracy, casualties were certain to be horrendous unless tactics changed. The increased killing power of even newer weapons introduced late in the war (breech-loading rifles, cavalry carbines, and the Gatling gun) underscored the need for more open tactical formations than Casey had called for in 1862. Various unit commanders gradually introduced such formations to reduce the vulnerability of their men to the increased volume and accuracy of enemy fire.

Taking note of those changing realities during the course of the war, Bvt. Maj. Gen. Emory Upton prepared a new manual to supplement Casey's. His *Tactics*, adopted as Army doctrine in 1867, placed greater emphasis upon simplicity of maneuver. His instructions could be taught more easily by NCOs to new troops, shortened training time, and increased the soldier's effective term of service.

The gradual elimination of linear tactics after the Civil War redefined the NCO's combat leadership role. Throughout the world, a technological revolution continued to sweep over all armies, supplying both the infantry and the artillery with weapons of ever-growing lethality. These weapons broke up the use of close-packed masses of troops, forcing them into a more open order of battle pre-

Attack at Dawn, *Charles Schreyvogel, 1904. Small patrols, often led by NCOs, proved the most effective way to patrol the West.*

ceded by lines of skirmishes. This change in tactics emphasized and expanded the role of small-unit leaders—the noncommissioned officers—in maintaining order on a more complex battlefield.

The Regular Army of the late nineteenth century was a small, tough, close-knit body of men. Except for some coast artillerymen, these soldiers had few connections with American society at large. Most noncommissioned officers were bachelors. At least one-quarter of the enlisted men were foreign born. In addition, elite black regiments (the 24th and 25th Infantry and the 9th and 10th Cavalry) played an important military role in frontier campaigning. All the NCOs in these units were black, and they enjoyed considerable prestige in black communities. Because blacks had few opportunities in civilian society, many able men enlisted and proved to be superb Indian fighters (in the 9th Cavalry, eleven noncommissioned officers won the Medal of Honor during the regiment's long campaign against the Apaches in the Southwest).

In addition to displaying ethnic diversity, the Army of the late nineteenth century consisted of enlisted men from a variety of occupational and social backgrounds. Company Descriptive Books listed not only the usual farm boys, but also craftsmen, scholars, and adventurers. Many served for more than one enlistment, creating in the process a Noncommissioned Officer Corps of stability as well as variety.

Regardless of personal background, military rank and individual worth mattered most in the widely scattered infantry or cavalry garrisons of the time. In Spartan barracks, corporals and privates lived together in one large room, with sergeants usually occupying a small cubicle of their own next to the main sleeping quarters or on the second level of two-story barracks. Under such circumstances, it was not surprising that isolated company-size units developed close bonds. Many company commanders and first sergeants felt a paternal concern for the men.

The first sergeant stood at the center of this "family" relationship. Enlisted men had to obtain his permission to speak to the company commander. The first sergeant kept the Company Descriptive Book— the family bible of the unit—and was chief adviser to the captain in all matters concerning the men. A few notorious sergeants took advantage of their special position to bully and brutalize their men, but most noncommissioned officers exercised their authority with restraint. In either case, the classic old Army of the Indian-fighting days did not last even until the end of the century. Already the nation was changing, and the Army had to change with it.

American Expansion Overseas, 1898–1902

As the Indian Wars came to an end and the nineteenth century drew to a close, Army officers began to consider the challenges the new century was likely to bring. Reformers, both within and outside the Army, agreed that a fundamental need existed for better-trained noncommissioned officers, like those found in the older, more experienced armies of other countries. In 1878 Bvt. Maj. Gen. Emory Upton, in his book *The Armies of Asia and Europe*, had warned of the inadequacy of NCO training in the United States. In travels over-

We Leave the Trenches, *Charles Johnson Post, 1898. Although short in duration, the Spanish-American War tested the ability of both Regular and National Guard NCOs to make a swift transition from peace to combat.*

seas, he had learned that all European armies accepted the notion that "a good noncommissioned officer can no more be improvised than an officer."

But the road to reform was long. Since the early years of the nineteenth century the Army had provided some technical training for noncommissioned officers of the artillery at Fort Monroe, Virginia. Hospital stewards, the senior NCOs of the Medical Service, had received special training since 1857. Since the 1870s Signal Corps noncommissioned officers had received instruction, first at Fort Whipple, Virginia, and later at Fort Riley, Kansas. Similarly, engineer NCOs received training at Fort Totten, New York. For a time, an Infantry School of Application at Jefferson Barracks, Missouri, and a Cavalry School of Application at Carlisle Barracks, Pennsylvania, trained noncommissioned officers in those branches. But such schools were not ready to meet the technological challenges the twentieth century would bring to NCO education. Their tradition-bound curriculums simply did not keep up with progress in the various skill fields.

At first, most company-grade officers opposed the establishment of more and better schools for noncommissioned officers. They argued, with some justification, that the company commander knew his men's capabilities and limitations best and therefore was in a position to provide them on-the-job training (OJT). A minority of officers expressed doubt whether OJT for combat-arms NCOs was adequate. They wanted more post schools, where instruction could be given in elementary mathematics, science, mechanical drawing, surveying, and engineering. But at first they could make little progress. Major improvements in NCO training and education would have to wait for World War I.

During the latter years of the nineteenth century, the United States began to emerge as a new world power. An increasing num-

14

ber of Americans were prepared to support imperialistic ventures overseas. Some were motivated by high ideals, others by a more basic quest for profit. Whatever the inspiration that drew Americans beyond the continental limits of the United States, it was only a matter of time before the nation's leadership called on the Army and the Navy to protect the nation's new overseas interests.

The United States now spanned from coast to coast and had even bought Alaska from the Russians. Now it focused on the Pacific and the Caribbean, as commercial and naval interests began to acquire coaling and repair stations for the nation's growing fleet of steam-powered cargo ships and warships. In the Caribbean, American economic interests blended with humanitarian concerns for the people of Cuba, who in 1895 rebelled against a repressive Spanish colonial regime. When the battleship Maine mysteriously blew up and sank in Havana harbor in 1898, war broke out. Secretary of State John Hay once referred to the war with Spain as America's "splendid little war." True, it was a short war (less than six months of actual fighting) that ended in unqualified victory for the United States, but for the average soldier and NCO there was very little that was agreeable—much less splendid—about the conflict.

The Last Stand, Frederic *Remington, 1900. As the United States entered the twentieth century as a new world power, NCOs faced duty on foreign shores in conflicts ranging from the Philippine Insurrection (shown here) to China's Boxer Rebellion.*

The Regular Army was almost totally unprepared to fight an overseas war. Its 26,000 officers and men were scattered around America in obscure posts and in company- and battalion-size units. For several years the Army had not been able to hold training for more than a regiment. The individual NCOs and privates were tough and experienced, but the Army lacked a mobilization plan. Moreover, it lacked experience in carrying out the joint operations with the Navy necessary to invade Cuba and the Spanish-held Philippines.

One problem the Army did not have was finding enough men. The sinking of the Maine caused a great surge of patriotic fervor. Congress expanded the Regular Army to nearly 29,000 and called for an additional 125,000 volunteers, mostly National Guardsmen. By the end of the war these numbers had grown into a total force of 275,000.

Mobilizing and supplying all these soldiers severely strained the ill-prepared War Department. The men assembled at fifteen campsites, mostly in the South, to be equipped, trained, and transported to Cuba. In the camps, the soldiers ate substandard food and lived in unsanitary conditions during the heat of the summer. Typhoid fever broke out, destroying thousands of lives in the camps. Once the men arrived in

Cuba after a delayed, uncomfortable trip on crowded transports, far more men died from a combination of typhoid, yellow fever, and malaria than in combat.

During the actual fighting in Cuba, the three American divisions (two infantry and one dismounted cavalry) were arrayed for battle for the first time in post–Civil War open tactical formations. Individual NCOs showed they could lead their men successfully in this new way of fighting. Most of the American troops were regulars, but some volunteer units were outstanding—including the famous "Rough Riders." The Spanish forces, isolated by the U.S. Navy, which had destroyed or bottled up their fleet, surrendered within a matter of days.

The Army learned a number of lessons from the operations in the Caribbean, including some valuable lessons on joint operations with the Navy. The painful experiences with tropical disease in Cuba led to a Medical Department investigation of the cause of yellow fever and the transmission of typhoid. Enlisted volunteers played a heroic part in the yellow-fever experiments, some winning stripes for their courage. A healthier Army was the result, with tighter sanitation rules that NCOs enforced in camp and field. Never again did the Army as a whole suffer such losses from disease. Significantly, during a war marked by poor food, the NCO Corps added a new specialist. Each company, for the first time, got a designated, permanent cook with NCO status.

In Asia, the Army learned other lessons. The Spanish forces in the Philippines were quickly pinned down by the American fleet, by the American VIII Corps (fresh from San Francisco), and by Filipino insurgents who were eager to win independence. The Spanish in Manila surrendered after a token resistance that cost the Americans only seventeen dead. But the U.S. forces soon found they had a new fight on their hands. The insurgents were no more willing to see their country run by Americans than by Spaniards. After a few months of uneasy collaboration, the Filipinos launched an armed insurrection against their new colonial rulers.

The Philippine Insurrection lasted over three and one-half years, with most of the fighting taking place in the mountains and jungles. The insurgents were excellent guerrilla fighters, and the Army had to rely on all of its experience gained in fighting the Great Plains Indians and the Seminoles to campaign successfully against them. The Americans suppressed the uprising, but casualties were heavy.

The fight against the Filipino insurgents was a soldier's war, with individual determination and warfighting skill counting for much more than strategy. Cpl. Leland S. Smith, serving with a Signal Corps photographic detachment attached to an infantry company, kept a diary that captured the flavor of the campaign. In October 1899 the company was pursuing the guerrillas and was in march column as it approached a bamboo jungle in which insurgents possibly were hiding. The inexperienced lieutenant ordered the men to form a company front and fix bayonets, intending to personally lead a bayonet charge crashing through the bamboo. The grizzled old first sergeant, after giving the lieutenant a pained look, suggested that the men might instead remove their bayonets and move cautiously through the dense growth. In the end, the lieutenant and the company followed the sergeant's lead.

The fighting in the Philippines was the longest and the hardest the Army experienced in Asia up to that time, but it was not the only crisis American soldiers faced there. American interest in China was an old story, and behind it was the usual mix of commercial and humanitarian reasons. China, then a weak nation riddled with corruption, had granted favorable trading concessions to a number of powers. But the exploitation of their country by both European and American traders caused some young Chinese nationalists to form a secret society that westerners called the Boxers. By early 1900 the Boxers had brought China to the verge of revolution with a campaign to get rid of all foreigners and non-Chinese influences. They murdered Chinese Christians and western missionaries and in June 1900 assassinated the German ambassador. Fearing for their lives, the remaining foreigners in Peking (Beijing) fled to the embassies. When a large force of Boxers and Chinese imperial troops laid siege to the legations, the United States joined Britain, France, Japan, Russia, Germany, Austria, and Italy in creating an allied relief force to move on the Chinese capital and rescue the foreign nationals trapped there.

Despite much sensational publicity, the hard fighting in China lasted only about a month. The Chinese nationalists were defeated, and the Manchu dynasty was forced to grant to the western powers concessions that were even more humiliating than before. But outstanding instances of bravery by individual soldiers, including Cpl. Calvin Titus of the U.S. Army, imparted some genuine heroism to this brief, spectacular episode (*see* Appendix B).

Perhaps the most important fact about the Boxer Rebellion for the United States was that it represented the first time since the American Revolution that the country had participated with other nations in an allied military operation. Like the war with Spain, the operation taught valuable lessons to an American Army inexperienced in fighting beyond the limits of the continental United States and in concert with other powers. But in other ways the events of 1898–1904 were misleading. Fighting the dispirited battalions of the fading Spanish Empire, the Filipino guerrillas, and the Chinese nationalists gave the Army, and its NCOs, no hint of the dangers they would face in a great modern war.

NCOs Enter the Modern Era: World War I

The decade and a half between the end of the Philippine Insurrection and the United States' entry into World War I were years of change for the Army. American institutions and policies adjusted to the country's new status as a world power. Although the United States did not become involved in any major conflicts, the armed services played a key role in administering the new overseas territories and in protecting American interests abroad. Along the Mexican border, U.S. forces pursued the bandit chieftain Francisco ("Pancho") Villa in what turned out to be a useful, though unintentional, training exercise.

The Army, remembering the problems that had emerged during the Spanish-American War and aware of the rapid technological changes taking place in warfare, began to modernize its weapons and equipment. The rod bayonet had proved too weak during the war with Spain and was replaced by a one-pound knife bayonet. The standard Army rifle, adopted in 1892, had already been made obsolete by clip-loading rifles with a higher sustained rate of fire. In 1903, therefore, the Army introduced the magazine-fed improved Springfield that served until World War II.

Though important, these advances in hand-held weapons paled in comparison with the impact on the Army and the NCO of two new inventions: the automatic machine gun and the internal combustion engine. The Army had used the manually operated Gatling gun since 1866. But by World War I several different versions of the fully automatic machine gun—a weapon that would revolutionize tactics during the war—had appeared in America. For both immediate and long-range impacts on warfare, even these weapons were less important than the gasoline-fueled motor that made possible trucks, tanks, and airplanes. As early as the Mexican border expedition in 1916, a few Army trucks had begun to replace the traditional mules. In time, mechanization would generate a whole new range of NCO specialist functions and have an immense influence on Army strategy, tactics, and organization.

Men in Rest Area, J. Andre Smith, c. 1917. Sergeants and corporals deployed to France as part of the American Expeditionary Forces (AEF).

Change resulted not only from technology. Starting in 1899 with the appointment of Elihu Root as secretary of war, the Army began a series of sweeping organizational and institutional reforms. Root's goal was to create a modern U.S. Army, with the commanding general replaced by a chief of staff and with a General Staff much like those found in European armies of the time. Congress approved these changes, but the new General Staff did relatively little genuine war planning and policy making at first, instead filling its days with administrative detail. In 1910, however, Maj. Gen. Leonard Wood became chief of staff and immediately began to eliminate many of the staff's time-consuming procedures so it could devote its energies to planning. Taken together, the Root reforms and the dynamic leadership of General Wood helped prepare the Army, and in turn the NCOs, for the age of modern warfare.

Realizing that the new Army would need the highest-quality NCOs, the Army's leaders took steps to improve the status of the NCO Corps. High on the list of reforms was pay. It had been a problem for generations, not only because it was low, but also because it differed very little from the pay of privates. Periodically throughout the nineteenth century—and especially after the Civil War—many officers warned that poor NCO pay was a continuing danger to morale. However, their voices were not heard in Washington. When Congress finally enacted a relatively comprehensive military pay bill in 1870, it did not address this particular problem. As a result, soldiers sometimes avoided the chance to obtain NCO stripes. Others, already promoted to NCO status, requested reduction in grade. Both were responding to the simple fact that a private could make more money than his sergeant by earning extra-duty pay for special details. NCOs were not eligible for such "overtime."

After the patriotic frenzy of the Spanish-American War had passed, the question of enlisted pay surfaced again as enlistments declined and desertions increased. By 1900 practically every unit of the Regular Army was understrength. For the rank and file, this meant more fatigue details and less time for training. Noncommissioned officers, instead of being experienced veterans, frequently had to be appointed from among men in their first term of enlistment. By 1907 the situation was so disturbing that Secretary of War William Howard Taft addressed it in his annual report to the president.

Taft argued that to recruit and hold skilled workmen such as foremen, mechanics, and clerks—men who could become NCOs— the Army had to compete successfully with industry. If a businessman expected to hire and keep foremen who could train unskilled laborers and make them work effectively together, he had to pay them far more than the unskilled workers. This fact held true for the Army as well.

Taft's strong plea for higher Army enlisted pay, especially for noncommissioned officers, finally moved Congress in May 1908 to pass the first Army-wide pay bill since 1870. The long-overdue legislation was a major step toward solving the problem that had for so long demoralized senior NCOs. It increased NCO pay, both in absolute terms and relative to privates' pay. Under its provisions, an artillery, cavalry, or infantry sergeant received $30 a month; corporals in these branches, $21; and privates first class, $18. The pay reform of 1908 was the Army's way of recognizing both the importance of the NCO Corps and the need to compete with the private sector for qualified people, an important step as the nation moved toward involvement in the First World War.

World War I provided many opportunities for noncommissioned officers to prove their skills both as technicians and as leaders on the modern battlefield. As casualties mounted on the Western Front, the Army, as it had in previous wars, commissioned outstanding NCOs to meet the need for company-level officers. But as the war dragged on, it also discovered that the problem of heavy losses among junior officers could be met by able noncommissioned officers' stepping in to replace the fallen. At the same time, technical units proliferated, and more NCOs demonstrated their skills as specialists.

The casualties of trench warfare also created shortages among noncommissioned officers. To meet the need for additional NCOs, the Army Staff recalled to active duty 648 retired men who, because of their age, mainly became recruit trainers instead of replacements in combat units. Most combat replacements came from draftees who trained for NCO positions in Army camps throughout the United States.

This infusion of recent civilians probably contributed to the criticism that soon developed among the allies.

On the Gas Alert, *Harry Everett Townsend, c. 1920. NCO roles in the Western Front trenches of World War I spanned the widest array of technical and tactical specialties.*

In their early contacts with the American Expeditionary Forces, Allied NCOs viewed American noncommissioned officers as half-trained and unsophisticated. When the first American divisions arrived in France, some French and British officers noted with distaste that American noncommissioned officers seemed to exercise little authority over their men. Part of the reason, the French concluded, was the American practice of throwing all the ranks together in garrison. The British and French had long set their noncommissioned officers apart, giving them special prestige and authority. From such comments, many Americans came to recognize the relatively low status of U.S. NCOs compared to those in other armies. And the NCOs themselves—regular and draftee—soon realized that trench warfare placed greater leadership demands upon them than their training had prepared them for.

As a result, General John J. ("Black Jack") Pershing, commander of the American Expeditionary Forces, recommended in April 1918 that NCO training in leadership skills be upgraded at once. The Army implemented his recommendations the next month. But when General Pershing recommended that special schools for sergeants be established immediately to improve leadership skills, schooling was provided, but only for noncommissioned officers in the American Expeditionary Forces—it was not institutionalized Army wide. Pershing's wartime expedient did not survive demobilization.

Nevertheless, during the last months of the war the strong performance of hundreds of noncommissioned officers showed the value of those reforms that Pershing had managed to institute. General Pershing summed up his views on the importance of NCOs as small-unit leaders in a message to Maj. Gen. G. B. Duncan, commanding general of the 82d Division: NCOs, Pershing wrote, "must love initiative and must hold what ground they gained to the utmost. It often happens that a sergeant or even a corporal may decide a battle by the boldness with which he seizes a bit of ground and holds it."

Indeed, the most important tactical lesson to emerge from the battles of the Western Front was the significance of small-unit actions. The European armies had learned the lesson slowly. The battle of the Somme and the horror of Verdun—a battle that cost hundreds of thousands of lives—taught the survivors on both sides to avoid mass formations. Usually led by a noncommissioned officer, small fire teams of infantrymen learned to take advantage of mist along river banks and every fold of ground, while providing covering fire for other groups nearby. At Pershing's insistence, Americans learned the lesson too. As weapons and tactics continued to evolve in twentieth-century warfare, the role of the NCO would continue to grow.

World War II and Korea

During the 1920s and 1930s, antiwar sentiments and isolationism swept America. The whole Army suffered, in particular the NCO Corps, whose numbers and pay were cut. Once again, the gap between a private's and a sergeant's pay narrowed. Despite the efforts of the War Department and the chiefs of staff to preserve a corps of experienced, professional soldiers and their special place within the Army, the Army could not build on General Pershing's wartime efforts to encourage the professional spirit of the NCO Corps. The Great Depression in particular brought further cuts in congressional funds for the Army and more hardships for those trying to make a living as career soldiers. Yet many civilians were going hungry, and the Army offered a career of relative security. Many competed for the few vacancies available.

World War II made more demands upon the Noncommissioned Officer Corps and had a greater impact upon the NCO's role and status than any previous conflict in American history. The war engaged a huge proportion of the nation's manpower: 25 percent, compared to 13.6 percent in World War I. This great mobilization not only increased the numbers of noncommissioned officers but also led to inflation in grade structure. As the eight-man infantry squad increased to twelve men, the squad leader became a sergeant. The corporal, once leader of the squad, became second-in-command and a fire-team leader. By the end of the war, 23,328 infantry squads in 288 active infantry regiments had two NCOs instead of one. More than 70 separate battalions, including armored infantry and rangers, raised the total number of such squads to over 25,000.

Along with the need for more small-unit leaders, the Army required thousands of new technical specialists to handle the more sophisticated weaponry of World War II. To identify and keep track of the numerous, complex skills appearing in the enlisted ranks, the Army introduced an important new managerial tool: the military occupational specialty (MOS) system. In World War I, personnel classification had included only initial identification of inductees' civilian work experiences. The MOS system went a step farther, using three-digit numbers to identify specific skills the Army needed, and it proved vital in handling the complexities of wartime personnel classification and assignment.

Yet the MOS system had its defects. It could identify specialties far better than it could identify men or women whose personal qualities would make them good noncommissioned officers. Furthermore, it soon became overspecialized, degenerating into a confusing maze of unrelated numbers, as each branch of the service developed its own series of special job skill requirements.

But the main problem was the proliferation of technicians/specialists, which became so great that it overwhelmed most units. Because these specialists received NCO status, a typical rifle company soon had only one private first class and seventeen privates—everyone else was a noncommissioned officer. This situation placed the burden for work details and guard duty on a shrinking number of soldiers. In late 1943 the Army leadership decided that technicians/specialists appointed after 1 December 1943 would share the duties of privates, while wearing the letter T under their NCO chevrons and drawing the pay of enlisted grades 3, 4, and 5. Thus the "techs" came into existence, the target of some joking at the time but an absolutely essential element in the winning of the war.

The large numbers of new NCOs were even more important. Drafted, trained, and promoted during the hectic months of 1942 and 1943, these citizen-soldiers carried out their duties as noncommissioned officers superbly in countless engagements on every front during World War II, but especially those where small-unit leadership was at a premium, such as the jungle warfare of New Guinea in the Pacific and the Hürtgen Forest battle in Europe.

When World War II ended, the great numbers of NCOs and techs presented a problem, for they were more likely to remain in the ser-

Machine Gunner, *Jes W. Schlaikier, 1943. From the steamy tropics of the South Pacific to the intense cold of the Ardennes Forest, NCO squad leaders coped with a wide variety of conditions during World War II.*

Kajon-ni, Korea, December 1952, *Don Spaulding, 1952. The 1950–1953 "police action" in Korea sent NCOs into combat as part of a United Nations force as the Cold War turned hot.*

vice than were privates and PFCs. While rapid demobilization reduced enlisted strength by 90 percent, NCO ranks were bursting at the seams. Numbers, however, were not the whole story. The World War II mobilization had permanently changed the character of the professional noncommissioned officer. No longer bachelors whose whole lives revolved around their units, many of the noncommissioned officers now were married men who lived in their own homes rather than sharing the barracks with their subordinates.

In the postwar era, the Army took some steps to improve NCO training and education. During World War II it had not revived Pershing's special schools for NCOs, although it had integrated some leadership training into the unit-training cycle before deployment. Decisive change came only after the war, as the Army took up its occupation duties in Germany and Japan and prepared to face the challenges of the Cold War. The Army Staff decided to develop service-wide standards for NCO training in peacetime. Although well-trained noncommissioned officers were still needed, few possessed the skills required for postwar duties.

The Army's answer was the NCO academy system. Beginning in 1947 and continuing throughout the 1950s, a small number of noncommissioned officer academies emerged, the first being the Constabulary Academy founded at Sonthofen, Germany. Probably the best known was the Seventh Army Noncommissioned Officers Academy in Munich. Although promising, the new schools had shortcomings: weak guidance from above resulted in a lack of uniformity in selection procedures, subject matter, quality of instruction, and length of courses. Moreover, most noncommissioned officers never attended an academy; for them, instruction continued to mean traditional on-the-job training.

For many NCOs, unfortunately, Army life in the late 1940s became merely a job like any other. Occupation duty in conquered Germany and Japan was soft, with the American dollar strong and food and recreation easy to obtain. During the late 1940s practical training was often neglected. Yet the onset of the Cold War in 1947–1948 ought to have warned all soldiers—in fact, all Americans—that the price of freedom was as high as ever.

The price had to be paid in 1950, when war broke out in Korea. During the first few months of desperate fighting, instances of poor combat leadership and discipline often led to panic. Yet during the shock of battle and the confusion of retreat, some NCOs, those veterans of World War II who had not forgotten what they had learned in combat, stood out. As survivors toughened up and as the Army brought in rigorous training once again, NCOs began to demonstrate a renewed spirit, and their leadership skills, never more important, began to reemerge.

Because of the irregular and compartmented nature of the Korean terrain (eroded hills, narrow valleys, and deep gorges), much of the fighting took the form of small-unit actions. As in earlier wars, capable NCOs took command when their officers became casualties. Combat studies of the Korean conflict show that noncommissioned officers participated significantly in every outstanding performance by an infantry company. During the Korean War NCOs became recognized as leaders in battle even more than in World War II. Their record, historian S. L. A. Marshall wrote, showed that "strengthening the prestige of the upper bracket of noncommissioned officers within the combat arms contributed more directly than all else to an uplift of the fighting power of the army."

After the war ended in stalemate in 1953, the readiness of the Army again declined. Congress cut military budgets, and the Army used the

Border patrol in Germany. The Cold War placed different demands on the NCO Corps than did conventional combat. Constant vigilance became a watchword for NCOs assigned to patrol the Iron Curtain in Germany.

NCO Corps as a holding area for officers who could no longer keep their commissions and who were awarded six stripes instead. But things never returned to the climate of the late 1940s. The nation had heard the warning, and it maintained the draft and at least the minimum forces it needed to meet a continuing Communist threat throughout the world.

Legislation gradually transformed the status of noncommissioned officers. One of the most significant acts was the Military Pay Bill of 1958, which created two additional pay grades, E–8 and E–9. This action emphasized the increasingly important role of senior NCOs in the post–Korean War Army and was one way of rewarding experienced E–7s who had performed in an outstanding manner.

The Korean War had shown the urgent need for more and better-trained small-unit leaders. The Army Staff began to see the deficiencies in a system that relied on ad hoc courses and on-the-job training to produce NCOs prepared for leadership in a nuclear age. This realization led to a belated attempt in 1957 (AR 350–90) to standardize the courses of instruction at the various academies.

The Army leadership wanted the curriculum to stress the increased responsibility that the new concept of the nuclear battlefield placed on the NCOs, since it expected scattered units and fire teams to operate in isolation from one another. This emphasis was especially necessary after the introduction of the so-called Pentomic division in 1957, a formation whose five battle groups required more NCOs as small-unit leaders than had the World War II division.

All phases of instruction now emphasized *how* to teach others, underscoring the NCO's role as instructor, trainer, and example. Methods of instruction were the largest block in the curriculum, with map reading—a chronic deficiency among inexperienced (and even experienced) troops—the second largest. The course of instruction was set at a minimum of four weeks.

Minimum standards proved harder to establish than a curriculum. For many reasons, the goal was never achieved. Various academies depended upon the budgetary fortunes of their parent commands, and the quality of both instructors and students varied from class to class and from academy to academy. Most combat-unit commanders were reluctant to release key senior noncommissioned officers to attend the academies, especially during maneuver periods. But perhaps the biggest weakness of the academies was that even as late as the Vietnam War period, they remained outside the Army's formal school system, and relatively few members of the Noncommissioned Officer Corps ever attended.

Vietnam and Beyond

When war broke out again it was in another poor and divided nation of the Third World. Although the nature of the Vietnam conflict differed considerably from the fighting in Korea during the previous decade, the NCO again was called upon to fill the traditional roles of skilled trainer and small-unit leader.

The first American soldiers arrived in the Republic of Vietnam not as fighting forces, but as military advisers to a non-Communist

American Advisers in Vietnam. Beginning in the early 1960s with small-scale deployments of advisers to help the Army of the Republic of Vietnam, the American presence grew to over a half-million soldiers.

government under siege by both domestic insurgents and infiltrators from North Vietnam across the so-called Demilitarized Zone, or DMZ. Working directly with the Army of the Republic of Vietnam (ARVN) in a variety of hands-on situations, Army NCOs proved their worth as trainers, teachers, and advisers, just as they had in earlier, similar assignments in the Philippines, Korea, and elsewhere. American sergeants and corporals helped the ARVN develop abilities ranging from how to operate bulldozers and other heavy equipment to how to use helicopters and sophisticated weapons supplied by the United States.

NCOs tackled this traditional role in a new land with skill and determination, and the effort quickly proved to be effective, both among the ARVN soldiers and the Hmong tribesmen of the Central Highlands. The people of Vietnam were willing to learn and to take a role in their own defense, and the American advisory effort—at least at the practical level where the noncommissioned officer operated—was a success.

Beginning in 1965, the American commitment in Southeast Asia began to change. The advisory effort, always supported by a small number of combat units for security, dwindled in proportion as the deployment of U.S. ground forces expanded dramatically. Thousands of additional American soldiers, along with allied forces from Korea, Thailand, Australia, the Philippines, and New Zealand, joined the ARVN in fighting the North Vietnamese and Viet Cong.

As American soldiers took on a major combat role, the character of the war became apparent: more so than in any other military involvement in American history, battlefield success in Vietnam depended on effective small-unit leadership. In this sense, Vietnam was the war of the platoon sergeant—of the squad, patrol, and fire-team NCO. The Korean War had provided many examples of such leadership, but the NCO role in Vietnam was much more pervasive, reflecting the enemy's own increasing emphasis on small-unit tactics and the diversity of the terrain. Now NCOs had to demonstrate their competence, judgment, and fighting skills in isolated actions in areas ranging from rice paddies and deep jungles to the Central Highlands of Vietnam. Their success in a succession of often-for-

Base Camp, An Khe, John O. Wehrle, 1966. During the Vietnam War, American forces took advantage of the helicopter to conduct multibattalion operations.

gotten day-to-day engagements was critical to the total American military effort. At the same time, their advisory role continued as they taught ARVN units to conduct their own search-and-destroy missions and large sweeps to clear areas of enemy forces.

U.S. Army commanders in Vietnam knew that a favorite Communist tactic was to infiltrate troops into a particular area until they outnumbered the ARVN defenders. The insurgents would then strike, overwhelming the government forces before reinforcements could arrive, and then fade back into the peasant population. Using this tactic, the Communists were able to muster a numerical superiority at almost any given point in Vietnam, even if they were outnumbered in the country as a whole. The Americans hoped to counter this tactic by making the maximum use of airmobility—moving troops quickly by helicopter. If there was one item of military equipment that symbolized American warfighting in Vietnam, it was the helicopter. Choppers enabled small combat units to move quickly throughout the Vietnamese countryside. The U.S. Army's extensive use of airmobility made the role of the NCO small-unit leader not only more effective, but also of greater tactical importance.

But if NCOs played a critical role in the Southeast Asia conflict, they did not find it an easy assignment. Operations in unfamiliar terrain, increasing and determined challenges from the enemy, and deteriorating morale on the home front—all these factors combined to place tremendous strain upon the Army's leaders, from generals to sergeants. But the sergeants had special problems.

For thousands of noncommissioned officers, the Vietnam War brought an identity crisis. Because of a chronic shortage of experienced NCOs, caused in part by rotation policies and the one-year tour of duty, many company-grade officers dealt directly with the men. Available NCOs were often bypassed, and their proper role as small-unit leaders eroded. The morale of the Noncommissioned Officer Corps thus declined at the very time when, because of the nature of the tactics employed in Vietnam, the small-unit leader was more important than ever.

Combat operations were often intense and resulted in large numbers of killed and wounded. These casualties, along with non-combat losses and the one-year rotation system, soon stretched the Army in Vietnam thin among the younger commissioned and mid-level noncommissioned officer grades. Promotions to captain and major, or to staff sergeant and platoon sergeant, came more rapidly than normal. To meet a critical shortage, the Army turned out thousands of so-called "shake and bake" NCOs. Often their personal qualities of bravery and talent overcame their lack of experience and training, but individual achievement could not conceal the fact that the Army had come to depend in great part on a hasty wartime expedient.

As the buildup in Vietnam continued, ill will within the American enlisted ranks also became a growing problem. During World War II, enlisted men usually directed their animosity toward officers' privileges. Even before Vietnam, however, the focus of enlisted hostility shifted toward the career NCOs, or "lifers." The problem was a growing polarization between the younger, junior enlisted men (E–1s through E–5s) and the older, professional noncommissioned officers (E–6s through E–9s). Junior company-grade officers, reflecting the national generation gap, also often found it difficult to identify with the older NCOs. The latter found themselves either completely isolated or siding with the attitudes of senior officers in their own age group. Unit discipline was the ultimate casualty.

Departure from Vietnam on a "Freedom Bird." The heavy requirement for small-unit tactical leaders, technical specialists, and trainers strained the available pool of NCOs. In addition, the typical 365-day tour of duty disrupted the customary ability of the corps to provide continuity and experience in the field.

Incidents of insubordination and violence toward senior non-commissioned officers and, in some cases, company commanders became more common as the Vietnam War continued. This is not to say that the Army was overwhelmed by insubordination or that non-commissioned officers overall lost control of their men. But incidents were frequent enough to contribute to an atmosphere of frustration and self-doubt among many experienced NCOs. The crisis of the corps was a part of the more general crisis of the Army itself and of the nation at large, a product of deep divisions that had developed over the war.

As the United States combat forces withdrew from Vietnam, the Army chief of staff recognized that raising the status of the Noncommissioned Officer Corps was the first, crucial step toward rebuilding the Army. In 1973 the president and Congress decided to end the draft (Selective Service). Instead of a mainly conscript Army, the nation would now have a truly professional, Modern Volunteer Army. As the term "modern" suggested, the intent was not to return to the lean, struggling "old Army" of the 1920s and 1930s—much less to the frontier and the Indian-fighting days—but rather to build an Army upon the most modern principles of personnel management, leadership, motivation, and training. After two hundred years of NCO evolution and development as trainers, technical specialists, and small-unit leaders, the Army was at last fully prepared to recognize, encourage, and reward NCO professionalism. No less was needed if the Army was to continue to serve the nation that depended upon it.

The Triumph of Professionalism

The Army's increased emphasis on NCO professionalism meant that the Noncommissioned Officer Corps' potential at last would be fully developed. From the days of George Washington's Army, non-commissioned officers had usually thought of themselves as professionals, for they did skilled work that was not easy to learn and they shared a sense of identity as leaders and teachers of the enlisted ranks. But the Army leadership had been slow to recognize and encourage NCO professionalism. Vietnam and the Volunteer Army compelled a recognition of the changes that advances in science, technology, and tactics had brought. The dark hours of Vietnam thus led in the end to a greater appreciation of the noncommissioned officer's proper role. The change that resulted affected the critical areas of NCO pay, training and education, and personnel management. Through fundamental changes in these areas, the Army gradually recognized NCOs as a distinct and essential group, separate from those they led, and provided them a career ladder to climb and the knowledge and training they needed to climb it.

Long a concern, NCO pay received close attention in the post-Vietnam era. The laws creating the Modern Volunteer Army after Vietnam ensured that noncommissioned officers would be paid salaries that reflected their professional status in the Army and in American society. Today, the Regular Army fully recognizes the professionalization of the NCO Corps in its pay scales, as it does in other crucial ways.

NCO training and education had also long been the focus of Army reform debate. All professional groups formally educate and certify their members. Doctors attend medical schools; attorneys, law schools; and commissioned officers, military academies and service schools. But for much of their history the Army's noncommissioned officers, other than technical specialists, did not receive professional educational opportunities. Instead, the Army's leadership considered on-the-job training adequate. Before 1971 a formal, standardized educational program for the Noncommissioned Officer Corps did not exist within the Army school system. For the great majority of enlisted men, regardless of rank, "training" meant nothing more than hands-on experience.

End-of-Month Inspection, Fort Riley, Kansas, c. 1900. The tradition of the formal end-of-the-month inspection and payday formation was central to NCO life for many years.

Vietnam brought NCO education and training to the point of crisis. Tactical operations depended upon small-unit leaders—on platoon sergeants and squad and fire-team leaders—even more than in Korea. As the American role grew, combat losses, the limitations of the 12-month tour in Vietnam, and the 25-month stabilized tour in the rotation base, plus normal separations and retirements, led to a severe NCO shortage.

In June 1967 Army Chief of Staff General Harold K. Johnson had created the Noncommissioned Officers Candidate Course (NCOCC) to train NCOs where the need was greatest—for the combat arms. The Infantry School at Fort Benning offered the first of these courses, followed shortly by courses at the Armor School at Fort Knox and the Artillery School at Fort Still.

To some extent the NCOCC paralleled the Officers Candidate School (OCS) that had served the Army well during and after World War II. Students in both programs were volunteers who were promoted to

Hands-on Instruction in the Field, 1922. Except for short periods of national emergency, the Army normally has had to operate with limited funds. Training continued during such lean periods because NCOs knew how to improvise.

corporal upon assignment. Following a 22-week course, the officer candidate received a commission as a second lieutenant upon graduation. The NCOCC student, after an intensive 10-week course, was promoted to sergeant (E–5), with the top 5 percent (honor graduates) promoted to staff sergeant (E–6).

All new NCOCC graduates received an additional ten weeks of practical training in grade as assistant instructors and tactical NCOs in a basic training center. After a total of twenty weeks of training, they were sent to units in Vietnam. The first reported for duty in the spring of 1968. Despite the fact that there is no substitute for experience, and despite some initial resentment from older, middle-grade noncommissioned officers, these "shake and bake" NCOs generally performed well. The Army leadership concluded, therefore, that the NCOCC was a good wartime expedient, but not a sound foundation upon which to base long-term NCO training.

The Noncommissioned Officers Candidate Course was important, not only because it met an immediate need in Vietnam, but also because its success stimulated fresh thinking about NCO education and training as a whole. Outside the academies, on-the-job training was still the norm in 1968. Unlike the system for officer candidates, no Army-wide standards or systematic procedures existed for developing noncommissioned leaders. The NCOCC led the Army in the right direction—toward permanent upgrading and reform.

The result was the Noncommissioned Officer Educational System (NCOES), implemented in 1971. NCOES began as a three-level (later four- and now five-level) education system for enlisted careerists. The program had four specific objectives: to increase the professional quality of the NCO Corps; to provide enlisted personnel with opportunities

10-inch Coast Defense Gun, *Thure de Thulstrup, 1900. Sergeants taught their men to master new weapons produced by the industrial and technical revolution at the turn of the nineteenth century.*

for progressive, continuing professional development; to enhance career attractiveness; and to provide the Army with trained and dedicated NCOs to fill permanent positions of increased responsibility.

The framework for achieving these objectives was a three-tier course of instruction designed to guide the NCO through a progressive series of skill levels in his or her primary and secondary military occupational specialties (MOSs). Each course included course work, on-the-job training, and periodic testing. NCOES courses attempted to present the proper balance of instruction in leadership, management, and technical skill. The basic course, which began in fiscal year 1971, provided E–4s and E–5s with training in all career management fields through forty-one service school courses. A year later, forty-three advanced courses opened, preparing over 4,000 E–6s and E–7s for E–8 and E–9 responsibilities in their MOS.

The capstone of the Noncommissioned Officer Educational System was the senior-level course, begun during fiscal year 1973 at the Sergeants Major Academy at Fort Bliss, Texas. Designed to prepare selected E–8s for duty as sergeants major and command sergeants major throughout the Army, the senior-level course at Fort Bliss, unlike the basic and advanced courses, was branch immaterial—dedicated to the broader professional perspective command sergeants major needed.

The 7th U.S. Army Noncommissioned Officer Academy, Sonthofen, Germany. Although formal instruction for officers began with the establishment of West Point, comparable leadership programs for NCOs began only after World War II.

With the maturing of the NCOES, the Army for the first time had put into place a formal, standardized system that educated enlisted men and women in step with grade progression. The senior-level course at the Sergeants Major Academy provided career enhancement for senior NCOs similar to that provided for officers by the senior service colleges. With NCOES, the professionalization of noncommissioned officer training was at last becoming a reality.

A professional NCO personnel management system, however, emerged very slowly. Like a juggler trying to keep several objects in the air at the same time, the Army Staff faced several manpower challenges in the mid-1960s. While operations in Vietnam required increasing quantities both of men and materiel, large field armies in western Europe and Korea also placed heavy demands on training and maintenance facilities. These burdens seriously challenged the Army's junior leaders, especially its NCOs. The Army tried a series of personnel management programs to sustain the professional capabilities and the morale of these leaders. But it was a scattergun approach.

As the 1970s began, the reduction of the Army from Vietnam's peak of 1.5 million men and women to about 775,000 and the emergence of the all-volunteer force caused the Army Staff to reconsider its piecemeal personnel management programs. Policies governing promotion, MOS classification, and testing and evaluation all affected a soldier's career pattern, morale, and likelihood of staying in the Army. Because the various programs were separate and sometimes contradictory in their effect, a soldier might well become confused and disheartened by the lack of clear direction in his or her career. Chief of Staff General Creighton W. Abrams directed a review to address the problem. In 1973 the Military Personnel Center and the Training and Doctrine Command (TRADOC) took the lead in initiating far-ranging studies.

The result was the Enlisted Personnel Management System (EPMS), implemented on 1 October 1975. It was designed to provide clear patterns of career development and promotion potential, whether a soldier served three years or thirty. Each career management field was grouped into a number of related MOSs and redesigned to provide a logical and visible road map to guide career-motivated soldiers along the most direct route from E–1 to E–9. The staff intended the new system to eliminate promotion bottlenecks and to provide a fair opportunity for advancement to all by centralizing promotions.

The EPMS had varied and powerful impacts. For one thing, dead-end military occupational specialties—those in which a soldier could progress only to sergeant or staff sergeant—were eliminated. Instead, the grouping of related responsibilities into career management fields enabled a soldier to merge one specialty into a related MOS at a certain grade. For example, a soldier with a Radio Operator MOS formerly peaked at the grade of sergeant and had to change jobs entirely to seek further promotion. Under the EPMS, the same soldier could merge into a related specialty (e.g., Tactical Communications System Operator/Mechanic) and continue along the same career path.

NCO education was also affected. The Noncommissioned Officer Educational System was one of the earliest programs to be taken over, integrated, and expanded. MOS skill levels were restructured for each enlisted grade, with a total of five levels. The branch schools developed training plans for each military occupational specialty, outlining specific tasks, the conditions under which tasks were to be performed, and the standards to be met for each skill level. Periodically, NCOs would verify through Skill Qualification Testing their ability to perform tasks at their required skill level. By achieving even higher qualifications scores in common-task testing, the MOS written test, and the hands-on evaluation, a soldier could attain the next higher skill level and thereby be considered for promotion.

In many ways the EPMS was like the Officers' Personnel Management System. Once the EPMS was adopted, the Noncommissioned Officer Corps had the kind of formal, service-wide system of professional career development that commissioned officers had long taken for granted.

But the EPMS was not the last word in noncommissioned officer career management. In 1980 the Deputy Chief of Staff for Operations outlined the Noncommissioned Officer Development Plan (NCOPD). The creators of the plan emphasized the need for commanders at all levels to conduct formal NCO leadership training. At the same time, the plan made the Sergeant Major of the Army responsible for overseeing noncommissioned officer professional development throughout the Army's major commands, the National Guard, and the Army Reserve.

Significantly, the NCODP complemented but did not displace the Enlisted Personnel Management System. The Noncommissioned Officer Development Plan enabled the NCO to put into practical application within his or her own unit the training and skills acquired through the EPMS and the NCOES. Instead of mere testing, this "doing" phase of training enabled soldiers to demonstrate their readiness to become truly professional NCOs.

Taken together, the Noncommissioned Officer Educational System, the Enlisted Personnel Management System, and the Noncommissioned Officer Development Plan meant that the Army had the doctrinal, institutional, and structural blueprint necessary to produce the professional noncommissioned officers needed for

Aerial View of the U.S. Army Sergeants Major Academy, c. 2001. A soldier's progression through the NCOES culminates in the Sergeants Major Academy. Inset: *Students of the Command Sergeants Major Course. Standardized classroom instruction is the hallmark of the current NCOES.*

a contemporary Army. Today NCOs in the U.S. Army enjoy the recognition as professionals they have earned. They receive respectable pay for a day's work; they can advance in rank through a career educational system; and they enjoy the benefits of centralized career management. NCOs now sit on promotion boards chaired by general officers and stand (symbolically at least) at the right hand of every commanding officer from platoon leader to the Chief of Staff. The way has been long, but a better Army has been the result.

DESERT STORM, Peacekeeping, and Beyond

The 1970s was a period that most veteran NCOs would like to forget. While Americans watched a quarter century of involvement in Vietnam come to an end with the fall of Saigon in April 1975, the Army struggled to maintain its effectiveness despite serious problems common to society as well. Illegal drugs flourished in many parts of the Army; 40 percent of the Army in Europe confessed to drug use. In some units, conditions approached mutiny as gangs used extortion and brutality to impose their will. Racial violence affected Army units around the world. Soldiers abused their officers and noncommissioned officers. Between 1969 and 1971 the Army recorded 800 instances of attacks involving hand grenades, resulting in the deaths of forty-five officers and NCOs. The low prestige of the Army in society at large forced the Army to accept recruits of inferior quality, when it could find them at all. By 1974 Army manpower levels were 20,000 below authorization, and only four of the thirteen active component divisions were combat ready. NCOs found themselves caught between undisciplined soldiers and efforts to build an all-volunteer force.

Through the efforts of leaders from the chief of staff to the NCOs in the field, the Army slowly regained its efficiency and esprit. Supported by superiors, NCOs attacked the problems in their units. The Army cracked down on drug dealers and gang leaders; in four months in 1973, the Army in Europe discharged over 1,300 undesirables. Racial awareness programs created a dialogue between blacks and whites that restored a degree of trust. The "enlisted men's councils" that had bypassed NCOs in the chain of command gradually disappeared. Savvy recruitment campaigns and long-overdue pay raises in the early 1980s helped draw more qualified soldiers. New combat training centers, notably the National Training Center at Fort Irwin, California, ensured that these soldiers would be better trained under conditions more realistic than ever before. New policies carried out by NCOs provided increased support for families of servicemen. And NCOs were in the vanguard as the Army rebuilt its doctrine and equipment for the future. A new AirLand Battle doctrine placed more emphasis on maneuver and leadership at lower levels on the battlefield. NCOs worked hard to incorporate the "Big Five" weapons systems that would execute this new doctrine: the UH–60 Black Hawk helicopter, the M1 Abrams tank, the AH–64 Apache helicopter, the Patriot air defense system, and the M2/3 Bradley fighting vehicle. New light divisions and special operations forces provided the Army with new capabilities at the lower ends of the conflict spectrum. The capabilities of the new Army were graphically demonstrated in the quick success of Operation JUST CAUSE, the invasion of Panama, in 1989.

One year after JUST CAUSE, the NCOs and the rest of the Army received the chance to show how far they had come in seventeen years. Within days of Saddam Hussein's occupation of Kuwait in

Desert Storm, *Frank Thomas, 1991. During the hundred-hour ground war in Southwest Asia, NCOs served proudly and capably as an integral part of the multinational force.*

Tank Doctors, *Robert Teachout, 1988. In the 1980s new equipment, new tactics, and new training centers kept the NCOs prepared for action.*

August 1990, NCOs deployed to Saudi Arabia with the rest of the 82d Airborne Division. For the next five months, NCOs were in the thick of Operation DESERT SHIELD, the deployment of 297,000 American troops with their food, equipment, vehicles, and big guns from the United States and Europe to the Persian Gulf region. When a United Nations resolution failed to induce Saddam to withdraw from Kuwait, the coalition launched Operation DESERT STORM on 17 January. From the tank gunners firing their Abrams guns with deadly accuracy to the engineer squad leaders supervising road construction in some cases ahead of their own combat forces, from the Special Forces sergeants training and performing liaison duties with Saudi and Kuwaiti troops to the grizzled command sergeants major providing veteran leadership for the young soldiers, the Army's NCOs covered themselves with glory during the hundred-hour ground war. With the conclusion of DESERT STORM, one of the most lopsided victories in American military annals, the Vietnam veterans among the NCOs could view with special pride the new Army that they had done so much to create.

The NCOs enjoyed little opportunity to rest on their laurels after the victory of DESERT STORM. With the collapse of the Soviet empire and end of the Cold War, the Army entered an era of downsizing. In fiscal year 1992 alone, the Army lost about 100,000 soldiers and inactivated such proud units as the VII Corps and the 3d Armored Division that had distinguished themselves in the Gulf. From 710,000 at the start of Fiscal Year 1992, the active Army had decreased to 529,000 by the end of FY 1994. To ease the strain of force reductions, the Army instituted a number of support programs—including payments, job searches, and counseling—for those leaving the Army. Still, the rapid reduction of force structure to 1950s levels created an immense challenge for NCOs as they struggled to maintain morale among soldiers uncertain about their futures with the Army.

As the Army shrank, it also was deploying more frequently to trouble spots around the world. The end of the Cold War brought into the open national rivalries and ethnic tensions that had been subsumed for years by the East-West contest. Within two years of DESERT STORM, the Army was deploying troops to Somalia to aid nongovernmental organizations in the task of ending the famine and restoring order to a society that had collapsed. In September 1994 the Army spearheaded an international force of 25,000 troops that landed in Haiti to restore President Jean Bertrand Aristide to power and to maintain order. In December 1995 American troops participated in a 60,000-man force that deployed to Bosnia to implement the Dayton Peace Agreements between the Serbs and the Bosnian Muslims. And, in May 1999, Task Force HAWK moved to Albania to support Operation ALLIED FORCE against Serb occupation of Kosovo. In between these deployments, American soldiers were deploying to other trouble spots from the Sinai to Macedonia. At the same time Army troops retained a forward presence in Germany, Korea, Kuwait, and Saudi Arabia.

Nor were American troops, including NCOs, going overseas merely to conduct peacekeeping missions or nation building. To an unprecedented degree, they found themselves conducting humanitarian missions, both foreign and domestic, and helping to interdict the flow of illegal drugs into the United States. In southeastern Turkey, Rwanda, Peru, Ecuador, and Honduras, NCOs aided those left homeless by warfare or natural disasters. At home, NCOs gave out relief supplies to victims of Hurricane Andrew in southern Florida, helped fight floods in the Midwest and Georgia, and assisted those affected by earthquakes in California. NCOs trained foreign and domestic law enforcement and helped with detection equipment in the effort to stem the flow of illegal drugs into the United States. The pace of activity, with many soldiers deploying overseas multiple times in a given period, increased the challenge for NCOs in maintaining morale, particularly given the growing number of enlisted men with families. It is largely due to the efforts of competent, confident NCOs that retention rates remained as high as they did.

In the rising number of overseas deployments, NCOs of the reserve component played a full share. The Army's force-structure reforms of the early 1970s had placed an ever larger share of combat support and combat service support functions in the hands of National Guard and Army Reserve units, to the point that it was hard to envision an overseas mission of any scale without the participation of such units. Reserve NCOs possessed a number of skills in such areas as medicine, military police, and civil affairs—skills that were valuable to the nation-building, peacekeeping, and humanitarian tasks that were becoming such a steady staple of the Army's activities

SMA Jack L. Tilley with 101st Airborne Troops in Afghanistan, 2002. Today's NCO safeguards standards and traditions, trains subordinates, and is both technically and tactically proficient—the backbone of the Army.

in the 1990s. A policeman from a Virginia town might find himself an NCO with a civil affairs unit in Bosnia, or a medical technician from Texas might find herself a medic NCO in Central America in response to a massive natural disaster. Never did the phrase Total Army have more resonance than in the active-reserve integration of the last years of the twentieth century.

With the beginning of the twenty-first century, NCOs joined the rest of the Army in bracing themselves for the changes wrought by the "revolution in military affairs." Through a sweeping "transformation," the Army sought to adjust to the information revolution and other major changes wrought by anticipated technological breakthroughs. The Army hoped that these breakthroughs would make possible an Objective Force that was more lethal, mobile, deployable, agile, survivable, and supportable than any force before it. These changes promised to make the intelligent, self-reliant noncommissioned officer more important than ever before to the Army of the future. NCOs were at the forefront of testing of the Stryker vehicle and other new systems of the Interim Combat Brigade Team at Fort Lewis, Washington. Just as they had contributed enormously to the Army that won the Gulf War, so they sought to build the Army of the new century.

On a September morning in 2001, however, the world of the NCO changed with the terrorist destruction of the twin towers of the World Trade Center and one of the outer walls of the Pentagon. In the halls of the Pentagon, NCOs performed heroically to rescue those at the mercy of the flames. Within weeks, Special Forces NCOs were making contact with allies in Afghanistan, cultivating the seeds for the upheaval that would eventually sweep al Qaeda terrorists and their Taliban allies from power. They helped train the fighters of the Northern Alliance and provided the air liaison parties that made possible the devastating aerial bombardments on Taliban positions. In

Operation ANACONDA, NCOs of the 10th Mountain and 101st Airborne Divisions led their troops through the rugged elevations and frigid weather of the Shahi Kowt (Shah-e-Kot) range in eastern Afghanistan to root out al Qaeda cells from their caves. In this war against terrorism, perhaps even more so than in previous American conflicts, NCOs figured to take a predominant role.

Never have the challenges for the Army's NCOs been more daunting, but never have the capabilities of those NCOs been greater. The NCO of the twenty-first century has come a long way from the file-closer of the Revolutionary War era. Today's NCO must deal with a more diverse body of soldiers than faced any of his predecessors. He finds himself in much more complex situations, at different times serving as ambassador, teacher, doctor, and technician, as well as disciplinarian. He deals with technology infinitely more complicated than the flintlock muskets and brass cannon of Washington's Army. But today's NCO has more training and education and more professional status than any of his predecessors. Furthermore, the most important factors, the intricacies of leadership and human relations, have not changed that much in 200 years.

Part Two

Portraits
of
NCOs
in
Action

"When someone pinned those stripes on your collar, you made a promise. You promised to take care of soldiers and teach them how to stay alive. You either did it consciously by reciting the NCO Creed or some other way during a ceremony....Look at your soldiers. Look at what's going on around you. Check, check, and correct. You should leave Sergeants Tracks behind you everywhere you go. They are the mark of a true professional."

—M. Sgt. Christopher J. Zimmer
NCO Journal, 2002

To Range the Woods, *Manuel B. Ablaza, 1988*

To
RANGE
THE
WOODS

NEW YORK, 1760

———————◆———————

Entering the fort made the ranger sergeant feel uneasy—too much saluting, too many people scurrying around acting important. Ever since this latest struggle against the French and their Indian allies had started in earnest, things had been this way. For the first time in anyone's memory British regulars had been sent across the ocean in large numbers, bringing a whole array of notions that had turned fighting upside down. Suddenly, officers everywhere were making an infernal racket and worrying about how you looked, not how well you could shoot. They even dressed wrong. Their red coats and shiny buttons stood out clearly in the bright summer sun, but that was hardly something that you wanted when you were trying to sneak up on an enemy outpost!

Although the scene at the fort always reminded him of an ant-hill after someone had kicked it over, he sighed and motioned to the private with him to proceed. They had a mission to carry out. Major Rogers had told him to deliver a message personally to the general, and it was best not to dawdle. Pausing only to ask directions to headquarters from the British sergeant (he was easy to spot—the one with the axe on a stick, called a halberd) at the gate, the two New Englanders set about their task. Although the private was young enough to be impressed by the fort, the sergeant had been in action for four years, and he wasn't about to let anyone forget that he wore the elite green uniform of a ranger.

The pride that he felt in his unit went hand in hand with the efficient arrangement of his weapons, uniform, and equipment. From his clean and well-maintained musket and hatchet to his leggings and moccasins, the sergeant projected an image of someone completely at home in the virgin forests that covered the frontiers of the North American colonies. Moving silently through the woods around Lake Champlain was second nature to this man—a fact that Major Rogers had noticed and rewarded, first by hand-picking him

The Battle of Rogers' Rock, J. L. G. Ferris. The fundamental American belief that soldiers are also citizens has always prompted those in authority to lead through example rather than through fear. Since Rogers' Rangers in the French and Indian War (depicted here), NCOs have used this personal approach to maintain discipline.

and then by promoting him. Leading a small patrol and acting as the army's eyes and ears carried a high degree of risk and the burden of making split-second decisions that could mean life or death for the soldiers serving under him, but that was what the sergeant wanted to do, and it was what he did best.

Background

From the late seventeenth to the mid-eighteenth century, Britain and France were engaged in a prolonged struggle for world dominance. Known loosely as the second Hundred Years' War, it pitted land and sea forces against each other around the globe. Colonists of both powers in North America and their Indian allies became embroiled in the conflict as well, establishing fundamental traditions in both the American and Canadian armed forces.

The term French and Indian War (1754–1763) refers to the portion of the contest between the two giants fought in the New World. To people of the time, North America formed a relatively minor theater compared with Europe, Africa, India, or even the Caribbean. But to Virginians or New Englanders or French Canadians the issue was far more immediate—survival. Earlier conflicts had involved relatively tiny contingents' raiding each other's outposts as the colonies expanded from their initial toeholds along the coastline and major rivers. By the middle of the eighteenth century, however, colonial growth had brought imperial interests fully into play. At stake was control over the rich resources of the continent, including the fur trade.

In 1754 the governor of Virginia raised a small contingent of full-time soldiers, known as Provincials to distinguish them from Royal regulars. He sent them under a former militia officer, George

Washington, to evict the French from the area that would later become Pittsburgh, Pennsylvania. The defeat of this Virginia force marked the opening round of the war. This initial disaster prompted the London government to send over two regular regiments of Redcoats the following year, while France dispatched similar forces to strengthen Canada. Although the outnumbered French and Canadians held the line for several years, the British marshaled increasing numbers of Provincials and Redcoats and prepared to bring the issue to conclusion.

Canada's security rested upon a network of defensive frontier fortifications that stretched from Louisbourg on the Atlantic, across the Great Lakes, and down the Ohio Valley. It also depended on the use of Indian allies in raids against the British colonies. For decades that combination had kept enemies at bay, but the British finally found a way to bring their superior resources into play. Columns of regulars and Provincials assembled annually on the disputed frontiers for campaigns targeting key forts. The first of these French forts fell in 1758. A year later the capture of Niagara cut the French off from the support of western tribes, while major British forces took Quebec City and finally punched through the Lake Champlain fortifications. The remaining French troops, now isolated, surrendered Canada in 1760.

Colonial military institutions took form during the period between the first landings by English settlers at Jamestown and Plymouth and that final victory over the French one hundred and fifty years later. Starting with Old World concepts, the settlers gradually modified their inherited traditions to fit the realities of the New World—a natural process as colonial society matured and grew. Whether political, legal, or military, all of America's institutions grew from English roots. Militarily, they traced their origins to the militia establishment created by the Anglo-Saxons over a millennium earlier. The militia tradition obligated each man who benefited

Rangers from the 2d Battalion, 75th Rangers, arrive by MH–6 Littlebird during training exercises at Fort Bragg, North Carolina, April 2002. Leading by example is especially important among Rangers, who have served with distinction since colonial times.

from society to protect it and, with certain exclusions, organized the able-bodied into part-time units on a local basis.

Colonists in North America created a defensive system to deal with two very different dangers: Indians and other Europeans. Contrary to popular myth, colonial military institutions did not evolve only with a view to the dangers of the forests; they also reflected the possibility of enemies' striking from the sea. The Indians posed a day-to-day problem only for frontiersmen; the Europeans, especially Frenchmen in the north and Spaniards in the south, formed a more significant long-term threat. America began as a maritime society and remained so until the Civil War. Because the art of war underwent dramatic change in Europe during the seventeenth century, as cannon and matchlock firearms improved and permanent professional armies emerged, the colonists had to adjust accordingly.

Conditions prevented early New World settlements from maintaining large standing armies, although they attempted to obtain the most modern weapons possible. Economic necessity required that everyone contribute to the production of food or essential products. The colonies could not afford to maintain idle manpower waiting for a possible war. At the same time, with little or no warning any colony or community could find itself under local attack from Indians or European raiders. The natural solution to this problem was to take the militia organization of England and infuse it with a new sense of urgency. Except for Pennsylvania, where a strong Quaker element objected to war on religious grounds, every English-speaking colony required free, able-bodied adult males to join their local military company and to provide their own weapons, ammunition, and basic field equipment. Regular unpaid training meetings—where training might be tough or casual, depending upon the current danger—provided basic skills, including an innovative emphasis on individual marksmanship. When it came to firing a musket, not every American was a Daniel Boone, but by the eighteenth century familiarity with and possession of firearms was more widespread in the English colonies than in almost any other place on earth.

In contrast to Europe, where the standing national army became all-important and local forces withered away, the American militia system remained vigorous. Although rarely mobilized in full strength, the network of local companies became a training agency and manpower pool from which full-time Provincial forces were raised. These Provincials enlisted for specific campaigns or provided garrisons in time of crisis for a network of small forts to protect key ports or frontier settlements.

A special category of Provincials represented colonial America's other original contribution to military science—the rangers. First appearing about 1675 as a type of scout to provide early warning of impending Indian attack by "ranging" or patrolling between forts, they (and their French-Canadian counterparts, the *coureurs du bois*) became masters of camouflage and woodcraft. Later their mission expanded when Capt. Benjamin Church of Massachusetts organized a mixed force of rangers and friendly Indians to conduct long-range raids during an Indian uprising called King Philip's War.

During the French and Indian War, the rangers reached a new level of importance. Robert Rogers of New Hampshire ultimately organized a force of about a dozen companies that accompanied the various British columns in the conquest of Canada. Their most daring achievement came in mid-September 1759 after General Jeffrey Amherst had captured Fort Carillon (Ticonderoga). Rogers personally led a strike force of about two hundred rangers on a deep raid designed to break the will of the last remaining pro-French Indians. Moving mostly at night, the column slipped through enemy lines and destroyed the village of St. Francis on the St. Lawrence River a hundred miles west of Quebec. The men then broke into small teams, often led by NCOs, and conducted a remarkable overland withdrawal to the New Hampshire frontier.

With such experiences behind him, the American soldier became markedly different from his European counterpart. His full-time service in any campaign became a matter of individual choice. Lacking the brutal discipline of continental Europe, Provincial leaders had to persuade militiamen to enlist and then they had to keep their confidence. Officers responsible for enforcing training and weapons-owning requirements knew they would meet their troops again as neighbors, as would their NCOs, who were responsible for the immediate supervision of the privates.

NCOs in Action

In the Old World, the noncommissioned officer emerged simultaneously with the concept of a permanent, or standing, army. With an officer corps drawn from the ranks of the aristocracy and privates from the lower classes, an intermediary group was required to bridge the social gap. Poorly paid, often unwilling troops needed constant supervision, and the new group of NCOs became the enforcers of discipline. Those duties carried greater weight in camp or garrison because actual combat remained relatively rare—few nations could afford the appalling casualty rates. Although no level of organization officially existed below the company, common practice divided the enlisted men into "messes" consisting of an NCO and eight or ten privates who ate and slept together—the origin of the modern squad.

Weapons in the seventeenth and eighteenth centuries were crude by modern standards. Poorly made and woefully inaccurate, the early matchlock and the later flintlock musket were effective only when fired at close range by large masses of troops standing shoulder to shoulder. Most nations raised their armies by contracting with captains and colonels to organize separate companies and regiments, uniform and equip them to a rough standard, and then recruit necessary replacements. When preparing for combat, the units would be grouped into brigades, battalions, and platoons, a process that often left the privates in a situation where they had to take orders from officers who were relative strangers. Under these conditions, sergeants and corporals exercised little independent authority. Their primary responsibility was to keep the men in line and force them to obey orders.

This use of the NCO in continental Europe peaked in the eighteenth century in the Prussian Army of Frederick the Great. During the Seven Years War in particular, relatively small Prussia held off the combined arms of three great powers—Russia, Austria, and France. Although he lost several battles, Frederick was a military genius, which accounted in part for his success. But contemporaries were quick to point to his NCO Corps as a secret weapon. Frederick knew that he would normally have to fight against superior numbers, but he realized that quality and determination frequently can triumph over quantity. He therefore set about training his regiments to a higher standard than did his neighbors, using sergeants and corporals to ensure absolute obedience. Frederick made no bones about it—he demanded that his privates fear their own NCOs more than the enemy.

American colonists, looking more to English practices, quickly made noncommissioned officers responsible for most of the training provided to new soldiers. But training was not based on large-scale units. Militia regiments existed as early as 1636, but they seldom could assemble in a single location for training. Instead, a town or village normally formed a single company, subdivided into squads patterned after the European messes. Although the fact that neighbors composed a squad helped to narrow the gap between NCO and private, the NCO had more immediate responsibility, and more opportunity than in Europe, for independent action in training and administration. Those enhanced powers inevitably translated into more responsibility on the battlefield, a trend reinforced by the need to adjust to the heavy woods and the hit-and-run tactics of Indians. Since large formations simply stood no chance of chasing and catching raiders, small units became the American norm. The result during the French and Indian War was the formation of ranger companies by Major Rogers.

A combination of factors, including the relative lack of rigid class lines in the New World, affected the evolution of a new kind of military organization in the colonies. Freed from the need to maintain large standing forces, with more economic and social freedom at a local level than in Europe, Americans quickly abandoned blind obedience as a foundation for their militia system. Instead, they created a new blend in which talent and competence mattered most. Leadership became a positive influence, not something enforced through brutal discipline.

From the very beginning, the notion that every citizen was expected to serve in the military if needed helped keep the armed forces clearly subordinate to civilian authorities. At the practical level, the local orientation of unit organization allowed the military to grow from the bottom up, guaranteeing that noncommissioned officers would form the backbone of any force. In fact, the practice begun during the colonial days of picking natural leaders to serve as NCOs still has an influence on how we train professional soldiers. And the passage of centuries has only confirmed the importance of the noncommissioned officer as small-unit leader, from the frozen wilderness of Lake Champlain in Rogers' day to the mountains of Afghanistan in our own.

An Ordered and Disciplined Camp, *Anita Y. Sonnie, 1988*

An
Ordered
and
Disciplined Camp

Virginia, 1781

———◆———

The quartermaster sergeant was caught up in the hustle and bustle of packing up his regiment's camp and loading the gear into wagons. To an outsider, the scene appeared one of total confusion, but not to the experienced eyes of veteran Continental Army noncommissioned officers. They knew that each man followed a careful script, so that no incomplete task would create problems down the road. Precision came from the routine itself, from a drill that defined specific tasks, allocated responsibilities, provided supervisors to correct any mistakes instantly, and, most important, took place each and every time the Army moved.

While uniforms might appear worse for wear, the regiments' weapons and equipment were immaculate—a fundamental change since the opening days of the Revolution. Thanks to training begun at Valley Forge by George Washington and his Inspector General, Baron Frederick von Steuben, officers and NCOs had standardized instructions and a sense of how each man fitted into the smooth functioning of the whole. One example of the improvement came from the "camp color men." Every day a dozen or so privates reported to the regimental quartermaster and his assistant, the quartermaster sergeant. In camp, this detail performed duties ranging from digging latrines to collecting firewood; on the march, they packed and unpacked the baggage wagons. Their nickname came from the small pennants, camp colors, used to mark both the wagons and the outlines of the camp. This systematic approach ensured that essential housekeeping functions were performed routinely without interfering with other important duties.

This morning General Washington broke camp shortly after dawn, pushing hard to cover as many miles as possible. For over a week, several American divisions and a French expeditionary force had been marching south from New York. Rumor had it that the units were on their way to a place called Yorktown in far-off Virginia. While the quartermaster rode ahead to mark out a new site, the sergeant supervised the detail and the baggage wagons. He knew that doing his job professionally would never lead to glory, but also that without his efforts the regiment would never reach its destination in shape to fight, a point he kept trying to make to the privates. The beautiful Indian summer weather and a compliment from Baron von Steuben himself made this particular morning special—and raised hopes that perhaps the campaign would end with a victory.

Background

The War of Independence began on 19 April 1775 at Lexington, Massachusetts, in a fight that the British had hoped to avoid. The British had sent a large garrison to Massachusetts after the Boston Tea Party to enforce the authority of the Royal governor. The angry citizens had countered by increasing militia training and gathering military supplies. The British column of regular light infantry that entered Lexington was on its way to destroy one such stockpile in nearby Concord. The Redcoats were met by the local militia company, commanded by a veteran of Rogers' Rangers, drawn up on the Common—a grassy open space. When the British attempted to disperse the citizen-soldiers, shots rang out, starting what proved to be the second longest war in American history.

Supply Depot, City Point, Virginia, 1864. Although combat operations attract public attention, it is the movement of troops and supplies, directed by technically competent NCOs, which ultimately has meant victory in a host of campaigns. During the Civil War, such activities revolved around horses, mules, and wagon trains.

By evening the British had been mauled and driven back into Boston, besieged by nearly 20,000 colonists. All four New England colonial governments reacted by replacing their militia and Minutemen with armies recruited to serve until the end of the year. At almost the same time, the Second Continental Congress convened in Philadelphia and quietly began creating a nation. On 14 June 1775, it assumed control of the existing military forces and established the regular Continental Army. To symbolize unity among all colonies, north and south, Congress promptly set about recruiting ten (later thirteen) companies of riflemen from the middle colonies and named a Virginian, George Washington, as commander in chief.

Over the next two years the growing Continental Army would experience both triumphs and defeats. Although it came to include regiments drawn from all thirteen colonies and Canada, it was plagued early in the war by instability, caused by relying on units recruited for only a single year at a time. That practice had been adequate during the French and Indian War, when the enemy remained on distant frontiers. It was also consistent with the colonists' deep-seated fear that professional, or standing, armies of the European kind posed a greater danger to civil liberties than any foreign invasion. Many Americans believed that militia units serving for limited periods would be sufficient to win independence, since militiamen could easily be mobilized to reinforce Washington and his generals whenever a crisis threatened. But Washington wanted a regular force as well. In the end both the militia and the regular Continental Army proved vital to victory.

Red Ball Express, H. Charles McBarron, 1978. During World War II, trucks like those of the famous "Red Ball Express" carried out the essential supply functions formerly conducted by wagon trains.

The Revolutionary forces quickly gained control over the countryside, dispersing attempts by those Americans still loyal to the King to assert themselves. Washington's units also succeeded in driving the British from Boston. Unfortunately, an American invasion of Canada ended in disaster, and in the summer and fall of 1776 a massive Royal fleet and army inflicted a string of humiliating defeats on Washington in New York. The largest expedition dispatched across a major ocean before the twentieth century, the British army mauled the continentals and militia attempting to defend Manhattan and Long Island. On Christmas Day 1776 the Revolution seemed to be on its last legs. The British and their Hessian auxiliaries had settled down in snug winter quarters to lay plans for the final conquest. Washington's remaining troops were huddled in rude camps, suffering the bitter cold.

But at dawn on 26 December the tide of the war turned back in the Americans' favor. The continentals suddenly struck across the Delaware River at a Hessian brigade in garrison at Trenton, New Jersey, destroying it as a fighting force while suffering only four casualties. Buoyed by that success the same troops, reinforced by Pennsylvania militiamen, slipped around the enraged British a week later and smashed a second brigade at Princeton, forcing the British to pull back.

Those twin victories, small though they were, along with the heartening words of Thomas Paine's pamphlet Common Sense, restored morale and enabled the Continental Congress to carry out a major recruiting effort. In a bold departure from earlier practices, the nation's leaders decided to match the British regulars with trained regulars of their own. They approved enlistments for the duration of the war, rather than for a fixed term. They also increased the Continental Army to a balanced force of over one hundred regiments of infantry, cavalry, and artillery, backed by technical specialists in military police, ordnance, and quartermaster units and by a sophisticated command and staff organization.

The Army did not achieve immediate success when it took to the field for the 1777 campaign. The new recruits lacked time for anything more than rudimentary training before operations began. Moreover, their weapons, imported from Europe, had to be routed to them through a complicated series of distribution points. In Pennsylvania, Washington fought hard against a British army brought by sea from New York to attack Philadelphia, but he could not prevent the loss of that city, then the nation's capital. In northern New York State, other Continental units, reinforced by large militia contingents, took advantage of favorable terrain in early fall and inflicted a serious setback on British invasion plans by capturing General "Gentleman Johnny" Burgoyne's army at Saratoga. In each case, some regiments performed well while others failed the test of battle.

Most of the Continental Army massed at Valley Forge, Pennsylvania, for the winter of 1777–1778, far enough from Philadelphia for safety, yet close enough to prevent the British from venturing into the countryside. Washington used the pause in active operations caused by the cold weather to institute a major reform of the Continentals. For the first time in the war he had time to standardize training programs. Taking advantage of European volunteers, especially Steuben, who had learned his trade in Frederick the Great's Prussia, the Americans crafted a coherent tactical doctrine that blended the ideas from the Old World with tried-and-true colonial experience.

Steuben, despite his German origins, agreed with Washington and the other leaders that the Army should follow the new French emphasis on flexibility and initiative and add to them the traditional American reliance on marksmanship. As Inspector General, he set about developing a comprehensive system to teach that doctrine to the troops assembled in snowbound huts at Valley Forge. Since the flintlock musket of the era lacked rifling and a rear sight, it was ineffective at ranges beyond one hundred yards. It also had a practical rate of fire of no more than three or four rounds per minute. To employ it efficiently, men had to be meticulously trained to stand in lines and load and fire in unison. Then they had to learn how to maneuver on the battlefield in those lines without losing their cohesion.

The system of instruction crafted by Steuben at Valley Forge was published in early 1779 under the title *Regulations for the Order and Discipline of the Troops of the United States, Part I* (better known to the troops as the *Blue Book* because of the color of its cover). It broke down the elements needed for combat success into individual tasks, each of which built upon mastery of preceding tasks. One of the simplest systems devised anywhere in the world, it was quickly absorbed by the soldiers. To speed that process along, Steuben displayed a genius at practical psychology. He assembled a "company of instruction" built around Washington's bodyguard and personally drilled it, encouraging all off-duty personnel to watch. Punctuated by a colorful array of epithets and jokes in several languages, his method of teaching made training enjoyable and challenged each soldier to excel. Members of the company then returned to their original units where, under the watchful eye of a select group of officers, they extended the system to the rest of the Army.

Beginning at the battle of Monmouth in June 1778, Steuben-trained continentals demonstrated a new battlefield competence. His system relied on skilled marksmanship (in fact, the Blue Book became the first drill manual in the world to use the command to take aim rather than simply instructing the private to point his weapon in the general direction of the enemy). It also called for new skills. Thanks to his instruction, Americans quickly mastered the techniques of bayonet fighting and learned to use cadenced marching and column formations to maneuver quickly under fire. Whenever possible, they practiced these skills on the same kind of broken terrain they would encounter on the battlefield, not on the kind of manicured parade grounds preferred by European armies.

By the late summer of 1781 the process set in motion at Valley Forge had achieved a measure of success on the battlefield. Moreover, Britain no longer faced rebellious Americans fighting alone, for France had declared war on England in 1778, followed in due course by Spain and the Netherlands. As the conflict spread around the globe, resources available to the British to carry on military operations in North America shrank. Commanders based in New York City, admitting that they could no longer risk challenging Washington on ground of his own choosing, shifted to a new strategy. All troops that could be spared from the British garrison in New York sailed south in an attempt to conquer the lower colonies one at a time. Despite a series of battlefield victories, the British could not crush the resistance there either. When the unanticipated arrival of a large French fleet from the West Indies created a decisive opening, Washington rapidly shifted his focus to Virginia, pinned General Charles Cornwallis against the water at Yorktown, and, in a textbook example of formal European siege warfare, forced Cornwallis to surrender.

NCOs in Action

Initial Continental Army tables of organization drew upon European ideas that had been modified by American experience, especially during the French and Indian War. They created an infantry regiment composed of eight companies and a small headquarters. At full strength, an ideal seldom reached, the basic 90-man company of musketmen had 4 officers, 4 sergeants, 4 corporals, 2 musicians, and 76 privates. The privates and corporals formed the "rank and file," the men who shouldered muskets in linear combat and fired in volleys. The fifer and a drummer drew the same pay as corporals and counted as NCOs. Despite their musician title, they actually functioned as the company's signal section, relaying commands through their instruments in the same manner as buglers in a later era.

If the basic company arrangement required by formal European-style combat formations appeared to minimize the importance of the NCO, administrative organization was quite a different matter. Camp routines revolved around four squads, each consisting of 1 sergeant, 1 corporal, and up to 19 privates. Soldiers ate and slept with their squad, sharing the burden of transporting unit equipment, such as cooking pots or axes, and occasionally splitting into two sections, each headed by an NCO. Appointment of sergeants and corporals remained the exclusive prerogative of the regimental commander, normally acting on the advice of the company commander, but great attention was paid to selecting men of demonstrated maturity and leadership. Subsequent changes in company organization preserved these same basic arrangements. In 1778 the company shrank to 3 officers, 2 musicians, and 3 squads with a total of 3 sergeants, 3 corporals, and 53 privates. In 1781 the fourth squad returned when the number of privates grew to 64. That final change did not alter the number of officers or musicians, but increased the sergeants to 5 and the corporals to 4. One of each continued to provide leadership for each squad. The extra sergeant, created by freeing the first sergeant from direct supervision, helped to augment the officers' command and control abilities.

As a product of the Old World, Steuben emphasized the importance of officer involvement in training and in tactical leadership. As an American, he integrated the noncommissioned officer into that system. A fundamental Continental Army concept after Valley Forge called for each NCO to be trained so that when emergencies arose in the heat of battle he could step forward and assume the duties of his immediate superior. That message was emphasized through the final chapter in the Blue Book that set out the duties and responsibilities of each individual in a regiment, from colonel to private.

Within an infantry regiment in the Steuben era, each staff function had two individuals assigned, one officer and one NCO. The quartermaster watching over transportation and logistics was backed up by his quartermaster sergeant, just as the sergeant major assisted the adjutant, while two senior musicians (called the fife and drum majors) provided technical supervision over their company-level counterparts. Similar relationships emerged within the line companies. When deployed for combat, a regiment's men stood two deep to take maximum advantage of the firepower of their muskets. Company-grade officers assumed positions in the front row to exercise command and control. A "covering sergeant" stood immediately behind each officer with the dual mission of protecting him or stepping forward in the event that he fell. The covering sergeant kept his musket at shoulder arms with bayonet fixed and did not shoot when the other troops did, but reserved fire as his last resort. Other NCOs provided a guard for the junior officers carrying the regimental colors or occupied positions behind the line as file closers.

Although no one realized it at the time, Yorktown was the decisive battle of the War of American Independence. News of the defeat broke Britain's political will to wage war, forcing the King to appoint a new government, which was committed to negotiating peace. While war dragged on for almost two more years as diplomats worked out complex arrangements acceptable to all of the parties involved, the Continental Army used the time to continue improving its training in the Steuben system. It even conducted maneuvers on the Hudson River in the summer of 1782 as a dress rehearsal for a planned invasion of Manhattan Island. An armistice went into effect on 19 April 1783, eight years to the day after the first shots at Lexington. The final peace treaty was signed in Paris the following September.

Demobilization began almost at once, introducing a pattern that would become typical of America's response to the end of any war. By the end of the year, Washington had returned his commission to Congress and had joined most of his former troops in civilian life. The last contingent of the Continental Army, a regiment in size, disbanded on 20 June 1784 at West Point, New York, proving that Washington had created not a standing army but, rather, a wartime emergency force. A lone company of artillerists provided a measure of continuity by transferring directly into the new, single-regiment Regular Army created by Congress that same month.

Over time that nucleus would expand and contract, as would the militia, whose citizen-soldiers provided an emergency reserve force under the Constitution. Each contingent preserved the Steuben system of doctrine and training relatively intact through the War of 1812. The practice of dispersing the regulars in coastal forts and small garrisons along the frontier and the militiamen in company-size units in individual towns, together with changes in weapons and equipment, eventually watered down the immediate battlefield practicality of the *Blue Book*. Ironically, these very same trends increased the Army's reliance on both the technical knowledge and small-unit leadership of the NCO Corps.

The Journal, *Michael Haynes, c. 2002*

ALONG
THE
FRONTIER

LOUISIANA TERRITORY, 1804

———————◆———————

The sergeant sat down at the end of a long day to write in his journal. As the senior noncommissioned officer of the expedition under "Captains" Lewis and Clark, he acted as the first sergeant, issuing the daily provisions after the company bivouacked in the evening and appointing guard and other details. When the two captains were absent, he commanded the expedition.

Under candlelight, the sergeant described the daily routine of the Corps of Discovery. The expedition usually "set off early" in the morning after breaking camp and loading its equipment aboard the boats. A corporal commanded the detachment that rode in the white canoe, while the civilian boatmen took the red canoe. On the keelboat, three sergeants rotated duties. One always manned the helm, another supervised the crew at amidships, and the third kept lookout at the bow.

Hard physical labor characterized each day, as the men navigated their "ungainly craft" up the powerful Missouri River. If the river was deep enough, the men rowed. If the current was too swift for rowing, the men fastened a 40-foot cable to the mast of the keelboat, came ashore, and pulled the boat upriver. If the wind failed and the river was shallow enough, the men walked to the bow of the keelboat, placed their iron-pointed setting poles into the river's bottom, and started walking to the stern of the boat, pushing it slowly upriver. They then returned to the bow and repeated this process. In every case, the men needed a total physical commitment to make every mile.

At the end of the day, while some kept watch and others danced to the fiddle, the sergeant faithfully described the events of the day in his journal. He noted that as the expedition traveled north, the men conquered every navigational hazard the Missouri River offered. The men also overcame a variety of physical ills: boils, blisters, bunions, sunstroke, dysentery, fatigue, injuries, colds, fevers, snakebites, ticks, gnats, toothaches, headaches, sore throats, and mosquitoes. At the same time the Corps of Discovery became the first Euro-Americans to

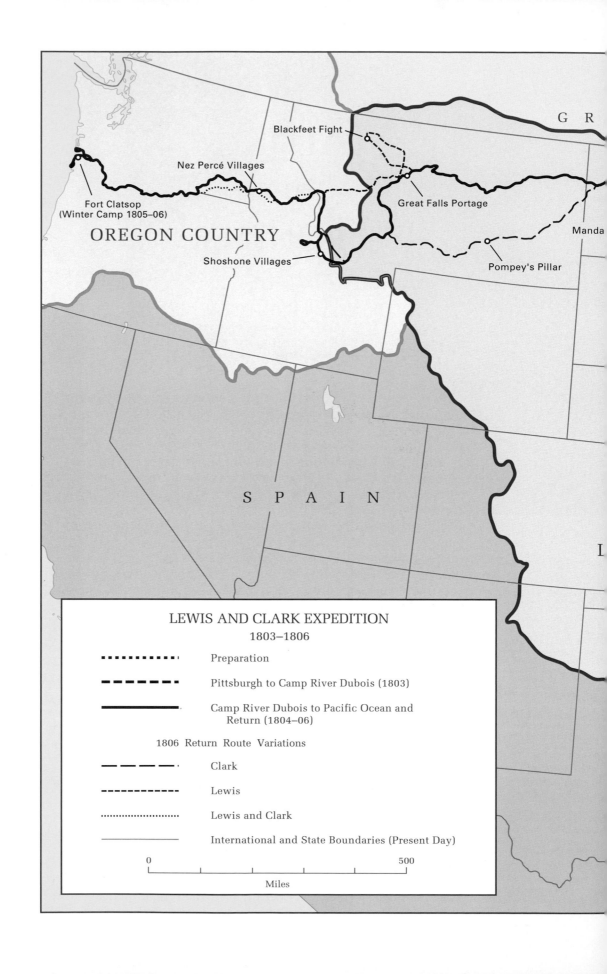

G R

Blackfeet Fight

Nez Percé Villages

Great Falls Portage

Fort Clatsop
(Winter Camp 1805–06)

Manda

OREGON COUNTRY

Shoshone Villages

Pompey's Pillar

S P A I N

L

LEWIS AND CLARK EXPEDITION
1803–1806

·············	Preparation
– – – – –	Pittsburgh to Camp River Dubois (1803)
——————	Camp River Dubois to Pacific Ocean and Return (1804–06)

1806 Return Route Variations

— – — – —	Clark
- - - - - - -	Lewis
··················	Lewis and Clark
—————	International and State Boundaries (Present Day)

0   500

Miles

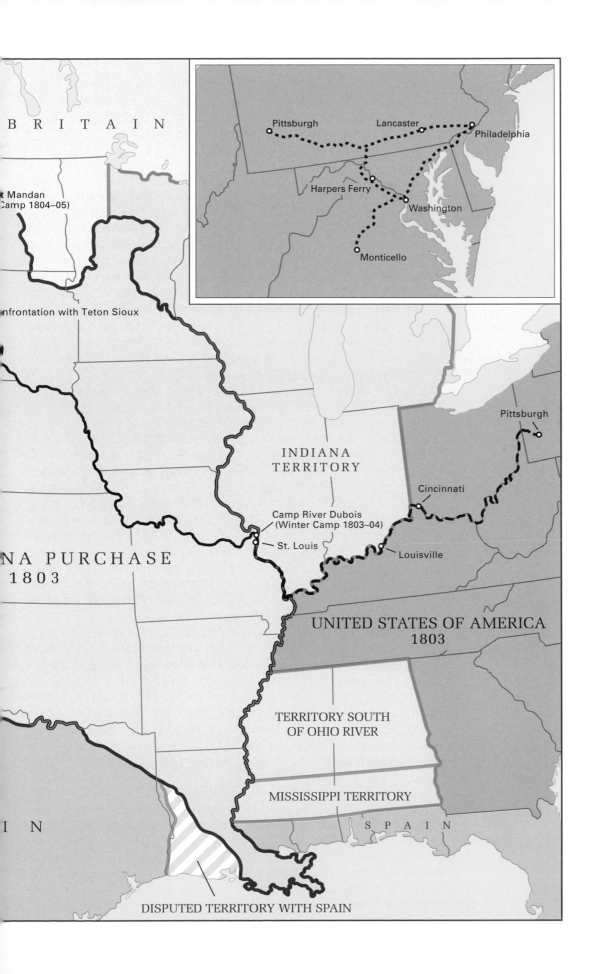

BRITAIN

Fort Mandan
(Winter Camp 1804–05)

Confrontation with Teton Sioux

LOUISIANA PURCHASE
1803

Pittsburgh   Lancaster
                              Philadelphia

Harpers Ferry
                    Washington

Monticello

Pittsburgh

INDIANA
TERRITORY

Cincinnati

Camp River Dubois
(Winter Camp 1803–04)

St. Louis
                    Louisville

UNITED STATES OF AMERICA
1803

TERRITORY SOUTH
OF OHIO RIVER

MISSISSIPPI TERRITORY   S P A I N

SPAIN

DISPUTED TERRITORY WITH SPAIN

see some remarkable species of animal life: the mule deer, prairie dog, and antelope. As the sergeant told his parents in a letter from Camp River Dubois at the start of the journey, "I am So [sic] happy as to be one of them pick'd [sic] Men [sic] from the armey [sic]."

Background

The Treaty of Paris, signed on 20 September 1783, formally ended the War of Independence and brought peace with Great Britain. With the end of hostilities, most Americans believed the United States had no immediate need for a standing army; indeed, most thought that the Congress had created the Continental Army only to fight the war. Even George Washington acknowledged that the new nation did not need nor could it afford a large standing army in time of peace. On the other hand, Washington noted that a few regular troops were "not only safe, but indispensably necessary" to support the rule of federal law. From the end of the American Revolution to the beginning of the War of 1812, the United States struggled to find the kind of army it needed "to provide for the common defense."

As most soldiers returned home from the Revolution, the Continental Congress considered the type of army the confederation of states required. In his "Sentiments on a Peace Establishment" (1783), Washington recommended a small regular army to garrison West Point and posts along the frontier. These soldiers would be "Continental Troops" who looked to Congress, not to the states, "for their Orders, their pay, and supplies of every kind." Washington envisioned four regiments of infantry and one of artillery, along with "artificers," a total of 2,631 officers, noncommissioned officers, and men. Each regiment of infantry would contain 26 noncommissioned officers, while the regiment of artillery would have 264 noncommissioned officers, including bombardiers and gunners. To supplement the regular army, Washington called for a well-organized, well-trained, and disciplined militia in which all male citizens from eighteen to fifty were required to serve.

Congress took no action on Washington's plan. Fearing that a standing army was "inconsistent" with representative government and "dangerous to the liberties of a free people," lawmakers on 2 June 1784 ordered Henry Knox, who had taken command of the army with Washington's return to civilian life, to discharge all remaining soldiers, except for twenty-five men at Fort Pitt (now Pittsburgh) and fifty-five at West Point. No officers above the rank of captain were to remain in the army, nor were there to be any noncommissioned officers. On 18 October 1784, Congress officially disbanded the Continental Army.

Meanwhile, events along the western frontier convinced the Continental Congress that the states required a military presence to protect their borders. Great Britain continued to garrison several forts in the Northwest in defiance of the Treaty of Paris. The British were also encouraging the Indians to resist the movement of Americans into the territory Great Britain had ceded to the Confederation. The problem of defending the nation's borders prompted Congress to authorize a peacetime regular army—the First American Regiment.

American soldiers greet local Afghan workers within the military compound, Kandahar, Afghanistan, May 2002. The NCO has often been one of the nation's most effective ambassadors, working with members of many nationalities and ethnic groups to get the job done.

On 3 June 1784, Congress asked Connecticut, New York, New Jersey, and Pennsylvania collectively to furnish 700 officers, noncommissioned officers, and men from their militias for this new formation. The First American Regiment was divided into eight infantry companies and two artillery batteries. Only Pennsylvania met her recruitment goal, and thus she chose the regimental commander, Lt. Col. Josiah Harmar. By the spring of 1785, Harmar had dispersed his small force among the tiny outposts along the Ohio River Valley to keep the peace between Americans and Indians.

While few Americans were affected by events along the frontier, many nevertheless felt that the Articles of Confederation did not vest enough authority in the central government. Border problems, an unfavorable balance of trade, the national debt, the specter of inflation, and Shay's Rebellion (1786) convinced most Americans that the states needed to form a more perfect union. From May to September 1787, fifty-five men met in Philadelphia and drafted the Constitution of the United States.

During the next two years, as the states ratified the new Constitution, Secretary of War Henry Knox directed the First American Regiment to restrain whites from settling Indian land. Unfortunately, by the end of the decade the Indians were feeling the press of white civilization as nearly 50,000 squatters entered their country. Although Harmar's men had taken steps to stop the encroachment of whites on Indian land, against so many lawless settlers the First American Regiment could do little to maintain the peace. Irritated by the intrusion of whites into their land, and encouraged by the British, the Indians became increasingly hostile. By the fall of 1789 a crisis in the Northwest was rapidly approaching. In response to the looming danger, Congress on 30 April 1790 voted to increase the number of enlisted men in the army to 1,216.

The infantry regiment was subsequently reorganized into three battalions of four companies each. Each company would contain four sergeants and four corporals.

Seeking to settle the Indian problem, Arthur St. Clair, governor of the Northwest Territory, directed Harmar to launch a punitive attack against the Miami tribal towns near what is now Cincinnati. Harmar's 1,453 troops were largely untrained recruits and militia, with a small core of only 320 veterans. Nevertheless, on 30 September 1790, Harmar moved his ill-trained force into the wilderness. By mid-October the Americans had destroyed the deserted Indian towns along the Maumee River and were on their way back to Fort Washington. But on 19 and 21 October Harmar's force suffered two successive defeats. During both actions, most of the militia panicked and fled, leaving the regulars unsupported. After a month of campaigning, Harmar returned to Fort Washington having lost a third of his pack train killed or stolen, nearly all of the militia (largely through desertion), and a quarter of his regulars. The first major military operation of the United States Army had ended in disaster.

The consequences of Harmar's defeat were immediately evident along the frontier. Angered by Harmar's attack and encouraged by their success, the Indians stepped up their raids. Determined to end these attacks, Congress authorized Governor St. Clair, old and in failing health, to raise and command a volunteer force of about 2,200 men. His mission was "to establish a just and liberal peace" with the Indians.

St. Clair had no more success than Harmar. Assembling his men and supplies at Fort Washington, He led his untrained and bickering force against the Indians on 7 August 1791. After three months of marches and the construction of two forts, the Americans encamped amid snow, ice, and rain near the eastern bank of the upper Wabash, about fifty miles from what is now Fort Wayne, Indiana. Although patrols had informed the command that Indians were nearby in great strength and were approaching the camp, security was surprisingly nonexistent. A half-hour before sunrise on 4 November 1791, approximately 1,000 Indians rushed from the forest and attacked the ill-prepared camp. The militia received the first impact of the attack and fled in panic, leaving the regulars and civilians accompanying the expedition to be slaughtered by the triumphant Indians. After three hours of fighting, St. Clair decided to abandon his camp rather than risk annihilation. Fortunately for the Americans, the Indians did not conduct a vigorous pursuit. Instead, they celebrated "the most one-sided, overwhelming victory" Indians have ever won over an American or European army. According to contemporary accounts, St. Clair had left nearly 650 soldiers and up to 200 civilians, including women and children, on the battlefield.

President George Washington was furious. What more proof did the Congress need in order to act on his "Sentiments on a Peace Establishment," written nearly ten years earlier? Now the president took steps to get Congress to act. He initiated, and Congress passed, laws to strengthen the militia and institute a legionary system for the regular army. The Militia Act of 8 May 1792 established in law the principle of universal military obligation, while the Congress on 27 December 1792 agreed to reorganize the regular army as a legion. Drawing parallels from the Roman Republic, the Legion of the United States consisted of four miniature armies called sub legions of 1,280 men each. Roughly analogous to modern battalion task forces, these sub legions were tactically flexible, self-sufficient combined-arms forces of infantry, light infantry, dragoons, and artillery. Regiments disappeared, as did the rank of colonel. Majors commanded the sub legions.

To train and lead the legion, Washington called upon Anthony Wayne, one of his ablest commanders during the Revolution. Washington knew Wayne possessed "a dominating desire to meet and annihilate the enemy." He was also "able, smart, and organized." For nearly two years, General Wayne recruited, trained, and disciplined the legion. Wayne placed a copy of Steuben's 1779 *Blue Book* in the hands of every company commander and saw that they used it. Noncommissioned officers drilled the men daily, teaching them to maneuver together in formation, to work as a team, and to react instinctively on the battlefield. Sergeants taught their men to handle their muskets, to use their bayonets, and to shoot accurately. Discipline was unrelenting and swift. Wayne's goal was to forge the Legion of the United States "into a strong, well disciplined striking force with one objective—to fight Indians in the wilderness and win." In 1794 the confrontation came.

At Fallen Timbers (near present-day Toledo, Ohio), on 20 August 1794, the Legion of the United States broke the power of the Indians in the eastern region of the Northwest, convinced the British to evacuate their garrisons below the Great Lakes, and gave the infant U.S. Army its first model of excellence. That Anthony Wayne had greater success against the Indians than did Josiah Harmar and Arthur St. Clair can be attributed to a number of factors. The Legion was twice as large as the forces Harmar and St. Clair marched against the Indians. Wayne's troops were also better paid and equipped. Most important, the Legion had nearly two years to prepare, due primarily to the fact that the government wished to exhaust all efforts for peace before giving Wayne permission to take military action.

The battlefield at Fallen Timbers was a mass of tangled thickets amid fallen and uprooted trees left by a tornado that had swept over the Maumee River Valley years earlier. Marching in combat formation, the Legion drove straight into the Indian lines. Expecting to launch their own assault against disoriented troops, the Indians suddenly faced a thundering volley of "close and well directed fire" from the American infantrymen, then a fierce bayonet charge, and finally, hard-riding Kentucky mounted riflemen slashing from the flanks. This was more than the Indian force could stand. In forty-five minutes the battle was over. The United States again had a victorious army. A year later, on 3 August 1795, the Indians agreed to cede most of Ohio and part of Indiana to the United States in the Treaty of Greenville.

Relative quiet reigned along the frontier for the next fifteen years. On 30 May 1796, Congress abolished the Legion of the United States and reduced the army to a corps of artillerists and engineers, two companies of light dragoons, and four infantry regiments of eight companies each. America's conventionally organized and reduced army now began dispersing to garrison not only the forts along the northern border that Great Britain finally relinquished in accordance with Jay's Treaty (signed in London on 19 November 1794), but also those outposts in the south that the Spanish surrendered according to the terms of the Treaty of San Lorenzo, signed with Spain on 27 October 1795.

With the election of Thomas Jefferson to the presidency in 1800, the Army received close attention. Contrary to popular opinion, Jefferson increased the size of the army, expanded its role in building the new nation, reformed its leadership, established the U.S. Military Academy at West Point, New York (1802), and paid particular attention to military affairs along the frontier. Jefferson was both determined to maintain peace with the Indians and fascinated with western exploration.

After the United States purchased the Louisiana Territory on 30 April 1803, Jefferson chose the Army to explore this region. It was no accident that the new nation and its president turned to the Army for this most important mission. Soldiers possessed the toughness, teamwork, discipline, and training appropriate to the rigors they would face. The Army also had a nationwide organization even in 1803 and thus the potential to provide requisite operational and logistical support. Perhaps most important, the Army was already developing leaders of character and vision: officers such as Meriwether Lewis and William Clark and the outstanding noncommissioned officers—John Ordway, Charles Floyd, Nathaniel Pryor, Patrick Gass, and Richard Warfington—who served with them.

NCOs in Action

Perhaps the greatest achievement of the Army during the Jefferson administration was the famous Lewis and Clark Expedition, officially "the Corps of Volunteers for North Western Discovery." Covering nearly eight thousand miles in two years, four months, and ten days, the expedition has become famous over the past two hundred years as an epic of human achievement. Although the Corps of Discovery did not locate an uninterrupted, direct route to the Pacific Ocean as Jefferson had hoped, it strengthened the nation's claim to the Pacific Northwest and paved the way for future Army expeditions, which helped to open the American West to commerce and settlement. The two captains and some of their men kept detailed journals and brought back invaluable geographic, hydrologic, and scientific data, including 178 new plants and 122 previously unknown species and subspecies of animals. The expedition also made friends with several Indian tribes and gave the nation a foothold in the region's fur trade. All things considered, it was a magnificent example of America's potential for progress and creative good.

Noncommissioned officers made a singular contribution to the success of the Lewis and Clark Expedition. Throughout the winter of 1803–1804, John Ordway, an experienced noncommissioned

Pursuit of the Sioux, February 16, 1805, *Michael Haynes.*

On February 14, 1805 four men, George Drouillard and privates Robert Frazer, Silas Goodrich and John Newman were on a detail from Ft. Mandan to collect and bring back meat. About 25 miles downstream from the fort they were stopped and robbed by a party of hostile Sioux, estimated by William Clark to number 106. After making their way back to the fort with this bad news, a force of twenty volunteers was quickly assembled and at dawn on the 15th, under the leadership of Captain Lewis, set off in pursuit. The next morning the near-frozen men saw a column of smoke rising into the frigid air. The Sioux, after overnighting in the earth lodges of an abandoned Mandan village, set fire to them as they left. Not finding the Sioux, the men then hunted to replenish their fresh meat supply.

officer from the First Infantry Regiment, assisted Clark in establishing Camp River Dubois. During the five months of the encampment, Clark and Ordway received, selected, trained, and disciplined personnel for the expedition. On several occasions Ordway commanded the camp in the absence of the two captains. He was the "top sergeant" of the expedition, expected to maintain order and discipline and to see that daily operations ran smoothly.

Both captains dealt firmly with any form of insubordination or misbehavior, especially when it was directed against a noncommissioned officer. The first time this occurred, Captain Lewis admonished the recruits and pointed out the importance of noncommissioned officers in the chain of command. He informed the men that he and Captain Clark would be derelict in their own duties if they were "to communicate our orders in person" to every member of the expedition. On two occasions, Captain Clark appointed Sergeants Ordway and Nathaniel Pryor as presiding officers of court-martial boards convened to try infractions of military law. These measures proved effective, as the Corps of Discovery recorded only five infractions during its two-and-a-half-year trek, a record unmatched by any other Army unit of the time.

On the return trip, Lewis and Clark split the Expedition into four groups and called upon the noncommissioned officers to lead separate detachments. According to the plan developed at Fort Clatsop during the winter of 1805–1806, once the Expedition crossed back over the Rockies, Lewis, Sergeant Gass, George Drouillard, and seven privates would head northeast to the Marias River. At the portage camp near the Great Falls, Lewis would leave Gass and two men to recover the cache left there. He, Drouillard, and the remaining privates would travel up the Marias to seek the Blackfeet Indians and establish friendly relations with them. Meanwhile, Clark would take the remainder of the expedition southeast across the Continental Divide to the Three Forks of the Missouri River. From there, Sergeant Ordway, nine privates, and the cache recovered from Camp Fortunate would proceed down the Missouri to link up with Lewis and Gass at the mouth of the Marias. Clark, five privates, the Charbonneau family, and York would then descend the Yellowstone River to its juncture with the Missouri River. As Clark and his party were descending the Yellowstone, Sergeant Pryor and three privates would take the horses overland to the Mandan villages and deliver a confidential message from Lewis to Agent Hugh Heney of the British North West Company. Lewis hoped to entice the North West Company into an American trading system he sought to establish. All detachments would unite at the juncture of the Missouri and Yellowstone Rivers in August 1806.

The willingness of Lewis and Clark to divide their command in such rugged, uncertain, and potentially dangerous country shows the high degree of confidence they had in themselves, their noncommissioned officers, and their troops. In addition to the physical challenges the expedition would certainly meet, war parties of Crow, Blackfeet, Hidatsa, and other tribes regularly roamed the countryside and threatened to destroy the expedition piecemeal. By dividing their command in the face of uncertainty, Lewis and Clark took a bold but acceptable risk to accomplish their mission.

Separated for forty days, the Corps of Discovery proceeded to accomplish nearly all its objectives. Lewis and his party successfully reached the Marias River without incident. While Gass and five men were recovering the cache at the portage camp, Lewis, Drouillard, and two privates traveled up the Marias, where they clashed with the Blackfeet on 27 July. As Lewis and his men hastily made their way across country to the Missouri River after their bloody encounter with the Blackfeet, Ordway's group had recovered the cache at Camp Fortunate, proceeded down the Missouri River, and linked up with Gass, whose team had already recovered the cache at the portage camp at the Great Falls and was awaiting Lewis and Ordway. Meanwhile, as Clark and his party set off in canoes down the Yellowstone River, Pryor's party took the horses overland to the Mandan villages. On the second night, a Crow raiding party stole all the horses. Demonstrating their ingenuity, self-sufficiency, and mastery of life in the wilderness, Pryor and his men kept their poise, walked to Pompey's Pillar (named in honor of Sacagawea's infant son, whom Clark nicknamed "Pomp"), killed a buffalo for food and its hide, made two circular Mandan-type bullboats (all four rode in one, while the second was a reserve in case the first sank), and floated down river to link up with Clark on the morning of 8 August. Four days later Lewis and his group found Clark and his group along the banks of the Missouri. The Expedition then proceeded down the Missouri, arriving at St. Louis on the morning of 23 September 1806.

———————————

The Lewis and Clark Expedition was one of the most daring and dramatic episodes in American history. The Army furnished the organization and most of the manpower, equipment, and supplies. Military leadership, discipline, and training proved crucial, both to winning over potentially hostile tribes and to overcoming the huge natural obstacles to crossing the continent. Noncommissioned officer leadership was pivotal to the success of the expedition. The versatility and flexibility of the noncommissioned officers enabled the Corps of Discovery to chart a course for later Army colleagues to follow.

Throughout the nineteenth century the Army was instrumental in exploring the West. Perhaps no other organization contributed as much to the development of the American West as did the U.S. Army. This is especially true of the Army Corps of Topographical Engineers, which mapped the West, laid out boundaries, constructed roads, improved rivers, and assembled vast amounts of scientific information about the interior of North America. These Army explorers were not amateurs, mountain men, or entrepreneurs. They were soldiers led by professional officers and noncommissioned officers. Indeed, the Lewis and Clark Expedition demonstrated, as today's noncommissioned officer continues to, that the noncommissioned officer has many roles and serves the Army in many ways.

Checking Cartridge Boxes, *Theresa L. Unger, 1988*

CHECKING

CARTRIDGE BOXES

CANADA, 1814

The 22d Infantry noncommissioned officers were tired when they reached the bivouac areas north of Buffalo on a warm Tuesday. Unlike other units of the division, which had begun arriving in mid-April, Capt. Sampson King's three companies of the 22d had left western Pennsylvania late. The NCOs could not pause to appreciate the beauty of the season. As soon as the companies linked up with Maj. Henry Leavenworth's 9th Infantry, they learned that they had to prepare their men for combat in a matter of hours, not months.

While the officers went off to receive their briefings, the regimental sergeant major of the 9th quickly outlined what had been done so far and told the 22d Infantry's sergeants and corporals what he expected them to do. The NCOs returned to their companies and began to settle the men into the camp's routine. The edge in each corporal's voice during the endless round of squad inspections and drills communicated to the recruits a sense of urgency and seriousness.

Background

The Army entered the War of 1812 with fewer than 12,000 men. Few of the soldiers had any previous combat experience, and only the most senior officers, veterans of the War of Independence, had fought a trained enemy. In small, isolated garrisons on the frontier, where the Army had conducted some major campaigns against sizable Indian forces, the ability to make do with field expedients, not any sophisticated understanding of military science, had been essential. When Congress declared war on Great Britain, the Army had to shift gears and attempt to relearn the hard lessons of the Revolution.

Mobilization in that era called for existing regiments to pull their scattered companies together, absorb new recruits, and deploy to meet the threat. Other regiments, added by congressional legislation, were raised from scratch. The Army had not yet discovered the value of promoting experienced junior NCOs to provide trained cadres for new organizations. Hence, regiments created in wartime

Battle of North Point, *Don Troiani, 1983. Each NCO owes it to his soldiers to ensure that they are equipped, trained, and motivated before they face the test of battle. During the War of 1812, Maj. Gen. Samuel Smith's defenders of Baltimore depended upon such careful preparations.*

trained sergeants and corporals in their duties and responsibilities at the same time that raw privates were learning rudimentary skills from the company officers.

The weapons and tactics of 1812 were unchanged from those of the Revolution. This was the age of linear warfare. To succeed, infantry units had to be highly disciplined and superbly drilled. Up to a thousand men had to move as one to get into proper position and then fire their smoothbore muskets in controlled volleys to inflict maximum casualties on the enemy. Each man, in essence, was a part of a lead-throwing machine whose strength and success depended on a rigorous form of teamwork. In this system, NCOs took positions as file closers on the flanks and in the rear of their units, where they could watch the men's performance and plug gaps appearing in the line.

The work of the NCOs in preparing the men for campaigning in the field had an equally important impact on battlefield success. The Army had clearly defined this role since Steuben first set the standards at Valley Forge in 1778. The regimental sergeant major was responsible for the performance of the NCOs below him. He monitored their conduct, made sure they were technically proficient, and instructed them when they were not. He was the enlisted expert on matters of drill. The sergeant major also inspected the books and records maintained by the company first sergeants, showed them how to solve problems, and gave a consolidated report to the regimental adjutant each month. The first sergeant knew every man in his company, watched their progress in camp, arranged duty details such as guard, and served himself as a file closer in the field.

Armies employing linear tactics, whether in the Old World or the New, found that a company's sergeants and corporals formed the backbone of any unit. Although officers were in charge of conducting training, the NCOs, in their constant supervision of the privates, had to see to it that the instruction became internalized, so the men would respond instinctively in any crisis. Picked because of their superior performance in the ranks, company NCOs served as examples to the men they were expected to lead. For day-to-day life, a company formed messes, or squads, each under a single NCO, who became responsible for the squad's well-being on and off the battlefield. His knowledge of camp life, equipment care, and drill determined the quality and performance of his unit. Each recruit learned his manual of arms, wearing of the uniform, and basic drill from his squad leader. If the squad leader did not measure up, neither could the company or the regiment.

The critical role of NCOs in preparing for combat during this era was highlighted in the third year of conflict. When the war began, few British troops could be spared from the crucial struggle against Napoleon in continental Europe to fight the Americans. Public opinion in the United States understood this fact and expected a swift victory to be won by an invasion of Canada. The task turned out to be far more difficult than anticipated. In 1814, after several inconclusive American victories and defeats, Maj. Gen. Jacob Brown's division drew the assignment to strike at southern Ontario as soon as the weather improved enough to allow operations. Learning from the failures of other commanders who had been repulsed, he refused to launch his invasion prematurely. That spring, as the bulk of the troops marched westward from Sacketts Harbor, New York, Brown concentrated on logistics and turned training over to Brig. Gen. Winfield Scott. The result was an intense program that produced the best force fielded by the United States during the War of 1812—an outnumbered contingent that crossed the Niagara, fought two battles, and later withstood a siege in Fort Erie.

In 1814 Scott's problems were compounded by the absence of standards for unit or recruit training. Part of the problem lay in a lack of initiative in many commanders, part in an absence of agreement on which drill manual should be used. Some commanders favored Steuben's original 1779 *Regulations*, still nominally the official doctrine; others leaned toward a variety of privately published books. Scott preferred the current French system, available in translation as *Rules and Regulations for the Field Exercises of the French Infantry* (1803). Like Steuben at Valley Forge, he trained his officers and NCOs first and then had them train the men.

Knowing that his men might face some British elite regiments, he initiated a vigorous program as soon as the troops settled into camp in the Flint Hill area north of Buffalo. Reveille came at sunrise, at which time the troops were expected to turn out under arms. Except

Paratroopers of the 82d Airborne Division prepare for deployment during the 1960s. Since the Army's early years, soldiers' lives have depended in large part on how carefully their leaders have enforced attention to detail during training and preparation for combat.

for a brief breakfast break, squad and company drill lasted until noon, followed by four hours of battalion drill in the afternoon. The only free time was between supper at seven and lights out at nine o'clock. Each Sunday he conducted a full field inspection of the entire force. Daily battalion and company drills, some personally conducted by the general, gradually expanded to fill the entire duty day. Officers and NCOs alike emphasized mass movements and instinctively developed the pace and cadence so important to maneuvering linear formations. Scott applied his routine equally to regulars and to volunteer militia units, rarely approving exemption from drill for reasons of bad weather or for special duties or commitments.

The tempo and sophistication of training picked up in June as the men mastered the basics. Scott then began to emphasize proficiency in the tricky technique of firing muskets while formed in three ranks instead of the Revolutionary War's two. He also instituted, like Steuben a generation earlier, the practice of forming a composite unit at full strength. The various officers and NCOs whose men were included then took turns running the unit through the different maneuvers. This exercise not only allowed the leaders to gain additional experience, it helped build confidence at all ranks. Throughout the training, General Scott and his fellow brigade commander, Brig. Gen. Eleazer W. Ripley, tried hard to impress upon the officers and NCOs the importance of enforcing division policies. The former were told to lead through example, by being prompt and attentive at each formation. The latter, in directly supervising the privates, became the key enforcers of regulations, which touched on almost all aspects of the soldier's life. For example, believing that good health and sanitation went together, Scott required the men to bathe three times a week, "in the lake, not in the creek."

Scott also stressed that each soldier was to learn to keep his weapons, equipment, and uniforms in the best condition possible. When he initially faced major shortages, especially in clothing, he encouraged units to make up in drill and discipline what they lacked in appearance. When supplies eventually caught up, Scott made the NCOs responsible for ensuring that the entire division marked and numbered clothing and unit equipment according to a single scheme and began prohibiting deviations from standards that had been justified as "field expedients." Division inspectors checked each individual knapsack to ensure that it contained 1 shirt, 1 pair of summer pantaloons, 1 pair of shoes, 1 pair of socks or stockings, 1 fatigue frock, 1 pair of trousers, and 1 blanket. A hairbrush and handkerchief were the only optional items authorized. Every man also carried a haversack with three days' bread and meat. Any deficiencies were reported to the quartermaster and requisitioned by the units.

The last missing element in the division's preparation for the campaign arrived on 23 June—the long-expected shipment of uniforms. Because of shortages, however, it did not include the standard blue coat. Instead, the troops received a newly designed summer fatigue uniform consisting of a gray woolen "round-about" (a short jacket with long sleeves) and gray-white overalls. Companies that had already obtained new uniform coats were told to box them up and turn them back in, each marked with the owner's name, as soon as the round-abouts were available. All other clothing items not authorized were to be similarly boxed and stored. Sergeants and corporals supervised this process and made one final inspection of their men's muskets, gun slings, and cleaning tools before the division took to the field.

NCOs in Action

On 3 July 1814, Brown's force crossed the Niagara River and captured Fort Erie opposite Buffalo. Two days later it collided at Chippewa with a British force that had confidently left Fort George to "restore" the border. The enemy commander took one look at the gray uniforms and concluded that he was facing only local militia. As the outnumbered but well-trained Americans swung into action and executed complex movements under fire with precision, he recognized his error and exclaimed, "Those are Regulars, by God!" That discovery came too late to prevent a British defeat. The weeks of relentless practice imposed on the soldiers by Scott and his NCOs paid off in this hard-fought battle.

The division did not rest on its laurels, but resumed Scott's program of drills and inspections. Each afternoon at four o'clock all men not on an operational mission underwent a full check of equipment. NCOs and officers closely monitored shaves and haircuts. Scott insisted that unit leaders enforce his standards of cleanliness and appearance or face disciplinary charges themselves for failure to exercise proper supervision. Later, during the Mexican War, that attitude would lead a younger generation of troops to nickname him "Old Fuss and Feathers."

The painstaking attention to detail paid off. Following a period of indecisive maneuver, Brown's forces collided again with the reinforced British at Lundy's Lane on 25 July. Fought mostly in the dark, the battle turned into a test of small-unit leadership and of the skill, discipline, and devotion of the soldiers on both sides. Once again, the American soldier gave as good as he got, fighting his red-coated foe to a standstill, although heavy casualties forced the U.S. troops to withdraw to Fort Erie after the battle. Both sides considered the battle a victory.

For over a month Brown's outnumbered division clung tenaciously to the fort as the British attempted a conventional siege—one in which the enemy attempted to approach and undermine fortifications by advancing a series of trenches. Fortunately, Scott had anticipated this possibility and had created a provisional combat engineer element by pulling one hand-picked private from each infantry company and one corporal from each regiment. These "pioneers" received special training, drew proper tools—saws, spades, and axes carried in special leather shoulder slings—and wore a linen apron that extended from neck to knee. During regimental drills the corporals positioned themselves with the regimental staff while the privates stood in the center rear of their companies. During the siege the pioneers, led by a handful of officers, supervised infantry work parties in maintaining and extending the fortifications. Finally, a brilliant sortie on 17 September forced the British to withdraw and along with the approach of winter ended the campaign.

Chippewa, Lundy's Lane, and Fort Erie, like the victories at Fort McHenry and New Orleans on other fronts—and some losses elsewhere—reminded the Army of an important point lost during long years in isolated garrisons: training and dedicated, competent NCOs were essential to military success. It was a lesson that the Army would long remember in the aftermath of Winfield Scott's vivid demonstration.

The Army underwent a drastic demobilization at the end of the War of 1812, and its surviving units returned to service along the frontier and in coastal defense fortifications. Most of the specialized units and duty positions were eliminated, leaving the bulk of the soldiers in infantry and artillery regiments. Senior leadership positions passed to a new generation of officers who had matured during the conflict. These men retained an important sense of the value of a quality NCO Corps to the Army's mission in the field. The new civilian leadership that worked with generals like Scott and Andrew Jackson also recognized the role of sergeants and corporals. Thereafter, when faced with political pressures to trim the regular establishment, they fought hard to preserve as many NCO positions as possible, knowing that a trained cadre could absorb raw recruits quickly. Formal educational programs comparable to the officer corps' Military Academy at West Point, New York, still lay far in the future, but by insisting upon literacy as well as technical competence for anyone selected to serve as a sergeant or corporal, they took the first step toward a professional corps as well. Similar changes began to appear within the ranks of the volunteer militia, as some units gradually transformed themselves into a true reserve component.

Elements of the daily duties of a corporal in Scott's 22d Infantry will sound familiar to any squad leader or team chief today. Like his or her predecessor, the modern NCO is the ultimate first-line supervisor. Every detail of the private's equipment, uniform, and personal hygiene still must be checked on a regular basis. Regardless of branch of service, all NCOs still learn the fundamentals of marksmanship, drill, and tactics and pass them on to new soldiers who serve under their immediate watch. That legacy is of far greater and more enduring importance to the nation than most people realize. Historians often dwell on Scott's later military career or point out facts such as his responsibility for the gray dress uniforms worn by the cadets at West Point and the country's other military academies. In a real sense, however, his most important legacy, going back to the War of 1812, is preserved within the NCO Corps.

Guardians of Standards, *Manuel B. Ablaza, 1988*

GUARDIANS
OF
STANDARDS

MISSOURI, 1820S

———◆———

The sergeant major and the first sergeant surveyed the dimly lit barracks. It was Saturday afternoon, and the soldiers had spent all day cleaning their quarters and equipment. Wooden floors had been mopped or sanded. Heavy wooden bunks had been dismantled, scrubbed, and reassembled. Mattresses were stuffed with clean straw. Polished and oiled muskets were placed in racks on the whitewashed wall. Each soldier had brushed clean his dress uniform, blanket, and pack and neatly placed them on his bunk, topped with the leather dress cap (called a shako) and canvas cover. While the barracks was empty, the senior NCOs began their weekly inspection.

They first inspected the room for cleanliness. Bedding was studied next to ensure the infamous "Army bugs" had been, at least temporarily, banished. Next, the soldier's clothing and equipment came under review. Because each man's kit was neatly placed according to regulation, it was more quickly and easily checked for accountability and serviceability. Shirts, socks, and underwear received the bug test. Buttons and insignia were checked to see that they were clean, polished, and serviceable. Missing and damaged items were noted. The flintlock muskets were examined to ensure that they were in working order. Flints and mainsprings came under close scrutiny. Weapons that failed inspection were noted, to be turned in to the armorer for repair or replacement. When the inspection had been completed, the NCOs returned to their quarters to prepare reports. Housecleaning was over for the company, at least until next Saturday.

Background

The American soldier of the early nineteenth century spent his career largely isolated from civilian influences. Assigned mostly to far-flung outposts on the frontier, the soldier led a harsh, uninspiring life, felt unappreciated, and too often could not recognize the

Stand-to Inspection, Virginia, 1914. Each noncommissioned officer placed in charge of a section, squad, or shift has the duty to enforce standards in soldiers' daily lives.

importance of his activities to the country. Attitudes within the civilian community contributed to his sense of estrangement. Many taxpayers and voters still clung to the notion that a soldier's usefulness ended with the close of a war. For much of the early nineteenth century, the nation turned its back on the Army and frequently sought to keep military strength at a minimum. Sustaining morale and combat readiness posed the greatest challenge to the Army's leaders in those years.

The Army had demobilized at the conclusion of the War of 1812 and returned to its traditional missions of policing the frontiers and manning fortifications along the coastline and borders. A new secretary of war, John C. Calhoun, took office in 1816 and immediately began studying the lessons of the preceding conflict to determine how the Army could better meet its obligations under the Constitution. He and the senior officers quickly concluded that the military's primary peacetime function was deterring future conflict by being able to mobilize rapidly and efficiently. Greater professionalism was the essential precondition to accomplishing that task.

Leaders, however, had to operate within a broader national context. A severe economic depression racked the country, forcing the president and Congress to make major cuts in the armed forces. In late 1820 Secretary Calhoun responded to the challenge, submitting a plan to Congress that would minimize the impact of the budget on the Army's ability to mobilize in the event of another war. To avoid the damage done by the traditional method of disbanding entire regiments, Calhoun proposed an "expansible army" concept. Under that scheme the Army would make cuts only in the number of privates in each company, not in the number of regiments or companies on the books, nor in the officer and NCO Corps. In wartime it could quickly add new recruits to the existing units, restore basic combat capabilities, and buy time for the formation of new regiments and the mobilization of the militia.

Congress rejected Calhoun's concept and in 1821 reduced the Regular Army from 10,000 to 6,000 men, comprising seven regiments of infantry and four of artillery. The third arm, mounted troops, disappeared from the force until 1832. Although nominally separate and distinct branches, most artillery companies served in permanent fortifications or frontier posts and really trained as foot soldiers; only a handful had the opportunity during the nineteenth century to function as mobile gunners.

Although Congress rejected expansibility, Calhoun still sought to instill professionalism into the small contingent of officers and NCOs. He knew that leaders trained to high standards could quickly adjust to greater responsibilities if mobilization came. That philosophy received a boost from the reality of life during an era of austere budgets. The limited numbers of officers quickly became overextended, creating a shortage at company levels and forcing senior NCOs to take up the slack. The Army started transferring functions from the commissioned to the Noncommissioned Officer Corps out of necessity, but as the NCOs demonstrated their abilities that process tended to accelerate. Some sergeants even found themselves temporarily commanding companies.

One distinctive feature of the United States' approach to military service set the Army apart from its European counterparts throughout its early history. Emphasis on the citizen-soldier concept even for the regulars mandated a much shorter term of enlistment than the lifetime service typical of Old World armies. Most signed up for single hitches of three to five years. Turnover placed a heavy burden on the career officers and NCOs, since they had to devote large amounts of time to training and teaching new men the basic skills of military life.

Ensuring a steady flow of high-quality replacements required effort even at the low strength ceilings set by Congress. For greater

Stand-to Inspection, Basic Training, 1985. Just as in the 1820s and 1914, regular inspections help to ensure that equipment will be in the best possible condition when the unit faces combat.

efficiency, the Army replaced the earlier practice of regimental recruiters with a centralized system of depots in major cities. The General Recruiting Service enlisted men into the Army at large, rather than into specific units. The Army sought to attract single men between the ages of twenty-one and thirty-five. A married man wishing to enlist had to obtain permission from the War Department. Although the Army actively sought white, English-speaking U.S. citizens, recruiters could and did accept immigrants. During the 1820s roughly one-fourth of the Army fell into that category, primarily Irish and Germans, but by the 1850s the immigrant ratio had grown to two-thirds. Although black Americans had fought well during the War of Independence, none were allowed to serve in the Army until the middle of the Civil War.

It was hard to persuade highly qualified individuals to join up or enlist—conditions were severe and pay rates low. An act of December 1812 set monthly enlisted pay at $12 for sergeants major and quartermaster sergeants, $11 for sergeants and senior musicians, $10 for corporals, and $8 for privates. Military base pay was generally less than that of civilians. Common farm hands at the low end of the economic spectrum made between $8 and $12 a month, and individuals with skills comparable to many Army jobs earned $1 to $2 a day. A small increase in pay scales finally cleared Congress in 1833 but failed to match rising civilian incomes. To compound the problem, soldiers often had difficulty in collecting their pay. Although troops were supposed to be paid every two months, a paymaster might take six months or more to make the rounds of the frontier outposts to actually hand out the money.

Despite its reduced strength the Army pushed westward, exploring, surveying, and building roads and military posts. It was during Calhoun's tenure as Secretary of War that the line of garrisons on the frontier was extended west of the Mississippi River. Policy called for the Army to form a buffer zone between the leading edge of settlement and the areas occupied by Indians and to prevent either group from harassing the other. Skirmishes and long expeditions to "show the flag" to distant tribes sometimes broke the monotony of frontier duty, but the average soldier spent most of his time doing construction work or, even more important in an era of limited budgets, raising livestock and growing vegetables for subsistence. So much time was taken by these chores—common in European forces, but unusual in the American Army—that one officer complained, "The axe, pick, saw, and trowel have become more the equipment of the American soldier than the cannon, musket, and sword."

The frontier outposts usually amounted to a handful of simple, even primitive, log or adobe structures. Since the skills and imagination of the troops themselves determined how the buildings were constructed, quality varied greatly from post to post. In fact, the Army did not issue comprehensive instructions on the construction of military barracks until 1838. Twelve men occupied each hut or room, sleeping in bunk beds. Two shared the lower level and two the upper, an arrangement that was most comfortable during the cold frontier winters. (Soldiers did not receive individual beds until the 1840s.)

Little activity that was soldierly broke the monotony of work and sleep. Because construction (even when new posts were not under construction, the old ones needed constant repair) and other chores consumed so much of the soldier's day, regular training suffered. When time was available, NCOs marched and drilled troops in impromptu sessions. Calhoun realized the need for a more formal approach to training and played a key role in the establishment of the Artillery School of Practice at Fort Monroe, Virginia, the Army's first service school. Unlike today's individual instruction the artillery school trained entire units. Companies rotated to Fort Monroe for the year-long program and then moved to a new duty station. In 1827 Calhoun's successor established an Infantry School of Practice at Jefferson Barracks, Missouri, but the Army eventually discontinued both operations for budgetary reasons.

NCOs in Action

The Army regulations of 1821 were the first to establish a systematic method of selecting noncommissioned officers. Each regimental commander appointed the NCOs on his staff and chose company NCOs based upon the recommendation of the respective company commanders. The grade of lance corporal, long recognized in practice though not in law, also acquired legal status under these regulations. When there were too few NCOs in a company, selected privates were given that title and appointed as substitutes. Privates desiring the additional responsibility could either be appointed by a commissioned officer or could appear before a monthly board to represent themselves. Those selected received no extra pay and were not exempt from privates' duties, but they commanded squads and detachments consisting of other privates. The lance corporal rank existed off and on until the beginning of World War I in the Army and still persists in the Marine Corps.

Calhoun's emphasis on standardizing NCO selection and appointment resulted directly from his desire to strengthen the corps' professionalism. Similar motives lay behind changes in the way uniforms indicated rank. After several years of experimentation with various types of insignia the Army adopted chevrons in 1821. The regulations of the time prescribed that they be in distinctive branch colors (white for infantry, yellow for artillery) and be worn on the sleeve with points up. Sergeants major and quartermaster sergeants wore their chevrons above the elbow, corporals below. Except for one brief use of epaulets, chevrons have remained the NCO's distinctive mark ever since. Different systems changed the direction of the points from time to time until finally a 1902 general order prescribed the current points-up practice.

NCO duties during the decades between the War of 1812 and the Civil War were set forth in *Scott's Infantry Drill Regulations*, named for the general officer (Winfield Scott) who chaired the board that drafted them. These regulations placed the ultimate responsibility for the training, well-being, and readiness of a company's enlisted men in the hands of its noncommissioned officers. The appearance and condition of barracks and the neat and soldierly look of the men who lived in them became "sergeants' business." As a first-line supervisor the NCO also became accountable for the status and serviceability of the troops' uniforms and equipment. This duty turned the NCO into the Army's "guardian of the standards."

The Army had a very specific reason for using sergeants and corporals to monitor closely the living conditions of the soldiers. Status of weapons and equipment related directly to survival in combat, but disease killed four or five men for every one lost on the battlefield. The causes of typhoid, cholera, yellow fever, and other illnesses remained a mystery until the late 1800s, but observant commanders dating back to biblical times had recognized that rates of sickness went down when troops kept clean. Army doctors were too few to serve the many scattered posts, especially those isolated on the frontier, sometimes leaving line officers and NCOs to enforce preventive measures that were the only way to fight disease. Scott's regulations, for example, required NCOs to ensure that their men washed their hands and faces daily, brushed or combed their hair, and changed underwear regularly (three times a week during the summer, twice a week the rest of the year). Scrubbing barracks and clothing on a weekly basis supposedly rid them of bedbugs, lice, and ticks or, at the very least, kept their numbers down.

The Army noncommissioned officer of the 1820s also had to consider his own welfare. NCO opportunities were limited. No sergeant or corporal could be transferred in grade from one regiment to another without the permission of the War Department in Washington and endorsements at every layer in the chain of command—a lengthy process rarely attempted. Consequently, to protect their grades, senior NCOs had little choice but to remain with the same unit throughout their military careers. These men often became almost legendary figures in their respective regiments, as generations of officers came and went while they stayed as seemingly indestructible fixtures held in awe by both officers and enlisted men.

Today, as always, the readiness and efficiency of the Army depend upon the readiness and efficiency of the individual soldier and his equipment. Whether troops occupy shacks with simple chimneys, as in the last century, or modern high-rise billets complete with sophisticated central heating and air-conditioning systems, the fundamentals of military daily life do not change. Standards of performance for cleanliness, accountability, and serviceability are as relevant to battle dress uniforms (BDUs) and M16s as they were to leather shakos and flintlock muskets.

The responsibility of the NCO inspecting enlisted billets in the current decade is basically no different from that of the sergeant major and first sergeant who went through a log hut in the 1820s. A section or squad leader is still accountable for ensuring that all personnel under his or her command present a neat and soldierly appearance and that they maintain their living quarters and work areas. Of course, the complexity and tempo of modern war has changed. In contrast to earlier eras, today's soldier is issued far more gear under applicable Tables of Organization and Equipment (TOEs), Tables of Distribution and Allowances (TDAs), and Common Tables of Allowances (CTAs). His or her efficiency and survivability depend in large part on the serviceability of that equipment, as does the unit's ability to deploy quickly during an emergency. The NCO plays the central role in ensuring that the individual soldier remains in a constant state of readiness, able to function to his or her highest ability.

For two centuries NCOs have been dedicating their energies and resources to the task of sustaining the Army's most potent individual weapon, the soldier. Today's NCO carries on that long tradition of being the guardian of the standards.

The Battle of Molina del Rey, *James Walker, c. 1847*

LAYING
THE
GUN

MEXICO, 1847

———————◆———————

The sergeant had drilled his gun crew incessantly since arriving in Mexico. He took great pride in his position as "Chief of the Piece," knowing that the Army had entrusted him with a great deal of responsibility. The captain expected him to guarantee that both his men and the brass gun, a smoothbore muzzle-loader that fired six-pound shot, were ready for action. When the sounds of battle grew louder, the sergeant and his assistant, a corporal, checked and rechecked the weapon, implements, and horses. The two NCOs were veterans, educated in a hard school—fighting Indians on the western plains and in Florida's swamps. Their calmness and quiet competence quickly steadied the junior enlisted men.

Soon the order came to go forward, and the team started toward the enemy at full gallop. The wheels of the gun, its accompanying caisson, and their limbers kicked up dust as they traversed the plateau to reach a new position. Once there, they placed the gun in battery, the horses and vehicles shifted to a more protected spot farther back, and the men took up their carefully rehearsed positions. The sergeant and gunner (corporal) stood near the rear of the gun, the rest of the crew where they could use the implements. "Load!" and powder and ball were brought up and rammed home. The gunner coordinated the aiming of the piece. "Fire!" and a solid iron ball streaked toward the enemy.

With each shot, the sergeant visually marked the range, calling out corrections. Sweating cannoneers sponged out the hot barrel between rounds to extinguish any sparks that might set off the powder charges prematurely. As the enemy approached, the crew shifted first from a single iron ball to grapeshot and then, at closer range, to canister, converting the piece into a giant shotgun, firing dozens of deadly pieces of metal. After the attack was repulsed, the horses were brought forward to limber up, the crew remounted, and the "flying artillery" raced to another part of the field.

Moving up to the Battle, *James Walker, c. 1847. Historically, the Chief of the Piece has been responsible for transforming a weapons system, such as the artillery of the Mexican War, into a lethal instrument.*

Background

After the War of 1812 the United States entered an era known as the "Thirty Years' Peace." No foreign enemy threatened the security of the nation. The Army kept busy policing the borders and engaging in sporadic conflicts with Indians. During the 1830s and 1840s the only sources of combat experience for the NCO Corps were the Seminole Wars in Florida, a bitter struggle against the skillful Chief Black Hawk across the Mississippi River, and occasional campaigns as the line of settlement started to push out onto the Great Plains. Because so much of this service was performed by company- and battalion-size elements drawn from scattered posts, junior officers and NCOs became involved in a much wider array of planning and execution than they would have in a conventional conflict. Fortunately, this training prepared them for leadership responsibilities when war broke out with Mexico in 1846.

In 1842, at the conclusion of the Second Seminole War, Congress cut the strength of the Army from 12,500 men to 8,600. This reduction differed from earlier ones in that the legislators finally decided to follow Secretary of War Calhoun's 1820 recommendation for an expansible military. Only the number of privates in each company was reduced. No regiments or companies were disbanded, and no noncommissioned officers were released. The new policy nurtured an experienced NCO Corps, which in turn set and maintained standards of training that would not have been possible otherwise.

The wisdom of this policy was soon apparent. Three years later the independent Republic of Texas became part of the United States, increasing the territorial area that the Army had to protect. The annexation also caused sharp tensions with Mexico, which still considered much of eastern Texas part of its own territory; and war, with its need for an expanded Army and a well-equipped and trained artillery arm, became a real possibility.

While most of the regular infantrymen and dragoons served in remote posts and camps isolated from the mainstream of American life, many artillerymen enjoyed a better lot. Although the Army had originally established the branch with a mobile battlefield mission, since 1794 it had become the primary element of the Army charged with protecting the nation's coastline from European attack. Busy port cities were the most important points along the Atlantic and Gulf shores and therefore became the sites of the forts built by Army engineers and manned by gunners. Artillery companies assigned to those locations were spared physical isolation, but most of their days were monotonous, as they divided training time between infantry drills and practice with the heavy guns emplaced in the brick fortifications.

Artillerymen in Europe had enjoyed special status throughout history. No other arm required enlisted men to master such special skills and techniques. Cannoneers sang their own songs and spoke their own jargon, a remnant of the early days of their craft when artillerymen were civilians on contract to the military. They even had a patron saint, Barbara, protectress from sudden death. (Legend has it that the choice of St. Barbara directly reflected the nasty habit of early cannon to burst when fired.) These traditions passed into the U.S. military during the American Revolution, when Continental Army artillerists quickly demonstrated expertise on battlefields from Boston and Trenton to Yorktown, winning grudging praise from the British.

The heavy weapons of the eighteenth and early nineteenth centuries were smoothbore muzzle-loaders, cast in iron or brass. Limited in range and highly inaccurate, most fired solid iron balls on a flat trajectory. Explosive shells existed, but they lacked reliable fuses, and they were restricted to high-angle fire by mortars and howitzers.

Multiple Launch Rocket System (MLRS) Deployed during DESERT STORM, 1990–1991. The NCOs of today are responsible for the greatly intensified lethality of artillery on the battlefield, which is now able to blanket a square kilometer in less than a minute.

Barrels and carriages were so heavy that it took a crew of up to fifteen to manhandle and service a single large gun in combat, severely limiting both tactical mobility and the rate of fire. For the early guns, achieving even limited success depended directly on the extent to which the crew worked as a well-trained team, under the supervision of an officer in command of each gun.

In 1818 the Army had divided artillery weapons into three categories according to intended use—field, seacoast, and siege or garrison—with a variety of calibers and types within each category. Mobility was a factor only in the case of the first. A system of mobile field artillery, adopted in 1839, introduced interchangeable parts and carriages with a single wooden trail. It remained substantially in place, with the addition of rifled cannon, throughout the Civil War.

Each of the Regular Army's four artillery regiments in 1846 contained ten companies, although one company functioned as light artillery, armed with four to six guns. The rest served as infantry when not garrisoning fortifications. When war broke out, expansion brought the regulars back up to full company strength as Calhoun had advocated.

The basic enlisted artilleryman's uniform in this era was the same as the infantry's—a light blue jacket and trousers. Distinctive branch markings included red trim on the dark blue cap and red stripes down each leg. Privates and corporals wore one stripe, sergeants and officers two. Regulations prescribed chevrons to be worn on the sleeve of the uniform, points up, as a means of designating enlisted rank—three for sergeant, two for corporal, and none for privates. Chevrons for artillery and cavalry were yellow, while infantry wore white.

During the Mexican War, the artillery tested two important changes, one involving organization and the other training. In the fall of 1838 Congress had authorized light artillery units to receive horses. The first to be selected was Capt. Samuel Ringgold's Company C, 3d Artillery. It served as a model for the units that were to follow, going into action with crew members sitting on ammunition chests carried on the caissons and limbers or riding some of the harnessed horses. Building on that precedent, select units switched to a "flying" configuration by taking cannoneers from the precarious chests and mounting them on saddle horses. The changes allowed commanders to shift the guns rapidly from one point on the battlefield to another and to employ them offensively as well as defensively.

The other innovation came in the standardized precision drill, which permitted the men to unlimber, load, fire, and limber up quickly to take advantage of the improved weapons and organization. Practice was the key, and the NCOs saw to it that their soldiers were cross-trained in all functions so that a few casualties would not knock the gun out of action. Rehearsals enabled each piece to fire two aimed rounds every minute for a sustained period. During the Revolution and the War of 1812 each gun had been commanded by a company officer; by the time of the conflict with Mexico that function had passed to a sergeant, designated as Chief of the Piece. Immediate command of each crew and the sighting of the gun were charged to the gunner, a corporal. Seven additional enlisted men completed the crew.

The tactical improvements made possible by the advances in weapons, organization, and training paid enormous dividends during the Mexican War. At the battle of Palo Alto, when Mexican cannon attempted to fire on American infantry, Brevet Major Ringgold's battery galloped to their defense. As the Mexicans were setting up their battery, the "flying artillery" unlimbered, loaded, and fired point-blank into the enemy guns, annihilating their crews. When the enemy broke through the American left flank at the battle of Buena Vista, Bragg's and Sherman's batteries quickly moved from point to point, mounting and dismounting, limbering and unlimbering, firing shot and canister at the enemy ranks. These batteries and the handful of others available to Maj. Gens. Zachary Taylor and Winfield Scott proved to be decisive, enabling American troops, although usually outnumbered, to stage two successful invasions and eventually force the Mexicans to sue for peace.

NCOs in Action

Although junior enlisted strength rose and fell, artillery tables of organization remained fairly consistent in allocating noncommissioned officers during the 1830s and 1840s. Whether there were four or six guns, each company contained 2 sergeants with special staff responsibilities, 4 to 6 sergeants (Chiefs of Piece), 8 to 12 corporals (the gunners and an ammunition NCO to support each piece), and 2 buglers. The latter ranked with and were paid as NCOs.

In this generally lean era, the NCO was treated far better than the private soldier, reflecting his close relationship with the commander who had picked him for promotion. For example, NCOs were rarely deprived of their whiskey ration as a disciplinary measure, a common punishment for the private soldier. Neglect of duty and conduct unbecoming a soldier—often due to drunkenness—were the most frequent charges NCOs faced. Reduction to the ranks for varying periods of time was the most common punishment.

Then, as now, a key role of the NCO in all branches was that of trainer. Because NCOs supervised daily drill, they worked with officers to master the "school of the soldier," as basic training subjects were called in earlier times. They then passed on that knowledge to the privates. To carry out training, a typical company in peacetime garrison organized enlisted men into four squads, each under the charge of an NCO. In these squads soldiers learned various drills, practiced maneuvers at the company level, and gained skill and confidence in handling artillery. The success these sergeants and corporals had in quickly training the large influx of recruits during the Mexican War confirmed the wisdom of the reforms advocated by Secretary Calhoun. Thereafter, policy makers never abandoned the notion that a relatively small number of qualified professionals could meet the requirements of mobilization.

By the mid-1800s the Army had moved so far down the road of transferring basic leadership responsibilities, especially in the area of training, that the NCO Corps began to earn the nickname "backbone of the Army." This process was accompanied by an effort to enhance the individual noncommissioned officer's prestige and authority. Every NCO received a certificate, or warrant, to document his status in a manner similar to the commission of an officer, and for the first time the sergeants and corporals were allowed to form their own mess separate from the private soldiers. To recognize special service, an act of 1847 authorized the president to award a brevet as second lieutenant to any NCO who distinguished himself, with the pay and benefits of the higher grade. The individual NCO had the option of accepting or declining the appointment, since it entailed transferring to a new unit.

NCOs also began to draw new assignments with less direct supervision by officers. This increase in responsibilities reflected both a trend within the Army toward greater technical specialization and the growth of professional attitudes among NCOs. Some of these changes came within the regimental staffs, while others gave sergeants the chance to work outside unit confines. A handful began to replace officers as recruiters in civilian population centers. Another important change during the 1830s allowed the ordnance sergeant to supplant an officer known as a conductor of artillery, who had performed important duties ensuring that weapons and other materiel were properly cared and accounted for. Choice assignments like these became the goal of many career NCOs.

Since Yorktown, the artillery service has had to keep pace with constant growth in the complexity of modern warfare. Technological requirements set the cannoneers apart from their fellows in the Continental Army. The pace of change accelerated so rapidly during the nineteenth century that by 1903 the branch had to be split in two. Those "redlegs" charged with manning weapons in fortifications became the Coast Artillery, and later the Air Defense Artillery when long-range bombers replaced battleships as the primary strategic threat to national security. The successors of Ringgold and Bragg became the Field Artillery and concentrated on improving their ability to provide support on the battlefield. The mobility of "flying artillery" is now seen in self-propelled howitzers and the Multiple Launch Rocket System (MLRS) and in the use of helicopters and parachutes instead of horses to move weapons into firing position.

The versatility and flexibility necessary for artillerymen in modern combat demand technical skills that the Mexican War soldier could scarcely imagine. At the same time, the sergeant in command of an MLRS on today's sophisticated battlefield still has the same basic responsibilities as a six-pounder's Chief of Piece under Captain Bragg at Buena Vista. That continuity is most apparent in the training of individual soldiers. In the artillery, as throughout the Army, the NCO of today is still the key link in transmitting skills and motivating junior soldiers to maintain the highest possible state of readiness.

Training in this sense is really the most fundamental form of leadership. Over the centuries the Army noncommissioned officer has been the person with the most direct influence over the soldier on a daily basis. The fact that missions are accomplished and work performed according to high standards reflects how effective sergeants and corporals have been in instilling a sense of professionalism and technical and tactical competence in the men and women they command.

Union Standard Bearer, *Don Troiani, 1983*

Dress

on the

Colors

Virginia, 1864

The wind-tossed Stars and Stripes wrapped around the color sergeant as he took up his position and planted its staff in front of his blue-clad regiment. Several hundred yards ahead stood the enemy breastworks. The battlefield was pandemonium. Clouds of drifting smoke and dust, the thud of artillery, the crackle of thousands of muskets, shouted commands, cries of the wounded—all combined to rattle even veteran soldiers. Still, the men could see the flag. It was more than a patriotic symbol. It was a fixed point, and like the calmness of its bearer, it steadied the men. Responding to orders, the blue line behind the color sergeant advanced with heads lowered, as if walking into the heart of a storm, advancing around comrades who had dropped as the Confederates began to find the range. When the men reached the colors, they halted to regain their alignment.

The regiments of the brigade approached the enemy field works through a series of such advances. Each time Old Glory led the way, allowing the line to maintain its formation. At a hundred yards, the men exchanged volleys with hardly visible opponents in butternut and gray. But as often happened during the Civil War, the advantage lay with defenders under cover. Canister and Minie balls ripped gaps in the ranks until finally the command "Fall back!" rang out. The impulse to run for safety was strong, but once again the color sergeant served as a steadying guide. The sight of the unit flag moving through the swirling battle imposed order on the chaos. Recovering the precision mastered on the parade ground, the battered unit withdrew from the field, surviving to fight another day.

Background

After the Mexican War, Congress reduced the Army to a small force of regulars with traditional peacetime roles. Initially set at slightly less than 10,000 officers and men, the size of the Army had

The Death of General Warren at the Battle of Bunker's Hill, 17 June 1775, *John Trumbull, 1786. Beginning with the defense of Bunker Hill, the Army used flags as rallying points that stood above the smoke of battle.*

grown to about 16,000 effectives by 1860, reflecting the need to secure the large territorial gains in the Southwest. Most of these troops were employed west of the Mississippi River; the rest were garrisoned at eastern coastal fortifications. Spread thinly in 130 garrisons, posts, and camps scattered over 3 million square miles, the regulars relied mainly on noncommissioned officers for junior leadership.

The military's most significant tasks after the war with Mexico lay in the West. The Army was involved in exploration, railway surveys, and mapping. In addition, troops assisted civil authorities during the 1850s in efforts to enforce federal law in Utah and to halt the fighting between pro- and anti-slavery forces in "Bleeding Kansas." The discovery of gold in California and the opening of the Oregon Territory's rich farmlands not only dramatically increased the westward movement, but also added to the Army's responsibilities. Wagon trains and routes had to be guarded by troops who protected the settlers from Indians and the Indians from the settlers. Combat experience gained during those missions came in the form of isolated small-unit actions.

The outbreak of the Civil War in 1861 brought a very different challenge. Congress promptly raised the strength of the Regular Army to over 22,000 men. Infantry regiments increased from 10 to 19, cavalry from 5 to 6, and artillery from 4 to 5, leading to immediate promotions to NCO rank for hundreds of soldiers. These events proved that Secretary of War John C. Calhoun had been right in the 1820s in urging Congress to organize the Army in peacetime on an "expansible" basis, but the regulars were never expected to deal with the crisis of secession by themselves. The Civil War would be fought by volunteers on both sides.

In 1861 President Abraham Lincoln, like the Confederacy's Jefferson Davis, issued a call for volunteers to be raised by the states and organized into regiments. Each side used various terms of enlistment; most men signed up either for a three-year stint or "for the duration." In either case, the obligation was different than the Regular Army's five-year hitch. So great was the response that by mid-1861 each army had formed several hundred infantry regiments and almost 500,000 volunteers had entered the federal service. Volunteer units, especially those raised early in the war, often depended upon existing militia formations for their cadres. They carried designations that included a number (each state employed its own numbering system), state of origin, and, in the North, the term "volunteer," all of which were emblazoned on the unit's colors. Common usage simply referred to the infantry regiments as the 2d Massachusetts or the 5th Virginia.

On paper, a Civil War infantry regiment consisted of a small headquarters element and ten companies. Each company included a captain, a first lieutenant, a second lieutenant, a first sergeant, 4 other sergeants, 8 corporals, 2 musicians, 1 wagoner, and between

Drill Sergeant at Attention in Front of the Colors, Fort Benning, Georgia, 1998. Army units now use flags only on ceremonial occasions; but in tribute to the NCO's historic role as color bearer in battle, today's color guards consist of noncommissioned officers.

64 and 82 privates. The minimum strength of a regiment was supposed to be slightly more than 850 officers and men, the maximum strength about 1,050. Actual numbers in the field were much lower, especially as units incurred losses from combat and disease. On the Union side, present and fit-for-duty strengths often fell into the 150- to 500-man range. Attrition took a heavier toll on Regular units than on volunteers because longer enlistments and lower benefits attracted few replacement recruits. The 2d Infantry, for example, consisted in 1864 of only seven officers and thirty-eight enlisted men, assigned mainly to guard duty.

One of the most honored and sought-after NCO positions in the regiment was that of color bearer. These men carried the national and regimental colors at the head of the unit in battle, a responsibility entrusted only to the most respected and courageous individuals. Regulations authorized each Union regiment of infantry two silk flags: the U.S. national color and an organizational color. Usually only the former went into combat at the head of the regiment, with the organizational color remaining with the trains for safety. Regulations also allowed a unit to inscribe on the colors the names of battles in which it had participated. Confederate regiments followed similar practices.

The true importance of the colors in the eighteenth and nineteenth centuries did not come from ceremonial use. They played a critical tactical role in this era of linear warfare, providing immediate visibility at the center of the unit. Vital as a key element in the command-and-control system, they also served as a rallying point during close combat. These functions related directly to the weapons of the

Noncommissioned Officer's Sash *The Army has used the sash to denote rank from early times. From 1840 until 1872, line sergeants and members of the noncommissioned staff were authorized to wear a sash of worsted wool as pictured.*

Shoulder Scales for Noncommissioned Staff *In the mid-nineteenth century brass shoulder scales protected soldiers from saber blows. Beginning about 1854, three patterns of shoulder scales came into use, one pattern of scales for noncommissioned staff as pictured, another for sergeants, and a third for corporals and privates. Scales of this type continued in use until 1872.*

Civil War Drum *Regimental Drum of the Civil War Period, 1861–1865. Drums, fifes, trumpets, and bugles conveyed the commander's orders in the noise and confusion of the battlefield in the eighteenth and nineteenth centuries. Drummers and field musicians not only needed the skill and talent to play but also had to maintain their composure under fire. Positions such as this would lead to the introduction of specialist grades at the beginning of the twentieth century.*

day. During the Revolution and War of 1812, smoothbore flintlock muskets required units to deploy in long lines two or three ranks deep to achieve maximum efficiency in the use of their cumbersome short-range firearms. The volleys were controlled in part through the use of the flags, which were then carried by junior officers called ensigns.

By the time of the Civil War, technological advances in weaponry had led to an accurate, dependable, muzzle-loading percussion rifle for general use. In 1855 the highly effective .58-caliber "rifled musket" had been adopted by the Regular Army. The new weapon was accurate to 600 yards, 500 more than the range of the old smoothbore. The new rifle underwent minor modifications during the war, but it would remain the standard infantry weapon until a breech-loader was adopted in 1873.

Although improved weapons allowed more emphasis on individual marksmanship and initiative, tactical manuals lagged in taking full advantage of the Minie ball's potential. Napoleonic concepts still dominated. Doctrine still called for infantry to stand shoulder-to-shoulder in two ranks. Loading, firing, and bayonet charges were all performed on command in drills involving many separate motions under rigid discipline. Decisive action continued to depend on platoon, company, battalion, and even regiment and brigade volleys. These were designed to bring the greatest mass of firepower possible to bear on a specific part of the enemy's line, softening it up for a charge. The goal of training became the "perfect volley," in which every soldier pulled his trigger at the same instant.

Under linear tactical systems, effectiveness depended heavily on the smooth and rapid alignment of a unit. Without proper control, maneuvers such as forming lines of battle from the march, wheeling, oblique firings, and bayonet charges simply degenerated into a mob of armed men, each acting on impulse. When the newly raised Civil War regiments received their baptism of fire and began to experience the far heavier casualties inflicted by rifled muskets, subtle adjustments began to appear. Given half a chance, units opened the distance between individual ranks and, if on the defensive, dug in or took ready cover to minimize losses. Those changes increased the burden on officers and NCOs and the importance of the colors.

By 1861 the ensign had disappeared from the U.S. Army. All company-grade officers were fully occupied with other duties. Responsibility for carrying the two flags devolved upon NCOs, and the Army added two color sergeants to the regimental headquarters to perform this special duty. To protect them in combat, a distinct color guard was also created, consisting of five to eight color corporals, depending upon the number of colors carried. Regulations stated that members of the color guard would carry their muskets with bayonets always fixed. Often, for added protection, a specially selected color company of varying size would accompany the color guard.

Through this natural evolution, the colors became a key factor in esprit de corps. The flags represented the honor and integrity of the unit. They symbolized the glories of the past, stood guard over the present, and provided inspiration for the future. Both officers and men fully understood that their colors could not be surrendered. To return from battle without them was the ultimate disgrace. For example, General Orders of the Army of the Potomac denied any unit that lost its colors in action the right to carry others without the authority of the commanding general. Permission would not be given in cases where a unit had lost its colors through misconduct, "until such troops shall, by their bravery on other fields, have fully retrieved their tarnished honor." Because of their tactical and psychological importance, and because of their visibility even in the smoke of battle, the colors often became the focal point of enemy fire and charges. Casualties among color bearers were high.

NCOs in Action

Of the more than 2 million men who served in the Union Army, over 1,925,000 were volunteers. Since about one in ten eventually became a noncommissioned officer, the wartime NCO Corps was also essentially a volunteer group. Like their Regular counterparts, volunteer NCOs held their rank through the action of the regimental colonel, who made selections based upon recommendations by the company captains. All appointments had to be announced in regimental orders. Once an NCO was appointed, he could not be removed from office except by sentence of court-martial or by the order of the regimental commander.

Pay increases made the NCO's life marginally more tolerable. During the early part of the war, when base pay for Union infantry sergeants was $17 per month, soldiers were considered well paid. However, wartime inflation cut into the buying power of military pay, as did the Army's decision to issue the troops paper currency that depreciated rapidly. In 1864, when the greenback dollar was worth only 39 cents in coin, Congress voted an increase in military pay, adding $3 a month to the income of a line sergeant. This still left him far behind civilians in terms of buying power, but his inadequate pay was partially offset by enlistment and reenlistment bounties. In 1864, when the three-year enlistments were about to expire, all members of veteran regiments, regardless of rank, received a $400 bonus to remain in service. Some states offered additional sums, so that by the end of the war some soldiers received up to $1,000 to reenlist. Foreign observers, accustomed to the low pay of European armies, were struck by America's generosity toward its soldiers.

Yet the sums of money involved, accentuated by the relatively small difference between the pay of a private and a sergeant, belied the important roles carried out by NCOs during the war. The tactics of the time called for officers up to the rank of brigadier general to lead their men in person, and in consequence officer casualties were high. As a battle went on, sergeants and corporals often found themselves assuming command of companies. In extreme cases, such as the charge of Pickett's Virginia division at Gettysburg in 1863, whole regiments lost all their commissioned officers. The demonstrated ability of the NCOs to handle the burden of leadership in such cases permanently affected the corps' future status.

The exposed position of a unit's colors and their tactical significance led to particularly high casualties among the sergeants and corporals carrying them—often wiping out the entire color guard. During the 1862 battle of Fredericksburg, for example, the 155th Pennsylvania was ordered to cross an exposed area and assault enemy-held heights that dominated the field of battle. When the color sergeant was killed, a corporal seized the flag. He soon fell, as did three successors. A fifth corporal grasped the banner and kept it aloft, an act for which he was promoted to color sergeant. In the battle of Antietam, the 62d New York lost sixteen color bearers in quick succession. Two years later at Spotsylvania, Sgt. Nathaniel Barker, 11th New Hampshire Infantry, took up the national and regimental colors after six predecessors had been killed and carried both throughout the remainder of the battle. Sergeant Barker's heroism led to the award of the newly authorized Medal of Honor, a recognition extended to many individuals who either protected their own colors or captured those of an enemy unit.

The accurate rifle fire of the Civil War changed infantry tactics. Based on the hard lessons of battle, the Army adopted a new system of open-order tactics after the war. Instead of advancing in rigid linear formations, soldiers now equipped with the new breech-loading rifles spent more time in small groups. Given the higher volume of fire, the Army achieved a more efficient use of manpower through skirmishing and attacking in rushes. That trend would continue in the Spanish-American War, which saw the introduction of high velocity, low trajectory clip-loading rifles, and would accelerate throughout the twentieth century as technology further increased the lethality of the battlefield. These advances in firepower, however, made it impossible to carry flags into combat, thus leading to the abolition of the rank of color sergeant.

At the same time, the utility of the old linear tactics as a tool for instilling the fundamentals of unit discipline did not diminish. Like colors and color guards, drill and formations have remained a key part of Army tradition and training after disappearing from combat. Flags and guidons continue to play an important role in the creation of unit identity, cohesion, and esprit de corps, with battle streamers replacing the old inscriptions. Their continued presence at the center of a formation symbolically represents their former position in the heat of battle. The retention of a color guard with fixed bayonets commemorates the earlier functional role of protecting the colors against capture.

The Army values traditions and relies heavily on the NCO Corps to preserve them. Drill and ceremony, including parades, reviews, retreat, and military funerals, add pageantry to military life but also symbolize for each soldier the shared values, courage, and self-discipline essential to any successful military organization. The high honor given to a unit's senior enlisted member as custodian of its flag or guidon and membership in the color guard reflect that continuity in a very personal way.

Ready for Patrol, *Theresa L. Unger, 1988*

READY

FOR

PATROL

NEW MEXICO, 1870S

———◆———

The NCOs were stern, the troops anxious; only the horses seemed calm. No quick once-over before the daily retreat parade, this was the last inspection before going out on a war patrol that might last a month or more, depending on how soon the Indians were found and whether they chose to talk or fight. The Apaches had been on the attack again, raiding settlements from across the Mexican border. Here at Fort Union, in the New Mexico Territory, the sergeants and corporals respected the Apache as a tough enemy who could find and take advantage of any weakness, any detail overlooked in garrison. Spit shine and polish would count for little in the coming months, but the tools of campaigning would. Experienced eyes ran over carbines, uniforms, boots, bridles, saddles, and cartridge belts and looked in every knapsack and saddlebag.

During the hours of preparation for the reconnaissance, as it was officially termed, the varied experiences of the men became obvious. The newer men were loudest, their excited talk filled with bravado. To them it was all high adventure and daring exploits. The veteran cavalrymen, some with Civil War experience, quietly continued their cleaning and packing for the campaign. They knew that the boasts of green troopers would provide no protection from Indian arrows and bullets. The NCOs used the inspection to quash as many youthful misconceptions as possible. "Why do you carry so much coffee? Are you going to offer the Apaches a cup?…Where are your extra socks? And where's the bar of soap? No, you're not taking any baths for a while—you soap your feet so you don't get blisters…and cut them fingernails and toenails…pack more bullets and salt…make sure your cantle and pommel rolls are balanced…when's the last time you cleaned this revolver?"

Background

Following the Civil War and a decade of Reconstruction duty in the South, a sharply reduced Army returned to its old tasks: enforcing treaties and trying to prevent fighting between Indians and settlers

A Cavalryman's Breakfast on the Plains, *Frederic Remington, c. 1892. Despite profound changes in the outward appearance of the cavalry during the last century, the mission to "get there fastest with the mostest" remains.*

on the frontier. The postwar Army split into small detachments and used both cavalry and infantry extensively to cover vast distances in pursuit of elusive adversaries. After demobilization, the Army would remain for the next thirty years at slightly under 25,000 troops, most assigned to twenty-five infantry and ten cavalry regiments. One positive result of the Civil War was the enlistment of black soldiers in the Regular Army for the first time since the Revolution. Though mostly officered by whites, the 24th and 25th Infantries and the 9th and 10th Cavalries were black units with a full complement of black NCOs.

In 1869 the Army administered its 255 posts through three major territorial departments: Atlantic, Pacific, and Missouri. Campaigns against the Indians were coordinated by the Department of the Missouri, headquartered at Jefferson Barracks near St. Louis. Although they sent soldiers into 943 engagements with the Indians in a thirty-year period, many of the Army's senior leaders remained largely unconcerned with the operations they directed. Interested in large-scale campaigns like those waged by Napoleon, Grant, Lee, and Jackson, they found few lessons of value in the Plains campaigns. The junior officers, NCOs, and troopers coping with the daily reality of the frontier, on the other hand, had a different viewpoint. They cared less about Napoleon and Lee than about Geronimo and Red Cloud. Learning in the saddle, they became experts in dealing with some of the world's greatest irregular fighters and in the process wrote a new chapter in the history of one of the Army's most important combat arms—the Cavalry.

The image of cavalrymen as soldiers in resplendent uniforms, charging across a plain on magnificent horses, with sabers drawn and guidons billowing in the wind has more reality in European than in American history. America's experience with mounted troops has placed much greater importance on the abilities and initiative of the noncommissioned officer to ensure that the men put in their "forty miles a day on beans and hay," chasing an elusive enemy over barren desert territories.

The use of mounted troops by the U.S. Army dates back to the Revolutionary War. Dense forests, stone fences to divide fields, and limited roads restricted European-style mounted charges. On the other hand, after being defeated in 1776 at the battle of Long Island by an undetected British flanking movement, George Washington recognized the value of reliable scouts mounted on horseback. The following winter Congress added four cavalry regiments to the Continental Army. Those regiments, really mounted infantry, originally received the designation light dragoons, a choice of terms that established the precedent for the use of troopers throughout the Army's history. Basically, Washington's cavalrymen performed reconnaissance missions. Their battles usually involved skirmishing, often dismounted, rather than charges. Like the colonial rangers, the light dragoons tended to spend most of their time in small patrols where NCOs played important leadership roles. Even in Nathanael Greene's campaign in the Carolinas in 1781, where the terrain lent itself more to European-style charges, the lives of the men serving under William Washington or "Light Horse Harry" Lee were filled with routine rather than glamour.

The pattern of service in the mounted arm in the decades that followed, like that of the infantry and artillery, built upon Revolutionary precedents. In the small Army, the nation maintained to police its interior border and to man a handful of coast defense forts, relatively few of the expensive horsemen were necessary, and European-style heavy cavalry was hardly needed at all. Those troopers that did exist spent most of their time caring for their horses and costly equipment and nearly all of the rest conducting patrols. NCOs supervised the former and provided much of the essential leadership for the latter functions. Even when they became involved in combat, the horsemen tended to be employed as mobile infantry who dismounted to fight. Only on rare occasions—such as at Resaca de la Palma during the Mexican War or at Brandy Station in the Civil War—did American

Bradley M2/M3A3 Tracked Armored Fighting Vehicle, 2000. From horses on the Great Plains to Bradleys in the twenty-first century, the essentials of small-unit leadership and, therefore, the duties of the NCO have remained the same.

cavalry conduct true mounted charges. On the other hand, the massive mobilization for the latter conflict brought more troopers into the Army than ever before, and such great cavalrymen as James E. B. "Jeb" Stuart, George Armstrong Custer, and Philip H. Sheridan emerged among the leaders on both sides of the fighting.

When the Army returned to the Great Plains and the deserts of the Southwest in late 1865, it kept a larger proportion of horsemen than at any time in its history. The vast distances and small total strength of the service mandated a larger share of responsibility for the troopers. Scouting, escorting the workers constructing the transcontinental railroads and telegraph lines, and enforcing treaties with various tribes were easier when mounted. Although charismatic officers like George Armstrong Custer frequently dominated the newspaper headlines, the quiet professionalism of long-term NCOs held units together during years of isolation at each of the dozens of forts established during a thirty-year period.

An example of a "hitching-post" garrison was Fort Union in the Territory of New Mexico. In the late 1870s responsibility for protection of that region fell to elements of the 9th Cavalry, a black regiment, and the 15th Infantry. Several companies occupied Fort Union, from which patrols set forth to prevent or punish Indian attacks on settlers and infringement on treaties by unscrupulous whites. A typical patrol would last up to several weeks, with infantry participating as escorts for a wagon train carrying reserve supplies, hardtack and salt pork for the men, and grain for the animals. As each day came to a close, a camp was established and sergeants and corporals organized the nighttime guard. Troopers cared for their horses and equipment before themselves, a crucial duty often enforced by the NCOs.

If the patrol met hostile Indians, the troops could expect frontier combat against a fierce and resourceful enemy. For the men of the 9th Cavalry in New Mexico Territory, the most formidable adversary was Victorio, an Apache who had never studied the campaigns of Napoleon or Frederick the Great. His relatively small band relied heavily on the element of surprise. Plains Indian warfare centered on the raid, intended to accomplish a specific purpose with a minimum of loss to the tribe. Taking maximum advantage of their intimate familiarity with the terrain and ignoring the boundary between the United States and Mexico, the Apaches often seemed to materialize out of nowhere, inflict considerable damage during a brief fire fight, and then disappear before an effective response could be organized. With no intertribal coordination and no systematic recruiting to replace casualties, Indians traditionally shunned set-piece battles, fighting at night or staging true ambushes. Their courage and preference for close battle cost them dearly against long-range rifles.

The Army took years to find a way to employ its advantages of firepower and discipline. Constant pressure gradually neutralized surprise tactics by wresting the initiative from the Indians, while the cumulative impact of casualties, losses of property and livestock, and slaughter of the buffalo wore the tribes down. Such warfare demanded high proficiency in basic military skills, especially marksmanship. Massive battles in the Civil War had placed a premium on artillery and sheer numbers of rounds fired, rather than individual accuracy. Out on the plains and deserts of the West, units initially found themselves blazing away until their ammunition was nearly gone then watching in frustration as most of the enemy escaped. The basic marksmanship problem was worsened by the fact that many of the recruits joining the Army in the 1870s were recently arrived immigrants from Europe, men who lacked experience with firearms. Budget restrictions prevented the Army from buying ammunition for frequent rifle practice, even had time been available for it, since so much of a soldier's day had to be spent on growing food, maintaining the buildings of his post, and caring for animals and equipment.

In the aftermath of Custer's stunning 1876 disaster at the Little Big Horn, changes were instituted. New regulations mandated that each soldier fire twenty rounds per month at targets set up at ranges of from 100 to 1,000 yards. Cavalrymen fired the carbine from a stationary position and the revolver while mounted, first at a walk, then a trot, and finally at the gallop. Officers and troops alike came to take pride in their new skills and soon formed teams for competitions between posts. The American soldier's international reputation for outstanding marksmanship dates from this period. More importantly for the men involved, the increased attention to training began to pay off in improved combat effectiveness against hostile tribes.

NCOs in Action

Noncommissioned officers on the frontier assumed positions of responsibility that went beyond the important roles that they had long filled. In addition to the familiar company-level positions and regimental-level NCO staff, a new category of assignments appeared. Post staff NCOs—the ordnance and quartermaster corps sergeants—emerged. Assignment to such a position was not part of a normal career pattern. An NCO interested in becoming a post ordnance sergeant had to have served at least eight years in the Army, four as an NCO; those interested in the post quartermaster sergeant duty had to have already completed at least four years in uniform. Applications, which had to be handwritten as a proof of literacy, were passed up the chain of command to The Adjutant General, who made the assignments.

The main purpose in appointing post NCOs was to ensure property accountability in a widely scattered Army. Secondary purposes were to reward long and faithful service among the NCO Corps and to encourage junior enlisted men to remain with the colors by holding out the chance for advancement beyond the company level. Charged with responsibility for government property at his post, each ordnance sergeant quickly became one of its most respected soldiers. He had to be honest as well as experienced, for the opportunity to make an illegal profit at government expense was always present.

His responsibility extended beyond the weaponry and ammunition implied by his title. He also had to keep each unit assigned to the post well supplied with all required equipment and clothing, assisted by the quartermaster sergeant. When a cavalry unit was present, the ordnance sergeant added all equipment related to horses and riding to his inventory. Post NCOs came to provide continuity in an environment made fluid by the mission of the Army in the West. Companies and regiments changed stations, but the post NCOs stayed. Beyond that, as they developed new skills and qualifications in an increasingly complex military system, they became forerunners of a whole family of specialists who later contributed to the development of the Army.

The rise in the status of NCOs in the West grew directly out of the nature of the fighting they encountered. Besides keeping unit records, overseeing daily fatigue details, and supervising training, sergeants and corporals often served as small-unit leaders without immediate supervision by officers. In the dusty expanses of the Plains or southwestern mesas, merely finding a hostile force could become a major undertaking, requiring patrols that lasted for weeks and covered hundreds of miles. To conduct patrols properly, infantry and cavalry squads and platoons often had to search independently and then reconcentrate promptly. NCOs, of course, led these squads and platoons, occasionally accompanied by a lone officer. If the reconnaissance confronted a hostile band, they then had to become combat leaders. Courage, skill, and brains were all requirements of the job. Just giving commands to their men was a problem in some units, where up to a quarter of the soldiers spoke little or no English. While American general officers thought about great battles of future wars, crucial innovations in practice were emerging from the warfare on the Plains. Gradually, the increasing use of heliostats and the telegraph for signaling and the railroad for shifting and concentrating forces made the Plains garrisons less isolated.

In the twentieth century, technology dramatically changed the cavalry, as it did warfare in general. The Noncommissioned Officer Corps coped with the new inventions, just as it had taken other developments in stride. The use of machine guns in World War I severely limited the combat role of horse cavalry. Small numbers of mounted soldiers did perform reconnaissance, liaison, and courier service in France, but the large-scale introduction of motor vehicles and tanks changed the scale, the pace, and the form of warfare. Army leadership in general turned out to be more willing to plan changes for the cavalry than Congress was to provide funding, but by 1932 the branch had its first mechanized cavalry regiment equipped with light tanks and armored cars. Large-scale cavalry training continued well into World War II, although most cavalrymen fought as infantry, in reconnaissance squadrons (troops that performed vital roles in screening the flanks of corps and divisions), or in the armored divisions and separate tank battalions of the combined-arms team. A decade later the introduction of assault and troop-carrying helicopters would extend that cavalry mission to the sky. NCOs met this new challenge by becoming the commanders of individual tanks and armored cars and mastering the technical skills to maintain the fleets of new war machines, just as they had led patrols and cared for horses and saddles.

It was the Noncommissioned Officer Corps that in many ways provided the glue that held the branch together during the wrenching changes from horses to the internal combustion engine. The sergeants and corporals found that when technology changes many functions continue, whether soldiers are mounted on chargers, tanks, or helicopters. Reconnaissance, screening, and raiding can be performed by armored vehicles and helicopters, shock action by main battle tanks and attack aircraft. In each case the fundamental techniques of leading and supervising troops on a day-to-day basis do not change.

Whether on horseback or in a turret, the cavalry NCO carries a great deal of responsibility. He must make quick decisions about deployment of forces on all types of terrain while remaining ready to respond quickly to mechanical breakdowns or the actions of hostile forces. He remains the immediate link between the officer and the private, translating planning into action. The Army on the western plains was an Army in transition, an Army preparing for a vastly expanded role in the twentieth century, although it did not know it at the time. Fittingly, NCOs helped to pioneer and achieve that transition.

Field Hospital Back of the Lines, *Charles Johnson Post, 1898*

AMBULANCE CORPS PROFICIENCY

CUBA, 1898

T he ambulance sergeant had never seen a situation like this. Ever since the V Corps had landed at Daiquiri nine days ago, one thing after another had gone wrong for the medical personnel. The landing itself had been a nightmare: supplies lost in the surf, hospitals unable to get ashore given the demand for the few available small boats. Then the shortage of baggage wagons had so hampered the march inland that surgeons had often abandoned medical chests along the route, hoping to retrieve them later. Now, as fighting raged along the slopes of a nearby rise the local natives called San Juan Hill on this oppressively hot July day, the few ambulances available had been posted near the corps headquarters, so that the corps surgeon could personally control their use. The sergeant could only watch the wounded trickle back to the field hospital by whatever means they could find, whether their own feet or the wagons that could navigate the few roads, which were already heavily congested.

Although the corps commander had believed that muddy roads would enable supply wagons to do the same work as ambulances, the sergeant was not so sure. Between the poor condition of the roads, the unruly behavior of the drivers and mules, and the resulting jars and jolts, more than a few patients had died trying to cover the four or five miles from the battlefield to the field hospital. There, they would encounter such a shortage of tents, cots, and bedding that many could only recline on the ground. It was the sergeant's responsibility to keep up the spirits of the young privates as they gawked at the confusion surrounding them. He knew that he must control his irritation at a moment like this and provide the sort of leadership that would bring order to chaos. Inwardly, he could only hope that future Army expeditions would take more care to organize their medical preparations than this one had.

Background

Formation of the Ambulance Corps represented another step in the accelerating specialization and professionalism of American society in the late nineteenth century. The Army joined this trend in spite

Pre–World War I Medical Training Exercise, Fort Benning, Georgia. NCOs involved in the care and treatment of battlefield casualties have always needed to make life-and-death decisions under fire.

of severely limited peacetime budgets. Just as doctors and lawyers developed their professional organizations and career training, career officers and NCOs in their own ways sought to upgrade their standards and adjust to new ideas and growing technological complexity. Engineers and artillerymen, for example, tried to adapt to a stream of inventions that changed the way in which the seacoasts were protected, rebuilding fortifications and introducing heavy artillery and telegraphic and telephonic communications to create an early centralized fire control system. Driving the change was the realization that the United States might one day have to face up-to-date foreign armies in the field, as the Army had done in the past.

The requirement for new skills was first reflected in the addition of individual specialists to combat units and post garrisons. In time, however, the Army created entire units with unique missions. Since the time of the Revolution the Army had set up such organizations in wartime, but now it considered permanent units necessary to enhance its capability to deter foreign aggression. The combination of technical developments and broadening awareness provoked reexamination of many long-accepted dogmas. A growing number of Army branches began to publish journals, discussing issues and spreading innovations among widely scattered units. Yet budget restrictions prevented the Regular Army from pursuing many promising leads. Hence the former state militias—now increasingly known as the National Guard—took the lead. Using state-appropriated funds and drawing on civilian skills, these citizen-soldiers, for example, created the first true Signal Corps unit in New York in the 1870s and the earliest permanent division organization in Pennsylvania in 1878. The trend continued in the early twentieth century with the creation of the Army Reserve, which had as one of its original missions the responsibility of maintaining a reservoir of technical specialists.

A field that changed dramatically was the initial care and evacuation of the wounded. Caring for casualties has always been a major problem in war. In the American Revolution, the recovery of casualties fell to the regimental quartermaster sergeant with a work party composed of fifers and drummers. No wounded man could call for a medic, for the trained medic and litter bearer did not yet exist. In the Civil War, two-thirds of the wounded died. Initial treatment came from a regimental surgeon in an often improvised aid station, but two men were needed to move each wounded soldier there. As a result, many casualties were untended for considerable periods on the battlefield. Commanders risked defeat if they diverted too many able-bodied fighters from the line to recover the wounded, whose chances were slim anyway.

The massive casualty figures of the Civil War highlighted a continuing problem in military medicine: how to move battlefield casualties to regimental surgeons without worsening their condition. Under policies in effect at the beginning of that war, each regimental surgeon was to be assisted by a maximum of 25 enlisted men: 15 bandsmen and no more than 10 men detailed from line companies, but no medical specialist. Problems quickly became apparent. The quality of personnel was often poor, because commanders did not send their best men to act as nurses, orderlies, pharmacists, and litter bearers. Those who went often lacked motivation as well as training. The detailed "hospital attendants" had to split their time between retrieving new battlefield casualties and caring for those already at the temporary facility. Ambulances were lacking. Although testing began in 1859, the Army had not yet adopted a standard design when the war broke out. Often the rough, springless wagons

Medicine Man, *Henrietta Snowden, 2000. Today's medical NCOs find themselves deployed on a wide range of missions, from combat duty in the Middle East and Afghanistan to humanitarian missions in the Balkans and Africa.*

pressed into service to fill that gap had civilian teamsters, not soldiers, as drivers.

Dr. Jonathan Letterman, an Army surgeon, made the first attempt to create a system of treatment and evacuation. When he became medical director of the Army of the Potomac in the summer of 1862, he centralized a large ambulance force—he used 200 men at the battle of Antietam in September—all under the control of officers or NCOs. A captain took charge of an army corps' vehicles, with a first lieutenant at the division level, and a sergeant commanding the two ambulances assigned to each regiment, each with a driver, plus two men and two stretchers. Another Letterman innovation welcomed by surgeons came from assigning better men to the ambulance crews, soldiers detailed from line regiments who had demonstrated that they were "active and efficient." Once in the new ambulance corps, they stayed with it and trained regularly. With the Army able to provide better treatment and more efficient evacuation for its wounded, an increasing proportion of the wounded were able to return to duty.

The Letterman system remained limited to the Army of the Potomac until March 1864. Tested in fierce battles, it finally became the basis for a new Army-wide ambulance service. Each regiment had between one and three ambulances. Two additional ambulances accompanied each corps headquarters, while two Army freight wagons supported each division's ambulance train. Field experience through the rest of the war showed that the only major problem with the Letterman ambulance corps was the chronic shortage of vehicles.

Noncommissioned Officer's Belt *The noncommissioned officer's belt was introduced in 1851 and used until 1902. It was authorized for noncommissioned officers of the line and staff who were authorized to carry the noncommissioned officer's sword. After 1872 the use of the belt and sword was relegated principally to members of regimental noncommissioned staff, including regimental sergeants major, regimental quartermaster sergeants, ordnance sergeants, principal musicians, and noncommissioned officers of the various staff departments, including the Medical, Subsistence, Quartermaster, and Ordnance Departments.*

Insignia for Regimental Noncommissioned Staff *Pattern 1896 Insignia for the Noncommissioned Staff of the 25th Infantry on Model 1895 Forage Cap. The crossed rifles indicate infantry branch, and the regimental number, in this case "25," denotes the unit. The lack of a company letter shows that the wearer served on the regimental noncommissioned staff, which should not be confused with noncommissioned officers of the various staff departments.*

Insignia of a Commissary Sergeant *Pattern 1896 Insignia of a Post Commissary Sergeant of the Subsistence Department on a Model 1895 Forage Cap from the Period of the Spanish-American War. A badge with a wreath is indicative of the insignia worn by noncommissioned officers of the various staff departments and indicates a specific position rather than a branch association.*

Unfortunately for the future of Army medical care, the Ambulance Corps with its now trained NCOs and enlisted men disbanded at the end of the Civil War. Low peacetime strength levels (no more than 25,000 regulars served at any one time for most of the rest of the century) forced the War Department to concentrate on policing Indians and settlers in the western territories, not on preparing for a major conventional war. Much of what the Army had learned in medical treatment and evacuation during the Civil War was forgotten. Critical specialties were eliminated, including nurses, medical storekeepers (druggists), and the ambulance men who provided initial treatment in the field. The only enlisted medical specialists retained were hospital stewards.

A comeback began on 14 May 1885, when the Massachusetts legislature created the Ambulance Corps, Massachusetts Volunteer Militia. Each of the militia's two brigades received permission to form a unit of 1 officer, 2 sergeants, and 13 privates. The officer in charge had to be a trained physician, able to pass the test as a medical officer in the Regular Army and to recruit and train his own enlisted men. Samuel B. Clarke, M.D., enlisted thirteen medical students in time to have his unit participate in its first "summer camp" two months later. The second ambulance unit completed organization in 1887. Wearing infantry uniforms and red crosses, Clarke's men carried modified cartridge boxes with medical supplies, special knives in lieu of weapons, and collapsible stretchers. In camp they not only trained but also demonstrated their immediate value to others by treating a variety of heat casualties. The Massachusetts Ambulance Corps went through a number of changes in the following decades, setting an example for other states and the regulars to follow. By the eve of World War I it had grown to the size of a battalion with 4 specialized companies, 2 of which manned ambulances while 2 provided the enlisted strength for field hospitals.

Action by the War Department came in 1887. Congress, approving an Army request, created the Hospital Corps within the Medical Department. It provided three grades for enlisted medical specialists: hospital stewards, acting hospital stewards, and privates. Serving as nurses, wardmasters, cooks, and assistants, these men would perform all "hospital services in garrison and in the field" and staff the wartime ambulance service.

The Hospital Corps marked a new departure in two ways. First, prospective enlisted members had to volunteer for the duty and to show real aptitude. Second, recruits now had a professional career pattern. Men who volunteered from line units received training in first aid and in the duties of a litter bearer for at least four hours a month. After working as litter bearers for at least one year, candidates could take an examination for selection as Hospital Corps privates. After a year of service with the Hospital Corps, privates would be eligible for appointment as acting hospital stewards. Following one year of service on a probationary basis and passage of another examination, they could be appointed permanent hospital stewards. In its first year some 600 privates transferred to the new corps, with 24 passing their examinations and receiving promotions to NCO status as acting hospital stewards. Such planned career development made the establishment of the

Hospital Corps important for the Army as a whole, for it launched the continuing development of various new specialties that allowed the Army to emerge as a modern, professional force.

Until the Spanish-American War, however, the Hospital Corps maintained a strength of only about 750, slightly more than one-quarter of whom held NCO rank. Additional responsibilities without commensurate pay raises, however, prompted many potential NCOs to opt for remaining with their line regiments. Others, trained by the Army, left at the end of their initial enlistments for better jobs in civilian life. When the Army assembled a divisional field hospital at Pine Ridge, South Dakota, in 1890, units in surrounding states and territories had to be stripped of stewards and corpsmen, leaving them almost without medical support for several weeks. Once at the divisional hospital, these corpsmen also revealed unacceptable variations in training. Both problems were addressed quickly. In 1891 two companies of instruction were founded (a third was added in 1893) to standardize training. With staffs of 3 medical officers, 7 NCOs, and 40 privates each, the companies produced competent "sanitary soldiers" by offering a curriculum of infantry drill, first aid, elementary nursing and pharmacology, field hospital setup, field cookery, care of animals, and ambulance driving. Beginning in 1892, recruiting rules were altered to allow direct enlistment into the corps, a policy aimed at attracting civilian druggists, teachers, and cooks, and base pay for a Hospital Corps private was raised from $13 to $18 per month.

The Spanish-American War provided a rigorous test for the Hospital Corps. Though the quality of corpsmen trained in the companies of instruction was excellent, the quantity was insufficient. The Army had no choice but to go back to its old system of detailing men from the line and trying to train them quickly. By the end of the war, 6,588 corpsmen, of whom 608 were NCOs, had served in the combined Regular and volunteer force.

In the years that followed, additional reforms again sought to standardize performance and grade structure. In 1903 the medics expanded to a five-rank grade progression, from private to private first class, corporal, sergeant, and sergeant first class. Beginning in 1904, annual maneuvers funded by the federal government brought National Guardsmen and regulars together for joint training. The Hospital Corps used these occasions to test its ability to perform its wartime mission. Each year, however, the companies of instruction had to cease normal operations to transform themselves temporarily for field service. Finally, in the spring of 1911, the corps reorganized on a permanent, specialized basis into four field hospital companies and four ambulance companies. On maneuvers, these companies supported units in the field. In garrison, they trained in all medical functions.

NCOs in Action

As hospital steward and assistant hospital steward, the NCO appeared in a new role in the late nineteenth century: the technical specialist. This development certainly was not restricted to the Medical Department. Already in the 1870s and 1880s technical specialists were well established in the artillery and coast artillery as fire-direction NCOs and electricians and in the Signal Corps as communications experts and weather observers.

But the Hospital Corps, reflecting advances in medicine as a whole, was particularly affected by the trend toward specialization. In its early stages, medical specialization meant teaching line soldiers the rudiments of field medicine and emergency first aid. Later, Hospital Corps NCOs and privates acquired the skills to perform an increasing number of complex medical procedures without close supervision.

Training methods also became more specialized, and the responsibilities of medical NCOs as trainers expanded. Before and during the Civil War the Army left the training of hospital attendants to regimental surgeons, but the need to train subordinates took surgeons away from their primary duties, while many of the soldiers detailed to medical service brought little or no interest to their informal apprenticeship. To eliminate these problems, the Army created the two companies of instruction in the 1890s to train personnel recruited directly for a medical military career. NCOs were a part of that process from the very beginning, using their practical field experience to supplement the technical knowledge of the doctors.

By the eve of World War I, skilled and specialized medical units had become an integral part of the Army. During the war each regiment or separate battalion had a sanitary detachment, reinforced by a division-level sanitary train capable of providing one field hospital and one ambulance company to support each line regiment. Additional units existed at corps and army levels. Growth in the overall size of the Hospital Corps was stimulated by additional pay increases and by the expansion of the grade system from five ranks to seven.

Technological change compelled further development of Army medicine as the lethality of the battlefield escalated dramatically. Fortunately, medical science kept pace. New inventions and improved knowledge allowed treatment to save lives that hitherto would have been lost. Late nineteenth century medical advances made possible the successful treatment of a greater range of illnesses and injuries. New drugs and antiseptics reduced pain and infection. Line commanders welcomed such developments, which held out the possibility of increased unit efficiency, higher morale, and less death and suffering. If large numbers of the wounded could be returned to duty, line units could regain experienced men and maintain manpower levels needed for continuous campaigning.

More was demanded of the medical enlisted ranks, especially the NCOs. They had to recover casualties rapidly, stabilize them, and move them safely to aid stations for treatment. During World War II, the Army's Medical Corps introduced the most sophisticated network of facilities and hospitals yet seen. Later, in Korea and Vietnam, extensive use of helicopters as aerial ambulances dramatically improved evacuation procedures and survival rates. The seriously wounded could be taken from a battlefield to a hospital in as little as twenty minutes. The Army medical NCO has come a long way from the Spanish-American War.

On the Trail of the Hun, *William James Aylward, c. 1920*

SUSTAINING
THE
OFFENSIVE

FRANCE, 1918

———————◆———————

The two American Expeditionary Forces (AEF) NCOs faced a familiar scene as the Meuse-Argonne offensive entered November 1918: deep mud, miserable weather, a hopelessly unrealistic schedule, and enemy harassing fire. Neither had enjoyed the luxury of a full night's sleep lately, and their tempers were short. Such problems had faced leaders throughout the history of warfare. But now NCOs had to deal with something new: traffic jams, like the one that the military police sergeant found himself trying to untangle.

"Before your truck can go," he told the sergeant from the Chemical Corps, "that ammunition convoy for V Corps has got to get through the intersection. And they aren't going anywhere until someone finishes changing that flat tire." Each day hundreds of vehicles tried to use the same road at the same time, with everyone claiming the highest priority. To hear convoy commanders tell it, General Pershing had personally ordered every driver to get to the front as fast as possible no matter what was in the way. Once again, the military policeman thought, it was the NCO on the scene who had to get things moving again. To be successful, he'd have to take full advantage of the authority that the "MP" on his arm and the pistol on his hip provided. At least the drivers had stopped yelling—they could see it wouldn't do any good—and the tire was just about changed. NCOs had straightened out difficult situations in earlier campaigns, and they were equal to the task again. For days and nights on end, they had moved ten divisions of troops and thousands of tons of weapons, ammunition, and equipment into position for this, the largest American offensive of the war. Now that the attack was under way, it was even more important to keep the convoys on schedule to sustain momentum and to achieve the victory that would let the men return home again.

Background

Soldiers performing specialized duties like military policemen and truck drivers are so familiar—and so essential—in today's Army that their presence is taken for granted. Every duty position requires

Transportation Problems in Italy, 1944. The application of the internal combustion engine to warfighting in the twentieth century led to a host of new technical specialties for NCOs.

specific skills and training beyond that gained in civilian life. This fact of life is so fundamental that people tend to forget that it has not always been the case. From the Revolution through the Civil War the Army was overwhelmingly infantry oriented, focusing on the ability to execute a handful of common tasks. Throughout its early history the military operated under very limited budgets and could set aside only about five percent of its manpower to perform specialized functions. Not even the late nineteenth century's explosion of new inventions produced a dramatic change. As late as the Spanish-American War, the combat arms still accounted for ten out of every eleven soldiers. The principle of effectiveness gained by division of labor had long been understood in industry, but it was slower in gaining recognition in the armed forces.

One important reason for the limited earlier reliance on technical specialists grew from the Army's restricted peacetime mission. During the late eighteenth and nineteenth centuries, it had served primarily as a constabulary force. Spread along the inland frontier or in small coast defense garrisons, it dealt with low-level threats and operated at a technological level based on the requirements of local conditions. The only constant requirement for experts tended to involve a few clerks, cooks, bandsmen, and the people to keep the horses and mules moving: farriers, blacksmiths, saddlers, and wagoners.

Within the combat branches, however, a small number of duty positions depended upon technical skills even in the days of the Continental Army. For example, effective use of artillery required experienced NCOs and enlisted men to assist officers in placing and aiming the guns. But these early specialists received no formal training in their duties. Instead, they learned on the job, as apprentices did, by watching an experienced NCO and carrying out his orders. Formal schooling for enlisted personnel appeared about a half-century into the Army's history when, in 1824, the Artillery School opened at Fort Monroe. Entire companies rotated assignments to that post, to allow both officers and soldiers to get classroom and practical instruction with heavy emphasis on the mathematics needed in gunnery. Although its creation was a significant breakthrough, the Artillery School suffered many interruptions. Budget problems and wartime priorities suspended classes from 1835 to 1858 and again during the Civil War and the Spanish-American War. The school enjoyed its greatest influence on the Army between 1868 and 1898, graduating nineteen classes of NCOs and officers.

Artillerymen had more choice than other enlisted specialists about higher-level positions they could hope to achieve. Most could aspire to a promotion sequence based on leadership and tactical proficiency that would carry them through the classification of master gunner to the rank of first sergeant or regimental sergeant major. If they opted to concentrate on the heavy artillery dedicated to coast defense, they could also benefit from a technological revolution that began in the late 1880s. Developments in the design of long-range guns and the use of the telegraph and telephone led to indirect-fire control systems and created duty positions for sergeant electricians and engineers. The Engineer School of Application at Willet's Point, New York, began informally training engineer NCOs as early as 1866, although the school was not officially recognized until 1885.

Among other branches in the nineteenth-century Army, the small Signal Corps became along with the Corps of Engineers one of the most technically oriented. Its small size enabled it to set and enforce high standards and to maintain a very high ratio of NCOs to privates. Enlisted applicants had to pass rigorous tests in mathematics, English grammar, and the history and geography of the

Saudi Arabia, January 1991, Jim Dietz, 1991. The Army has always relied on NCO leadership and technical skills to keep the convoys rolling. This painting depicts potable water supply in DESERT SHIELD/DESERT STORM.

United States before being allowed to attend the Signal School at Fort Whipple (now Fort Myer), Virginia. Most graduates went on to serve at weather stations, where they received further on-the-job training in the highly technical field of meteorology. After at least one year in the field, enlisted men could compete for vacant sergeant-observer slots. In 1887 Congress fixed the enlisted force of the Signal Corps at 150 sergeants, 30 corporals, and 270 privates.

By the end of the nineteenth century, a number of discoveries and inventions promised to change the material base of life—and warfare—among industrializing nations. During the first decade of the twentieth century the Army, now faced with overseas responsibilities as the nation began to emerge as a major world power, reexamined the way it had to organize and fight. The results were dramatic increases in technical specialists in both new and old occupations. As part of a series of reforms requested by Secretaries of War Russell A. Alger and Elihu Root in the aftermath of the Spanish-American War, Congress authorized additional technical personnel, regrouped them by function to make training more efficient, and revised the enlisted grade structure to give regular NCO status to many specialists.

No single invention had a greater impact on the Army than the internal combustion engine, which promised to free troops from the slow pace of horses and mules. In 1906 the Quartermaster Corps bought its first six automobiles, and experiments with trucks soon followed. Army trucks quickly demonstrated their value following the San Francisco earthquake. In 1907 the Army formed an "aeronautical division" in the Signal Corps and two years later bought its first experimental powered aircraft from the Wright brothers. Both applications of the engine received field testing during General John ("Black Jack") Pershing's expedition into Mexico in 1916. The service was hard, as Army units pursued the elusive bandit and Mexican folk hero Pancho Villa through forbidding terrain. Despite crashes and maintenance problems, cars and trucks proved superior to horses and mules, and the eight planes then in service performed reconnaissance and carried messages. Aviation was definitely now a part of the Army, even if the planes did have a tendency to break down with some regularity.

Beginning in 1904, with the issue of new Field Service Regulations and with the motivating force of the Root reforms, the Army also changed to meet the needs of an expanded overseas mission. Basic was the planning for a permanent divisional organization. The Army's support functions also underwent extensive reshuffling. In 1912 the Quartermaster, Subsistence, and Paymaster Departments merged as a single Quartermaster Corps, with its own body of enlisted men to perform tasks previously done by civilian contractors or by line soldiers on detail. Changes extended to the infantry regiments, which created units to sustain their riflemen: sanitary (medical) detachments and headquarters, machine gun, and supply companies. As a result, the regimental commander now controlled a wide array of technically proficient NCOs and specialists. His headquarters company still included such traditional noncommissioned staff positions as the sergeant major and the color, mess, and stable sergeants, plus cooks, bandsmen, and administrative clerks.

When America entered the war in Europe in 1917, specialization increased. Long-established technical functions required more personnel, so that the engineers, to take one example, jumped from 1.6 percent of the Army's total strength to 10.8 percent by the end of the war. New kinds of units grew rapidly. The Medical Service Corps was formed in 1917 and the Chemical and the Tank Corps in 1918. In addition, the scattered truck companies of 1916 were gathered and expanded into the new Motor Transport Corps, and the first air squadron, formed in 1913, became the 185-squadron Air Service in 1918.

The "square" infantry division formed the main American tactical unit of World War I. Its basic structure demonstrated how deeply dependent the Army had become on noncombat specialists. Each division deployed tactically in 4 infantry and 3 field artillery regiments, supplemented by 3 machine gun battalions. Supporting them were a field signal battalion, an engineer regiment, and a variety of headquarters and trains units. The sheer number of personnel and vehicles requiring coordination led to the addition to the trains of two companies of trained military policemen, a return to a practice first conducted during the Revolution, but abandoned thereafter. These MPs replaced details of infantry or cavalry performing traffic control and headquarters security missions. Tables of organization for the standard division required 64 mechanical draftsmen, 64 electricians, 142 linemen, 10 cable splicers, 156 radio operators, 29 switchboard operators, 163 telegraphers, 360 telephone repairmen, 52 leather and canvas workers, 118 surveyors and assistants, 62 topographers, 132 auto mechanics, 128 machinists, 167 mechanics, 67 blacksmiths, 151 carpenters, 691 auto and truck drivers, 128 tractor operators, 122 truckmasters, plus men for 68 other trades. These technology-driven changes reduced ground combat troops to a minority in the Army for the first time in history. Infantry, artillery, and tankers ended the war accounting for only 42 percent of the men in Army uniform. In contrast, the technical services—engineer, medical, signal, quartermaster, ordnance, transport, and chemical—grew to 31.6 percent of the Army's strength.

The increase in new specialty occupations (a jump from 57 to 704) overwhelmed the prewar rank and pay structure, prompting a host of experiments and temporary adjustments. The experience of the Tank Corps is typical. When tank battalions were added to the AEF, General Pershing simply made up new occupational titles such as "tank commander" and "tank driver" and assigned them grades that he thought matched their responsibilities—in these cases, sergeants. This method met the Army's needs in the early months of the war, but it gradually led to many inconsistencies. Efforts to devise an Index of Occupations and accompanying pay tables that would rationalize the system of matching grades to jobs ended with the Armistice and did not resume until World War II.

These wide-ranging changes in the Army had a profound impact on the NCO Corps. From colonial times, American NCOs had filled certain well-defined roles as trainers, enforcers of discipline, small-unit leaders on the battlefield, and keepers of company-level records. But as NCOs became specialists in new technologies as well, a split started to emerge between the specialists and traditional troop leaders.

The supreme test of the new specialist-oriented Army came during the Meuse-Argonne offensive. A major assault on the German lines began on 26 September 1918, when nine divisions moved out across a 24-mile front, and it lasted until the Armistice on 11 November. Before the first troops jumped off, over 80 depots and 34 evacuation hospitals had to be built, hundreds of miles of roads and railroads put in operating condition, 40,000 tons of ammunition stockpiled, and hundreds of guns and some 800,000 men moved into position—all at night, to avoid detection by the enemy's aircraft. Several thousand military policemen alone were needed to handle traffic control during fourteen days of frenzied activity.

Once the specialists set the stage, troop-leading NCOs took over the initiative as American troops joined the huge Allied offensive along the Western Front. The American zone of attack was along the Meuse River and through the Argonne Forest in German-occupied northeastern France. The aim was to cut the enemy's strategic rail network supporting most of the Western Front. Difficult terrain and the complexity and depth of German defenses promised a long, costly fight. Interlocking artillery and machine gun positions arrayed in up to five belts covered all approaches to the key heights. Although the Germans had failed to detect the buildup, a stalemate developed, as the offensive turned into an endless series of firefights between squads, platoons, and companies. Bayonets, hand grenades, shotguns, rifles, and even entrenching tools served as weapons. NCOs leading these desperate assaults might not have been well versed in the fine points of staff briefings, but they knew what had to be done. With a disregard for their own survival that inspired their countrymen, these NCOs and their troops pressed forward.

When the fighting ended, the Americans could look back on an extraordinary achievement. After 47 days of combat, the 21 divisions and 324 tanks of the First and Second Armies had gained over 30 miles and defeated 47 German divisions. Artillerymen manning 2,417 guns had fired over 4.2 million rounds, while 821 aircraft, employed for the first time in large numbers in a ground attack role, had dropped 100 tons of bombs. But the cost of the huge offensive was heavy—120,000 American casualties.

NCOs in Action

Contrary to popular opinion, the "doughboys" did not try to overwhelm German machine guns with human waves. At Pershing's insistence, they placed reliance on traditional American strengths—marksmanship and individual initiative—and the employment of skirmishing tactics to seek out soft points in the system of trenches and to isolate strongpoints to be neutralized later. In this process sergeants and corporals found themselves performing as small-unit leaders at the squad and platoon levels. As lieutenants fell, NCOs had to control much of the actual fighting. Both casualty rates and decorations reflected their achievements.

But those infantrymen, cannoneers, and machine gunners were not alone in the great effort. Heroism on the battlefield was matched by the less-publicized efforts of specialists behind the lines. Specialists from long-established technical branches such as engineers and medical corpsmen joined with military policemen, truck drivers, and chemical service personnel to keep the offensive moving.

In each case the NCOs, many of whom owed their stripes to civilian skills rather than service longevity, stepped forward to exercise independent judgment and supervision over work details, filling a potential void. The long-anticipated war of movement taxed support specialists to the limit. The artillery alone required twelve to fourteen trainloads of ammunition every day. Thousands of replacement troops had to be moved toward the front and thousands of casualties back to field hospitals. Trucks, locomotives, and rolling stock had to be maintained around the clock, roads and tracks had to be repaired, supply dumps had to be organized, and convoys had to be directed and controlled. In each case myriad decisions had to be made on the spot by NCOs tasked with immediate supervision over work details.

The Army's experiences during the Meuse-Argonne offensive marked the culmination of the nation's first involvement in modern mass mobilization. From recruitment through training and movement overseas to combat, the War Department had to make dramatic adjustments to the needs of technology. The number of motor vehicles in the inventory, for example, jumped from 500 in 1916 to over 118,000 by the war's end. Enormous traffic jams developed on shell-cratered roads, and troops sometimes had to push and pull disabled vehicles. Thanks in large measure to the important part played by technically proficient NCOs, the supplies and equipment got through to the frontline troops.

The new specialist-oriented Army proved itself the most effective fighting force in American history. A fast-growing number of specialists—over 700 separate occupational titles by war's end—performed many jobs that no one in the Army had even been aware of only a few years earlier. Outstanding among the specialists were those involved in transportation—drivers, dispatchers, and their supervising NCOs—and the small army of military police, mechanics, and fuel handlers who supported them. Their work in pre-positioning troops and equipment, and then keeping them supported during the fighting, was essential to victory.

Although the Army inevitably cut back its forces after World War I, it could not, and did not, turn its back on the lessons it had learned. The need for modern technology and for specialists able to use it effectively had continued to be a hallmark of the twentieth-century Army. Recognition of the important role played by specialized units culminated in permanent status for selected branches. On 26 September 1941, the Military Police Corps reached this plateau, followed a little over a year later by the Transportation Corps. In World War I the Army clearly left behind the horse-and-wagon pace of the past.

A Hidden Resource, *Manuel B. Ablaza, 1988*

A
HIDDEN RESOURCE

PHILIPPINES, 1920S

——◆——

Teaching a class to a group of civilians is not an activity usually associated with the duties of a corporal in the U.S. Army.
In the early decades of the twentieth century, however, that
is exactly what several hundred noncommissioned officers found
themselves doing in the Philippine Islands. NCOs had not been sent
across the Pacific to teach. They went overseas to perform a very traditional role: to fight the enemies of their country and to deter potential
enemies. But Army tasks had been changing as the nation expanded
beyond the limits of North America and emerged as a world power. In
the aftermath of the Spanish-American War and World War I, soldiers
began to perform duties in what would later be called civic action.
This was a new kind of battle, sometimes as important as skirmishes
in the jungle—perhaps even more important.

The corporal entering the primitive classroom for the first time
knew he had to apply his Signal Corps technical training and basic
leadership skills in new ways. Like NCOs who had drawn similar
assignments in the 1920s in other villages, his job was to work with
the local population in a program to build roads and bridges, dig
wells, set up medical care, improve hygiene, and teach English. The
goal was to prepare the Filipinos for eventual independence and
democracy. Now it was up to him to make things happen. He took
off his campaign hat, looked at the expectant faces sitting in the
audience, and started to work.

Background

In 1898 the United States fought a war with an overseas power,
the kingdom of Spain, for the first time in nearly a century. The
struggle was short, but operations were worldwide, stretching from
the Caribbean to the western Pacific. Victory left America responsible for a number of new territories, including Puerto Rico and the
Philippines. Along with increased international prestige came the
responsibility to protect those possessions. Yet the new international
standing did not alter an old American tradition: pressure from the
voters to demobilize after the end of hostilities.

Although American reluctance to maintain a large peacetime
Army predated independence, this traditional attitude had not

128

been a significant problem throughout most of the years since the Revolution. A small force of regulars, backed by militia, was usually ample for protecting selected ports and policing western frontiers. The vast expanse of the Atlantic Ocean and the capabilities of the Navy made it difficult for any European nation to threaten the country. Although technological changes in the late nineteenth century started to alter the dynamics of these basic conditions, most soldiers who fought against Spain in 1898 did not realize that the world was becoming a more complex and dangerous place. They volunteered for a year and, like their citizen-soldier predecessors in every American war, wanted to go home as soon as the fighting ended.

That left the War Department with a dilemma. Anti-Spanish Filipino groups sought immediate independence and took up arms when the American occupation forces did not depart. Thus began an unexpected and unwanted conflict that lasted until mid-1902. The Army faced a growing insurgency at a time when demobilization was draining available manpower. In the face of the simple fact that not enough troops were available to occupy and administer every town and village, American civilian and military officials in Washington and Manila adopted a new approach. The Army began to develop a policy designed to win over the Filipino people, and this policy introduced the Army to large-scale civic action programs.

The new approach tried to address long-standing problems of life in the islands: inefficient public administration, unhealthy living conditions, and lack of educational, economic, and political opportunity. The Army would use force only against active insurgency. Congress and the President told the Army to use three guidelines in working out its difficult and delicate assignment: maintain law and order, respect local laws and customs, and remember that the United States hoped ultimately to extend to the islands the basic ideals of self-government expressed in the Declaration of Independence and the Constitution.

The commander of American ground forces on the scene, Maj. Gen. Wesley Merritt, had taken the first steps in developing a civic action policy immediately after the Spanish surrendered Manila in August 1898. He directed that all municipal functions except policing the city were to remain in Filipino hands as long as public order was preserved and American interests respected. Merritt promised protection for churches, schools, and libraries and reopened the port to revive the economy. The Army's direct participation came

Soldiers distributed medical supplies, food, and clothing to the people of Cap Haitien, Haiti, in Support of Operation UPHOLD DEMOCRACY in 1994. Relationships formed with local civilian populations have proved of lasting value to America's foreign policy.

in the area of law enforcement. Soldiers policed the streets of Manila and the Army set up a military court system—Superior and Inferior Provost Courts—to replace the Spanish colonial judiciary.

Public health was a major concern of the Army from the beginning. Manila had undergone a two-month siege before surrendering, leaving its 70,000 inhabitants vulnerable to malnutrition and epidemics. The problem was magnified by the fact that local health conditions had always been poor. For centuries rivers and the moat that surrounded the old city had been used as open sewers. Army specialists quickly went to work. Merritt's chief surgeon instituted a policy of inspections, vaccinations, and scientific sanitation procedures. Army engineers cleaned the reservoirs that served the city water system, pumped water at increased pressure, and monitored contamination levels. Manila residents were urged to change traditional patterns of behavior that threatened public health. New sanitary standards were enforced and legal action taken against violators.

These early civic action projects largely sought to relieve immediate problems by reducing crime and disease and reviving commerce. But the Army also took action that would have long-lasting effects. American soldiers in the Philippines became teachers in khaki.

They were surprised at the Filipino hunger for education. Whenever an American in uniform began explaining anything, even something quite ordinary, crowds of Filipinos quickly gathered on street corners or in tiny villages. Americans discovered they

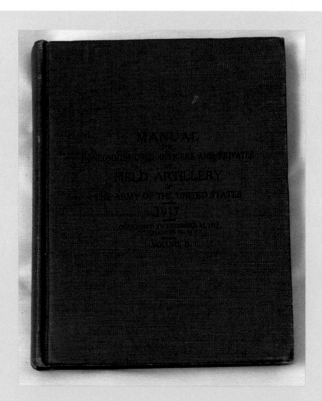

Manual for Noncommissioned Officers and Privates of Field Artillery of the Army of the United States, 1917 *As the duties and technical requirements for noncommissioned officers increased at the beginning of the twentieth century, the need for education and professional development also increased. This manual dates from World War I.*

would have to do more than simply revive the Spanish colonial system, which had reserved education to a small male elite. The Army moved quickly to build a public school system.

General Merritt assigned the chaplain of the 1st California Volunteers as administrator of education in Manila. Schools in the capital began to reopen in September 1898, only three months after the Army arrived in the islands, and by the end of the month several were in session. Since Catholicism was no longer the official state religion, as it had been under the Spanish, courses in religion were eliminated, although Manila's Catholic teaching orders were allowed to supervise secondary and higher education programs as long as they did not oppose the new policy of religious pluralism. The English language was taught in each school, typically by an American soldier. Americans—first soldiers, later civilians—supervised primary and intermediate instruction. Within a few months the number of schools increased from seven to thirty-nine with over 3,700 students enrolled.

In time, Manila served as the laboratory for a civic action campaign throughout the Philippines. The same four-part policy—law enforcement, public health, public works, and education—was extended to hundreds of villages. The character of the physical environment and the dispersal of the population over thousands of islands ensured that civic action could not be the monopoly of officers; there were simply too many villages to contact. From the outset civic action depended on the participation of noncommissioned officers and enlisted men.

Noncommissioned Officer's Small Implements Pouch *Throughout the eighteenth and nineteenth centuries, junior noncommissioned officers in positions of trust were required to carry and maintain tools and implements to maintain the weapons and equipment of the squad. The NCO small implements pouch M1910 carried by squad leaders during World War I represents the last vestige of this responsibility.*

Company Whistle *The advent of longer-range weapons in the mid-nineteenth century resulted in a change to small-unit tactics. The introduction of whistles at company, battalion, and regimental levels improved the conveyance of movement orders. The whistle is symbolic of the changing role of the noncommissioned officer: as the battlefield became larger and more complex, the NCO increasingly took on the role and responsibilities of the small-unit leader.*

Policymakers in faraway Washington were products of their times. With the best intentions, they viewed events in the islands from a traditional cultural and racial perspective, even describing the Army's new mission in the Philippines as part of the "white man's burden" to carry civilization to "backward" Filipinos. NCOs and troops on the scene, however, thought in terms that were much more down to earth. To them, civic action projects were not crusades but tasks to be accomplished in the face of obstacles: armed opposition, jungle heat, monsoon rains, and shortages of money and equipment. In other words, they accepted the new mission as part of everyday life, and applied the same leadership and technical skills to accomplishing it that they would have used for any task at a stateside post.

In supervising civic action projects, NCOs brought to their new mission the enthusiastic "can-do" attitude typical of their own training and of the Progressive Era and got the job done. They took off their shirts and got down in the mud, pushing roads through the jungle to give isolated villages access to markets. They dug wells, built bridges, and deepened harbors. They drained swamps and taught hygiene to villagers who had long believed illness the work of mysterious fate. They loaned equipment and donated building materials to towns and villages, and then ensured that donated materials did not become the personal property of town and village council members. And, with the realization that civic action reforms could not succeed in an insecure environment, NCOs trained local police forces.

By 1900 the educational component of the program emerged as the most effective tool to defeat the rebels. This command policy was reflected at all levels throughout the Philippines. Typically one of the first projects undertaken when an American unit moved into a town was the organization of a school. NCOs supervised construction of necessary facilities, while commanders detailed officers and enlisted men as principals and teachers. The education program grew so rapidly that by the spring of 1900 the headquarters in Manila organized a Department of Public Instruction under Capt. Albert Todd. He instituted a centralized system employing basic American methods: compulsory attendance, free primary and secondary schools, and specialized schools to prepare industrial workers for jobs and Filipinos for careers in education. To overcome the barrier posed by an array of local dialects, all instruction beyond the primary grades used English.

The Filipino people were remarkably receptive to their new American-style schools. Only five months after the Department of Public Instruction began operations, over 100,000 students were enrolled in about one thousand schools. In the same brief period, the Army distributed over $100,000 worth of school materials, including arithmetic, geography, American history, and English-language texts, as well as ink, workbooks, pens, paper, chalk, blackboards, and slates. Captain Todd and his assistants in the field were surprised and delighted that compulsion was virtually unnecessary in the new education system. In many areas, adults were willing to meet for night classes. Obviously, the Army's soldier-teachers were responding to a desire for knowledge long unsatisfied by the Spanish.

The image of the Army NCO as a teacher no doubt surprised the Filipinos in the early months of the American presence in the islands. To them, education had always been a function of the church, and teachers had always been priests or nuns. Now teachers were appearing in the uniform of a foreign army. Just as surprising, the new soldier-teachers were bringing new subjects into classrooms and villages: English language, hygiene, and the rudiments of citizenship in a democracy. NCOs overcame their lack of formal preparation by teaching subjects in which they had excelled during their own school years or in which they simply had an off-duty interest. Army soldier-teachers were providing needed instruction, and they were appreciated for it.

Their successes reflected the fact that civic action called on them to perform a familiar role, albeit in a new environment. NCOs had always been instructors, the ones responsible for teaching recruits everything from the wearing of a uniform to the operation of highly technical equipment. In a larger sense, NCOs had been instructors for all enlisted personnel, because they translated the orders of officers into specific instructions to the troops. In the islands their audience was civilian, and they began communicating a variety of subjects which, taken together, comprised a primary course in what Americans would regard as modern citizenship. Army NCOs helped to transform the Filipino people from the burdened subjects of a foreign colonial power into the citizens of the independent democracy that would emerge in the islands after World War II.

Once the basic security and health needs of villagers were answered, Americans went on to teach some of their favorite customs and recreations as well. Filipinos proved receptive to the American-style Christmas party, especially when it included a soldier-Santa with gifts for the local children. NCOs also introduced American sports to the Filipinos. Baseball and basketball soon became—and remain today—enormously popular in the islands. Although American soldiers were simply an occupation force in the first phase of U.S. involvement, they soon opened up the country to knowledge and many other positive characteristics of contemporary societies.

NCOs in Action

Competence and adaptability have always been important attributes of Army NCOs. Duty in the Philippines highlighted the importance of those qualities by placing sergeants and corporals in a demanding situation, midway between military and civilian status. Fortunately, the Army turned to the NCO Corps just at the time when the trend toward technical specialization was expanding the reservoir of skills in its ranks. While many NCOs led small-unit patrols tracking insurgents in the steaming heat of Philippine jungles and hills, others played vital roles in civic action programs that won over large segments of a potentially hostile population. The Philippine War cost the lives of over 4,200 soldiers, but the Army's improvised civic action program proved to be one of the most successful efforts of its type in history.

The fact that NCOs could perform and ultimately excel under such conditions grew directly not only from their function as teachers, but also from their long tradition of on-the-job training. NCOs had always learned how to do their jobs in part from more senior noncommissioned officers. The immediacy and informality of this process required NCOs to give full play to their imaginations and to improvise. In pursuing the American mission in the Philippines, they had ample opportunity to exercise these abilities.

The end of the Philippine War did not mean that the Army's civic action program was over. A garrison remained in the islands until World War II broke out; its NCOs continued teaching the Filipinos useful skills even after the Army handed most of the responsibilities for public health, public administration, civil engineering, and education to American civilians and eventually to trained Filipinos. That experience paid dividends during and after World War II.

Beginning in 1942 America and its Allies began liberating countries occupied by Nazi Germany or imperial Japan. As the principal ground force, it fell to the Army to assume initial responsibility for bringing order to areas recently cleared of hostile forces. As in the case of the Philippines, the Army had the talents and resources needed to restore sanitation and fight disease in ruined Naples, to clear the war-damaged port facilities of Amsterdam, and to dig wells in Okinawa. Nowhere were these skills more important than in Manila, virtually destroyed in the battle to liberate it. In each case, the Army undertook the mission as a temporary adjunct to its primary combat role and sought to turn responsibility over to civilians as soon as possible.

One difference from the Philippine experience was that during World War II the Army established staff sections and entire units dedicated to civic action programs and other functions of military government. These were manned by officers and NCOs selected on the basis of civilian backgrounds or because of special skills. When the war ended and American troops continued occupation duties in Germany and Japan, that expertise remained in place in a scaled-down form and played a key role in turning former enemies into allies. That same technique would be attempted again in Korea and Vietnam when the Army had to compete with ideologically motivated enemies for the hearts and minds of civilian populations.

From an extemporized beginning in turn-of-the-century Manila, through occupation duties in Japan, Germany, and Korea after World War II, to the global deployments of the 1950s and 1960s, the Army has built upon the proven concepts of complementing combat skills with a dedicated program of civic action. Consistently it has made the direct involvement of NCOs the cornerstone of its efforts.

Rome, Italy, June 4, 1944, *Greg K. Olsen, 1944*

TEAMWORK, FIREPOWER, RESPONSIBILITY

ITALY, 1944

———◆———

The infantry sergeant and the staff sergeant commanding the M4 Sherman tank were both anxious, yet cautiously optimistic. The Germans had taken cover in some of the picturesque streets and buildings of the Italian capital of Rome. As the two veteran sergeants well knew, urban fighting was a hard, methodical, dangerous business. But they also believed in the ability of their combat team to survive and function—they had the experience, the men, and the weapons to work their way through the streets and do the job at a minimal cost.

Taken together, the tank crew and the attached infantry squad made up a small unit—fewer than twenty men. But between them, the two noncommissioned officers commanded a combined-arms organization with more firepower than an entire Civil War regiment. The Sherman contributed its 75-mm. main gun and three machine guns to the team; one of the infantrymen carried a Browning Automatic Rifle (BAR), and the rest had the clip-fed Garand semiautomatic rifle. If the sergeants had done their job properly, ensuring that each man attained proficiency with his individual weapon and that all understood the tactics of employing armor alongside foot soldiers, they could handle whatever the Germans threw their way.

When they had distributed the resupply of ammunition and C-rations and after the tank commander checked in with higher headquarters on his radio, the NCOs decided that the unit was ready for its next mission. The squad leader issued the terse command "Mount up!" and the Sherman tank started down the outwardly deserted street.

Background

Had they faced this same situation a few years earlier, these same men might well have lacked the equipment, the combined-arms training, and the experienced NCO leadership necessary to fight the

Maneuver Exercises, Manassas, Virginia, 1904. Team building is an essential goal of training, and as in 1904 the Army builds teams through maneuver exercises in realistic settings that resemble the face of war.

Germans. The armistice of November 1918 that ended the fighting in World War I also ushered in the traditional return to low peacetime manpower levels that meant hard times for the Army.

The War Department tried to avoid that drawdown. After evaluating wartime performance, especially the problems encountered in the first massive mobilization since the Civil War, the Secretary of War asked Congress to approve a force of about 600,000 men and universal male military training. Officials argued that this approach, almost a return to the colonial militia concept, would help to deter future wars. Since most Americans had understood that World War I was the "War To End All Wars," Congress did not accept the argument. After all, the defeat of Germany and the exhausted condition of the other European powers meant that another large-scale land war was very unlikely for many years to come. Beyond that, an isolationist spirit prevailed in the United States during the interwar years.

Rapid demobilization from the wartime high of 3,250,000 men continued until it finally bottomed out in the early 1920s at 12,000 officers and 125,000 men, grouped in nine skeleton divisions. In the years that followed, Congress rarely appropriated enough money to sustain the training needed to prepare even this small force for the possibility of combat. The reductions compelled many experienced noncommissioned officers to return to civilian life. Yet this was the time when the Army needed them the most. As John C. Calhoun had recognized after the War of 1812, a small peacetime Army needed a professional NCO Corps to preserve the knowledge essential to train recruits in any future mobilization.

Tight budget restrictions—which became even tighter when the Great Depression arrived in 1929—prevented the Army from doing much about new weapons and tactics. In fact, Congress, acting upon General John ("Black Jack") Pershing's recommendation, deprived the Tank Corps, created during World War I, of its status as a separate combat arm. As late as 1938, while German armor experts were developing advanced tanks and Panzer tactics, the major general in charge of the Army's cavalry urged the country not to be misled into believing an "untried machine" could replace the "proven and tried horse."

In 1933 the Nazi dictator, Adolf Hitler, came to power in Germany. Within three years, Germany renounced the Treaty of Versailles and began to rearm. America responded slowly at first to this potential threat. Beginning in 1935 Congress started to increase appropriations for the armed forces, giving priority to the Navy and the Army Air Corps. Active enlisted strength in the Army crept back up toward 165,000 men, and increased funds permitted the resumption of summer maneuvers that involved National Guard units as well as regulars.

In the fall of 1939 Hitler invaded Poland, launching a new war in Europe. Reluctantly, the United States began to accelerate its military preparations. At the same time, a new leadership team gradually took over in the War Department with the appointment of General George C. Marshall as Chief of Staff in September 1939 and Henry L. Stimson as Secretary of War in July 1940. In September 1940 the National Guard entered federal service for a year of intensive training; and in the same year, after bitter debate, Congress voted the nation's first peacetime draft. Other reforms introduced at this time were the creation of a general headquarters to coordinate training, the establishment of the Armored Force at Fort Knox, Kentucky, and the creation of a small airborne force. By the autumn of 1941 the Army had grown to 27 infantry, 5 armored, and 2 cavalry divisions, plus a host of supporting units. This sudden growth placed a heavy burden on the small professional NCO Corps that had endured the lean years.

In July 1940 Chief of Staff Marshall selected Brig. Gen. Lesley J. McNair as his deputy at general headquarters and later at Army

Infantry troops surround an M1A1 Abrams main battle tank. The precedent of combining arms and blending Regulars with reserve components continues today.

Ground Forces (AGF). McNair pushed hard to improve both weapons and tactics. In particular, he sought to maximize resources by designing lean but flexible organizations that balanced mobility and firepower. McNair also ardently supported the development of armor, favoring mass production of a maneuverable medium tank and self-propelled tank destroyers. But above all, General McNair was a trainer. He insisted on progressive training, beginning with the fundamentals for individual soldiers, then moving on to combined-arms operations, and finally to maneuvers involving whole armies and corps.

His capacity for work was prodigious. McNair oversaw the creation of new tables of organization for the entire Army, the formation of thousands of units, the staging of twenty-seven large-scale domestic maneuvers, and the preparation of hundreds of thousands of soldiers for combat. Under his guidance, AGF also perfected the tactical doctrine that these forces would carry overseas. Significantly, both training and battlefield doctrine stressed teamwork. McNair himself observed that "you cannot use men against Hitler, you must use fighting units." This emphasis on trained teams contributed directly to the growth of the NCO's small-unit leadership function.

For all of McNair's preparations, however, the battle was still the payoff. As Michael Doubler has argued, "The American Army was

Combat Leader's Stripe on a Wool Field Jacket, Pattern 1944 *A wool field jacket, sometimes referred to as the "Ike Jacket," of a technical sergeant of the Tank Destroyer Force in World War II. The green stripe under the chevrons on each sleeve indicates that this technical sergeant was not only a platoon sergeant, but also a leader within a combat organization. After the war the technical sergeant became the sergeant first class, and the combat leader's stripe evolved into the combat leader's tab.*

successful because it proved itself capable of quickly adapting to new and sometimes unexpected circumstances." In Europe and the Mediterranean, the Army faced a tested enemy that often enjoyed the advantages of favorable terrain and fortified defensive positions. Inexperienced compared to their German foes, American soldiers also found some of their doctrine, training, equipment, and organization to be flawed. But even the Germans were impressed with the resourcefulness of the U.S. Army—its ability to adopt new tactical techniques, technology, and organization in the midst of a campaign. For this resilience in adjusting combined-arms tactics, the Army owed much to its NCO Corps.

NCOs in Action

The U.S. Army had much to learn about infantry-armor coordination and street fighting when it joined the war in Europe. Very few infantry formations had trained with tank units, and Army doctrine said little about combined-arms tactics against village strongholds. In the initial actions in the Mediterranean, tank-infantry coordination was generally poor. The infantry often failed to exploit armored mobility and firepower; many times, tankers found themselves on the objective while the infantrymen who were supposed to accompany them had bogged down against pockets of German resistance. Those infantrymen who did manage to keep up with the tanks often were killed or wounded by enemy fire directed at the armor. For their part, tankers, concerned about antitank obstacles, often showed a reluctance to advance and take the burden of pressing the attack from the riflemen. Inadequate communications between the two arms further hindered cooperation. The infantry had no way to alert tanks of antitank traps or heavy weapons, while the tank crews could not point out enemy positions to the infantrymen.

Fortunately, the flexibility of the Army on doctrinal matters enabled small-unit leaders to develop specific techniques to solve specific battlefield problems. The Army placed no restriction on sources for ideas. Learning and adapting to tactical situations generally took place at lower levels, with field armies, corps, and divisions primarily collecting "lessons learned" and distributing them in the form of bulletins. Rarely did the higher echelons dictate new tactics; they focused on providing ideas and information and then holding commanders responsible for results. Freed to act on their own initiative, NCOs developed tactical solutions on the basis of their own experience. These lessons then spread, whether by higher level bulletins or demonstrations issued by higher levels or, quite frequently, by word of mouth among the NCOs themselves.

Depending on the situation, NCOs either creatively applied doctrine or disregarded it entirely while improvising new combat formations and tactics. As tanks and infantry trained and fought together in the theater, they learned to advance together—the infantry clearing antitank obstacles, the tanks providing close fire support to the infantry assault. Short, quick armored thrusts followed closely by infantry proved effective, whether in the advance up the

Italian peninsula, the fighting in the hedgerows of Normandy, or the struggle to penetrate the West Wall along the German border.

The process of learning at lower levels is particularly illustrated by the Army's experience with street fighting. Soldiers soon learned that the worst place to be in urban combat was along the boulevards, swept by enemy fire. They adopted the approach of advancing from building to building in succession by blasting holes through adjacent structures. Once they had cleared a particular house, soldiers would call on engineer teams to place explosives against the wall adjacent to the next building. The resulting explosion would clear a hole in the wall while generally surprising and incapacitating the enemy in the next room, enabling the unit to pour through the hole, clear the room, and then clear the building. To carry out these tactics, platoons and squads changed their configuration. Under the overall leadership of squad leaders, assault parties moved quickly and aggressively through the buildings, clearing each floor in succession. Covering parties provided fire support, assisted where needed, and remained ready for any counterattack. Meanwhile, from the streets, tanks, tank destroyers, and self-propelled guns provided heavier fire support where necessary.

NCOs also showed their resourcefulness in their improvisation with technology. In the fierce battles for the hedgerows of Normandy, the Army installed phones on the back decks of tanks, so that infantry small-unit leaders could communicate with their armored counterparts. Sgt. Curtis G. Culin of the 102d Cavalry Reconnaissance Squadron developed his famous hedgerow cutter that enabled tanks to plow through the embankments of the hedges blocking the American advance in Normandy. Soldiers developed creative ways to use explosives to blow gaps through hedgerows, walls, or buildings. They also used bazookas and bangalore torpedoes, as well as pole and satchel charges, to blow gaps in the enemy positions. Finally, NCOs learned to use tanks, tank destroyers, and even antiaircraft guns for heavy-caliber fire at point-blank range. Battering strongpoints with direct fire by supporting heavy weapons not only soon reduced those fortifications to rubble but also had an electrifying effect on the morale of the riflemen attacking the defenses. Through such means, the NCOs and their soldiers carried out the timeless task of inflicting maximum damage on the enemy while minimizing their own losses.

The Army has continued to develop and refine combined-arms tactics. Today's team (except in light divisions) looks very different from its 1944 predecessor. No longer must an infantry squad hitch a ride, exposed, on the outside of a tank. Now mechanized infantry ride inside their own armored M2 Bradley infantry fighting vehicle, capable of keeping pace with the M1 Abrams main battle tank. Furthermore, the team can call directly for support not only from self-propelled artillery pieces but also from specialized antitank weapons carriers, helicopter gunships, and Air Force A–10 close-support strike aircraft. That combination, fighting under AirLand Battle doctrine, possesses a mix of speed and firepower that would make the World War II NCO shake his head in amazement, although he would still recognize the basic concepts being used.

No matter how the modern combined-arms team is constructed, however, it still must be competently led and properly trained if it is to achieve its goals. Highly sophisticated technology has been placed in the hands of every soldier. Each junior leader, therefore, must be both technically and tactically proficient. Now as never before, the role of the trained professional NCO is central to the success of the team's mission.

Keeping the System Moving, *Anita Y. Sonnie, 1988*

KEEPING

THE

SYSTEM MOVING

SOUTHWEST PACIFIC, 1945

For most Americans in 1940 the South Pacific was an exotic place. The movie screen and magazines depicted it as a romantic realm of palm trees and moonlit beaches. The next five years radically changed that image—especially for the troops stationed there. For soldiers working in a nondescript G.I. Quonset hut near the equator, their little island with the strange-sounding name was hot, humid, and buggy. But their sense of purpose helped them overcome any immediate discomforts.

To the Tech. 5 and dozens of other troops waiting in line for processing, this was simply another stop on a long journey toward the front lines of the war against Japan. Already they had endured the boredom and discomfort of life on a crowded troopship that had spent weeks crossing thousands of miles of ocean. Since leaving ports of embarkation in the United States, few of the enlisted men had even known exactly where they were going. The ship had been full of rumors throughout the voyage, but all the officers would say about their destination was that it was "somewhere in the Pacific theater of operations."

To the Women's Army Corps first sergeant, the island was the front lines and the Quonset hut her place to serve in the war effort. Her job was to ensure that the Tech. 5 and everyone else in that long line went through processing "by the numbers." She had volunteered to don a uniform and carry out duties that would free men for combat. If the Army felt that her talents were best used in keeping the paper flowing, then she would see to it that the clerks under her supervision efficiently and correctly filled out each form so that the replacements would not be held up unnecessarily. The waiting men were merely part of a seemingly endless line of troops heading for the next island invasion. Moving them along was the first sergeant's job, and the stripes and rockers on her sleeve gave her the authority and standing to accomplish that mission. No soldier or NCO would ever become careless at that processing point—she saw to it that they all realized quickly that the operative word in Women's Army

Clerks of the Union Army's 1st Division, IX Corps, at Petersburg, Virginia, 1864. Behind the lines of every battle in the Army's history, the largely unsung combat service support troops have carried out unglamorous but essential functions under the supervision of their NCOs.

Corps was Army. Her steady stream of orders coordinated the clerks, replacements, and the blizzard of paper work.

Background

The Noncommissioned Officer Corps contributed in many ways to defeat the Axis armies in World War II. Many sergeants, corporals, and technicians did not serve on the front lines, but in critical behind-the-scenes roles in a host of fields, expanding upon the corps' well-established tradition of furnishing the Army with the expertise to keep pace with technological change. NCOs delivered fuel and ammunition to the tankers, cannoneers, and riflemen. They built airfields, installed communications networks, operated weather stations, and maintained and repaired all kinds of equipment, including items that had not even been invented by the time of Pearl Harbor.

This period also saw the emergence of the female NCO. During World War II the U.S. Army for the first time officially enrolled women other than nurses. In 1942 the War Department established a modest force that rapidly grew into a Women's Army Corps almost 100,000 strong. The WACs, as they came to be called, filled important roles in all theaters of the war, primarily clerical and administrative. WACs under their own noncommissioned officers quickly became a vital cog in the machine that moved millions of troops and mountains of supplies and equipment all over the world.

Allied strategy gave primary importance to the defeat of Nazi Germany, making it imperative for commanders in the Pacific Theater to make the most of their limited resources. General Douglas MacArthur, Admiral Chester W. Nimitz, and Lt. Gen. "Vinegar Joe"

Stilwell coordinated forces in the Southwest Pacific, Central Pacific, and China-Burma-India Theaters in a drive toward Tokyo. In the process they sent troops, including WACs, to some of the most remote locations the Army had ever seen. The MacArthur-Nimitz technique of conserving resources by bypassing many of the strongest Japanese garrisons came to be known as "island-hopping." That process required the Navy to move marines, soldiers, and equipment over vast distances on precise timetables. After assault forces fought desperate battles for vital terrain, support elements carved supply dumps, roads, and air strips from coral atolls, volcanic lava, and jungle valleys. These bases, connected by ships and planes, formed a gigantic "pipeline" stretching from training camps and manufacturing plants in the continental United States to the front lines. Many Army women found employment along these support and supply arteries.

An administrative NCO from the 254th Base Support Battalion handles a variety of paperwork, c. 2001. A successful military operation requires that soldiers and equipment arrive at a precise location when needed, a task that depends largely on administrative and logistics NCOs and their soldiers.

The Army's use of the WACs was part of the largest mobilization in American history. But American women had contributed to the Army since the founding of the nation. As early as 1775, General George Washington employed female civilians in staff hospitals. In so doing, he confronted certain basic issues that would resurface frequently until the mid-twentieth century. One problem was internal: placing any group of civilians within a military organization created administrative complications. The second problem had more to do with society at large than with the Army. Too often civilians belittled the women working for the Army as "camp followers," rather than regarding them as patriots. Those same issues plagued each tentative experiment to integrate females into the Army that followed. Until the twentieth century, even female nurses were excluded from military service except in wartime, both by public opinion and by Army doctors. Then came Pearl Harbor. The enormous demands of World War II simply overwhelmed the old objections and forced the military to find new solutions at a time when America's British and Soviet Allies had vast numbers of women in uniform.

On 15 May 1942, President Franklin D. Roosevelt signed a law that established a Women's Army Auxiliary Corps (WAAC). Although its creation launched a new era in American military history, the WAAC took time to develop. In its early days it had a civilian director, Oveta Culp Hobby, but no officers, NCOs, or recruits. Nine weeks later the first WAAC officer candidate school (OCS) convened at Fort Des Moines, Iowa, followed shortly by the first enlisted basic training course. Six months later female OCS graduates began reporting for duty, and during 1943 women took over full responsibility for training new WAACs. But no schools existed anywhere in the Army to create sergeants and corporals. The War Department filled that gap by turning to the traditional Army practice of company-based promotion, making temporary adjustments to fit the special circumstances of the WAAC.

After finishing a four-week basic training cycle, WAAC recruits learned specific skills at one of four schools: Administration, Motor

Transport, Telephone Operator, and Cook and Baker. During this phase the training company cadre selected a number of recruits to serve as acting NCOs for the remainder of the cycle. Upon completion of the specialty courses, most WAACs formed all-female companies. The Army filled most leadership positions with officers who had finished OCS, NCOs transferred from training staffs, and graduating recruits selected for permanent NCO rank. A few graduates remained with the training cadre as instructors or administrative clerks, usually becoming NCOs for later classes. The newly formed company then went as a unit to its first duty station.

Initially the WAAC enlisted structure differed radically from the rest of the Army. WAACs could attain four ranks: auxiliary, junior leader, leader, and first leader. This contrasted with the seven ranks found among male NCOs. The lowest WAAC ranks, auxiliary (subdivided into first, second, and third classes) and junior leader, roughly translated as private and private first class, respectively. Equivalents for the two upper WAAC ranks were less precise. Their responsibilities spanned the spectrum from corporal through master sergeant. Despite these differences, WAAC NCOs performed the duties of squad and section leaders, platoon sergeants, and company first sergeants. Comparisons became easier on 1 April 1943, when the WAAC expanded to seven enlisted grades that differed from the rest of the Army only in the titles: auxiliary, junior leader, leader, staff leader, technical leader, first leader, and chief leader. Holders of the top five ranks were considered NCOs.

Organizationally the WAAC became part of the Services of Supply in the continental United States. Many of the first units (twenty-seven companies by October 1942) drew assignments with the Aircraft Warning Service, where they helped to operate a primitive tracking system along the East Coast. WAAC NCOs assigned to duty there primarily provided first-line supervision during around-the-clock operations. WAAC NCOs also were involved in the full range of the corps' activities outside the Aircraft Warning Service. Because nearly two-thirds of the women performed administrative and office duties, the majority of their NCOs naturally served in clerical fields as well. At the same time, over 13 percent of the WAACs were assigned to technical and professional duties, which put NCOs in charge of photographers, medical technicians, weather observers, and other specialists.

Although the units deploying to assignments provided a valuable addition to the Army's capabilities during the second full year of World War II, WAAC NCOs still retained important functions as instructors. The final table of organization for a training company at the five WAAC centers provided the unit with sixteen NCOs, but only five officers. A company contained between 150 and 200 recruits. Training needs ensured that several thousand WAAC NCOs would remain on training duty during the last three years of the war.

NCOs in Action

Important and varied as these responsibilities were, NCOs performing them labored under a handicap. As originally constituted, the WAAC was an auxiliary to the Army, not a part of the Army. This legal distinction meant that WAAC personnel did not have military status; the only real parallels to the Army were the WAAC chain of command, pay scale, and uniform. Neither NCOs nor anyone else in the Auxiliary enjoyed the array of benefits extended to male soldiers—from pensions to burial with military honors. Gender was not the issue, for the members of the Army Nurse Corps, part of the Medical Department since 1901, did receive benefits. The lack of status also affected WAAC legal standing. Since women were not subject to court-martial, questions arose about jurisdiction over disciplinary infractions. If WAACs had to be confined, they required separate facilities and guards.

The resolution of these issues came on 1 September 1943, when the War Department granted full military status to the Women's Army Corps (WAC). The name change, dropping "auxiliary," carried more than symbolic meaning. The Army had gained a large group of trained and dedicated new soldiers. On its first day, the new WAC numbered 51,268, of which 1,811 were serving outside the continental United States. The corps grew as senior commanders discovered the value of using women in military roles. General Dwight D. Eisenhower in Europe became the first major overseas commander to specifically request WAC units. After his request was filled in January 1943, plans to employ Army women accelerated, and WAC NCOs took up supervisory activities in more locations with each passing month. WAC strength climbed as fast as volunteers could be processed, peaking at 99,288 in April 1945, just before the surrender of Germany.

During World War II, WACs and their NCOs served in every theater of operations, although most remained at bases within the forty-eight states. The Army used them in a large number of jobs, but not in slots related to combat, since public opinion held that women should not be on the front lines. The bulk of WAC jobs were administrative, and most WAC NCOs headed clerical sections, but some detachments carried out assignments that ranged from operating targets for antiaircraft artillery gunners to rigging parachutes for airborne units.

At major installations in the United States, WAC headquarters companies assumed most of the routine support functions of "post overhead." Sergeants and corporals had traditionally supervised such day-to-day activities; WAC NCOs took over from their male counterparts without friction. Diversity came from assignments to the various technical services; the Signal Corps was the first to request WACs, and it employed most of them in communications centers or in signal intelligence. Other WAC NCOs worked in the Chemical Warfare Service as pharmacologists and toxicologists; under Corps of Engineers control on the Manhattan Project (the highly classified effort to develop the atomic bomb); and at the Transportation Corps' eight ports of embarkation as mechanics, photo technicians, tailors, movie projectionists, and even butchers.

So many WACs served with the Army Air Forces—nearly half of the total WAC strength—that throughout the war a number of War

Department officials persisted in thinking of the WAC as an organization established for Air Forces use exclusively. Female NCOs in this line of work carried out assignments that included weather observation, Link trainer instruction, control tower operation, cryptography, bombsight maintenance, and sheet-metal work. A lucky few even drew flight duty.

One of the most important WAC contributions to the war effort came in the Medical Department, which by the end of World War II employed one-fifth of the corps. Because medicine by its nature requires a high degree of individual competence, WACs in this field became something of an elite group. To be eligible for training in one of the medical specialties (such as pharmacist, Braille instructor, optometrist, bacteriologist, or therapist), women needed superior scores on a screening test and a high school diploma. Because prior civilian technical training was necessary for many medical duties, WAC recruiters had to offer more than junior enlisted status and pay to attract women with the requisite talents. WAC psychiatric workers, for example, became staff sergeants upon completion of basic training. These special arrangements began to change the character of the WAC NCO Corps by creating two types of NCOs: those who had come up the rank ladder one rung at a time, and "instant" NCOs who possessed critical skills. In both cases, these female leaders represented an infusion of new talent and leadership into what had long been exclusively a man's Army.

The Army had established the Women's Army Corps to free men for duty on the battlefield. WACs actually moved far beyond that relatively limited objective and became a vital part of the trend toward specialization that has marked the twentieth-century Army. During the war, women in uniform did so-called feminine jobs, such as typing personnel records and operating telephones, but they also repaired truck engines and changed tires, functions traditionally considered strictly masculine. Despite this steady expansion into traditional Army roles, however, WAC NCOs in many respects were all specialists because of their exclusion from combat, and their NCO Corps in many ways retained an identity separate from that of the male NCOs.

As a noncombat component, the female corps never developed the sharp division between NCO troop leaders and skilled technicians that became so pronounced elsewhere in the Army. In an effort to control the negative effects of that division among male soldiers, the Army had favored first specialists, then troop leaders, in a series of rank and pay adjustments stretching over several decades. The need for such adjustments never arose in the WAC, where the closest thing to troop leaders was training company NCOs, whose numbers steadily declined as more WACs took positions in the field.

The greater homogeneity of the WAC NCOs in many ways reflected the nature of the WAC as a whole. Female recruits differed from their male counterparts in several notable respects: all were volunteers and most were older than the average newly sworn-in male. As in later years, they were also better educated. Young male draftees usually came to the Army with little or no work experience, whereas many WACs had held a job of some kind between high school and enlistment. Most women brought to the Army valuable skills, even advanced degrees. Although some officers used WACs only reluctantly, many commanders recognized them as an asset and sought to place them in positions where their experience could be maximized. Women who had been secretaries or hospital laboratory technicians in civilian life needed little training to perform similar tasks in the WAC. The contribution made by American women in World War II was never a mirror image of that made by men; the Women's Army Corps was narrow in purpose but high in quality and experience, and its NCO leadership reflected the overall characteristics of the corps' membership.

At the end of World War II, the War Department began demobilizing all components of the wartime Army. The important contributions to victory made by the WACs and their NCOs were recognized by all, but the idea of retaining women in a peacetime Army initially met the same objections that had always been raised. Alarm at the rapid loss of skilled personnel soon forced a reassessment. When Congress granted Regular Army status to the WAC in 1948, female NCOs were assured of the Army careers many desired. Although the prominence of Army women in administrative positions caused most to be identified with the Adjutant General Corps, WAC NCOs proved they could perform any noncombat specialty held by male NCOs. By the time the WAC was fully integrated into the Army in 1978, female corporals and sergeants were respected members of the Army NCO Corps.

From Information to Intelligence, *Anita Y. Sonnie, 1988*

From Information
to
Intelligence

Korea, 1952

———◆———

The intelligence sergeant from division G–2 waited impatiently in the bunker for word that the reconnaissance platoon was safely back inside the barbed wire. He knew the importance of talking to the patrol, and especially the platoon leader, while the night's work was still fresh in everyone's memory. Even though the men might be tired, hungry, and dirty, they had to be debriefed immediately. Taking time to wash up or wolf down a C-ration might make someone forget a critical detail that experts could use to piece together the enemy's intentions.

Once the infantrymen reported in, the two NCOs settled down in front of the maps and began working their way through a systematic question-and-answer process. Did the patrol uncover any features not on the map? Did it locate the enemy? Were they North Koreans or Chinese? What kinds of equipment did they have? These and a host of other questions formed a list carefully constructed by senior intelligence analysts to ensure that nothing was overlooked and that every point was covered. Fortunately, the corporals and sergeants assigned to the reconnaissance element usually brought back something of value each time they went beyond the regiment's outpost line.

Even now, with the Korean War two years old, Communist units still conducted operations with a single-minded inflexibility surprising to senior American noncoms who had experienced World War II. That predictability gave the intelligence specialists their most valuable tool. It created patterns, patterns which created a framework that tied together otherwise isolated facts uncovered by repeated patrolling—things like finding fresh tread marks along a dirt road or watching a new trench complex being slowly extended. When analyzed, that kind of information became intelligence that often predicted what the North Korean or Chinese troops across the valley would do next, as well as when and where. Such nuts-and-bolts work, rather than the glamorous discovery of a key document or the decoding of some message, actually held the greatest satisfaction for

Sgts. William Major and Joe Kessay, the Last of the Famous Apache Scouts of the Post–Civil War Years, Stationed at Fort Huachuca, Arizona. Through- out the centuries, NCOs have acted as the eyes and ears of their commanders by collecting and interpreting intelligence data.

most of the senior NCO specialists. When their attention to detail allowed regimental, battalion, and company commanders to make adjustments that saved lives and brought the chances of peace that much closer, they had turned in a good day's work.

Background

Only five years after the conclusion of World War II, the Cold War turned hot. Encouraged by America's former ally, the Soviet Union, Communist North Korea launched a surprise attack on pro-Western South Korea in the early hours of 25 June 1950. Its leaders hoped to overwhelm the Republic of Korea (ROK), and expected no armed reaction from the United States. Instead, Americans acted decisively. President Harry S. Truman immediately recognized that unless free nations met aggression with force, the pattern would be repeated endlessly around the globe. At his orders an emergency task force was pieced together from units on occupation duty in Japan and rushed across the narrow strait to Korea. Other units, unprepared and inadequately armed, arrived in time to join a general retreat southward that halted only when ROK and American forces took a final position against the sea in a small pocket behind the Naktong River—the so-called Pusan Perimeter.

In opposing Communist aggression on the Korean peninsula, the United States entered a new and different kind of war. This war did not begin with a dramatic declaration by Congress and did not have as its objective the capture of the enemy's territory. Instead, Washington sought to "contain" communism and restore a border along the 38th Parallel. To avoid escalation into a possible full-fledged global conflict, possibly involving nuclear weapons, President Truman opted not to order a general mobilization or to risk opening other fronts in Asia, although reinforcements were dispatched to Europe as a precaution. One of the earliest signals that the struggle would be limited in nature came in official references to it as a "conflict" or a "police action," not as a war. After the United Nations gave its blessing to the American policy, eighteen U.N. member nations sent forces, from platoon to brigade in size, to aid in the fight.

During its first year the struggle approximated the war of maneuver common in World War II. Within two months of being pushed south, U.N. forces, led by the U.S. Eighth Army and X Corps, coordinated a daring amphibious landing behind enemy lines at Inch'on with a simultaneous breakout from the Pusan Perimeter. The North Korean People's Army shattered under the dual blows. U.N. forces invaded North Korea, and remnants of Communist forces retreated toward the People's Republic of China. Alarmed as the allies approached its Manchurian border, China intervened, sending massive forces of so-called volunteers into the peninsula. The November onslaught defeated the allies and drove them back to positions south of the South Korean capital, Seoul.

AN/TSQ–138 Trailblazer, a Mobile, Ground-based Electronic Warfare Signals Intelligence Intercept System. As a tactical direction-finding and intercept system to provide support to the tactical commander, it performs many of the former functions of the Apache Scouts.

Stalemate ensued. When truce talks began in the summer of 1951, the war of movement ended. For the next two years both sides traded blows and registered limited gains along a generally stable front stretching 150 miles from coast to coast on the Korean peninsula. The war now began to look like a replay of World War I, with the opposing armies dug into strongpoints and ridgelines. Minefields, barbed wire, and artillery duels completed the image of a Western Front in the Far East. Deliberately stalling the truce talks, the Communist side intensified small-unit actions in an effort to improve its bargaining position.

In its first battlefield clash with Communist powers, the Army came face to face with strange new conditions. More than at any time since the Revolution, Americans fighting in Korea had to be aware of the political effects of their actions. The impact of each operation on President Truman, the Joint Chiefs of Staff, and the American public (and to a lesser extent on other U.N. combatants) became a prime consideration behind each enemy move. Because their attempts to erode American public support for the war outweighed other factors, Communist forces frequently preferred to inflict small setbacks on isolated units rather than mount a large-scale campaign aimed at a major objective. Americans fought back by withdrawing and counterattacking enemy troops, rather than focusing exclusively on the capture or retention of terrain, and attempted to avoid heavy losses. Unfortunately, while preserving lives, this tactic confused a public conditioned by World War II to expect a series of territorial gains that added up to victory. On the other hand, the Army's long experience with civic action programs gave it a decided edge in winning the support of the Korean people.

Within this context, exploiting the potential of military intelligence became extremely important. Although spying is often referred to as the second oldest profession, military intelligence as a dedicated specialty was a new phenomenon in the Army. Until World War II the function involved a handful of detailed personnel, mostly officers, operating at the highest levels. Beginning on the eve of that conflict, however, advances in technology made it possible for experts to gather a massive volume of information, process it rapidly, and give it to units in time to influence ongoing operations. Taking advantage of the new advances in signal intelligence required a dramatic organizational change. In addition to a vastly expanded and functionally specialized collection and analysis capability at the national and theater levels, the demand for usable intelligence required other staff positions at echelons down to the battalion.

Such growth meant more than just adding bodies. As the equipment and techniques of war became more sophisticated, intelligence production became more complex. All personnel assigned to the newly formed Counter Intelligence Corps (CIC) and their counterparts in the Signal Corps involved in intercepting communications had to meet high standards of competence and to remain constantly in touch with new developments as technology advanced. To meet the sudden demand for proficient NCOs, the Army turned to an old mobilization technique: recruiting people with relevant aptitudes and offering them extra technical training. That approach, retained even after World War II ended, produced intelligence specialists, especially within the NCO Corps, capable of carrying out very complex tasks requiring unusual attention to detail with only a minimum of direct supervision.

NCOs in the intelligence field in Korea met the challenges posed by new Communist tactics in several ways. CIC detachments assigned to each division, usually operating as teams composed of one officer and three enlisted men, produced combat intelligence. Other NCOs found themselves working in rear areas to counter enemy propaganda, sabotage, espionage, and subversion efforts. CIC NCOs working with the South Korean Army became especially adept at uncovering low-level North Korean agents attempting to infiltrate the lines by posing as civilian refugees. Others in the signal field maintained the security of friendly radio traffic through the use of codes and ciphers. The members of communication reconnaissance companies operated powerful radio equipment designed to intercept or jam enemy communications. The value of intercepts often went beyond message content. If at least two units intercepted the same transmission, they could pinpoint the location of an enemy command post, then inform an artillery or air unit for an attack mission.

The NCOs working in the field of combat intelligence drew less attention but in many ways exceeded even the high standards set during World War II. Thanks to American air superiority over the entire Korean peninsula, observers could photograph enemy activity from above. Film came back to intelligence units, where NCOs studied the prints through magnifying lenses. All features of military significance—firing bunkers, trenches, weapons emplacements—were identified and labeled, and prints distributed to units operating in the area. Other NCOs specialized in producing technical intelligence from weapons, equipment, and documents captured by line units or developed tactics to more effectively counter enemy strengths. Linguists at the enlisted level interrogated refugees, suspected agents, and prisoners and translated documents to learn enemy operational plans.

Solving the language problem became one of the more enduring intelligence triumphs of the war. Although in the two world wars large numbers of Americans had spoken the languages of the enemy, Americans fluent in Korean were very rare in 1950. At the outbreak of hostilities only two members of General MacArthur's G–2 staff spoke Korean. As a temporary measure he turned to the Japanese-Americans who had proved invaluable in World War II. Since most Koreans had to learn Japanese during the decades before 1945, when their country was occupied by Japan, Japanese became the linguistic bridge between Korean and English. However, this three-language system caused delays that lowered the value of information collected. A crash program of language training instituted during the first year of the war eventually filled the gap.

Captured enemy soldiers turned out to be one of the most valuable intelligence assets in Korea, just as they had been in every other war in history. Primary responsibility for exploiting this source fell to the intelligence specialists within the NCO Corps. It quickly became apparent that a sudden increase in enemy stragglers and deserters foreshadowed an offensive, and NCO interrogators soon uncovered the reason. Communist doctrine stressed building unit cohesion by furnishing troops with very detailed information on upcoming tactical plans except the date for the attack. Once this practice was discovered, a team of interrogators and analysts could easily connect items of information extracted from a number of individuals and fill in the missing pieces.

The close relationships established between American and South Korean soldiers in the intelligence field were matched elsewhere. Very early in the war the Army adopted a policy of pairing officers, NCOs, and other enlisted men of the two national armies at all echelons as a way swiftly to improve the Korean ground force. At the company level and below, the policy took the form of the Korean Augmentation to the United States Army (KATUSA) program. A number of ROK soldiers were assigned to each American line company. Training and fighting within a "buddy" system, American troops taught South Korean soldiers the use of infantry weapons, small-unit tactics, and basic English terms and phrases. In return the KATUSAs became invaluable assets for squad and platoon NCOs. They were adept at reading terrain accurately, detecting signs of enemy activity, and serving as translators.

The use of KATUSAs recalls the experience of earlier generations of NCOs working with Indian scouts to conduct cavalry operations on the western plains. The result in both eras was the same: NCOs became more effective small-unit leaders.

NCOs in Action

Throughout World War II and Korea the number and functions of intelligence specialists within the Army grew, eventually giving rise to the formation of a permanent, distinct military intelligence branch. During this process a basic distinction emerged, based on rank: enlisted personnel collected and recorded relevant information, while officers analyzed it. In accordance with this tradition, NCOs occupied critical middle positions in the chain. They transmitted finished intelligence from division-, corps-, or army-level G–2 staffs downward to the regiment-, battalion-, and company-level units engaged in field operations. And during operations the NCOs gathered information and equipment from small-unit actions for transmission to higher-echelon intelligence sections to be analyzed. The historical practice in the intelligence field of reserving to officers the function of analysis did not bar NCOs from interpreting evidence they handled. On the contrary, NCOs were required to look for changes or trends and to bring them to the attention of superiors.

But before intelligence NCOs could examine any prisoners, equipment, or documents and begin extracting information from them, they had to receive evidence from the field. That process depended on an even older military skill: reconnaissance. Ever since Maj. Robert Rogers' men ranged the woods in the mid-eighteenth century, the observations of such specialists within the combat arms had formed the primary source of the raw information on which intelligence was based. If modern intelligence specialists owed much to the revolution in technology that produced sophisticated photographic and communications intercept equipment, the reconnaissance field remained solidly grounded in time-honed fundamentals. Patrols conducted in Korea, like Rogers' sweeps along the shores of Lake Champlain, could succeed only if carried out by hand-picked, highly motivated, and well-led soldiers with the training to collect relevant information over all types of terrain and through all types of weather.

The combination of traditional reconnaissance expertise with a highly technical information-processing function made for a very effective intelligence-producing operation by the time of the Korean War. Information derived from patrols and intercepts became very valuable in frustrating new tactics introduced by the Communists. As the Army tried to adjust to America's new role as the leader of the

Free World, it returned again and again to techniques pioneered in the Korean War. In succeeding decades, the ground component of the military focused increasing attention on the need to operate in underdeveloped areas, creating in time a host of special operations forces to carry out that mission. Each step along the way reaffirmed the importance to ultimate success of competent, professional NCOs.

Together, the intelligence specialist and the reconnaissance NCO were also a fine example of the twentieth-century cooperation between the specialist and the troop leader. The Army created its technical specialists largely by giving them special training. The troop leader, in the absence of schools for enlisted men, was a product of on-the-job training. In combat, however, the two worked together to accomplish a single mission, the patrol maintaining close contact with the enemy while the intelligence expert used technical tools to collate and analyze the reports on enemy units to produce a single picture. On both sides of the equation, the NCO was an essential member of the team, contributing not only to a more versatile and professional corps, but also to a more flexible, modern, and effective Army.

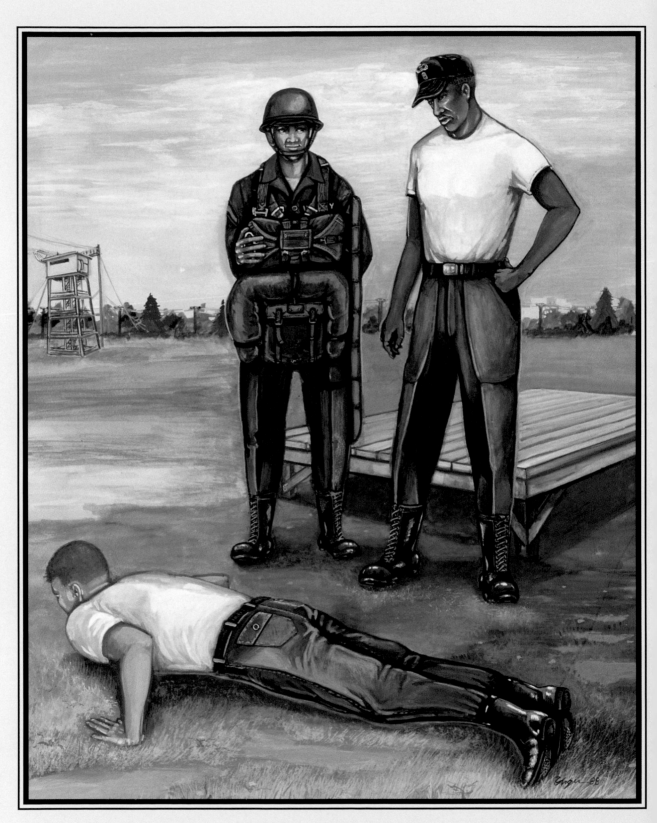

Give Me Ten, *Theresa L. Unger, 1988*

GIVE ME TEN

GEORGIA, 1960

———◆———

The NCO instructor wore a black hat, spit-shined jump boots, and a scowl on his face. Aided by a demonstrator in the standard T–10 "chute," reserve parachute, weapon, and full field gear, he had just given a careful explanation of how to hit the ground safely even while carrying a great weight. But when the students attempted to practice what they had been taught, one of them committed a bad mistake—all the worse because, although he wore no rank insignia on his white T-shirt, the offender was a brand new lieutenant.

Fortunately, the sergeant was an old hand at this game. He had the job of ensuring that trainees' mistakes were corrected on the practice field, before they cost a life. The Army had equipped him with a sure-fire method to make his points—physical exertion.

"You!" he bellowed. The offender came to rigid attention. "Drop!"

The class was only part way through the first phase of a three-week course, yet that simple four-letter word already carried a special meaning. The lieutenant understood exactly what was expected. He assumed what was commonly known as the "front leaning rest" position and began knocking out strenuous four-count pushups.

For him, it was a tough moment in a tough day—in fact, the lieutenant found airborne training the most physically demanding experience of his life. Up at dawn, he had gone through an hour of intense exercise. With his fellow students, he double-timed everywhere he went. At every moment he was subject to close supervision, iron discipline, and immediate on-the-spot corrections by tough NCOs. Yet the young officer endured and in time came to respect and even admire his taskmaster. He knew that he must learn fast in a game where errors could be fatal.

The payoff came later, when he made a series of five jumps from transport aircraft over the Fort Benning drop zones. He learned the whole experience, from the butterflies in his stomach before each jump to the exhilaration that followed a successful landing. He made the transition from "leg" to paratrooper and earned the right to wear jump wings and the distinctive glider badge. And he, with

Practice Jump at Fort Benning, Georgia, 1940. While most soldiers never attend jump school, since 1940 the physical fitness of the paratrooper has set the standard for all soldiers.

his fellow students who did not "wash out," went on to become teachers of others.

Background

The Army got into airborne warfare through a series of limited experiments. When World War II erupted in Europe at the end of 1939, the United States faced the task of suddenly modernizing and expanding its armed forces after years of low peacetime budgets. Army planners had to address a host of new or emerging technologies and to uncover ways to exploit them on the battlefield. The task ranged from employing primitive automatic data processing equipment to studying recent improvements in tanks and airplanes. Fortunately, the Army had time to assess experiments carried out by the European powers, especially by Germany and the Soviet Union. Experts also studied the operations of the recently concluded Spanish Civil War and the opening campaigns of World War II.

Exploring the airborne forces' potential fell to the chief of infantry and the Infantry School at Fort Benning, Georgia. Although the Germans successfully employed paratroopers while overrunning Holland in 1940 and Crete in 1941, questions remained. Did these victories warrant the heavy losses? Could transport aircraft parachute enough men and weapons in the right place at the right time to accomplish a combat mission? Or was the concept only another hoped-for breakthrough in the art of war that in practice would prove to be a dead end? The Army needed to find answers quickly, before it wasted precious resources required elsewhere.

Initial tests conducted in 1940 by a platoon of volunteers at Fort Benning proved that airborne troops had a role to play. But which organization would control them? A vigorous turf battle followed, pitting the ground forces against the aviators. The Infantry argued that paratroopers were basically infantrymen who, although transported to the battlefield by aircraft, would fight as part of a large traditional ground combat force. The Army Air Forces, noting that most German paratroopers were part of the Luftwaffe, emphasized the need for close coordination between parachutists, troop carrier aircraft, and tactical fighters and bombers providing fire support before, during, and immediately after a landing. The Corps of Engineers also entered the fray. They envisioned small-scale operations, commando assaults, intended to seize or destroy specific military targets behind enemy lines.

The 82d Airborne Division troops depart for Grenada, 1983. Drill sergeants and other trainers throughout the Army have adopted the same physical training approach as their airborne counterparts, guaranteeing that no new recruit would ever escape the dreaded words "Give me ten!"

The War Department chose the Infantry as proponent in late 1940, setting in motion a full-fledged program to develop tactical doctrine and tables of organization. Early in 1942 a special command within the Army Ground Forces assumed centralized control over the planning process and the training of individuals and troop units. Although problems of air-ground coordination persisted throughout the war, the first of five airborne divisions took its place in the Army's order of battle in August. Three (the 17th, 82d, and 101st) conducted combat jumps in the European Theater of Operations, while the 11th saw action in the Pacific. Each combined parachute units capable of jumping directly into enemy-held areas with more heavily armed glider-borne elements intended to follow up the initial landings and provide staying power until armored or motorized forces could punch through and relieve the airhead.

In the process of readying these units for battle, a standard training scheme emerged that was heavily dependent upon NCOs. In July 1941 the Infantry School institutionalized its airborne training in the Parachute School at Fort Benning. The direct predecessor of today's jump school, it remained in service throughout the war. The 82d and 101st Divisions introduced an alternative form of parachute or glider training in August 1942. Conducted as part of a fourteen-week unit training cycle, the divisions led each soldier in a sequence of steps through to company-level training. Practical work devoted to mastering the techniques of jumping was integrated with physical training, parachute maintenance, weapons proficiency, and land navigation.

When the Airborne Command (later redesignated the Airborne Center) moved to Fort Bragg and nearby Camp Mackall, North Carolina, in May 1942, the training functions split. The small Parachute School remained at Fort Benning as a component of the Infantry School and continued to produce individual replacements. By 1943 it was turning out an average of 700 trainees per week to be sent to units elsewhere in the United States or to overseas commanders. Meanwhile, the Center, a subordinate element of the Army Ground Forces, carried out airborne unit training. It constantly revised and upgraded both doctrine and curriculum to include lessons learned in combat and took over from the Parachute School training in collective skills.

The results of the trainers' work soon became apparent on the battlefield. The Army's first airborne drops took place in North Africa in November 1942. Relatively small operations conducted at night, they were marked by mass confusion in the drop zones. Larger efforts involving both parachutists and gliders followed in Sicily and at Salerno in 1943, and two full American divisions and one British division dropped into Normandy during the early hours of D-day, 6 June 1944. Three months later the newly formed 1st Allied Airborne Army employed American, British, and Polish units in the most ambitious use of the new striking power during the war—a series of daylight landings and drops in the Netherlands intended to seize a series of bridges and perhaps avoid a costly battle to cross the Rhine River farther south. Other airborne actions took place in southern France, western Germany, New Guinea, the Philippines, and Burma.

By the end of the Sicily operation, airborne troops had become an acknowledged elite force of highly trained and capable individuals. They enhanced their reputation in Normandy and the Netherlands and again in the distant Pacific, where—dropping from 300 feet—they recaptured from the Japanese the island fortress of Corregidor. In each of those drops, innumerable feats of initiative and heroism contributed to the eventual success of the mission. In airborne warfare, forces often scattered widely in drops. The initiative of NCOs in forming units and taking the offensive was essential. During the night jump on D-Day, for example, some units of both the 82d and 101st landed miles from their designated drop zones. Junior leaders had to think on their feet, rallying available troops into squad- and platoon-size units and moving out to occupy critical bridges, villages, and crossroads before the confused Germans could react. In the first hours of airborne operations, even more than in traditional combat, NCOs leading the way were crucial in hundreds of small actions.

Having demonstrated its worth during World War II, the new force survived the demobilization that followed, despite deep personnel and budget cuts. Gradually, technical improvements—introduction of a new generation of Air Force transport aircraft such as the C–119 "Flying Boxcar" and improvements in the parachute—replaced the vulnerable gliders. The split between the two types of airborne forces disappeared, and their ability to sustain combat dramatically increased. Since the airplane gave an airborne division unparalleled mobility, the Army made the 82d, based at Fort Bragg, North Carolina, its strategic reserve.

When the Korean War broke out, the Army had to fight the Communist enemy in Asia while it remained alert to the possibility of hostile Russian actions in Europe. Hence, the 82d remained at Bragg throughout the war, ready for swift deployment to reinforce Europe, while a special force, the 187th Regimental Combat Team (RCT), went to Korea. In October 1950 the RCT made two combat jumps behind North Korean lines near Pyongyang in an attempt to liberate prisoners of war and a third drop on 23 March 1951 at Munsan-ni near the Imjin River to disrupt enemy defenses. It also suppressed two riots among enemy captives at Koje-do. The rest of the time it provided the United Nations Command with an operational reserve of unmatched mobility.

Service in both wars confirmed the resourcefulness of the individual airborne trooper as well as the superb leadership abilities of his NCOs. Just as the prestige of being a member of an elite organization attracted soldiers of high quality, so too did the emphasis on initiative and judgment, the extra jump pay, and the chance to work with an all-volunteer force. Outstanding corporals and sergeants who intended to make careers in the profession of arms were quick to join. In airborne units, many of the Army's best NCOs found the ultimate challenge of their careers.

NCOs in Action

The Army changed in many ways in the decades after the chief of infantry created the first experimental airborne platoon. The technical skills each soldier had to master continued to grow as the military became more and more dependent upon sophisticated weapons and support systems. While many of these modifications promised to improve combat power and the ability of senior commanders to influence the course of a battle, they did not guarantee that the confusion faced by the 82d Airborne Division during the Normandy night drop could be prevented. The only true solution to that problem lay in the professionalism and competence of individual squad, section, and platoon NCOs.

By 1963 the Army's educational system for enlisted personnel was changing and expanding rapidly, as it became clear that NCOs, while retaining their traditional leadership role, would also work increasingly as technicians. Soldiers performing an array of jobs needed a host of technical skills to sustain and operate everything from rockets and missiles to field kitchens and the still-ubiquitous Jeep. Unprecedented numbers of men (and more and more women) in both the Regulars and the reserve components attended centralized or unit-level schools or participated in increasingly structured on-the-job training.

The expanding array of technical fields led to a reorientation of the NCO Corps that actually marked the culmination of a long trend. In the late 1950s the Army revised and expanded its system of enlisted rank and grade distinctions, attempting to differentiate between the large number of individuals who carried responsibility because of their mastery of specific tasks and those who filled positions that required them to exercise leadership on a constant basis. A new sequence of specialist ranks marked by an eagle insignia and a pattern of "rockers" emerged to provide the pay and prestige factors necessary to support the former group. The much smaller leader category continued to bear the "hard stripe" of sergeant or corporal.

Airborne training as it had evolved by 1963 offered a key example of how deeply the Army had come to depend on its Noncommissioned Officer Corps' functioning as technical experts, small-unit leaders, and instructors. Ironically, just as the Army was distinguishing between NCO skills and functions in its insignia, more and more NCOs, including airborne instructors, could see that the truly professional NCO had to be prepared to carry out all three functions on any given day.

In 1961 all basic parachute training in the Army was consolidated at Fort Benning. Within two years the course was turning out 24,000 qualified jumpers annually, sending them through three weeks of progressively more difficult instruction. Ground week led into tower week and finally to jump week. During each step the NCO instruc-

Moment of Truth, *Al Sprague, 1988*

tor, wearing his distinctive black hat, not only imparted the necessary information, but also served as a role model. An expert jumper with obvious technical knowledge, this handpicked individual carried out 98 percent of all instruction, whether the trainees were officers or enlisted men.

Guardians of a well-deserved reputation, the NCOs ruled the Airborne School with an iron hand, ensuring that trainees were constantly alert and maintained the proud bearing of elite soldiers. Many officer students who attended Airborne School remarked that what impressed them most about the training was the unshakable professionalism of the black hats. Young lieutenants and privates still new to the Army saw airborne sergeant-instructors as what an NCO was supposed to be, much as basic trainees during World War II had accepted the feared drill sergeant. When new paratroopers left Fort Benning and reported to duty assignments around the world in a host of military occupational specialties, they extended that ideal throughout the Army.

For a decade after the Korean War, national planners were preoccupied with the military implications and dangers of nuclear weapons. Within the Army, tactical considerations placed a premium on dispersion and flexibility, implying a series of basic organizational changes. Simultaneously, the superpowers shifted their attention to underdeveloped countries, and the Cold War became a contest for the support and resources of newly emerging nations. These impulses created a situation in which the Army and its NCO Corps had to be prepared to go anywhere at any time.

Although the entire post–Korean War Army had to be ready to meet the kind of challenges reserved primarily for paratroopers in World War II, the 82d and 101st Airborne Divisions now served as the heart of an elite mobile reserve (including "leg" divisions)—the Strategic Army Corps (STRAC). The painstaking attention to detail and to soldierly bearing absorbed by the men who formed those two divisions so dominated the corps that the acronym STRAC became the slang term identifying any outstanding soldier, unit, or military activity. A second element of the Airborne School training regimen also spread far beyond the limits of Fort Benning. The physical training (to the troops, PT) established an Army-wide standard. The push-up and the school's distinctive sustained running style (the "airborne shuffle") permeated all echelons.

The pride, self-discipline, and high standards of a paratroop platoon in 1940 set a standard that eventually affected the way in which the entire Army, active and reserve, saw itself and sought to accomplish the global missions assigned by national leaders. NCOs can and should recognize that their skills as trainers and their time-honored role as the institutional guardians of standards drove that change.

Into the Provinces, *Manuel B. Ablaza, 1988*

INTO

THE

PROVINCES

VIETNAM, 1965

———◆———

During the previous twenty-five years the Army had sent the master sergeant to many different locations—from Fort Belvoir, just down the highway from the Pentagon, to Berlin, Ethiopia, and Korea. Along the way, it had issued him many different uniforms. Now, as he stood in the muggy Vietnamese heat on yet another tour of duty far from his family, he took in stride the new boots, bush hat, and jungle fatigues. He prided himself on being a dedicated professional. If Uncle Sam wanted him to test some new items of equipment before they became general issue, he was happy to oblige.

The roar of the road grader's engine pushed thoughts of clothing out of the NCO's mind. As he was always trying to tell the young soldiers assigned to his work details, operating heavy equipment was serious business, and failure to concentrate could get people hurt. Especially in Vietnam. A war was going on—not like World War II, his first experience in combat, nor even like the Korean "police action"—but a real war nonetheless. The field manuals said that construction engineers were supposed to do their jobs behind the front lines; in Vietnam, no one knew where those lines might be at any given time. No American could distinguish Viet Cong guerrillas from the local farmers or predict where the enemy would strike next.

The sergeant realized that one of the reasons why "the brass" had sent his engineer unit to Southeast Asia to turn an ancient path into a road had to do with that very problem—separating the farmers from the enemy. How could the poor village people be convinced that freedom rather than communism would make their lives easier? If the Army could prove to the peasants that Americans were here to help them, then the Communists may yet be beaten. The sergeant aimed to make that happen.

Background

Army engineers played a key role in supporting American foreign policy efforts after World War II. By the mid-1950s the United States

A Civil War Ponton Bridge, c. 1863. Whether assigned to combat or construction duties, NCOs of the Corps of Engineers enable the Army to reach its destination and support the troops on the way.

and the Soviet Union had emerged as superpowers heading alliances. While limited conventional wars such as the Korean conflict still took place, the danger of mass destruction posed by thermonuclear weapons introduced a new kind of struggle: a Cold War fought with a spectrum of methods, including psychological warfare, to determine whose social and economic system would prevail. In large measure this change took the form of a contest between West and East for influence in the so-called Third World of poor, nonindustrialized countries.

As European countries, at times reluctantly, granted independence to their former colonial possessions, the United States offered assistance to the newly liberated peoples. Successive presidents and Congresses tried to improve the quality of life and to secure protection for human rights in the emerging nations as a way to block the growth of Soviet influence. In Southeast Asia, this process began in earnest after Viet Minh insurgents defeated French troops at Dien Bien Phu in 1954. Resulting peace talks split Indochina into Communist North Vietnam, pro-Western South Vietnam, and neutral Laos and Cambodia.

The Communists never intended that arrangement to be more than a temporary pause. When they resumed their advance in 1956, they avoided their mistake in Korea. Instead of launching a conventional invasion, they relied on guerrilla warfare. The United States countered by offering the Saigon government diplomatic and economic aid, a policy that met with only limited success. Eventually, President John F. Kennedy concluded that the mounting Viet Cong threat had to be met by military assistance as well.

The Corps of Engineers is among the oldest branches of the Army and one of the first to place reliance on technically competent noncommissioned officers. The roots of NCO technical professionalism reach back to the three companies of sappers and miners formed during the Revolution. These early engineers demonstrated their worth at the siege of Yorktown, where NCOs took charge of the working parties that dug the trenches, built the batteries, and led the light infantry assault columns in the capture of British-held Redoubt 10. The Regular Army's first permanent combat engineer company came into being during the Mexican War, expanding to a battalion during the Civil War. By 1917 the engineers had become leaders in technological innovation, forming highly specialized units to meet the needs of modern warfare.

Engineers' work with civic action programs overseas dated back to the early years of the twentieth century in the Philippines. There, they had refined their special skills while supervising the construction of everything from roads to barracks. They became crucial to the success of the Army in working with the local civilian population. Sixty years later, their assignments in South Vietnam continued a well-established tradition. Most experienced engineer NCOs served during the early years as members of the Military Assistance

Armored vehicles move across the Sava River on a ribbon bridge constructed by a U.S. Army bridging unit, Bosnia, 1996. Combat engineers routinely overcome obstacles that civilian engineers seldom encounter.

Command, Vietnam (MACV). Their backgrounds in such specialties as construction, equipment maintenance, and terrain intelligence made them invaluable trainers for the Army of the Republic of Vietnam (ARVN). Other engineers served with the Special Forces that President Kennedy had made the spearhead of his effort to win over the Vietnamese people. Among the Green Berets, engineer NCOs worked as demolition specialists with "A" detachments in the bush or as foremen constructing fortified camps in the most remote parts of the country.

The Army also created civic action mobile training teams to assist the ARVN's rural pacification program. Some teams were dispatched from Okinawa with engineer sergeants trained in public utilities to create public works programs from scratch. Usually an officer was teamed with the NCO. While the officer concentrated on working with the Vietnamese bureaucracy, the NCO used his ingenuity and experience to "scrounge" vital equipment and supplies. From the Montagnard settlements of the Central Highlands to the steamy Mekong Delta, just as other NCOs had done in the Philippines more than a half-century earlier, these teams provided a variety of technical services such as obtaining drinkable water by digging or repairing wells.

In 1963 the Army formalized much of the experience it had gained through the creation of engineer control and advisory detachments (ECADs). These detachments began to augment Special Forces groups all around the world, with the ECAD based in Okinawa sending teams throughout the Far East. In Vietnam its engineers worked closely with other military and civilian advisers and the Green Berets in people-to-people projects. The small but talented ECAD included a number of senior engineer NCOs ranging in rank from staff sergeant to sergeant major. Contact teams systematically eliminated a water supply crisis that had developed in both South Vietnam and Thailand, setting up installations and teaching military and public works employees how to operate and maintain equipment. Later, ECAD personnel also participated in flood relief operations to alleviate the suffering caused by a typhoon.

However, initial American support for the South Vietnamese government was more than matched by the Communist regimes that backed the Viet Cong as North Vietnamese regular regiments moved into South Vietnam. In early 1965 President Lyndon Johnson and other national leaders reluctantly decided to commit major U.S. forces. Engineer units and NCOs became some of the first Army elements to deploy to Southeast Asia as part of the new commitment. Their technical skills, honed through years of on-the-job training, were essential ingredients for the massive construction program required to create base complexes, port facilities, airfields, and road networks needed to support the arriving divisions and brigades. Combat engineers, with experienced sergeants occupying leadership positions as first-line supervisors, extended the American reach out into the countryside, while mobile forces started search-and-destroy missions to bring the enemy to bay.

In March the ECAD in Okinawa dispatched reinforcements to the small contingent of engineers already in South Vietnam supporting American advisers. They provided the know-how to supervise U.S. and Vietnamese contractors at the first eleven sites selected for development. Designs developed at this time for everything from tropical billets and mess halls to bunkers and helicopter pads became standard for the rest of the war. In June the first major engineer unit—the 864th Engineer Construction Battalion—arrived and began the dramatic transformation of Cam Ranh Bay, a sparsely settled natural harbor, into one of the most elaborate logistical bases in the world. The battalion commander later credited his senior NCOs with getting the program off the ground.

The Engineer Command in Vietnam reached a peak strength of 33,000 men in 1969. They served in 2 brigades, 6 groups, 28 combat and construction battalions, and 40 separate companies. Several thousand more engineers served with the engineer battalions assigned to the divisions and other tactical units (brigades and armored cavalry regiments) and the logistical command. The commitment of major U.S. forces had paid dividends, forcing the Viet Cong remnants and their regular North Vietnamese Army allies to abandon conventional operations, withdraw to sanctuaries in Laos and Cambodia, and revert to small-unit guerrilla action. At that point, under the American government's policy of Vietnamization, U.S. forces began to withdraw, and the ARVN, now trained and equipped, gradually took over the main fighting effort. To help prepare for that transition, the engineers embarked on a massive road restoration program. In this, as in the preceding phase, engineer NCOs at every level played key roles.

NCOs in Action

Bulldozers and their operators literally changed the face of South Vietnam. Many engineer NCOs began their Army careers as 'dozer operators or soon became intimately acquainted with their proper use. In Vietnam this experience enabled sergeants to receive instructions from officers and translate them into action. It also made the NCOs alert to the vital though unglamorous job of maintaining equipment, a duty that had to be constantly stressed to the younger troops and one that taxed the NCOs' leadership skills.

The addition of a special blade and protective cab turned the standard D7 'dozer into a "Rome Plow," a vital tactical weapon. Escorted by armored cavalry or infantry, Rome Plows—eventually organized into special land-clearing units—cut swaths through selected enemy-held areas of South Vietnam, denying the guerrillas the use of formerly secure base areas hidden from aerial observation. Operators had to be trained to run and maintain the machines, and keeping them on their toes was "sergeants' business."

NCO leadership was also at the forefront in the divisional and nondivisional combat engineer battalions. These units swept roads of mines, carved out temporary patrol and fire support bases in remote areas, and, when time allowed, took care of grass-roots civic action projects. Such assignments drew the engineers into situations that stressed the "combat" in their designation. The fire-support bases turned out to be especially vulnerable, for the enemy preferred to attack them, rather than larger and more formidable installations. Frequently, engineers working in such locations, often a small work party under NCOs, had to drop their equipment and grab rifles to repel enemy assaults.

Although the most familiar images of engineers in Vietnam involve scenes of construction and heavy equipment, their secondary role as infantry became more pronounced during the closing years of the war. Line units tended to be the first withdrawn from Vietnam, while engineers remained behind to work on a massive highway-rebuilding program. Engineer soldiers provided their own security, as technically expert NCOs led traditional combat squads and platoons. Locating and destroying bunker and tunnel complexes or setting up ambushes was tough, rugged duty, but it demonstrated once again the fundamental versatility of the career sergeants.

Among the engineer NCOs' last assignments in Vietnam was preparing the ARVN for the task of protecting its country without outside assistance. For the engineers this task involved establishing and conducting an on-the-job equipment-training program, dubbed Project Buddy. As in earlier advisory efforts, the veteran engineer NCO emerged as a key player, this time as a teacher.

The technically oriented branches played a critical role during the decade-long involvement of the U.S. Army in Southeast Asia. Nine of every ten soldiers deployed to that theater served in supporting roles rather than in the basic combat arms. Signalmen, medics, truck drivers, and clerks matched the engineers in contributing vital skills required to sustain a modern army and assist an ally in its struggle to survive as a nation. They also endured tropical heat and humidity and faced tropical diseases such as malaria to carry out the civic action program. By and large their activities attracted little public attention and gained no glory. Their efforts were not always recognized or appreciated by the riflemen, even though many support troops also did field service and came under attack in a war in which there was no front or rear area. Thus, the Vietnam experience challenged the NCO Corps' technical and leadership skills to the fullest extent.

Decades of increasing dependence upon technology to win wars and to prevent needless loss of life had created a Vietnam-era Army in which a professional soldier advanced mainly by adding to his skills as a specialist. Engineer promotions came to the noncommissioned officer who mastered a specific occupation: erecting buildings and bridges, making roads, turning jungles into airfields, surveying, or even diving. In paddies and isolated hilltop bases the NCO Corps, entangled in a formless, unconventional war, confronted the fact that leadership was still a basic part of wearing stripes. From section chief or squad leader through platoon sergeant to first sergeant and sergeant major, each NCO relearned that essential point.

Today's Army has been shaped by a conscious effort to examine the meaning of Vietnam—of what went right and what went wrong there. The renewed emphasis on the NCO Corps is a product of that reexamination and analysis. In both active and reserve components, formal training programs have dramatically expanded to improve professionalism, while constantly stressing basic troop-leading skills.

Swamp Patrol, *Felix R. Sanchez, 1966*

WAR
IN A
MAZE

VIETNAM, 1969

———◆———

The young NCO waded slowly through the knee-deep, stagnant paddy water. His squad had not taken any fire yet, but the tension seemed to surround him like a fog. There could be booby traps buried under the mud among clumps of rice shoots, grenades with pins pulled halfway out on those vines just an arm's reach away. There could be a punji pit just ahead, its floor a carpet of sharpened bamboo spikes covered with excrement, or an unexploded shell that had been rigged with a pressure detonator in that dry patch off to the right, just waiting for a man who wanted to get out of the stinking muck for a few minutes. If that wasn't enough, somewhere out there, a sniper might be drawing a bead on the squad members.

But the sergeant kept his emotions under control and managed to convey a sense of confidence that inspired the patrol's Spec. 4s and PFCs. He wore the stripes and he had the experience. They counted on the sergeant to teach each "newbie" how to spot the telltale signs of the enemy—the trip wires, the cut bark, the color contrasts in the dirt and leaves, and the silhouettes that were so hard to see in the green maze of Vietnam's delta country. More than that, they relied on him to keep them on their toes in the ferocious heat—over 100 degrees already, and it wasn't even noon—when a weary man could easily begin to ignore details. Everyone just wanted to get to the objective and clear it. The squad leader had to convince them that the constant care and vigilance were worth it, especially when the alternative could be a life without legs or arms—or no life at all.

Now he could hear the radio telephone operator (RTO) on the horn with the platoon leader. At first the sergeant was angry—the squad was already alert, its weapons locked and loaded; he didn't need reminders. Then he realized that the lieutenant was merely passing on the word from the company commander. Earlier this morning, the men of Alpha Company had been hit by a couple of snipers in the tree line. Every other company in the battalion had heard it—they were just on the other side of that stand of rubber

178

Road to Fallen Timbers, *H. Charles McBarron, 1952. Since the early days of the U.S. Army it has been the small-unit leader, the sergeant caring for and inspiring soldiers in the face of the enemy, who represents the essence of warfighting.*

trees over there, no more than a "click" away. Alpha got both snipers, but only after suffering five wounded themselves. The dust-off choppers had come and gone, and now the count was known: one had died in the air on the way back to the field hospital; the other four would make it, though only two would probably ever return to duty in the bush. This was everyday life in the III Corps Tactical Zone, South Vietnam, 1969.

Background

No branch of the Army can claim a longer history than the Infantry. Through the centuries and across national boundaries its experience has an almost timeless quality. Foot soldiers retain their central position in the profession of arms. For only the infantryman can achieve the ultimate measure of battlefield success—taking and holding ground. Other branches facilitate victory, but only the infantrymen can occupy and hold the objective once it is taken.

Infantrymen have always faced the most difficult work of war: marching long distances, digging defensive positions, holding the line in the face of enemy fire, and tolerating a wide range of adversity, from thirst and hunger to fear and loneliness. American soldiers and their NCOs have performed those thankless tasks for over two centuries, regardless of how the Army has changed the way it fights the nation's wars. Down in the mud, it hasn't always been easy for the infantryman to appreciate the impact of technology and scientific progress on his immediate role on the battlefield. Other branches have seen the changes more clearly. Signal Corps specialists and their NCOs have watched semaphore flags and torches become microwave relay communications equipment; cavalrymen have made the transition from horses to tracked vehicles and then to helicopters. So far-reaching have been some of these changes that entire new branches of the Army have resulted, including the Army Air Forces, which achieved separate status in the mid-twentieth century as the U.S. Air Force.

Yet the infantry certainly has not been immune to the influence of advancing technology. Both weapons and equipment have changed considerably over time. Infantrymen of the Revolution and the War of 1812 struggled to master the primitive smoothbore flintlock musket. Over succeeding decades that basic small arm evolved through rifling, percussion firing mechanisms, metallic cartridges, and breech-loading, magazine-fed, semiautomatic, and finally automatic capability. Other equipment kept pace, as industry and science produced protective helmets, lightweight uniforms, prepackaged individual rations, and comfortable, durable boots. By the height of the Vietnam War the foot soldier possessed the lightest and fastest-firing rifle ever issued to the Army, scientifically designed field gear, and a uniform specifically tailored for the tropical climate in which he had to fight. As valuable as these improvements were, however, they did not alter the fundamentals of how he performed his mission. The Vietnam-era infantryman remained what he had always been. He still had to walk the hills and valleys, rifle at the ready.

In the 1960s the Army's infantrymen adapted their traditional skills to support a new Army doctrine: counterinsurgency. Supported by Communist regimes elsewhere, North and South Vietnamese insurgents were well into their second decade of struggle to unify the country under Communist leadership. Having defeated French colonialists, they now sought to topple the pro-Western Saigon gov-

Soldiers await the arrival of helicopter transport during the Vietnam War. Whether fighting the Indians of the old Northwest or insurgents in Southeast Asia, NCOs ensured the success of operations in remote locations against an unconventional enemy.

ernment. To accomplish that aim, they followed the example set by Mao Ze Dong in China, creating a guerrilla movement that survived by melding with the peasant population. Reinforced at first by cadres who infiltrated from the North, and later by entire military units, the Viet Cong built an infrastructure by drawing rice, recruits, and information from the hamlets and villages.

After several years of giving advice and support to Saigon, the United States began to commit combat units in 1965 to offset the growing rebel pressure. Striving to buy time for the South Vietnamese to build a military force that could stand on its own, the U.S. Army, Vietnam (USARV), moved out of the cities and into the countryside to deprive the enemy of support. Counterinsurgency exposed the infantrymen of the combat divisions and their NCOs to battle in terrain that ranged from delta swamps to harsh, jungle-covered mountains. To survive and win, American NCOs had to learn skills that could not be taught at stateside bases like Fort Benning or picked up during routine overseas tours in Korea or Germany.

With its different character in different places, the war demanded different approaches. The 9th Infantry Division, deployed in the south along the watershed of the Mekong River, invented special riverine tactics to cope with the maze of rice paddies and streams. In the country's Central Highlands, the 4th Infantry Division dealt with a population of different ethnic background and language, in terrain where temperatures could fall far below the tropical range characteristic of the delta. And in the north, in I Corps, troops of the 23d (American) Infantry and 101st Airborne Divisions, operating alongside U.S. marines, contended with landscapes that ranged from wet lowlands to sharp hill masses. The 1st Cavalry Division, which ranged throughout the country, adapted its airmobile capability to all situations. The remaining divisions, particularly the 1st and 25th Infantry Divisions, occupied positions in what was known as the III Corps Tactical Zone. Together with a host of smaller formations and key elements of the Army of the Republic of Vietnam (ARVN), they formed a barrier of men and guns between Communist base areas in neighboring Cambodia and Saigon, the capital of the fragile, developing Republic of Vietnam. NCOs of the "Big Red One" and "Tropic Lightning" divisions and their men learned to fight in rice paddies, rubber plantations, and patches of bamboo and jungle crisscrossed by irrigation canals and small streams.

At first, counterinsurgency strategy adapted conventional techniques to the tropical environment. When units embarked at American ports, they left behind bulky equipment and some of their heaviest weapons, but they added many more helicopters and much technical support. After arrival in country and initial orientation, the forces fanned out to confront the Viet Cong. In strengths ranging from a brigade to several divisions, the Americans attacked enemy elements that threatened to cut off inland rice-producing areas from the urban centers along the coast. By late 1967 the Viet Cong and the North Vietnamese Army had been stopped in their tracks in most areas. Then their high command made a desperate gamble to regain the initiative during the lunar new year holiday in early 1968. This Tet offensive cost them grave losses, but back home in America, antiwar sentiment accelerated after the bloody fighting of Tet. The fact that the Communist forces could still mount such a major attack loomed larger in the public mind than the enemy's defeat.

Convinced that superior American firepower could not be met head on, the enemy high command changed tactics. Most large formations withdrew westward to sanctuaries in Cambodia and Laos to reconstitute their manpower and prepare for an eventual return. In the meantime, thousands of small detachments moved back and forth across the border, planting caches of weapons and equipment for subsequent operations or carrying out hit-and-run attacks on American and ARVN bases. By early 1968 the big multidivision operations of the war were over, at least as far as the Americans were concerned. While brigade-size operations continued, small-unit actions on both sides became the norm, giving even more importance to the role of the NCO.

Ambushing enemy elements and seeking out the thousands of supply points required skilled and courageous small-unit leadership. The smallest hamlets and streambeds had to be searched, and virtually every fold in the landscape had to be examined again and again in an effort to uncover every stockpile, cave, and tunnel complex. In the process the war became an endless series of search-and-destroy missions.

For thousands of NCOs and their infantry squads, sections, and platoons, search and destroy came to mean not only patrolling and sweeping through areas of suspected enemy strength, but dealing face to face with villagers. In supervising the search of individual huts for weapons, documents, and hidden supplies, NCOs had to act with great tact to accomplish their mission without alienating the rural Vietnamese people whose support was fundamental to winning the war.

At the village level, counterinsurgency demanded unit reorganization. Throughout Vietnam, units as small as battalions activated an additional staff section, Civil Affairs (S–5). It continued the Army's earlier programs of civic action and helped to integrate them into the flow of combat operations. While a sweep was under way, for example, one or two squads would escort medics or engineers into a village to provide otherwise unobtainable treatment and assistance. NCOs and their men often stood guard as Army materials and expertise were employed to construct hospitals, schools, wells, and roads, all in an effort to bind the villagers to the central government.

Civic action, of course, was a very old technique for the Army. So too were the skills of small unit combat and patrolling. In fact, each soldier arriving in Vietnam received a pocket-size card containing "Rogers' Rules of Ranging." Written during the French and Indian War, these rules were still applicable two centuries later.

In Vietnam, American soldiers and their NCO leaders enjoyed one key advantage over Major Rogers' men—the helicopter. The "chopper" gave Americans and their allies unprecedented mobility, largely neutralizing the Communist tactic of ambush that had helped to defeat the French in the early 1950s. Announcing their arrival by the sound of rotor blades slicing through the humid air, these machines served as transports, gunships, and aerial ambulances, and successfully demonstrated the tactical value of airmobility. Major terrain obstacles were no longer a deterrent. Infantrymen could now land at an objective with little warning and be fresh for combat. Once a ground commander pinned down an elusive enemy, he could use helicopters to "pile on" additional friendly forces, bring direct and precise fire to bear, and conduct resupply and "dust-off" operations rapidly. On the ground, the infantryman and his NCO squad leader were cut from traditional cloth, but supporting them was the most advanced technology seen in any war.

NCOs in Action

The Vietnam War and the needs of counterinsurgency doctrine gave NCOs a prominent role in Army operations. Terrain, enemy methods, and political reality combined to place a premium on small-unit leadership. The Vietnamese land surface includes dense jungle, with a double or even triple canopy of trees in some areas; towering hill masses; and many rivers and streams. These features often forced larger units to break up into smaller elements, in close but not direct contact—moving along parallel ridges or valleys, for example. This pattern was reinforced later in the war when the enemy shifted to small-scale forces conducting localized ambushes and population-control operations.

The Army carried the battle to the enemy by trying to maintain the maximum number of maneuver battalions in the field and by breaking them down into companies, platoons, and even squads whenever advantageous. This meant that throughout the second half of the war, NCOs carried a major share of the leadership burden. They ran the squads and fire teams on patrol, constructed listening and observation posts, and set ambushes. Thanks to the superiority of American firepower, the troops could usually offset any initial enemy advantage in numbers once they made contact. The squad leader in Vietnam had more firepower under his control than an entire platoon in World War II. At his side was the modern counterpart of the color sergeant, the ever-present radio telephone operator (RTO) with a PRC–25 radio. Weighed down with a full infantryman's basic load as well, the radioman was the squad's link to artillery, armed helicopters, and tactical air strikes—as well as to prompt medical attention and occasional hot food and clean clothes. The enemy realized that fact, regularly targeting the RTO first in any firefight or ambush.

But while some aspects of the war enhanced the status and authority of the Noncommissioned Officer Corps, others diminished them. The Vietnam War was the nation's longest struggle, lasting over eight years, and it became steadily more unpopular the longer it lasted, especially among young Americans. Tension soon developed between draftees and long-serving NCOs. More ominous to the NCO Corps was the lack of experience that began to emerge among its younger members. Rotation on a fixed one-year tour sent personnel home often just as they acquired useful experience. Many first-term enlistees won their stripes rapidly and then rotated out before they could become mature, fully rounded NCO leaders.

The cumulative effect produced a crisis among troop-leading

NCOs. As early as October 1967 one brigade noted in its quarterly Operational Report—Lessons Learned (ORLL) that it was short over 300 sergeants and staff sergeants. The Army tried to fill that void in Vietnam by changing training cycles. Recruits identified during basic training as having leadership potential were used in advanced individual training as additional cadre, to cut down on the number of experienced NCOs dedicated to daily operations. Others were dispatched to a special six-week course after finishing their advanced training to receive formal instruction in basic leadership techniques. Upon completion of that program, they received immediate promotion to sergeant and were sent to line units. These improvised efforts succeeded in large part in meeting the Army's need for NCO leaders, but they also revealed the need for a permanent system of NCO education.

A centralized program was needed to distill the lessons earlier generations of NCOs had learned on the job and to transmit this knowledge in a systematic way to the Army's future junior leaders. At a time when seven specialists in support and service roles in-country backed up every soldier in the combat arms, the growing gap between the technical specialist and the troop leader had to be bridged. After Vietnam, it was clear to everyone that all troop leaders in the modern, high-tech Army had to be technical specialists in order to contribute to an effective combined-arms team. At the same time, it was understood that traditional leadership skills remained an essential part of any technical specialist's abilities.

Training the Trainers, *Theresa L. Unger, 1988*

TRAINING
THE
TRAINERS

CONUS, 1975

———————◆———————

I f anyone had told the sergeant major when he enlisted that he would find himself sitting, like some recruit, in a classroom with other senior NCOs as he approached the end of a thirty-year Army career, he would not have believed it. But today he was attending a refresher course in something he had either been doing, or supervising, for over ten years: records management. The sergeant major had joined the Army during World War II. In a way, the classroom symbolized how much things had changed since then.

One of the most obvious differences was the instructor. For most of the sergeant major's career, he had seen only male officers or NCOs carry out that function. The female soldiers of the Women's Army Corps (WAC) with whom he had come in contact had been involved mainly in administrative duties. Now WACs and WAC NCOs could be seen in the most visible leadership and technical positions. The grade insignia on the instructor's sleeve marked another major change—the introduction in 1954 of specialists (replacing the "Techs" of World War II) with their insignia combining an eagle and stripes.

Whether in garrison or in the field, the Army had always needed NCO instructors, to teach everything from the correct way to wear the uniform to the proper employment of weapons. This tradition had been strengthened by twentieth-century developments. As the Army adopted ever more sophisticated equipment, the need for trained personnel to teach young soldiers how to use it, and to supervise its use, increased. To keep their expertise current, NCOs in the Army of the 1970s now had to return to the classroom several times in their careers, either to update knowledge in an established field or to learn a new subject.

This new all-volunteer Army had no lack of courses, old or new. There were the standard subjects that the Army had long needed to support field operations—the Morning Report, Unit Supply Procedures, Preventive Maintenance Checks and Services, Range Safety Procedures, and Principles of Instruction. But the flood of

Wireless Operator's School, Camp Vail, New Jersey, c. 1920. NCOs, who for generations had been the trainers of combat skills, found themselves learning and teaching new technical specialties in the early twentieth century.

new technology since World War II had led to a parallel stream of courses for NCOs in electronics and communications. The coming of the computer had added a new list of skills to those considered necessary for basic NCO effectiveness. The information explosion in the Army affected more than course content. Training itself had become a specialty, involving much more than a loud voice and a half-dozen posters. NCO instructors now had to be familiar with a growing variety of instructional techniques, such as movie projectors, closed-circuit television, individually paced skills training, and video cassette recorders.

Background

In the late nineteenth and early twentieth centuries, an accelerating succession of inventions had created a new technology for the Army. The most dramatic invention was the internal combustion engine, which enabled the Army to move faster in a variety of vehicles and aircraft. But others appeared as well: radios and other electrical devices, improved metals for lighter and more dependable weapons, refrigeration to preserve food, and improved and more effective explosives. This new technology dramatically changed the personnel structure of the Army. The traditional field army structure—dependent on infantry and artillery, backed by a minuscule service and support system—was reversed in less than half a century. At the end of the Spanish-American War, only about 8 percent of the Army's manpower was engaged in service and support specialties. By the end of World War I, that proportion had increased to 58 percent, by the end of World War II to 67 percent.

Another long-term trend well under way by the 1970s was personnel integration, a term implying more than the elimination of racial barriers. Until 1948 the black experience in the Army had been restricted to segregated units commanded largely by white officers. An executive order issued by the president in that year started the forces of change in motion, and within seven years all segregated units had disappeared. In succeeding years, large numbers of other ethnic groups turned to the military as a way to improve their opportunities in life, and the Army's overall personnel composition began more closely to mirror that of society at large. In addition, World War II had seen the creation of the Women's Army Corps. For the first time, the Army directly recruited large numbers of women and gave them a variety of duties, several of which had long been considered as masculine. Having clearly demonstrated that women could perform many tasks in the military, the WAC was continued after the war.

A more recent event shaping the Army in the 1970s was the Vietnam War. As the nation's ground force, the Army bore the brunt of the fighting in Southeast Asia. Although the Marine Corps' loss ratio was higher, the casualty totals recorded the heavy price paid by the senior service. Of approximately 58,000 Americans who died in that war, 38,000 were soldiers. The effects of the war on small-unit leadership and personnel policies were pronounced. The one-year tour disrupted both small-unit cohesion and leadership in Vietnam and training in the United States. Fire-team leaders, squad leaders,

Conducting the After Action Review (Hotwash), *Sieger Hartgers, 1995. Increasingly, NCOs have had to master and teach a host of subjects far removed from traditional military skills such as marksmanship.*

and platoon sergeants in many cases had barely learned their duties when they rotated out of the war zone, only to be replaced by less experienced men. As the war continued, finally becoming the longest in American history, a severe shortage of NCOs developed. In an effort to alleviate the situation, the Army assigned fewer experienced NCOs to training camps and attempted to cover that deficiency by appointing temporary NCOs from among recruits, a policy that inevitably degraded the effectiveness of the training.

Rapid changes in civilian society also affected the Army during the Vietnam War. Drug abuse, racial tensions, and resistance to traditional authority developed in the streets and on the campuses and inevitably spread into the Army as the draft continued. The results were distressing to commanders in and out of the war zone. Discipline and unit effectiveness at all levels were threatened. Alarming for the future of the Army was the decline of public esteem for all the uniformed services, a change of attitude reinforced by continued publicity about their internal troubles.

Of all the post-Vietnam developments in American military policy, the most influential in shaping the Army was the coming of the Modern Volunteer Army (VOLAR). The Army faced the most difficult transition of all the armed services in attempting to rely on volunteers to maintain a large, quality force. In previous eras, an all-volunteer Army had meant a small domestic force carrying out limited missions during times when the nation's main defense had been its remoteness from the quarrels of Europe and Asia. After World War II, however, the Army received international missions that its leaders believed could be fulfilled only through continuous reliance on a manpower draft. To answer the need, the federal government had extended Selective Service into peacetime. Except for a fifteen-month period in 1947–1948, the draft remained in effect from September 1940 through most of the Vietnam War period.

The Modern Volunteer Army of the 1970s was supposed to strengthen both the Army and the national defense in several respects. For the short term, VOLAR would answer charges that the draft during the Vietnam War drew too heavily on the economically disadvantaged and on ethnic minorities in the population. For the longer term, the Army Staff hoped that VOLAR would make the Army a higher quality force. Enlistment standards would be raised; enlisted personnel, especially NCOs, would receive more specialized training; and the retention rate would increase. At the same time, the training base and the administration required to handle draftees would be reduced. Achieving these goals implied not only improving the professional qualifications of personnel already in the Army but also altering recruiting methods to enlist young people who possessed higher aptitude levels. To attract quality recruits, many traditional features of Army life changed dramatically. Pay increased to make the Army competitive with entry-level positions in the private sector. Once in uniform, soldiers were offered a range of benefits previously unheard-of in the military. Soldiers had more military occupational specialties (MOSs) from which to choose during initial enlistment and, after making their initial choice, a greater opportunity to change. Soldiers now found the Army more sensitive to quality-of-life issues such as privacy in the barracks, grooming standards, and more variety in the PX and club systems. To retain quality junior enlisted personnel, the Army offered generous reenlistment bonuses and a peacetime GI Bill.

The initial reaction of the NCO Corps to the Modern Volunteer Army was negative. At first glance the changes from a drafted to a volunteer Army seemed to represent a loss of authority for platoon- and company-level NCOs. Rumors abounded that the new Army would be manned by long-haired rebels swilling beer in the barracks. Many of these fears, however, were quickly dispelled as exaggerations. The reforms brought about by the Modern Volunteer Army dramatically improved communications up and down the chain of command. The Army initiated an extensive counseling effort at the lowest command levels to ensure that every soldier understood his or her unit's mission and individual role within the unit. At the other end of the chain of command, officers, including corps and army commanders, became more aware of the attitudes and concerns of subordinates at all levels. Local commanders instituted human relations programs to speed responses to legitimate grievances not only from soldiers but also from their spouses. NCOs came to see that the reforms represented not a loss of authority but a different method of applying their own traditional leadership. The result of the new policy of tying discipline to counseling was a better informed and more highly motivated Army.

NCOs in Action

Throughout the history of the U.S. Army, instruction has remained a fundamental responsibility of NCOs. The subjects of instruction have always covered the full range of knowledge required by both recruits and experienced soldiers to function in the Army. Since the Revolutionary War the newest soldiers at any post have spent their first months in the Army following the instructions of their NCOs: learning how to wear the uniform, how to make a bed, how to prepare for inspection, how to use and care for weapons, and how to stand guard duty. As the soldier gained experience, he needed more sophisticated skills. But the primary instructor was still an NCO who led the soldier through squad, platoon, and company tactics and through whatever specialty training he needed in artillery, communications, or other fields. In time many soldiers became NCOs themselves, learning from senior members of the corps. When he or she reached the top NCO rank, there were still lessons to be learned, such as preparation of the morning report, maintenance of company personnel records, and supervision of larger bodies of troops.

As the advance of technology in the twentieth century began to affect the way the Army did almost everything, the functions of NCOs changed dramatically. In addition to exercising their historic role as small-unit leaders in the field and instructors in garrison, NCOs became technical specialists. This development set in motion permanent changes in the NCO Corps. Trained in essential areas of technical expertise—as radio operators, aircraft maintenance specialists, tank drivers, ordnance specialists, motor pool sergeants, and so forth—NCO specialists became as indispensable as traditional troop leaders. At the same time, the NCO's traditional role of instructor took on new importance as modern research resulted in an endless stream of new technology.

But before new technology can benefit the Army, it has to be disseminated down the chain of command to individual soldier-specialists. This continuous upgrading of technical skills throughout the enlisted ranks is the responsibility today of every supervising NCO. Before they can instruct their troops in the latest technology, NCOs must learn it themselves at formal schools where they are instructed by other NCOs. The NCOs who begin the process of disseminating new technology are truly "training the trainers."

Over the course of a twenty- or thirty-year career, NCOs in every specialty need periodic refresher training to keep up in their fields. Refresher training amounts to a significant investment by the Army in the career development of each NCO. The loss of such highly trained people would seriously threaten the ability of the Army to carry out its varied missions. To preserve the talents of its NCOs, the Army during the Vietnam War began to emphasize retention, vigorously backing up the campaign with substantial financial benefits and quality-of-life reforms. The "Re-Up!" theme of the 1970s became much more than a slogan in the transition from draft to Modern Volunteer Army, when there was real concern about the loss of specialist NCOs to private industry. By making service in uniform attractive to all elements of the general population, the Army achieved not only the goal of retaining talented NCOs but that of integration as well. Women and minorities moved into large numbers of NCO billets in the Modern Volunteer Army, joining the corps' leadership and becoming role models for others.

In the Army of the 1970s, the teaching function of NCOs became, like the courses offered, more technical and complex. NCOs had to learn new things and new ways of teaching. Training in all specialties was reorganized and presented in the Tasks-Conditions-Standards format. After explaining the task within a certain specialty, the NCO instructor outlined the conditions under which the task was to be performed and the standards by which the performance of the soldier was to be judged. The new methodology allowed for individualized training on a more extensive scale than ever before. Soldiers and NCOs could draw "tech tapes" from their unit libraries to remain current in their specialties or to prepare for annual skills and promotion tests.

In addition to the NCOs' role in introductory and refresher instruction, they also began administering a series of individual and unit tests. The three phases of the Skill Qualification Test (SQT)—common task testing, written test, and hands-on evaluation—determine each soldier's position in the system of five skill levels. NCOs test units under the Army Training Evaluation Program (ARTEP), which examines each component of a command as well as the entire unit. ARTEP foreshadowed the even more sophisticated evaluation methods of the

1980s, such as MILES (Multiple Integrated Laser Equipment System) and BTMS (Battalion Training Management System).

In all of this, NCO students and instructors alike found an increased emphasis on professionalism. When the shortage of NCOs developed in the later years of the Vietnam War, tasks that normally would have been carried out by experienced NCOs often were taken over by company-grade officers. To prepare NCOs to resume these tasks, instruction was increased, not only in occupational specialties but in rank responsibilities as well. Before or during promotion to E–5, most young NCOs are enrolled in the Primary Leadership Development Course, followed successively by the Basic and Advanced Noncommissioned Officer Courses. This professional education sequence culminates with attendance at the Sergeants Major Academy. The changes set in train by the switch to the Modern Volunteer Army have turned out to be extremely important to both the NCO Corps and the Army. Every effective NCO leader is a skilled trainer, and every skilled trainer is an effective leader.

Mighty, Mighty Fine Slingload, *Carl E. "Gene" Snyder, 1996*

READY

TO

RESPOND

GERMANY, 1987

———————◆———————

"**B**ravo Two-Niner this is Tango Three-Five. Permission to land. Out." From a camouflaged tent, well hidden in a treeline on the north German plain, those cryptic words informed the pilots and crew chiefs of two low-flying Army helicopters that they could take on the aviation gas that they needed to carry out the next phase of a complicated training mission. Each year a large contingent of troops came over from the United States to test the nation's ability to react quickly to international crises by reinforcing other members of the North Atlantic Treaty Organization (NATO). Once in place, the troops conducted a series of maneuvers alongside Americans permanently stationed in West Germany and the Low Countries and allied contingents. In 1987 those exercises, under the names Return of Forces to Germany (REFORGER) and Certain Strike, gave units from Fort Hood, Texas, the opportunity to train with forces from four other countries. The crew chiefs on the helicopters and the forward air controller in the tent—all wearing NCO stripes—were part of this huge and complex effort.

These NCOs were true professionals. Each had mastered a complicated subject, attended periodic refresher courses to stay abreast of changes, and undergone regular tests to demonstrate technical proficiency. But none was a specialist only. Each had also learned to lead, supervising work parties of soldiers and giving instruction to their highly trained subordinates. Each NCO acted as a small-unit tactician, a function formerly associated only with combat arms squad leaders and platoon sergeants. On the highly lethal battlefields of modern war, there are no rear areas; every leader must shoulder the dual responsibilities of protecting his or her unit area as well as performing an assigned mission. Every NCO must be proficient as both technician and leader. The men and women of this Forward Arming and Refueling Point (FARP) had to be ready to operate close to the enemy, in some cases behind his lines, to sustain in continuous operation a new generation of helicopters. In performing their

A 1908 Wright Military Flyer at Fort Myer, Virginia. Airplanes have transformed the battlefield from a relatively shallow area in which opposing forces can see and shoot each other into a deep zone stretching hundreds of miles on either side of the forward line.

jobs they reflected two new realities of the post-Vietnam Army: the emergence of a mature NCO Corps and the ever-growing importance of Army aviation to battlegrounds of the present and future.

Background

When the Army left Vietnam in the early 1970s, it began one of the most sweeping and decisive transitions in its long history. In Korea and again in Vietnam, soldiers had fought so-called little wars. Tactics in Vietnam had been unconventional, while those in Korea had often featured pitched battles like those of the two world wars. Throughout both conflicts, however, national leaders had been aware that American strategic interest centered on Europe, where the Soviet Union and the Warsaw Pact nations had their main forces, and on the Middle East, from which America and its allies drew much of their oil. The end of the Vietnam War reemphasized these basic strategic facts. At the same time, the partial breakdown in morale that resulted from Vietnam, and the end of the draft, forced Army planners to do some basic thinking about the future.

Drawing upon historical examples, the Army's leadership reviewed the Vietnam experience to identify those things that the Army had done well and those that were in need of improvement. Once again, government policymakers felt considerable social and economic pressure to make dramatic cuts in the military. Many citizens called for the nation to withdraw from its role as an active world power and to turn its resources to domestic problems. In the media, criticism of the armed services was intense and often unfair. The American people, accustomed to an unbroken string of clear-cut triumphs in war, viewed the stalemate in Vietnam as a defeat, especially when the South Vietnamese government collapsed following the U.S. withdrawal. Leaders in the Department of Defense recognized the great need to return to military fundamentals and at the same time to embrace the social changes that were transforming the status of women and minorities in the country as a whole.

The result, though not a revolution, was fundamental change. Officer and enlisted training programs underwent wholesale revision to apply the best aspects of modern educational programs to military instruction. The Army reallocated resources between the active and reserve components, revised unit tables of organization and equipment wholesale, and reviewed basic doctrine. The Women's Army Corps was abolished, and women were integrated into the total force. From a low in the early 1970s, the Modern Volunteer Army expanded over the next decade and a half to include twenty-eight divisions drawn from the Regular Army, Army National Guard, and Army Reserve. Other combat, combat support, and combat service support elements provided a balanced structure capable of sustained operations. Equipped with the latest in technology, officers and NCOs began to develop new training programs that were as realistic as pos-

Attack on the Comandancia, Al Sprague, 1990. This painting depicts infantrymen deploying from an armored personnel carrier. Exploiting the potential inherent to AirLand Battle while guarding against an enemy's ability to do the same has required NCOs to master complex systems and equipment.

sible—a concept as old as Steuben's efforts at Valley Forge. Nowhere did the resurgence of traditional military values emerge more clearly than in the Noncommissioned Officer Corps.

One effect of the rapid changes during the 1970s and 1980s was the elevation of Army Aviation to branch status. Such recognition had been long in coming. Soldiers first took to the skies during the Civil War in gas-filled observation balloons often piloted by civilian aeronauts. But serious battlefield applications of flying came only after the invention of fixed-wing aircraft. Early in the twentieth century a detail of Signal Corps personnel received flying instruction from the Wright brothers themselves. By the time of World War I Army aces were performing reconnaissance missions, dropping bombs, and fighting aerial combats with German fliers like the Red Baron. Already in those early days of Army Aviation, NCOs were supervising ground crews and directing maintenance of planes.

Army Aviation suffered under the same budgetary restrictions as other parts of the armed forces during the interwar years. But throughout Europe and America, military planners knew that air power would play a major role in future wars. As the 1930s came to a close, the growing power of a rearmed Germany underlined the urgent need to develop fighters and bombers, both for tactical support of ground operations and for strategic destruction of enemy bases. In 1937 the U.S. Army received the first B–17s, the famous Flying Fortresses, on which NCOs served as gunners.

During World War II the relatively tiny Army Air Corps blossomed into the biggest air organization in the world, the Army Air Forces. Dozens of NCOs in ground crews and at maintenance facilities supported each air crew. But the difference in viewpoint between the fliers and those who fought the war at ground level was profound. Those who saw the war from the air really did not feel they were part of the same team. They agitated for a service of their own and eventually won a separate Air Force in the National Security Act of 1947.

This law established the basis for Army Aviation as it exists today. It allowed the Army to retain some organic aviation, but disputes between the two services were quick to develop. Basically, the Air Force wanted to limit the Army to a few light observation planes, used for liaison and artillery spotting as in World War II. The Army sought instead to develop aircraft that it could use for direct support of ground troops. Despite strong Air Force resistance, the Army became particularly interested in exploring the potential of the helicopter, which had just started to enter service in a few limited roles, mainly in medical evacuation.

In 1949 Army and Air Force representatives reached a preliminary agreement that sought to divide responsibilities by restricting Army aircraft, whether fixed wing or helicopter, to certain maximum weights. The agreement did not resolve the problem of direct support for the soldier on the ground, however, and was quickly outdated by the battlefield realities of the Korean War. Commanders who cared about their troops insisted on taking advantage of aircraft, particularly helicopters, to overcome the obstacles posed by Korea's harsh, hilly terrain. Speedy helicopter evacuation of the wounded to hospitals attracted the most attention, because it increased a G.I.'s chances of survival. But the Army also began to move troops and supplies throughout the combat zone by air.

The Korean War was still raging in 1951, when Secretary of the Army Frank Pace, Jr., and Secretary of the Air Force Thomas K. Finletter signed a new memorandum of understanding that dropped earlier weight restrictions. Army aviators were allowed to support land operations as long as they did not infringe upon functions historically assigned to the Air Force, especially assault transport and troop carrier airlift missions to deploy paratroopers. Despite this so-called Magna Carta of Army Aviation, time was still needed to work out interservice relationships and to clarify ambiguities. The Army continued to depend on the Air Force for close-air support, reconnaissance, and transport to and from the combat zone, while expanding its own aviation capabilities within the forward area.

By 1966 experiments and new executive decisions finally provided a solution to the interservice rivalry. The Army essentially gave up its larger fixed-wing planes in exchange for a free hand to exploit the capabilities of the helicopter, both as a means of transportation and as a fire support asset. In Vietnam, the decision paid dividends that revolutionized warfare. The air ambulance replaced ground vehicles as the primary means of battlefield evacuation, while the UH–1 Iroquois (better known to the troops as the Huey) was so common that it became a symbol of the Army's Southeast Asia war.

On the ground and in the air, NCOs played an ever-stronger role in supporting aviation, and soon they were fighting from the air as well. First developed at the aviation school at Fort Rucker, Alabama, armed helicopters made their debut in combat during the 1960s. From jury-rigged machine gun mounts on unarmed reconnaissance and evacuation helicopters, the gunship evolved into a sophisticated attack platform with the introduction of the AH–1 Cobra in 1967.

By this time members of the NCO Corps had pervaded Army Aviation. In Vietnam, the crew chief, usually a sergeant or NCO-level specialist, also became a gunner. Arming the Huey, for example, involved mounting two machine guns in the troop compartment doorways. The crew chief manned the one on the left side of the aircraft while a junior enlisted man handled the one on the right. Other NCO duties included supervising maintenance, operating the radio, acting as an extra set of eyes for the pilot, and ensuring that the aircraft was ready to perform its mission. Army airmen went where the action was the hottest and emerged from Vietnam as some of the most decorated soldiers in the service.

NCOs in Action

By the mid-1980s all the pieces had come together. Agencies such as the Natick Research and Development Center designed and fielded a host of new items that took advantage of technological breakthroughs to meet the practical needs of the soldier on the battlefield. Changes appeared in scores of familiar items: the soldier's ration; the duty uniform; a new regimental system and a training program that emphasized the importance of unit cohesion; lightweight load-bearing equipment; Gortex cold-weather clothing; a new armored vest and the Kevlar helmet; an improved M16 rifle; the Abrams (M1) main battle tank; the Bradley (M2 and M3) infantry and cavalry fighting vehicles; and the Multiple Launch Rocket System.

Army Aviation kept pace with the change. The helicopter's role as a symbol of Vietnam gave many people the impression that Army Aviation existed primarily to fight in guerrilla wars under the umbrella of Air Force fighters that provided total control of the skies. In point of fact, the Army had originally developed the basic doctrine of airmobility with a conventional war in mind. When the Army shifted its focus back to Europe and the Middle East in the 1970s, the only doctrinal changes needed involved updating to take advantage of a new generation of equipment. In addition to several fixed-wing aircraft that provided liaison and intelligence-collection capabilities, upgraded Cobras, Hueys, CH–47 Chinooks, and OH–58 Kiowas were joined by new AH–64 Apaches and UH–60 Black Hawks. Sustained by maintenance crews trained to the highest standards in the world, the Army's fleet of attack, utility, observation, and cargo helicopters turned its attention to addressing the challenge of high-intensity conventional combat.

Serving the new air fleet was an enlisted force and NCO Corps that had been transformed by a new educational system and a new emphasis on professionalism. In reality many of the changes in hardware and personal equipment reflected changes in outlook that had been building through the era of the world wars and after. No longer was the volunteer professional soldier to be viewed as an outcast, as had all too often been the case in the past. American society now demanded that all soldiers be motivated as citizens and treated as such, not as a caste apart. In exchange for the soldier's loyalty to the Constitution, the American people insisted that he or she be given the best possible materiel so that his or her life or health would not be wasted. By emphasizing these elements in recruiting and retention programs, the Army was able during the 1980s to attract the highest quality of personnel that it had ever enjoyed.

Good people, using good equipment, demanded good leadership. Since the leader must understand both the soldiers and the machines under his or her control, the old distinction between specialist and NCO no longer had much meaning. Recognizing that every supervisor had become a leader, the Army abolished the last vestiges of the distinction between "hard stripe" sergeants and technical specialists. It then sent the force to test its enhanced skills in realistic, objective, performance-oriented maneuvers to determine how well the men and women and the equipment would interact to execute a doctrine called AirLand Battle.

This was the underlying significance of the 1987 exercise called REFORGER. Plans called for the largest single overseas movement of U.S. troops since World War II—active and reserve units comprising the heart of a corps—and their employment in northern Germany under allied control as part of a five-nation war game with official Soviet observers. The success of the operation was a tribute, above all, to the new Army that emerged from the Vietnam experience and to the men and women who led it.

No armed service can succeed in modern combat without men and women who are capable of understanding and employing items of equipment that not long ago were considered science fiction. While today's Army NCO faces challenges similar to those faced by his or her predecessors for over the last two hundred years, there is a difference of degree. The stakes today are higher, and both the rate and the quality of the technological change are much greater. The Army NCO who serves as crew chief on a multimillion-dollar helicopter, acts as an air traffic controller to bring it home safely, or provides the forward support that keeps it in the air has a tremendous responsibility, both for lives and for an expensive and sophisticated weapons system. Today's NCO has to be both leader and technician, for modern war demands both current knowledge and the timeless qualities of leadership and courage.

Night Attack, *Mario H. Acevedo, 1991*

"Hell Night"
on
Objective Norfolk

Kuwait, 1991

❖

The M1A1 tank platoon sergeant pressed his head against his sight and braced for the recoil as his gunner shouted, "On the way!" In an instant the green glow of his thermal sight splashed white, first with the heat of the 120-mm. cannon's discharge, then with the thermal signature of an Iraqi T–62 tank bursting into flames at 300 meters' distance. His curt "Target, cease fire" barely stopped the gunner from sending another round into the already burning target; the loader already had another round in the tube. Grasping the tank commander's override control, the platoon sergeant quickly swiveled the turret to the right to affirm that his wingman's tank had destroyed its target as well. Two T–62s had literally popped out of the ground in front of them, backing out of revetments that had hidden them from view. Fortunately, the Iraqis had oriented their revetments to the south in the direction of an expected American attack up the Wadi al Batin, whereas the American tankers actually had approached from the west after a deep left hook. It took the Iraqis a few seconds of exposure to reposition their tanks to face this attack from an unexpected direction. A few seconds was all it took for superbly trained American gunners to find their marks.

That night every soldier in the battalion was grateful that their platoon sergeants had been strict with respect to maintenance and gunnery. Despite the hundred-plus kilometers of swirling dust and intermittent combat through which they had traveled to reach this point, every tank in the battalion still rolled purposefully forward through the darkness, skimming across the soft desert sands on quick, wide tracks, scanning for obstacles, enemy, and even landmines with thermal sights and methodically traversing turrets. Drawing on years of training and experience, the sergeants had enforced a rigorous routine of maintenance checks and services every day during their preparations for war and at every pause during their inexorable advance. Whatever mechanical problems they found were quickly resolved by the tank crews themselves or by NCO-led maintenance teams trailing them by a few hundred meters. One particularly meticulous process

202

The Tanks at Seicheprey, Harvey Dunn, 1918. Armor NCOs encountered their first challenges maintaining and operating tanks in a combat zone during World War I, when the fledgling Tank Corps of the American Expeditionary Forces went into action for the first time.

was that of sustaining main-gun boresight and zero, the mechanical relationship between the gun tube and the sights necessary to assure accuracy. This required executing a sixty-plus-step checklist morning and evening with continuous updates in between to accommodate both the great distances traveled and the extreme differences of temperature between night and day. The results of this attention to detail were awesome. The morning would reveal dozens of Iraqi tanks precisely drilled at the turret ring from distances over a mile away.

Although the platoon sergeant did not fully understand it at the time, his actions on Objective NORFOLK were part of a much-more-massive attack that crushed the elite Iraqi Republican Guard. He could get some idea of the scale of operations when he looked through his vision blocks to the left and right and saw a vast tableau of advancing American armor eerily illuminated by burning Iraqi vehicles as far as the eye could see. The chatter on the radio nets also provided a sense of scale. Depending upon the circumstances, either the platoon leader or the platoon sergeant would be speaking on the platoon net directing the actual employment of its vehicles while the other would use the company net to coordinate with and report to the company team leadership. Both men could monitor both nets. The radio traffic was a reassuring blend of familiar voices working through chaotic circumstances. Here was the flanking platoon sergeant reporting three T–62s they had encountered and destroyed; there was the motor sergeant reporting that the recovery NCO had pulled the platoon leader's wingman out of an antitank ditch. A little earlier the first sergeant had reassured the company commander that he had direct control of the fuel Heavy Expanded Mobile Tactical Trucks (HEMMTs) and was leading them through the landmines precisely in the tracks of tanks that had been through earlier, and a bit after that the NCOIC of the medics confirmed he had returned to duty a slightly injured soldier. The communications sergeant had already replaced one vehicle's radio and another vehicle's auxiliary receiver, and the mortar platoon sergeant had dismounted some of his men to serve as infantry securing Iraqi prisoners. The fire-support NCO offered the company commander yet another illumination round from time to time—not necessary for vehicles with thermal sights to see in the dark, but nevertheless a wonderful way to keep the multitude of vehicles oriented in the midst of confusion and darkness. All along that fifty-kilometer front of vehicles beetling purposefully forward through the wreckage of the battlefield, the voice of America was the voice of its NCOs.

Background

The Cold War ended rather suddenly in 1989, when first the Warsaw Pact and then the Soviet Union disintegrated due to domestic dissatisfaction with Communist rule. This was certainly not the end of threats to world peace, however. Iraqi dictator Saddam Hussein equally unexpectedly seized Kuwait with an armored blitzkrieg beginning 2 August 1990. President George H. W. Bush immediately asserted that this aggression would not stand and rushed American

The Final Push through the Rumayiah Oil Field, *Mario H. Acevedo, 1991. NCOs played a key role in the success of the biggest armored corps in American military history: the VII Corps in* DESERT STORM.

forces to reinforce Saudi Arabia against follow-on attacks while organizing a worldwide coalition to resist and then reverse the Iraqi invasion. After several months of DESERT SHIELD, the operation to defend Saudi Arabia, it became apparent that this containment coupled with diplomatic efforts and economic sanctions would not suffice to force Saddam Hussein out of Kuwait. President Bush and his coalition of allies decided to forcibly liberate Kuwait, and deployed the additional forces necessary to do so. On 17 January 1991, DESERT STORM, the campaign to liberate Kuwait, began with an air campaign to destroy enemy air defenses, neutralize strategic targets, incapacitate Iraqi command and control, and attrit Iraqi combat units. On 24 February the ground campaign began with an armored feint up the Wadi al Batin and supporting attacks from Marines and Arab allies. Meanwhile, the main effort, consisting of the American VII Corps flanked by the XVIII Airborne Corps, had driven deep into the desert and swept around the Iraqi right flank. The ground war lasted only 100 hours and left the Iraqis in Kuwait annihilated or in full retreat.

DESERT STORM had many of the features of the dramatic campaigns of liberation during World War II, but it also demonstrated the considerable recent change that had occurred in the Army. This change included the further evolution of expeditionary combat, the affirmation of an American training revolution, the maturation of precision-guided munitions, the introduction of battlefield digitization, the fluidity between conventional combat and operations other than war, and the reinforcement of a concept known at the time as the Total Army. Noncommissioned officers were key players in each of these accomplishments.

Some critics have argued that the DESERT STORM deployment was lethargic and that the coalition was successful only because Saddam Hussein passively waited six months while the allies mustered their forces. Actually, there were two distinct deployments: one to implement the defensive posture of Operation DESERT SHIELD and the other that followed the decision to implement DESERT STORM. Each deployment consisted of a heavy corps and lasted about two months. Each progressed twice as quickly as previous efforts to deploy heavy forces on such a scale, albeit half as fast as the standard now set for the Objective Force of 2015. American light forces were alone, except for their Saudi allies, on the ground for only a matter of weeks before American heavy forces joined them. The early inclusion of such tank-killing assets as Apache helicopters, main battle tanks, and Multiple Launch Rocket System (MLRS) artillery was a departure from more customary hasty deployments of light forces alone. Evidence suggests the Iraqis were surprised by the pace and resolution of the American buildup. Within two months they had lost all reasonable prospects for invading Saudi Arabia or seriously interfering with the allied deployment.

DESERT SHIELD and DESERT STORM represented a significant advance in the evolution of expeditionary combat along a continuum from World War II through 2015. The logistics involved were striking; the 22d Support Command offloaded and moved over 12,447 tracked vehicles, 102,697 wheeled vehicles, 1 billion gallons of fuel, and 24 short tons of mail. Innovations over previous wars included state-of-the-art roll-on, roll-off rapid sealift, modern containerization, an efficient single-fuel system for all vehicles, and extensive use of computers. A revolution over previous wars was exemplified by the technique of shipping vehicles and heavy equipment and then flying soldiers into the theater just in time to intercept them at the port of debarkation. This allowed troops to arrive physically fit and recently trained. When battalions arrived overseas during World War II, their soldiers often had not fired a crew-served weapon in five months. When battalions arrived in Saudi Arabia from Europe in 1991, they were only days removed from having fired a challenging gunnery regimen off the tanks of a sister unit at Grafenwöhr, Germany, the most sophisticated range complex in the world at the time.

Many have noted the renaissance within the Army following the Vietnam War. Much of this renaissance was a return to premises the Army had long held: readiness derives from appropriately allocating resources for training, logistics, and personnel; state-of-the-art equipment yields battlefield advantages when coupled with doctrine appropriate to its use; and leadership must be thoughtfully honed by commanders at every level. Ample budgets throughout the 1980s restored muscle to an Army declared "hollow" in the 1970s. Development and procurement of the then-futuristic M1A1 Abrams tank, M2/M3 Bradley fighting vehicle, Patriot air defense missile, MLRS, and Black Hawk and Apache helicopters—and tightly synchronized AirLand Battle doctrine to employ them—gave American heavy forces a decisive edge. The post-Vietnam formation of the Training and Doctrine Command (TRADOC) breathed new life and energy into the Army school system, and the maturation of a Noncommissioned Officer Educational System (NCOES) established a parallel ladder for refining enlisted leadership. One should also mention the extensive participation of numerous foreign soldiers in Army educational and training programs throughout the Cold War. The Gulf War was an enormously successful example of coalition warfare, enabled in part by shared appreciation of tactics, techniques, and procedures.

As dramatic as all this technological and educational progress was, the advances in training enabled by Multiple Integrated Laser Engagement System (MILES) gunnery and computer simulations were even greater. Post-Vietnam training developers constructed thoughtful and comprehensive "task-condition-standard" programs not unlike the comprehensive Mobilization Training Programs of World War II. MILES enabled this training to leap beyond subjective evaluations into realistic engagements wherein opposing forces maneuvered against and hit each other as they would in battle. By the mid-1980s battalions at the National Training Center fought wide-ranging direct-fire battles with realistic consequences under the careful scrutiny of pointedly critical observer-controllers. Many veterans of DESERT STORM characterized fighting against the Iraqis as more frightening but otherwise less challenging than at the National Training Center.

Computer simulations broadened such surrogate combat experience still further. Tank crews in M1A1 tank Unit Conduct of Fire Trainers (UCOFTs), for example, experienced a range and number of engagements otherwise impossible to duplicate short of the

206

Sherman Tanks Passing
Streams of German Prisoners,
Ogden Pleissner, 1944. Without thousands of skilled armor NCOs, the famous St. Lô breakthrough, the race across France, and the destruction of the German Seventh Army in World War II would have been impossible.

battlefield. Similarly, brigade and division staffs engaging in the computer-driven Battle Command Training Program (BCTP) experienced combat decision-making at a pace close to that of actual combat in an environment wherein their decisions led to realistic consequences. BCTP simulation also allowed for an appreciation of joint warfare otherwise impossible to introduce into Army training. The radically increased realism and pace rendered feasible by laser gunnery and computer simulations amounted to nothing less than a training revolution, a revolution affirmed by Desert Storm.

Lasers and computers were revolutionizing more than training, of course. Their contribution to the maturation of precision-guided munitions was transforming warfare itself. Much has been written concerning the sophistication of cruise missiles and "smart bombs" dropped from over 15,000 feet. Army munitions in this category of weaponry include the long-range, artillery-delivered Army Tactical Missile System (ATACMS) and the "fire-and-forget" television-guided Hellfire missiles. Similar technological advance is represented by the Patriot missile, an air defense weapon so fast and accurate that it not only could intercept planes but was on the verge of reliably intercepting missiles. Less well appreciated than the precision-guided munitions was the ability to deliver "dumb" munitions with ever-greater accuracy. One M1A1 tank battalion, for example, routinely engaged at ranges greater than 2,000 meters and destroyed over three hundred Iraqi tanks and armored vehicles while expending fewer than six hundred rounds. Advances in delivering dumb munitions were of considerable import when inventories of smart munitions were so expensive and so readily depleted. DESERT STORM's precision-guided munitions and precisely delivered munitions were a dramatic demonstration of an increasing capability, along a continuum extending at least as far back as World War II, that seems likely to continue with further upgrades well into the twenty-first century. Woe betide the army that engages in a pitched battle with an adversary a generation or more ahead in these capabilities—as did the Iraqis.

The Gulf War imparted as dramatic an impetus toward battlefield digitization—the lightning-fast network-wide sharing of vast data files via computers and their accessories—as it did toward the further maturation of precision munitions. Glimpses of the possibilities of the new technology appeared in the detailed real-time intelligence on enemy vehicular movement offered by the Joint Surveillance and Target Attack Radar System (JSTARS) and the theaterwide accountability of air missions afforded by the Airborne Warning and Control System (AWACS). These contrasted sharply with the uncoordinated pictures of the battlefield available to DESERT STORM ground commanders once the attack was rolling. These commanders shared information via techniques little different than those of World War II: face-to-face discussions over maps, radio conversations, and acetate overlays updated by grease pencil. Information lags and the inevitable "Murphy's Law" led to widely differing impressions of what was going on, from battalion commanders on Objective NORFOLK convinced they were fighting for their lives to staff officers in Riyadh opining that VII Corps should speed up its now risk-free advance.

A dark aspect of confused battlefield awareness was the harrowing incidence of fratricide. Ultimately, twenty-one of ninety-eight American battle deaths were attributed to friendly fire. Virtually every brigade that became involved in serious intermingled combat experienced engagements wherein friendly troops fired upon other friendlies, grim testimonials to weapons that can precisely engage at ranges greater than crews can reliably identify targets. In most cases the victims were located where the perpetrators anticipated no friendly units. Postwar efforts to redress the horrors of fratricide include steadily progressing use of computers to achieve digitized battlefield awareness, and the less successful search for vehicular identification friend or foe (IFF) devices analogous to those carried on warplanes.

After defeating Iraq, the Army quickly found itself responsible for a host of operations-other-than-war (OOTW) missions: humanitarian relief, refugee control, prisoner of war repatriation, peace enforcement, de-mining, civil administration, reconstruction, and others. These missions were not new to the Army, but they had not received much attention in a generation—certainly not by the heavy forces dominant in DESERT STORM. Now these heavy forces found themselves spending more time in OOTW than they did in combat—even in a theater where they had just fought a conventional conflict. This placed extraordinary requirements firmly upon the small-unit leadership, and thus upon NCOs.

DESERT SHIELD and DESERT STORM also witnessed a maturation of trends integrating the reserve and active components. Although the Reserves and National Guard had participated in larger numbers in earlier wars, they had never been as thoroughly integrated, as was the case during DESERT STORM. Through the Vietnam War the traditional view had been that the active component would be the first to fight and that the reserve component would add mass with similarly structured forces. In the aftermath of Vietnam, service chiefs believed that a major factor in plummeting support for the war had been the administration's decision not to activate the reserve component. In addition, the proliferation of combat support and combat service support required by modern war made it unrealistic to maintain the full required panoply of such forces on active service.

In part by accident and in part by design, the Army—an all-volunteer force since the 1970s—evolved into a force that could not sustain major operations without activating the reserve component. During DESERT STORM the active Army achieved a total force of 871,948, of which 60,427 were activated National Guardsmen and 79,118 activated reservists. Of the 227,800 soldiers deployed to Southwest Asia, 37,692 were National Guardsmen and 35,158 reservists. Rather than simply adding similar units to a steadily growing force, reserve component soldiers often filled complementary roles, in many cases bringing transferable civilian skills with them. Subsequent deployments have demonstrated that the reserve component is ever more integral to active component operations, leading Chief of Staff General Eric K. Shinseki in 1999 to abandon the term Total Army in favor of simply "The Army" when describing a force where active and reserve components are working together.

NCOs in Action

Noncommissioned officers were critical to the success of each of the major advances represented by DESERT SHIELD and DESERT STORM. The working mechanics of deployment have always been the business of NCOs, and the great strides in expeditionary combat reflected their efforts as well. NCOs prepared troops and equipment for overseas movement, inspected and supervised deploying contingents, designed and inspected load plans, and supervised every facet of unit and individual deployment. As technology and strategic circumstances dictated an increasingly deployable Army, NCO supervision made it possible.

NCOs made other contributions as well. The revolution that harnessed simulations and MILES laser gunnery for increasingly comprehensive and realistic training was implemented by NCOs. They, for example, were the direct supervisors in the case of UCOFT gunnery and they personally directed the installation, maintenance, and utilization of the MILES. Precision-guided munitions and precisely guided munitions may have represented radical advances in technology, but the experts who would prepare and use this equipment were NCOs—as had long been the case whenever newly fielded equipment transitioned from experimentation to general use. Similarly, the equipment necessary for digitization and the small-unit leadership necessary for operations required NCO supervision as well. Capable noncommissioned officers were as critical to activated reserve component units as they were to their active component brethren. In many cases the nature of their specialties scattered reservists and National

A sergeant of the 1st Cavalry Division climbs aboard his M1 during a training exercise. The leadership, technical expertise, training skills, and standards of the armor NCO continue to provide the margin between victory and defeat.

Guardsmen in small numbers across the breadth of the battlefield; in these cases effective NCO supervision of tiny contingents of soldiers proved doubly critical. It is clear that the major improvements in Army capabilities manifested during DESERT STORM were largely the result of the noncommissioned supervision that brought them into effect at the soldier's level.

As significant as their contributions to this makeover of the post-Vietnam Army were, the most memorable contributions of NCOs during DESERT STORM fell along more traditional lines. Many NCOs performed heroically, leading by example. On one occasion, two Iraqi T–55 tanks appeared immediately behind the fuel trucks in the combat trains of an armored task force. These rose in revetments within a hundred meters of the task force's command sergeant major (CSM), who had retraced the route of advance with three drivers armed with M16s to flush out what they thought was a single sniper. The CSM had seen green tracers—American tracers are red—and was concerned for the security of the fuel trucks. What followed became a confused melee as the tiny contingent was drawn first to one antitank guided missile (ATGM) position and then to another. The Iraqis revealed themselves by firing ATGMs, and the M16 marksmen cut them down. The ATGM positions featured bunkered larders of munitions; these the Americans methodically blew up with thermite grenades. At one bunker, the CSM met an Iraqi departing as he was entering and killed him at the muzzle of his .45-caliber pistol. When the T–55s rose up, the CSM clambered aboard the closest and tossed a thermite grenade into its hatch. The second T–55 was destroyed by fire from an unknown source. For a few moments the most critical action on NORFOLK was one NCO and three soldiers fighting totally outnumbered in the dark.

Most NCOs fighting on NORFOLK demonstrated painstakingly developed gunnery skills. Gunnery—preparatory maintenance, boresighting, simulations, drills, and the tank tables themselves—is NCO business. Gunners are generally sergeants, and most tank commanders are senior NCOs. The battalion master gunner, an NCO charged to facilitate gunnery training, is a revered figure at the pinnacle of technical proficiency. All this professional expertise paid off in the extraordinary marksmanship demonstrated on NORFOLK. Tank commanders made lightning-fast decisions in adverse circumstances. One M3 scout platoon sergeant was riding the interval between two task forces when a T–55 jerked out of a nearby pit and had him in its sights. Before the T–55 made the final lay of its gun, two M829 sabot rounds whistled past, one over the platoon sergeant's front slope and one past his rear ramp. The T–55 burst into flames and the sergeant continued his mission, truly appreciative of precision gunnery.

In one battalion task force, eleven tanks fell into tank ditches or through the roofs of Iraqi bunkers. Eight self-recovered under the supervision of their NCO tank commanders. The three that did not self-recover offer even more striking testimony to NCO expertise. One M1A1 crashed through the roof of an Iraqi bunker, collapsing into an excavation that almost precisely fit the dimensions of the tank. The wingman tried to assist with a tow, but another Iraqi bunker was aligned with the first in such a manner that the wingman would have fallen through it in his approach. The M88A1 medium recovery vehicle, called forward by the stricken tank commander from its position 300 meters behind the leading tanks, soon arrived. That vehicle's commander jockeyed around to create mine-safe footpaths with his vehicle tracks and then got out onto the ground to examine the "stick." Out came the M88A1's main cable, manhandled through a half-dozen vehicle lengths of tortured ground and then forced onto the M1A1's tow fixture, which had been hastily exposed by the digging of the crew. Down went the M88A1's blade and up went its front slope, perching the great drum of its main winch in the most advantageous position. A few quick instructions to the tank commander, and a carefully choreographed sequence began: the cable pulled taut; the winch inched the rear of the tank toward the lip of the ditch; at precisely the right point of purchase, the M1A1 assisted (not too fast, or it would have pitched into the second bunker) with its tracks. As the M1A1 teetered on the saddle between the bunkers, the winch quickly let out the cable, the tank spun into a 90-degree neutral steer and then pitched clear of both excavations even as the saddle between them collapsed under the violence of its maneuver. This vehicle save would have been a credit to the Recovery MOS (military occupation specialty) in any circumstances. It was phenomenal when executed under fire in the dark.

The catalog of NCO contributions on NORFOLK cannot be measured. Postwar debriefings established that virtually every NCO did some amazing thing to keep that great mass of armor moving forward through the inferno. Those with thermal sights guided those without them through the minefields. Dozens of hasty maintenance saves—some by mechanics and most not—brought every single combat vehicle not destroyed by fire through the entire night intact. Command, Control, and Communications (C³) NCOs jumped nets and spelled each other to keep the volume of coordination flowing. Medical NCOs snatched the wounded from flaming vehicles, while combatant counterparts conducted local counterattacks to secure the area. The advancing tanks talked to each other, covered each other, and hosed each other down with machine-gun fire when Iraqi infantry came too close. As sources of fire became apparent, M1A1 commanders talked lighter vehicles into the lee of their tanks, shielding them like great pachyderms protecting their young. In the immediate wake of the M1A1s and the Bradleys, HEMTTs rolled along with the fuel and ammunition upon which all future success depended. In each of these miniature serials, crossing the battlefield with no more protection than one would have in one's personal car, the lead driver was an NCO.

════════════════════

It in no way diminishes the contributions of officers and private soldiers to assert that the characteristic that most distinguished Americans from their late-twentieth-century adversaries was the caliber of their NCOs. No army exceeded and few approximated the combination of experience, leadership, and technical knowledge represented by pay grades E–5 through E–9. The battlefield is a complex and confusing place. An incredible number of miniature—but life-threatening—crises erupt simultaneously. Small clusters of men must accomplish extraordinary things with no notice, little help, and under adverse circumstances. Bulling across NORFOLK was an arduous task for all parties involved. America would not have succeeded if the only tactical circumstances resolved had been those of which commanders were aware.

Waiting To Go to War [Operation ENDURING FREEDOM], *Henrietta M. Snowden, 2000*

EXPEDITIONARY OPERATIONS

AN APOD IN
CONUS, 1990s

———————◆———————

The air defense battery first sergeant ambled congenially among the numerous soldiers in the Aerial Port of Debarkation (APOD) holding area. As was his habit during a deployment, he used inevitable waiting periods such as this to good advantage, circulating among the troops and quietly talking with first one and then another. As he departed, one cluster engaged in animated conversation about last night's ballgame, he saw his next conversation sitting on a helmet. The only one on the floor, the young soldier seemed a pensive figure sitting alone in a forest of legs.

It did not take the first sergeant long to discover that the man was a maintenance augmentee from another unit, one of a few from his unit deploying, and a stranger to the men around him. The first sergeant changed that quickly, introducing the augmentee to a half-dozen soldiers who would be working with him and to the young NCO who would be his immediate supervisor. Every private needs an NCO, especially in times of uncertainty. It turned out that this young soldier's wife was newly pregnant with their first child, and the couple had never been apart for any appreciable period since they had first married. She lived off post, far from their parents in Minnesota. She had a local job and he was worried that she might need help getting to the places and doing the things she might need to do. To the first sergeant, this was a variation on a familiar theme, and he reassured the private that a robust family-support group existed in the battery and that the spouses would do a great job of looking out for each other while the soldiers were away. Indeed, the battery commander and executive officer were bachelors; the first sergeant's wife had assumed the lead of the family support group herself. The first sergeant gave the private a cellular phone and told him to call his young wife and tell her that his own spouse would be calling in thirty minutes. As he walked away, it was invigorating to hear the confidence and hope in the young man's voice as he began his cellular conversation.

As an air defender the first sergeant deployed often. The pace began to accelerate with the Gulf War, when his Patriot battery had

Embarking for Cuba, *Charles Johnson Post, 1898. For NCOs, "deployment" means a seemingly endless string of tasks to accomplish in a hurry, as NCOs of the V Corps found when they boarded ships for Cuba in 1898.*

deployed to protect Tel Aviv from Iraqi Scuds and keep Israel out of the war. Since that time he had deployed twice to Saudi Arabia to protect that desert kingdom against any residual threat of Iraqi aggression. This did not include frequent exercises to demonstrate the capability to secure the skies above Turkey, Sicily, and South Korea. His brother, a military police platoon sergeant, seemed to be deployed almost as often, having logged tours in Somalia, Haiti, and Bosnia. Surprisingly his sister, a water purification specialist, seemed even more frequently deployed than either of them, if not for as long. She numbered among the first assets required for every hurricane, natural disaster, desert contingency, and failed regime that required U.S. intervention.

Preparation for overseas movement, or POM, has always been the business of NCOs. The enormous detail involved in seeing that each soldier has all the required immunizations, medical checks, dental checks, weapons qualifications, uniform inspections, equipment inventories, personnel actions, legal precautionaries, and counseling sessions represents an enormous undertaking. In addition, all unit vehicles and equipment must be properly serviced, packed, and dispatched and individual and collective training must reach the highest possible standard and then remain there. As the Air Force load masters arrived at the APOD holding area to tell the battery commander and first sergeant that departure was imminent, both men took considerable satisfaction in looking out over a congregation of soldiers as well prepared for the upcoming mission as anyone could reasonably have hoped. Both men knew they had reached that elevated state because each and every noncommissioned officer had done his job.

Background

The first sergeant awaiting overseas movement was representative of America's changed military responsibilities in the 1990s. As the Cold War ended and first the Warsaw Pact and then the Soviet Union itself disintegrated, the world became perhaps less dangerous but certainly more volatile. The threat of a massive global war or even a nuclear exchange with another superpower receded, but involvement in lesser conflicts became ever more likely. Indeed, despite a radically downsized Army, Americans averaged 30,000 soldiers deployed away from home stations into seventy countries at any given time during the 1990s—and found themselves under fire far more often than had been the case between the end of the Vietnam War and the fall of the Berlin Wall.

The shape of things to come became apparent in Panama a number of months before the Berlin Wall came down. The villain was Manuel Noriega, a murderous dictator who had subverted democratic process, hijacked the government, ruled by terror, and enriched himself from the drug trade. He responded to the United States' criticism and countermoves by bullying American citizens in the Canal Zone and ultimately killing an American soldier in an unprovoked shooting. This proved to be the last straw; 13,000 heavily armored soldiers from a half-dozen posts in the United States flew to Panama, joined the 13,000 soldiers and marines already there, and overwhelmed the Panama Defense Force in eight hours of fierce fighting. The American soldiers were generally welcomed as liberators by the population, and quickly set about the tasks of restoring law, order, public utilities, and civil government.

The local unrest, poverty, subversion of legitimate government, criminal organization, and drug involvement that complicated circumstances in Panama illustrated the complexities of the post–Cold War era. The Soviets had maintained order, if not necessarily law, in their far-flung empire. As the Soviet Union collapsed, historic ethnic tensions and local rivalries escalated into armed conflict. This conflict was much abetted by the ready availability of surplus Cold War–vintage arms in international markets. Arms purchases throughout the Third World and newly emerging states ballooned, and nations like Iraq without arms industries were able to equip themselves with formidable panoplies of modern weapons. In much of the Third World, population growth outstripped economic development, adding to unrest, desperation, and violence. Violence joined natural disaster in disrupting food and water supplies and precipitating humanitarian relief crises, sending huge waves of refugees across borders in search of sustenance and security. These refugees themselves became a source of instability when thrust upon nations unprepared to handle them.

The diverse threats of the post–Cold War era rarely could be resolved by straightforward military solutions, and in many cases the military component per se was less consequential than civilian efforts they supported and secured. Humanitarian relief efforts had long involved an international cast of characters spearheaded by such nongovernment organizations (NGOs) as the Red Cross and Doctors without Borders. The increasing globalization of the world economy was accompanied by globalization of organized crime, with international drug cartels leading the way. International terrorists followed suit, carrying their quarrels far beyond the geographical issues that had originally defined them. Particularly pernicious in this regard were extremist Islamic fundamentalist terrorists who chose to define U.S. interests anywhere as hostile to Islamic peoples everywhere.

None of the diverse threats and missions undertaken by the U.S. Army in the 1990s was altogether new, but they had increased in scale both absolutely and relative to the military means available. In the euphoria following the Soviet collapse the United States had radically reduced its armed forces and cut funding for them. Similar reductions among America's European allies were even more severe. Missions easily handled by robust Cold War–vintage defense establishments suddenly became major undertakings given the diminished military resources available. Although easing the weight of defense

Load 'Em Up, *Marshall Williams, 1991. The myriad details and complexities involved in deployment have only increased for the NCO in the century since the Spanish-American War.*

MARSHALL T. WILLIAMS 1991

expenditures upon the citizens of the Free World was wise, governments should have devoted more attention to residual threats, pace, and balance when doing so. Adversaries decided to try their luck against democracies they viewed as weaker, less resolute, and more vulnerable.

After the liberations of Panama and Kuwait, major deployments came so frequently they tended to overlap. In 1991, 11,000 soldiers and marines deployed to Turkey to assist Kurdish refugees and to restore them to their homelands. In 1992, 13,000 American soldiers and marines deployed to Somalia to guarantee the distribution of food to a starving people plagued by warlords and banditry. During their deployment famine decreased and Somali agriculture partially recovered, but the contingent ultimately left the country after ugly factional fighting left eighteen Americans slain by the very people they had come to assist. In 1994, 16,000 soldiers and marines overthrew a dictatorial military junta in Haiti and restored a democratically elected regime. In 1995, 20,000 American soldiers joined 40,000 allied soldiers in enforcing the Dayton accords that ended brutal civil strife in Bosnia. In 1999, 7,500 others advanced into Kosovo to support the eviction of Yugoslav dictator Slobodan Milosevic's forces from a province he was ethnically cleansing of its Albanian majority. In 2001, suicide attacks on the World Trade Center and the Pentagon

led to American intervention in Afghanistan. In addition to these major deployments, a host of lesser ones also occurred, as did the rotation of sizable contingents through such significant undertakings as the air defense of Saudi Arabia, peacekeeping missions in the Sinai and Macedonia, counter narcotics efforts in Columbia and Peru, and confidence-building maneuvers in Korea and Thailand.

The traditional forward basing of large forces in Germany and Korea proved inadequate to support new strategies of expeditionary combat. Bases in the continental United States and even in Europe became platforms from which the United States could launch forces to anywhere in the world. Pre-positioned sets of unit equipment, including a panoply of tanks, armored vehicles, support vehicles, equipment, and supplies of all types, had long existed in or near Germany to facilitate the rapid reinforcement of that country. Now the Army distributed brigade sets to the Mediterranean, Kuwait, Qatar, and Korea and even pre-positioned sets on ships that could move anywhere quickly. The Department of Defense gave considerable attention to increasing the numbers, capacity, and efficiency of modern sealift and airlift capabilities. Particular advances included the dramatically increased use of barcoding and automated information systems to facilitate smooth unit movements, accurate visibility of assets en route, and the delivery of supplies and equipment "just in time" rather than contributing to huge inefficient stockpiles "just in case." Since American forces were both smaller and busier than before, cooperative ventures with allies and friends became ever more important. All of the major American deployments were into multinational settings, and multinational training exercises such as those of Partnership for Peace established relationships that later proved useful when actual operations were under way.

The increasingly expeditionary nature of the U.S. Army and the multinational nature of its operations evolved through the decade. In October 1999 Army Chief of Staff General Eric K. Shinseki called for a radically accelerated pace of adaptation, a "Transformation" that would make the Army heavy forces more mobile and the light forces more survivable and lethal. He also set the standards of having a brigade anywhere in the world in 96 hours, a division in 120 hours, and a corps of five divisions in 30 days. These capabilities, wedded to the latest in technology and doctrine, promised to adapt the Army to the diverse nature and locations of emerging twenty-first-century threats.

NCOs in Action

The new direction taken by the post–Cold War Army necessarily made NCOs even busier. The preparations for and execution of overseas movement put extraordinary demands upon junior leaders. Troops must be inspected, conditioned, equipped, immunized, processed for departure, and trained to high standards in their individual and collective skills. The Army must care for families so their concerns will not become a distraction to soldiers already under duress. Equipment and supplies demand inspection, service, inventory, packing, and shipping. Administrative records of all types—personnel, supply, maintenance, transportation, etc.—must be current and consistently available to the many who need them. All of this has traditionally been NCO business, and it proved no different in an era wherein expeditionary operations assumed overwhelming significance.

Once deployed, NCOs performed all of their traditional combat functions but acquired even more responsibility in the small-unit environment of operations other than war. Many of the routine security, compliance, and reassurance missions took place at the squad level or below, and few circumstances demanded elements larger than a company at a time. This relative autonomy of small units—and thus of NCOs—was particularly significant in multinational settings. Responsibilities for direct coordination with allies and potential adversaries descended to a lower level than had ever been the case before. It was not unusual for small units of Americans to support larger allied or multinational contingents for long periods. Relative casualty rates can illustrate the focus of the lion's share of the action during the full-spectrum force operations of the 1990s. During World War II, Korea, and Vietnam, ground casualties consisted predominately of junior enlisted men, with officers and NCOs experiencing a proportional share. The battle casualties from Somalia, Bosnia, Kosovo, and Afghanistan thus far total forty-one, of whom well over half were NCOs. It seems clear that the immediately visible American leadership was largely noncommissioned.

As modernization progressed the successful fielding of new equipment depended upon the noncommissioned officers who supervised its maintenance and use. During this period, the Army made the most dramatic progress in the field of digitization, both for automating information systems and for increasingly accurate precision-guided munitions of several types. The new equipment thus fielded went to only a few units at a time, particularly when it was in an experimental status. Significant initiatives such as the Louisiana Maneuver (LAM) task force, Task Force XXI, and the Interim Brigade Combat Team involved the relative few rather than the many. Given the rotation of officers into and out of such units, relatively junior NCOs—allied with contractors and industrial representatives—often provided the continuity that allowed the experimentation and fielding to progress on schedule. The role of the NCO as an immediate supervisor of men and equipment alike remained unchanged.

During this period of change, successive Sergeants Major of the Army redoubled their emphasis on NCO education. The hierarchical Noncommissioned Officer Education System (NCOES) that had matured during the 1970s and 1980s became even more instrumental to a soldier's career success, with promotion to the next grade generally denied if relevant courses had not been completed. Given the ever-increasing reliance upon the reserve component, the Army made every effort to assure that all NCOs were trained to the same standard regardless of component. Civilian education received increasing emphasis as well, with steps taken in reenlistment packages, distance learning, and other initiatives to give each NCO the opportunity to improve his or her education. As the Army increased in operational tempo and technical sophistication, the noncommissioned officers who led it kept pace.

101st Airborne Division Troops Deployed to Afghanistan, 2003

War Against Terror
in the
Mountains

Afghanistan, 2002

———◆———

The platoon sergeant surveyed his soldiers as they walked down the ramp of the CH–47 helicopter. After days of trudging up and down the ridges of Shahi Kowt (Shah-e-Kot) fighting the Taliban and al Qaeda, his soldiers were now relaxed after days of pumping adrenaline, and he listened to stories of home and what they were going to do first.

They were light infantrymen who took pride in their craft, their buddies, and their organization. There was nothing flashy or fancy about them. They were like every other doughboy, dogface, grunt, or crunchy who fought with his boots on the ground. Today they were bearded, dirty, and tired, but their weapons gleamed. As infantrymen, they lived under the stars and got wet when it rained, shivered when it was cold, were excited when moving to contact, exhausted when moving to daylight, and scared when shot at. The radios and night-vision devices were much better than when the platoon sergeant had entered service, and everyone wore the latest in body armor. Each man carried more weight than recommended in FM 7–8, the infantry platoon manual, but that was normal, as a light fighter had no vehicles and carried everything necessary on his back. In the dark, everyone looked like a rucksack with legs.

The platoon sergeant had been a light infantryman since 1987, when he had enlisted as part of a cohort battalion at Fort Drum. Now, fourteen years and several assignments later, he had deployed again, this time with his soldiers to Afghanistan. He had been away from home a lot, with deployments to the Sinai, Haiti, Somalia, and twice to Bosnia; although he had been shot at before, Shah-e-Kot was the first time he and his soldiers had experienced combat.

His soldiers had trained well and hard. Since 11 September 2001, when his platoon was on a rifle range and the word came over the radio to check if any soldiers had relatives working at the World Trade Center or the Pentagon, they had been preparing for combat. Although everyone said this was a new kind of war, at the squad and platoon level, it was much the same as any other.

Yorktown, 14 October 1781, H. Charles McBarron, c. 1976. More than most units, light infantry demands courage and initiative from its NCOs, as exemplified by those who led the storming party that breached the British defensive line at Yorktown.

After the attacks, his division responded to the nation's call with some battalions immediately departing overseas to fight terrorism, while others, including his, prepared for combat through combat drills and combined live-fire exercises. Although he did not know the timing, the platoon sergeant knew they would deploy, and he worked hard to ensure that his soldiers and subordinate leaders were properly trained in their individual tasks, while the platoon leader concentrated on the platoon's collective tasks. No one had any regrets about deploying: they wanted to avenge the terror attacks against the United States.

He remembered when they left the United States the charter aircraft's circling the devastation of Ground Zero and the quietness of the soldiers within the cabin. Like him, they were lost in thought over why they were going to fight.

They began their six months' deployment guarding an air base. The platoon sergeant and other leaders continually stressed that although they must observe strict rules of engagement while guarding the perimeter, no one should lose sight of the reason they were there and of the basic light infantry mission—to close with and destroy the enemy. Every day might entail boarding an aircraft or helicopter to go into a fight. Many times they received on-order missions and the soldiers would prepare, go through rehearsals and inspections and then stand down. These ups and downs wore constantly on each man's psyche, and it was hard to keep focused. Even though they were far from any headquarters, the battalion commander continued to stress that leaders not compromise standards and not walk by something wrong without correcting it.

At the end of February his company and another, along with the battalion headquarters company, boarded Air Force C–130s for the flight to Bagram Airfield, Afghanistan, for high-altitude acclimatization. There, they road-marched with heavy loads and conducted more marksmanship, live-fire battle drills, and combat lifesaving. They trained for the worst possible scenario. Because of that hard training, the soldiers knew what to do when clearing caves. They were used to throwing grenades and firing live rounds.

The platoon sergeant submitted the daily status report and ensured that his soldiers were fed and kept their equipment serviceable. When the packing list for the upcoming operation arrived, he directed all the soldiers to repack their rucks, and then he and his squad leaders inspected each. It felt like he had done this a million times, both as a private laying his gear out and as an NCO inspecting it. The rucksacks were loaded with ammunition, batteries, night vision and communications gear for the operation itself, water and food, as well as "hawk" gear consisting of Gortex, fleece liners, and polypropylene underwear to keep warm when the "big heat tab in the sky" went down. Early in his career, the platoon sergeant had carried inoperable communications and night-vision equipment because the batteries had a shorter life span in the cold; this time he made sure his men had enough spares.

When they boarded the CH–47 for the flight into combat, the platoon sergeant checked each man's name against the manifest as they quietly filed by, each lost in his own thoughts and mortality. So many things could happen in combat: being killed or wounded or seeing one's comrades die. Everyone had vowed they would stick together and allow no one to be captured.

Inside the helicopter, everyone sat on their stuffed rucksacks like turtles on rocks. The smell of aviation gasoline and transmission fluid hung in the air, and red fluid dripped from fittings. During the long flight soldiers dozed to the drone of the engines, heads bouncing against their chest, back against the cabin wall, or leaning on another soldier's shoulder. The helicopters skimmed the desert floor until they entered the mountains, where they began gaining altitude to traverse between the high peaks. Five minutes from the landing zone, the signal came to get ready and soldiers passed back the word by yelling and splaying their fingers wide. Soldiers shuffled and arranged their

Light infantry troops scan the ridgeline during Operation ANACONDA, March 2002. In Afghanistan, light infantry has shown its ability to operate in some of the world's most forbidding terrain and most severe weather conditions.

equipment. The platoon sergeant made his final check, received the thumbs-up from his squad leaders, and passed it on to his platoon leader. He could see the stress on the faces around him and hoped that his own did not reveal his thoughts before landing. The nose of the CH–47 rose abruptly and the crew chief yelled "One minute!" A load whine and shock on landing, the ramp drop, and soldiers spilled into the whirlwind of gravel and dust kicked up by the rotors.

They landed in what appeared an onion patch high up on one of the ridgelines, so they would not have to fight as far uphill. The soldiers moved into traveling overwatch formation for their move to the blocking positions they were to secure and began their ascent. The rough terrain was more an obstacle than the elevation, although breathing was a task. They were above 9,000 feet and it was a real effort to hump the rucksack or even just to move around at that altitude. The sergeant's lungs burned and he saw that everyone was breathless with any exertion. Everybody did his job, and nobody quit. Although they had been warned to expect altitude sickness, none occurred in the sergeant's company, nor did anyone suffer from cold-weather injuries. The junior NCOs kept watching their soldiers and telling them that "altitude is the enemy, so's the weather."

The platoon sergeant observed small stacks of rocks, which intel had told them were predetermined al Qaeda aiming points for mortars. Looking down, he could see the ragged shale cliffs that ringed the valley below and the deep shadows that hid the many crevices and caves their commander had told them about.

The platoon sergeant controlled the two M240 machine guns assigned the platoon. When the enemy bullets and mortar rounds began impacting in their vicinity, the soldiers dropped rucks and executed Battle Drill 2, React to Ambush. While the platoon sergeant directed the fires of the machine guns and one squad against the target, the platoon leader and other squads maneuvered forward. No one hesitated in moving up to the high ground. Later, many wished they had the "hawk" gear they had left behind.

One day turned into the next, and soon they all seemed to merge. When the platoon located enemy positions they called in "fast movers," gunships, and attack helicopters to suppress and hopefully destroy the tunnel. The infantry maneuvered forward to attack. Just as in clearing a bunker or trench line, the platoon sergeant focused the fires of the support element on the tunnel opening, driving any enemy deeper into the hole, until the clearing team was near enough to toss in a grenade and, once it exploded, to rush inside. Throughout the operation, the platoon sergeant kept daily accountability; arranged for Medevac of wounded soldiers; kept his men resupplied with ammunition, water, and rations; and then ensured that everyone ate. On the tenth day he and the other members of his platoon boarded helicopters for the return flight to their initial staging area. As the platoon sergeant watched his soldiers move toward their tents at Bagram Airfield, he knew they had accomplished their mission.

War is never easy at the individual level. Although heavily supported by precision munitions, it will always take infantrymen moving forward under fire to clear rough terrain and caves of the enemy, and Operation ANACONDA was no exception. Infantrymen, in a bloody and close-in battle inching up rocky mountainsides, shivering in the cold, blasting the enemy one-by-one out of caves and rock piles, achieved what others could not, victory over a tenacious foe long used to fighting in this terrain and climate.

Background

The war on terror began in earnest on 11 September 2001, when commercial aircraft plowed into the twin towers of the World Trade Center and the Pentagon. Within days, soldiers from every branch were deploying overseas to hunt down and destroy those who had attacked or harbored plans to attack the United States or its allies.

This was a different kind of war, a world war, where deployments took soldiers from the United States to the mountains of Afghanistan, the desert of Saudi Arabia, the jungles of the Philippines, Bosnia, Kosovo, and any other locations to which terrorist bases had relocated. Battles could range from the sands of the Iraqi desert, where Abrams tanks and Bradley fighting vehicles reign supreme, to the 10,000-foot peaks of Afghanistan, where foot-slogging infantry is king and no terrain impassible in the search for a hard-to-pin-down terrorist foe. It was to the light infantry that the main fight against terrorism would fall.

Throughout U.S. history, light infantry forces have exhibited self-reliance and independence of action. In August 1777 General George Washington formed selected soldiers from each of his brigades into the Corps of Light Infantry. Specially trained in the use of the bayonet, it was with this elite formation that Brig. Gen. Anthony Wayne conducted the successful night attack against Stony Point in 1779. In July 1781 the Corps spearheaded the chief American assaults against the British works at Yorktown.

Later, during World War II, ranger, parachute, and glider infantry carried on the light infantry tradition. Although light divisions also appeared during World War II, none but the 10th Mountain Division saw combat as such. All these units emphasized physical fitness, expert weapons proficiency, and hard strenuous training that stressed self-reliance and development of junior leaders. With the advent of the Cold War, light units lost favor with those heavier organizations better able to fight against Soviet armored formations.

Only in the 1980s, after the successful British campaign in the Falkland Islands, Israeli operations in Lebanon, and U.S. operations in Grenada, did light forces demonstrate utility in "little" wars and under certain circumstances, in higher-intensity conflicts. General John Wickham stressed both the strategic value and the battlefield utility of these "highly deployable, hard hitting combat units" capable of demonstrating the United States' "resolve and capability," particularly in responding to low- to mid-intensity conflict threats and where a U.S. presence might well "prevent the outbreak of war." Early doctrine for light infantry units emphasized the need for rapid deployment: light infantry divisions would quickly deploy by air into operational areas using no more than five hundred C–141 sorties or their equivalents.

As part of the Army buildup of the 1980s, the Army activated three divisions (the 6th, 7th, 10th), and reorganized two others (the 25th and the National Guard 29th) as light divisions. Battalions were austere, with only a few vehicles in the headquarters company mortar, antitank, and support platoons. The three rifle companies contained no vehicles, and their weapons had to be light enough for soldiers to carry them over long distances.

However, the seismic changes occurred not in organization or equipment, but in mindset. The spirit and philosophy of the light infantry ethic comes through tough, demanding training that develops small-unit leaders who are capable of taking independent action within the overall framework of the commander's intent. Here, with the emphasis on the platoon and squad, good-quality training means the difference between life and death and self-reliance becomes second nature.

Comfort and luxury in the field are unknown, and soldiers learn to do without the usual amenities: hot rations, a chance to dig into duffle bags for clean and dry clothes, or rides to rifle ranges. Rain and cold adds to the misery, as rucksacks can only carry so much, with priority going to ammunition and other squad or platoon gear. Light infantrymen and their leaders learn self-reliance by doing without and challenging the limits that they think they can endure, then going beyond, with much of the training conducted by platoon- and squad-level NCOs. Soldiers develop initiative through live-fire exercises at squad and platoon level, patrolling, infiltration, and other small-unit tactical exercises day and night, as well as constant rehearsal of battle-drills to "what ifs." Darkness is the light infantryman's friend, and soldiers learn to operate at night as if it were daylight, using the darkness to both maneuver and fight. Marksmanship is vital, because every round fired is a round carried by the soldier and, not knowing when the next resupply will arrive, he husbands his ammunition. This austere, demanding training ultimately produces high self-confidence, trust, and cohesion within the units. Leadership by example and mutual trust derived from shared experiences of danger and deprivation characterizes light infantry.

Light infantry units have no room for those unfit. A soldier dropping by the wayside on a road march is just as much a casualty as one who is wounded in combat. Long marches with heavy rucksacks are commonplace, as are exercises involving high-risk live-fires. Long,

The portion of the Pentagon that was hit by a hijacked airplane on September 11 was illuminated by artificial light as round-the-clock recovery efforts continued, 2001.

sleepless days in the field develop endurance, with the ultimate goal of soldiers with a dogged, wiry endurance able to persevere regardless of their circumstances. Light infantry soldiers often find that combat conditions are actually less severe than the conditions they experienced in training.

During the late 1980s and 1990s, light forces—to include elements of the 7th, 10th, and 29th Light Infantry and the 82d and 101st Airborne Divisions (the latter airmobile) and 75th Ranger Regiment—have participated in numerous missions. They have participated in combat in Panama, Kuwait, and now in Afghanistan. They have also served as peacekeepers and peace-enforcers in Haiti, Somalia, Bosnia-Herzegovina, and Kosovo. This ability to perform different missions demonstrates the utility of light forces, especially considering the type of enemy they will now fight. It underscores the importance of boots on the ground and the limits of sterile missile strikes from above.

NCOs in Action

With the ongoing combat operations in Afghanistan, soldiers are performing in conditions once considered the operational environment and realm of well-trained special operations forces. The United States has never fought at such high altitudes where physical conditions are as unforgiving as the human foe and where the enemy is on familiar ground, fighting at a distinct advantage due to weather, terrain, and elevation.

That U.S. conventional light forces are able to operate in such terrain is a tribute to their leadership and training. Mountain terrain is harsh, movement slow, and hazards to health and physical well being ongoing. Conducting combat and maneuver at high altitudes is mentally and physically taxing, and small-unit leadership is of particular importance. The harsh living conditions, ongoing physical deterioration, and psychological depression inherent in mountain combat requires leaders, although suffering the same effects as their soldiers, to be vigilant in ensuring their soldiers not skip meals, drink potable water to prevent dehydration, perform basic hygiene, and check for cold-weather and high-altitude sickness. The Indian and Pakistani armies are probably the most experienced at fighting at high altitudes over long periods, yet almost 80 percent of their casualties there resulted from cold or high-altitude injuries. Analysts told the U.S. ground-force commander during ANACONDA to expect 40 percent casualties from altitude sickness alone; however, there were fewer than ten casualties, and cold-weather casualties were negligible even with his soldiers' carrying a minimum of warm-weather gear. It was all about soldier training and discipline.

Combat is primarily at small-unit level, where squads root from cave to cave and the difference in success and failure is what individuals and teams learned through hard training. Basic marksmanship skills and M4 rifles allowed soldiers to consistently hit targets at distances greater than 300 meters, and the rigorous physical training programs enabled soldiers to carry their heavy rucksacks up steep slopes in the thin mountain air. It proves that emphasizing basic soldier skills, with specialty skills added as missions require, serves the Army well in any situation.

Exceptional units stand out simply because their training allows them to do ordinary things well, resulting in self-confident and self-reliant soldiers who believe in their leaders and trust the soldiers they serve alongside. The cornerstone of this success revolves around discipline and adherence to standards. Both are an NCO's basic responsibility.

NCOs today do what they have always done, that is, take care of soldiers. They check and inspect packing lists and the myriad other details that go into preexecution operations. They talk with soldiers, listening to their concerns and passing on the good and the bad, in combat leading them ably and well. Confident in their leaders, soldiers then take care of their comrades on their right and left and accomplish the mission.

All these things found successful during Operation ANACONDA—physical conditioning, marksmanship, and cold-weather-injury prevention—are NCO business. NCOs looked out for their soldiers and enforced standards and discipline, this at a time when they were just as tired and disoriented by the conditions as everyone else. They did not let soldiers die from something that could have been prevented.

The discipline and mastery of an era's battle drills have served the Army well during this nation's previous wars: whether going in with the bayonet at Yorktown, remaining in ranks while facing British cannons at Chippewa, leaving perfectly good cover to perform an oblique march so they might pour fire into Confederate forces charging the copse of trees at Gettysburg, executing battle drills to take out a bunker under heavy fire at Normandy, reacting to an ambush in Vietnam, or clearing a wire obstacle at night during DESERT STORM. The tradition of a firm grounding in the basics continued and contributed markedly to the Army's success in Operation ANACONDA in the mountains of Afghanistan.

An NCO's focus, most especially at platoon and squad levels, is on the training that keeps his or her soldiers alive in combat. Fundamental training with the basic building blocks applicable to all soldiers (weapons, physical training, first aid, and chemical) as well as those necessary for their duty position go far in that regard. Combat wears soldiers down; after a short period of rest, training resumes with the added lessons learned in combat.

Nothing is more important than a solid foundation in leader and individual tasks. They are the foundation upon which successful operations rest. NCOs ensure soldiers meet standards for the individual tasks that contribute to mission success. Officers rely on NCOs to put the training intent into tangible individual and leader tasks that build the collective tasks to support mission accomplishment. When missions fail, it is often because leader and individual tasks are not properly accomplished.

Combat proves the rule. In the mountains of Shah-e-Kot, two soldiers lay exposed for hours manning their machine gun, keeping Taliban soldiers away from a mortar positioned to rain fire on their comrades. They did not want to let their comrades down. In another place, at another time, a reporter covering the air-assault landing into Haiti watched soldiers jump out of their helicopters, run ten paces, and then flop down into prone positions behind their rucksacks. He went to one young soldier lying on the hot tarmac, his rifle pointed around the right side of his rucksack, and asked the young soldier why he was doing this when no one was firing at him. The soldier replied, "That's what my sergeant taught me to do."

Noncommissioned officers at the cutting edge of combat live by the adage "Deeds not Words" in leading their soldiers from the front. Of the eleven leaders in an infantry platoon, ten are NCOs ranging in grade from sergeant team-leaders to a sergeant first class platoon sergeant. They deal daily with soldiers and each other; they represent tens of years of experience with numerous assignments and deployments under their belts. By personal example, they play a key role in affecting their soldiers' values and behavior so that when the test of combat comes, all are determined to see the mission through to completion. The words "We don't do that in this organization" go far in establishing a unit's "command climate."

Each enlisted leadership position has specific duties, as well as practicing the professional Army ethic; enforcing Army standards on appearance and conduct; supervising maintenance of equipment, living areas, and work places; and instilling discipline and esprit de corps within the organization. Also important are the intangibles of knowing each of their soldiers, not only whether they can perform the prescribed individual and collective tasks, but also whether they embody Army Values. NCOs know the difference between errors of omission, such as not knowing how to do something, and errors of commission, such as submitting a doctored report or lying to protect oneself. One receives little notice outside of additional training and the other results in immediate punishment.

Current trends suggest that the exercise of independent leadership will become increasingly important to noncommissioned officers who lead soldiers in combat. As our Army fights the war on terror and becomes more involved in operations other than war, the "battlefield" becomes defined in new ways, and many decisions will be made by soldiers operating in environments away from their superiors. Training junior leaders to take the appropriate action on their own initiative in support of the commander's intent will always be an important part of the senior NCO's duties.

Seen through a night-vision device, a soldier takes up a defensive posture after being engaged by the enemy in the Sadamia area of Baghdad, Iraq, July 2004.

THE FUTURE

After thirty years, it was over and the sergeant major was standing his last parade, this time as an honoree. How things had changed in what now seemed such a short period! He had experienced service in a draftee army withdrawing from Vietnam, the growing pains of the modern Volunteer Army, and the joy of serving in a professional army for his remaining years of service. Most of the uniforms and equipment of the seventies were long gone—the fatigues replaced by BDUs, the WWII-style "steel pot" by first a Kevlar helmet and now the new Land Warrior assault headgear that looked a bit like that worn by a bicyclist. The venerable M60 machine gun had been replaced by the M240B machine gun and the M16 by the M4 rifle. Moreover, where once only the platoon leader had a radio, today radios were standard equipment for squads and teams, and plans for the future envisioned digitally linked soldiers.

What he had found more important than equipment and organizational changes were the changes that had occurred within the Noncommissioned Officer Corps. During the early seventies, while he was on detail in the orderly room, he had listened to his first sergeant tell stories of army life during the fifties. "Top" administered the "beans and bullets," while the "field first" took care of the company in the field. It was not like that now, nor could it be in the future.

He knew that soldiers today and in the future would expect much from their leaders, and the leaders would have to earn their respect through performance, confidence, trust, and closeness between leader and led. The Army would need NCOs who were innovative, imaginative, flexible and tough minded and who had a sincere concern for their soldiers without pandering. Today, when their companies were in the field, the first sergeants were there also, attending to beans and bullets and assisting the company's platoons in their individual and small-unit training. In 1993, AR 350–41, *Training in Units*, was changed to reflect that: "Battalion-level and company-level commanders will assign primary responsibility for collective training to officers, and primary responsibility for soldier training to NCOs. NCOs will also train most sections, squads, teams and crews." Now accountable for individual training, these NCOs of fifteen to twenty-five years of service and the beneficiaries of the Army's Noncommissioned Officer Education System were easily the equivalent of the guild masters of the Renaissance, responsible for training and upholding the standards of the profession.

The sergeant major had realized early on that for units to progress past platoon training with a "Trained" rating, tasks had to be separated. When assigning him responsibility for a gunnery range, one of his old bosses had once told him that the unit would never get to Tank Table XII if officers became too involved in Table VIII. Now with the Objective Force on the horizon, delineation of tasks was even more important.

Although the sergeant major felt the Army was on the right track for the future, possessing superior leadership and the most highly skilled soldiers in the world, he knew more would be expected in the future. Training leaders was and always would be the most important task for the Army, whether in peacetime or war, and the Army's values-based leadership was the foundation upon which all else stood.

He realized that the Objective Army lay far in the future, and that the privates today would be senior sergeants when it became reality. He expected that within units of the Objective Force, NCOs would typically have wide latitude and more responsibility because of dispersed operations. He recognized that the "new" NCO would have to be self-aware and adaptable, comfortable with ambiguity and change, even more so than in the present. He knew that this would require a coherent approach to developing leaders through a mix of institutional training, unit-level training, Combat Training Center (CTC) rotations, operational experiences in both small and large units, education, and a process for self-development and mentoring.

Although the sergeant major loved the light infantry and everything associated with it, he knew there were drawbacks. During the early 1990s its motto was "Too light to fight, too heavy to run," and during the early days of DESERT SHIELD, members of the 82d Airborne Division referred to themselves as "speed bumps in the sand." He had watched soldiers riding in the backs of open Humvees conduct the initial operations in Kosovo, protected by little more than their Kevlar vests.

The fundamental objective of the Army ground combat mission had not changed during his service, and with what he had read about the Objective Force, it would not change in the future. Even with new technology, all Objective Force operations ultimately focused on tactical success in close combat, with one purpose—to close with and destroy the enemy.

Although organized as battalions, companies, platoons, and squads, the new Army, in the sergeant major's opinion, would face a tremendous difference in application. His study of the Objective Force operations reminded him a bit of the science fiction book, *Tactics of Mistake* written by Gordon Dickson, about small tactical groups that were modular in structure and designed for agile, decentralized operations. From the crew or squad-like fighting unit through the platoon to an expanded number of all-arms maneuver formations, the Objective Force "teams of teams" approach depended upon each grouping to focus on a specific set of tactical tasks, with each element easily plugging into any Objective Force organization. The future appeared challenging, and the sergeant major wished that he could begin again as a private as the Army modernized toward the Objective Force of the 2020s.

LEADERSHIP

Storming of a British Redoubt,
Eugene Lami, c. 1840

The Skirmish Line (Union Soldiers at Cold Harbor), *Gilbert Gaul, c. 1890*

Above: *Members of the 45th Infantry Division on Board a Troopship Bound for the Mediterranean Theater of Operations, 1943.* Right: A First-Class Fighting Man, *Frederic Remington, 1899.*

Full Study of Corporal, 15th New York Infantry, *Raymond Desvarraux, 1918*

An Antiaircraft Artillery Position along the Siegfried Line, December 1944

A squad deploys from an M113 armored personnel carrier north of Saigon, October 1965.

ers return to Fire Support Base JAMIE, Vietnam, September

An Army Recruiting and Retention School instructor demonstrates the counseling skills that will be needed during the course of an NCO's career, 2001.

Trainees under the Watchful Eye of Their Drill Sergeant

Above: *A drill sergeant gives his troops a sign of encouragement during basic combat training, Fort Leonard Wood, Missouri, 2002.* Right: *A medic out of Camp Comanche with Task Force* PEGASUS *2d Battalion, 224th Aviation, completes the twelve-mile road march, the last event of the Combat Med Challenge at* EAGLE *Base, Bosnia.*

TRAINING

Above: The First Muster, Salem, Massachusetts, 1637, *Don Troiani, 1985*

Right: *Soldiers of the 10th U.S. Cavalry conduct bayonet drills, Fort Huachuca, Arizona, c. 1920.*

A drill sergeant gives hands-on weapons instruction during basic training, Fort Benning, Georgia, 1998.

Ranger training involves practice in hand-to-hand combat.

A soldier participates in airborne training at "The Tower," Fort Benning, c. 1985.

Steuben at Valley Forge, *Edwin Austin Abbey*

Give me ten!

A 24th Infantry Division tank crew trains at Grafenwöhr, Germany, c. 1964.

Scaling the Wall with a Little Help, *Sieger Hartgers, 1991*

TECHNICAL

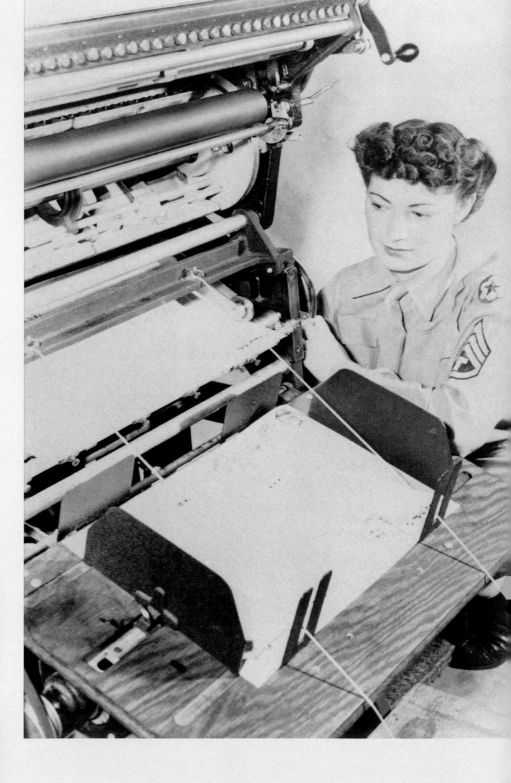

A Women's Army Corps NCO operates a small printing press during World War II.

NCOs slice tissue samples for study by a pathologist at Dewitt Army Community Hospital, Fort Belvoir, Virginia, 2002.

A medic stows equipment before his aircraft leaves for a training mission, 2002.

A Civil War Regimental Aid Station Sketched in Action for Harper's *magazine.*

U.S. Army Signal Corps Radio Tractor and its Crew, 1915. Below: Soldiers from Fort Lewis, Washington, refit their Stryker Infantry Carrier Vehicle after rolling off a C–130 aircraft at Bicycle Lake Army Airfield, Fort Irwin, California, 2002.

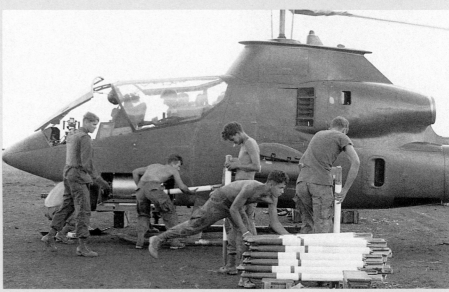

Left: A microwave repair specialist stationed in central Europe works on a radio designed to NATO-wide specifications, 2001. Above: Troops Rearming an AH–1G Cobra at Mai Loc, Vietnam, 1969.

STANDARDS

Basic trainees and their drill sergeant march to the mess hall, Fort Riley, Kansas, 1966.

A First Lesson in the Art of War,
Frederic Remington, 1898

Troops of the 9th Cavalry stand at attention by their pup tents, Fort Riley, 1941.

A drill sergeant teaches recruits how to fold the national colors.

Sentinels from the Old Guard keep 24-hour watch at the Tomb of the Unknowns, Arlington National Cemetery, c. 1989.

Three Breaks to the Ground, Ready, Go!, *Carl E. "Gene" Snyder, 1996*

An NCO surveys the edible creations on display at the 27th Annual U.S. Army Culinary Arts Competition, Fort Lee, Virginia, 2002.

An Old Guard drum major leads the fife and drum corps through a rehearsal, 2001.

A staff sergeant guides an enlisted forklift operator, Afghanistan, 2002.

DEPLOYMENT

A soldier of 69th Regiment, New York National Guard, leaves his family behind for service in World War I, 1917.

A corporal bids his family goodbye as he departs for Korea, 1950.

A mother weeps as her husband departs for Southwest Asia during Operation DESERT STORM, 1990.

ve: Joyful soldiers aboard a train going home. Right: The 17th
try traveled by rail to the front during the Spanish-American War.

Troops of the 82d Airborne Division start to board a C–5B for the long flight to Saudi Arabia, 1990.

Unloading HMMWVs from a C–130 in Sarajevo, Bosnia-Herzegovina, during Operation JOINT ENDEAVOR, 1995

Soldiers load a cannon for transport to Cuba during the Spanish-American War.

An HMMWV of the 10th Mountain Division drives onto the tarma Mogadishu, Somalia.

Soldiers of the 10th Mountain Division prepare to board aircraft in Haiti, 1994.

Happy veterans prepare for their return home from France at end of World War II, 1945.

Family and friends greet members of the 82d Airborne Division upon their return from Operation DESERT STORM, 1991.

Part Three

Selected Documents

"The sardgente…must read and write, be well trained in martiall matters, yea and of soe great importance that more tolerable it were that all the other officers of the company and the captaine himself to be rawe men and of little experience, but the Sardgente not soe."

—*A Discourse of Militaire Discipline, 1634*

Selected Documents

As suggested by the author of this 1634 treatise on the organization of an effective military force, the noncommissioned officer has always shared leadership responsibilities with his commissioned superiors. In fact, for more than two hundred years NCOs have served as leaders in the U.S. Army, not only in the barracks and on the parade ground but, most importantly, in the face of the enemy. In both peace and war they are the key to unit morale and esprit de corps and the mainstay of discipline and efficiency.

Although obvious to us today, the role of the NCO was not always clearly defined. Only in recent years has the Army become concerned with the professionalism of its noncommissioned officers and set service-wide standards for their training. This growing recognition of the role and status of the NCO has been reflected in official documents and publications, as in the extracts that follow.

It should be noted that, beyond minor deletions, as indicated, because of space limitations, these documents appear without any historical editing on our part.

Responsibilities

Throughout its history, the Army has entrusted those who wore stripes with duties and responsibilities that required leadership skills and technical proficiency. These duties and responsibilities have appeared in official documents ranging from Steuben's Blue Book *to* Army Regulation (AR) 600–20. *It is clear from these documents that advances in technology and the resulting changes in tactics have made the duties of noncommissioned officers more complex, but their fundamental responsibilities have remained the same.*

Extract from Frederick von Steuben, *Regulations for the Order and Discipline of the Troops of the United States, Part I,* **1789.**

Instructions for the Serjeant Major

The Serjeant major, being at the head of the non-commissioned officers, must pay the greatest attention to their conduct and behaviour, never conniving at the least irregularity committed by them or the soldiers, from both of whom he must exact the most implicit obedience. He should be well acquainted with the interior management and discipline of the regiment, and the manner of keeping rosters and forming details. He must always attend the parade, be very expert in counting off the battalion, and in every other business of the adjutant, to whom he is an assistant.

Instructions for the Quarter-Master Serjeant

He is an assistant to the quarter-master of the regiment, and in his absence is to do his duty, unless an officer be specially appointed for that purpose. He should therefore acquaint himself with all the duties of the quarter-master before mentioned. When the army marches, he must see the tents properly packed and loaded, and go with the baggage, see that the waggoners commit no disorders, and that nothing is lost out of the waggons.

Instructions for the First Serjeant of a Company

The soldier having acquired that degree of confidence of his officers as to be appointed first serjeant of the company, should consider the importance of his office; that the discipline of the company, the conduct of the men, their exactness in obeying orders, and the regularity of their manners, will in a great measure depend on his vigilance.

He should be intimately acquainted with the character of every soldier of the company, and should take great pains to impress upon their minds the indispensable necessity of the strictest obedience, as the foundation of order and regularity.

He will keep the details of the company, and never warn a man out of his turn, unless particularly ordered so to do.

He must take the daily orders in a book kept by him for that purpose, and shew them to his officers.

He must every morning make a report to the captain of the state of the company, in the form prescribed; and at the same time acquaint him with any thing material that may have happened in the company since the preceding report.

He must parade all guards and detachments furnished by his company, examine their arms, ammunition, accoutrements and dress, before he carries them to the parade; and if any man appears unfit, he must supply his place with another, and have the defaulter punished: For this purpose he must always warn a man or two more than ordered, to serve as a reserve, who, if not wanted, will return to their companies.

He will keep the company book (under the inspection of the captain) in which he will enter the name and description of every non-commissioned officer and soldier; his trade and occupation; the place of his birth and usual residence where, when and for what term he was inlisted; the bounty paid him; the arms, ammunition, accoutrements, clothing and necessaries delivered him, with their marks and numbers, and the times when delivered; also copies of all returns, furloughs, discharges, and every casualty that happens in the company.

When each soldier shall be provided with a small book, the first serjeant is to enter therein the soldier's name, a copy of his inlistment, the bounty paid him, the arms, accoutrements, clothing, and necessaries delivered him, with their marks and numbers. For this purpose he must be present at all distributions in his company and as often as arms, clothing, etc. are delivered, he must enter them in the soldier's as well as the company's book.

The first serjeant is not to go on any duty, unless with the whole company, but is to be always in camp or quarters, to answer any call that may be made.

He is never to lead a platoon or section, but is always to be a file-closer in the formation of the company, his duty being in the company like the adjutant's in the regiment.

Instructions for the Serjeants and Corporals

It being on the non-commissioned officers that the discipline and order of a company in a great measure depend, they cannot be too circumspect in their behaviour towards the men, by treating them with mildness, and at the same time obliging every one to do his duty. By avoiding too great familiarity with the men, they will not only gain their love and confidence, but be treated with a proper respect whereas by a contrary conduct they forfeit all regard, and their authority becomes despised.

Each serjeant and corporal will be in a particular manner answerable for the squad committed to his care. He must pay particular attention to their conduct in every respect; that they keep themselves and their arms always clean; that they have their effects always ready, and put where they can get them immediately, even in the dark, without confusion; and on every fine day he must oblige them to air their effects.

When a man of his squad is warned for duty, he must examine him before he carries him to the parade, obliging him to take all his effects with him unless when specially ordered to the contrary. In teaching the recruits, they must exercise all their patience, by no means abusing them, but treating them with mildness, and not expect too much precision in the first lessons, punishing those only who are wilfully negligent.

They must suppress all quarrels and disputes in the company; and where other means fail, must use their authority in confining the offender.

They should teach the soldiers of their squads how to dress with a soldier-like air, how to clean their arms, accoutrements, etc. and how to mount and dismount their firelocks; for which purpose each non-commissioned officer should always be provided with a turnscrew, and suffer no soldier to take his arms to pieces without his permission.

On a march the non-commissioned officers must preserve order and regularity, and suffer no man to leave the ranks without permission of the officer commanding the platoon. A corporal must teach the sentinels to challenge briskly, and every thing else they are to do in their different situation; and when he relieves them, must make them deliver the orders distinctly.

When a guard is relieved, the non-commissioned officers take the orders from those whom they relieve; when sent to visit the sentries, they should instruct them in their duty. They should reconnoitre the roads they are to patrol in the night, that they may not lose themselves. They must make their patrol with the greatest silence and attention, and where necessary, send a faithful soldier a-head to look out. If they meet a detachment of the enemy stronger than their own, they must retreat in order to their own post. In the night they must stop all strangers that approach. They must not suffer their men to make the least noise with their arms or accoutrements, and every now and then stop and listen. On their return from patrolling, they must report to the officer what they have seen or heard.

When a non-commissioned officer is a file-closer, he must take care to keep the ranks and files properly closed, and when too much crowded, make them incline from the centre. When the files of his platoon are disordered by the loss of men, he must exert himself to dress and complete them afresh, with the utmost expedition. He must keep the greatest silence in the ranks, see that the men load well and quick, and take good aim. He will do all in his power to encourage the soldiers, and use the most vigorous means to prevent any from leaving the ranks, unless wounded.

Extract from An Act Establishing Rules and Articles for the Government of the Armies of the United States; with the Regulations of the War Department, 1812.

Art. 2. It is earnestly recommended to all officers and soldiers diligently to attend divine service; and all officers who shall behave indecently, or irreverently at any place of divine worship, shall,...if noncommissioned officers or soldiers [so behave], every person so offending shall, for his first offence, forfeit *one sixth of a dollar*, to be deducted out of his next pay; for the second offence, he shall not only forfeit a like sum, but be confined twenty-four hours; and for every like offence shall suffer and pay in like manner; which money, so forfeited, shall be applied by the captain or senior officer of the troop or company, to the use of the sick soldiers of the company or troops to which the offender belongs.

Art. 3. Any non-commissioned officer or soldier who shall use any profane oath or execration shall incur the penalties expressed in the foregoing article....

Art. 5. Any officer or soldier who shall use contemptuous or disrespectful words against the President of the United States, against the Vice-President thereof, against the Congress of the United States, or against the chief magistrate or legislature of any of the United States in which he may be quartered,...if a non-commissioned officer or soldier, he shall suffer such punishment as shall be inflicted on him by the sentence of a court martial....

Art. 8. Any officer, non-commissioned officer, or soldier, who, being present at any mutiny or sedition, does not use his utmost endeavor to suppress the same, or coming to the knowledge of any intended mutiny, does not without delay, give information thereof to his commanding officer, shall be punished by the sentence of a court martial with death or otherwise, according to the nature of his offence....

Art. 10. Every non-commissioned officer, or soldier, who shall enlist himself in the service of the United States, shall, at the time of his so enlisting, or within six days afterwards, have the articles for the government of the armies of the United States, read to him, and shall, by the officer who enlisted him, or by the commanding officer of the troop or company into which he was enlisted, be taken before the next justice of the peace, or chief magistrate of any city or, town corporate, not being an officer of the army, or where recourse cannot be had to the civil magistrate, before the judge advocate, and in his presence, shall take the following oath or affirmation: "I, A.B. do solemnly swear or affirm, (as the case may be) that I will bear true allegiance to the United States of America; and that I will serve them honestly and faithfully against all their enemies, or opposers, whatsoever, and observe and obey the orders of the President of the United States, and the orders of the officers appointed over me, according to the rules and articles for the government of the armies of the United States."

Art. 11. After a non-commissioned officer or soldier, shall have been duly enlisted and sworn, he shall not be dismissed the service without a discharge in writing; and no discharge granted to him shall be sufficient, which is not signed by a field officer of the regiment to which he belongs, or commanding officer, where no field officer of the regiment is present; and no discharge shall be given to a non-commissioned officer or soldier, before his term of service has expired, but by order of the President, the Secretary of War, the commanding officer of a department, or the sentence of a general court martial....

Art. 12. Every colonel, or other officer commanding a regiment, troop, or company, and actually quartered with it, may give furloughs to non-commissioned officers or soldiers, in such numbers, and for so long a time as he shall judge to be most consistent with the good of the service...for time not exceeding twenty days in six months, but not to more than two persons to be absent at the same time, excepting some extraordinary occasion should require it.

Art. 13. At every muster...the commanding officer of every troop, or company, shall give certificates, signifying the reasons of the absence of the noncommissioned officers and private soldiers, which reasons, and time of absence, shall be inserted in the muster-rolls opposite the name of the respective absent officers and soldiers. The certificates shall, together with the muster-rolls, be remitted by the commissary of musters, or other officer mustering, to the department of war as speedily as the distance of the place will admit....

Art. 21. Any non-commissioned officer or soldier, who shall, without leave from his commanding officer, absent himself from his troop, company, or detachment, shall, upon being convicted thereof, be punished according to the nature of his offence, at the discretion of a court martial.

Art. 22. No non-commissioned officer or soldier, shall enlist himself in any other regiment, troop, or company, without a regular discharge from the regiment, troop, or company, in which he last served on the penalty of being reputed a deserter, and suffering accordingly....

Art. 26. If any commissioned or non-commissioned officer commanding a guard, shall knowingly or willingly suffer any person whatsoever to go forth to fight a duel, he shall be punished as a challenger....

Art. 27. All officers, of what condition soever, have power to part and quell all quarrels, frays, and disorders, though the persons concerned should belong to another regiment, troop, or company; and either to order officers into arrest, or non-commissioned officers or soldiers into confinement, until their proper superior officer shall be acquainted therewith....

Art. 37. Any non-commissioned officer or soldier, who shall be convicted, at a regimental court martial, of having sold, or designedly, or through neglect, wasted the ammunition delivered out to him, to be employed in the service of the United States, shall be punished at the discretion of such court.

Art. 38. Every non-commissioned officer or soldier, who shall be convicted before a court martial, of having sold, lost, or spoiled, through neglect, his horse, arms, clothes, or accoutrements, shall be put under such weekly stoppages (not exceeding the half of his pay) as such court martial shall judge sufficient, for repairing the loss or damage; and shall suffer confinement, or such other corporal punishment as his crime shall deserve....

Art. 39....if any non-commissioned officer [shall be convicted before a court martial, of having embezzled, or misapplied any money with which he may have been entrusted, he] shall be reduced to the ranks, be put under stoppages until the money be made good, and suffer such corporal punishment as such court martial shall direct....

Art. 41. All non-commissioned officers and soldiers, who shall be found one mile from the camp, without leave, in writing, from their commanding officer, shall suffer such punishment as shall be inflicted upon them by the sentence of a court martial....

Art. 43. Every non-commissioned officer and soldier shall retire to his quarters or tent, at the beating of the retreat; in default of which he shall be punished according to the nature of his offence.

Art. 44. No officer, non-commissioned officer or soldier, shall fail in repairing, at the time fixed, to the place of parade, of exercise or other rendezvous, appointed by his commanding officer, if not prevented by sickness, or some other evident necessity, or shall go from the said place of rendezvous, without leave from his commanding officer, before he shall be regularly dismissed or relieved, on the penalty of being punished according to the nature of his offence by the sentence of a court martial.

Art. 45. Any commissioned officer, who shall be found drunk on his guard, party, or other duty, shall be cashiered. Any non-commissioned officer or soldier so offending, shall suffer such corporal punishment as shall be inflicted by the sentence of a court martial....

Art. 59. If any commander of any garrison, fortress or post, shall be compelled, by the officers and soldiers under his command, to give up to the enemy, or to abandon it; the commissioned officers, non-commissioned officers, or soldiers, who shall be convicted of having so offended, shall suffer death, or such other punishment as shall be inflicted upon them by the sentence of a court martial....

Extract from William Duane, *A Hand Book for Infantry*, 9th ed., 1814.

It is too much practice to commit the charge of the elementary drills to non-commissioned officers, by which many great evils are produced....By devolving these first duties on non-commissioned officers, the commissioned officers remain ignorant or timid; and the chance of finding non-commissioned officers, who can clearly comprehend and explain the principles of a good discipline, is not one in twenty; from which cause it is twenty to one that the recruits are imperfectly or erroneously taught....

The Serjeant Major

This is a very useful and indispensible officer—it would be desirable, and would conduce to the perfection of discipline, if there were one to every company. The duties are very heavy on a single serjeant major to a battalion, and it is not easy to find men every way qualified. He is to the serjeants and corporals, what the major is to the platoon officers. He has charge of the details of serjeants, corporals, privates, and musicians for every service, guards, drills, fatigues, etc. and is an indispensible aid to the adjutant.

He should be a complete master of all the exercises of the battalion from the first drill to the movements in line of battle. A serjeant major who feels a pride in his station, and whose conduct is exemplary, may expect with propriety, military promotion.

Serjeants

The non-commissioned officers should be selected from among the most orderly and best qualified men—upon them will depend very much the order and good conduct of the company. They should each have a squad composed of an equal distribution of the men, who should form messes, over which the serjeants and corporals should preside and be responsible for the good and orderly conduct of the mess, the dressing of provisions, the cleaning of their persons, arms, quarters, and clothing.

The serjeants in rotation should see the parties daily turn out for guards—inspect them and their arms—that their clothing be clean—arms in good order—flints good and well fitted—ammunition sufficient and in good condition.

The serjeants make a morning report, one copy for the captain, the other for the serjeant major, who delivers them to the former.

The serjeants make weekly reports of the company, men and arms—reports are delivered to the serjeant major on a stated hour of the day every week, but they must be ready to make report at any hour required, and the corporals aid the serjeants in this duty.

At roll call they should report all who were absent—when upon guard arrange the sentinels, and never be absent from the head quarters of the guard. The serjeants perform orderly duty, once a week in rotation, of which the serjeant major keeps a roster; the duty of the orderly serjeant is to attend upon and execute such orders as the officer to whom he is attached shall order. The serjeants act as guides and pivots in the evolutions of battalions.

Corporals

These are in fact deputy serjeants—they have the charge of squads in quarters—there is an orderly corporal in quarters always dressed, and whose duty it is to execute such orders as the orderly serjeant is required to have executed. The corporals keep each a roll of the company, and they warn the men for duty. They teach the recruits the manual exercise, instruct them in cleaning arms and accoutrements, and see that they perform this duty each for himself—they take their share of duties in guards, fatigues, the care of ammunition and provisions and storage.

The serjeants and corporals call the rolls at *taptoo* time—and are the first on daily parade, and are exemplary in the neatness of their persons and their sobriety and good demeanor.

The corporals plant the sentinels, the elder corporal has the choice of the route, after an equal distribution.

Extract from General Regulations for the Army of the United States; also, The Rules and Articles of War, and Extracts from Laws relating to them, 1835.

Article IX
Appointment of Adjutants and Non-commissioned Officers

12. Each colonel will appoint, from the subaltern officers of his own regiment, his Adjutant, and report the same to the Adjutant General. He will also appoint the non-commissioned staff of his regiment; and on the recommendation and nomination of the Captains of the companies, he will, should he approve thereof, appoint the Sergeants and Corporals of their respective companies.

All these appointments are to be announced in regimental orders.

13. The officers and non-commissioned officers thus appointed, are not to be removed from their respective places, except by the sentence of a court martial, or by order of the Colonel or permanent commanding officer of the regiment.

14. A non-commissioned officer having been duly appointed, cannot, at his pleasure, resign his place or relinquish his duties as such, and return to the ranks. If he have been regraded, in consequence of misconduct, he shall not be re-enlisted within a period to entitle him to the additional bounty allowed to such privates and musicians, as may re-enlist under the provisions of the act, section 3, of the 2d March, 1833.

System of Responsibility

15. Nothing more essentially tends to the maintenance of good order, than that chain of responsibility, which should extend from the highest to the lowest grade. To effect this, each company must be divided into four squads, each to be put under the charge of a non-commissioned officer, who will be responsible to the subalterns of the company. Should there be a deficiency in the number of non-commissioned officers, required to assist the subaltern officers in the discharge of this duty, Corporals may be appointed to act as lance-sergeants, and the most approved private soldiers as lance-corporals, who, if they conduct themselves with propriety, should be promoted to the first vacancies.

18. As far as practical, squads will be kept separate, whether in tents or quarters; and the men of each will be numbered according to their qualifications, in order that the highest in number present, may, as lance-corporal, command the squad in the absence of noncommissioned officers and lance-corporals....

42. As an allowance is made by law to officers for private waiters, no non-commissioned officer or soldier is to be employed in any menial office, or made to perform any service not strictly military, for the private benefit of any officer or mess of officers.

Extract from General Regulations for the Army of the United States, 1847.

Article XIII

Non-Commissioned Officers

117. It is of essential importance to the service that the station and respectability of the non-commissioned officer be upheld. It is, therefore, earnestly recommended, and enjoined upon all officers, to be cautious in reproving non-commissioned officers in the presence or hearing of privates, lest their authority be weakened in the eyes of their inferiors. It is also directed that non-commissioned officers, in no case, be sent to the guard-room and mixed with privates, during confinement, but be considered as placed in arrest, except in aggravated cases, where escape may be apprehended.

118. When non-commissioned officers are appointed and announced in the manner prescribed by paragraphs 96 and 97, they are not to be removed from their respective places except by the sentence of a court-martial, or by order of the permanent commander of the regiment. If reduced to the ranks by garrison courts, at posts not the head-quarters of the regiment, the company commander will immediately forward a transcript of the order to the Colonel.

119. A non-commissioned officer having been duly appointed, cannot, at his pleasure, resign his place, or relinquish his duties as such, and return to the ranks.

120. Every non-commissioned officer shall be furnished with a certificate or warrant of his rank, assimilated to the commission of an officer, signed by the Colonel and countersigned by the Adjutant. The first, or orderly sergeant, when selected by the captain, will be entitled to a separate warrant as such, in addition to the appointment he may hold as a non-commissioned officer of the company.

121. Whenever circumstances may make it necessary, lance-sergeants may be appointed from the corporals, and lance-corporals from the privates, who, if their conduct be good and evince capacity for the discharge of such duties, should be promoted to the first vacancies. The appointments will be made in the same manner as that already pointed out for non-commissioned officers.

122. Independent of the particular duties required of non-commissioned officers, (sergeants and corporals), when in the ranks, according to the systems of tactical instruction, it is also their duty, at all times, to observe the conduct of the privates, and to report immediately to the proper authority, every breach of the general regulations of the service, or of the particular orders of the post....

Article XIV

144. Unless under special circumstances, Saturdays will be particularly appropriated to police. The chiefs of squads will cause bunks and bedding to be overhauled; floors dry rubbed; tables and benches scoured; arms cleaned; accoutrements whitened and polished, and every thing put in the most exact order.

145. Bathing is promotive both of comfort and health; and where conveniences for it are to be had, the men should be made to bathe at least once a week. The feet are to be washed at least twice a week.

146. It is essential to cleanliness and health that the soldiers should change their linen at least three times a week in mid-summer, and twice a week during the remainder of the year. The hair must be cut close to the head, and always be kept short.

147. Non-commissioned officers, in command of squads, will be held more immediately responsible that their men observe what is prescribed above; that they wash their hands and faces daily—habitually, immediately after the general fatigue; that they, at the same time, shave themselves (if necessary) and brush or comb their heads; that afterwards, those who are to go on duty, put their arms, accoutrements, dress, &c., in the best order, and that such as have permission to pass the chain of sentinels are in the dress that may be ordered....

Extract from Maj. Gen. Winfield Scott, *Infantry Tactics; or, Rules for the Exercise and Maneuvers of the United States Infantry, 1854.*

Article I

Posts of Company Officers, Sergeants, and Corporals

19. The company officers and sergeants may (as on a war establishment, with ranks filled) be ten in number, as follows: 1. Captain. 2. First lieutenant. 3. Second lieutenant. 4. Third lieutenant. 5. Ensign. 6. First sergeant. 7. Second sergeant. 8. Third sergeant. 9. Fourth sergeant. 10. Fifth sergeant.

20. If the whole ten be under arms with the company, they will be posted as follows:

21. No. 1 in the front rank on the right of the company, touching with the left elbow.

22. No. 6 in the rear rank, touching with the left elbow, and covering No. 1. In the manoeuvres, No. 6 (first sergeant) will be denominated covering sergeant, or right guide of the company.

23. The remaining officers and sergeants will constitute the file closers, and be posted in a line two paces in the rear of the rear rank, measuring from heels to heels, as follows:

24. No. 2 equidistant between the positions, which will be assigned to Nos. 4 and 7.

25. No. 3 opposite to the centre of the first platoon.

26. No. 4 opposite to the centre of the second platoon.

27. No. 5 equidistant between No. 3 and the right of the company.

28. No. 7 (with an exception to be immediately made) opposite to the second file from the left of the company. No. 7, (second sergeant), in every company, will, in the manoeuvres, be denominated left guide of the company.

29. No. 8 opposite to the second file from the left of the first platoon.

30. No. 9 opposite to the second file from the right of the second platoon.

31. No. 10 equidistant between Nos. 3 and 8.

32. No. 7, in the left company, will be posted in the front rank, on the left of the battalion, touching with the right elbow, and be covered by a corporal in the rear rank. This sergeant will, in the manoeuvres, be sometimes designated as the closing sergeant, and the corporal behind him the covering corporal....

Article II

Instruction of Sergeants and Corporals

72. This will comprehend the Schools of the Soldier and Company. The sergeants and corporals will be held to know, not only how to execute with precision the manual of arms as sergeants, but, also, every thing relating to the manual of arms, as rank and file, the firings and marchings.

73. The adjutant and sergeant major, under the supervision of the field officers, will be immediately charged with the instruction of the sergeants and corporals. This will commence with the exercises in the School of the Soldier, followed by the manual of arms as sergeants.

74. When the sergeants and corporals are well established in the foregoing, they will next be formed into the semblance of a company, and four of the sergeants designated as captain, covering sergeant, left guide, and file closer, respectively. Every sergeant will, in his turn, fill each of those positions, and, if practicable, each corporal also.

75. This instruction having principally for object to qualify the sergeant to instruct the men, and the corporals to replace sergeants, the adjutant will explain to them all the principles of the first two schools, at first on the ground, and next in a course of theoretic instruction. The two modes will comprehend all the various duties of guides in the manoeuvres of the battalion.

76. The colonel will frequently cause to be exercised, by a field officer, the colour-bearer, the colour-guard, and the general guides in marching in line. The endeavour will be to make them contract the habit of marching in a given direction with the most scrupulous accuracy, and of preserving, in like manner, the length and cadence of the pace....

Colour-guard

50. In each battalion the colour-guard will be composed of eight or five corporals, according as the battalion may be formed

in three or two ranks, and be posted on the left of the right centre company, of which company (for the time being) the guard will make a part.

51. The corporals will be selected by the colonel, who, nevertheless, will take but one at a time from the same company, and not one from the rifle, unless the rifles have bayonets. (In battalions with less than five companies present, there will be no colour-guard and no display of colours, except it may be at reviews.)

52. The front or colour rank of the guard will be composed of a sergeant, (to be selected by the colonel), who will be called, for the time, the *colour-bearer**, with a corporal on his right and left; these places will be given in preference to the corporals of grenadiers and light infantry, respectively, as often as they compose a part of the guard.

53. The two other ranks of the guard will each consist of three corporals; or, if there be but one other rank that will be so composed.

54. When the guard consists of three ranks, the centre rank will be composed of the three corporals the most distinguished for regularity and precision, as well in their positions under arms as in their marching. The latter advantage, and a just carriage of the person, are yet to be more particularly sought for in the selection of the colour-bearer.

55. The corporals of the colour-guard will carry their muskets within the right arm, as will be prescribed at the end of Title III—bayonets always fixed....

*The colour, in bad or windy weather, except in saluting, will be borne furled and cased. The heel of ferrule of its lance ought to have for support, a leather stirrup or socket, suspended from a belt, the latter buckled around the waist of the colour-bearer.

Extract from Regulations for the Army of the United States, 1904.
Article XV

The Post Noncommissioned Staff

93. The post noncommissioned staff consists of master electricians, Artillery Corps, ordnance, post commissary, post quartermaster, and electrician sergeants. They are appointed by the Secretary of War after due examination, as follows: Master electricians Artillery Corps from the Army or from civil life; ordnance sergeants from sergeants of the line who have served at least eight years in the Army, including four years as noncommissioned officers, and who are less than 45 years of age; post commissary-sergeants from sergeants of the line who have served five years in the Army, including three years as noncommissioned officers; post quartermaster-sergeants from sergeants of the line who have served four years in the Army; electrician sergeants from the Army or from civil life.

94. An application for appointment must be in the handwriting of the applicant, and will briefly state the length and nature of his military service, and for what time and in what organizations he has served as a noncommissioned officer. The company commander will indorse thereon the character of the applicant and his opinion as to his intelligence and fitness for the position. The application so indorsed will be submitted to the regimental or artillery district commander, who will forward the same, with his remarks as to the merits of the applicant, to The Military Secretary of the Army.

95. While the law contemplates in these appointments the better preservation of public property at the several posts, there is also a further consideration—that of offering a reward to faithful and well-tried sergeants, thus giving encouragement to deserving soldiers to hope for substantial promotion. Commanding officers can not be too particular in investigating and reporting upon the character and qualifications of applicants.

96. Regulations for the examination of applicants for appointment as post noncommissioned staff officers will be published from time to time in orders by the War Department.

97. A post noncommissioned staff officer will assist the officer of his department, and will not be detailed upon any service not pertaining to his proper position, unless the necessities of the service require such detail, in which case the post commander will note the fact, with reasons therefor, on the sergeant's personal report.

98. A noncommissioned staff officer at an ungarrisoned post or station will be responsible for the property of his own department, and for such other property as may be intrusted to him for safe-keeping. For all public property committed to his charge he will account to the heads of the staff departments concerned, and if the means at his disposal are insufficient for its preservation he will report the facts.

99. The military control of post noncommissioned staff officers serving at posts not occupied by troops is vested in the commander of the territorial department in which they are serving. All matters relating to them as soldiers subject to military command, as distinguished from the administrative duties imposed upon them by regulations and orders, will, except in cases of reenlistment, be determined at department headquarters, where their descriptive lists and accounts of pay and clothing will be kept. When they are discharged a copy of the descriptive list, upon which will be noted the fact of discharge, with the date, place, and cause, and the character given on the discharge certificate, will be forwarded to The Military Secretary of the Army.

100. Each post noncommissoned staff officer will make such personal reports as may be required by the head of the corps or department to which he belongs. The officer under whose orders these noncommissioned officers are serving will indorse on each separate report his opinion of the manner in which the noncommissioned officer has performed his duties, and the commanding officer will forward the report direct to the chief of the proper bureau or corps.

101. A post noncommissioned staff officer may be reenlisted, provided he shall have conducted himself properly and performed his duties in a satisfactory manner. If, however, his commanding officer should not deem the reenlistment to be for the best interest of the service he will communicate his reasons to The Military Secretary of the Army in time to receive the decision of the War Department before the soldier's discharge. If serving at an ungarrisoned post application for reenlistment will be made by the soldier to The Military Secretary through department headquarters. The reenlistment paper will immediately be forwarded direct to The Military Secretary, except in the case of soldiers stationed at ungarrisoned posts, in which case it will be forwarded through department headquarters. A post noncommissioned staff officer will be furnished with a warrant signed by the chief of the proper bureau or corps. The warrant will remain in force so long as the soldier is continuously in the service, i.e., if he reenlists the day following that of his discharge. Every such reenlistment will be noted on the back of the warrant by the officer who reenlists the soldier, as follows: Reenlisted (date); warrant continued.

102. Post noncommissioned staff officers, though liable to discharge for inefficiency or misconduct, will not be reduced.

Article XVI

Detached Soldiers: Descriptive Lists

103. When an enlisted man is detached from his company, a descriptive list will be prepared and forwarded to his new commanding officer. On the descriptive list will be shown the pay due the soldier, the condition of his clothing allowance, and all information necessary to the settlement of his accounts with the Government. When it can be avoided, the descriptive list will not be intrusted to the soldier, but to an officer or noncommissioned officer under whose charge he may be, or it may be forwarded by mail. The date of the last vaccination of the soldier and its result will be noted on the descriptive list. Articles of ordnance equipment in possession of a detached soldier will be transferred as prescribed in paragraph 1564....

Article XXIX

Regiments and Battalions

244. The adjutant, quartermaster, and commissary are, under the regimental commander, responsible for the discipline and efficiency of the noncommissioned staff and band.

245. The quartermaster will perform the duties of quartermaster of the regiment when

in the field, and may be required to perform the duties of quartermaster of the post where he is stationed. The commissary will perform the duties of commissary of the regiment when in the field, and may be required to perform the duties of commissary of the post where he is stationed.

246. A regimental staff officer may be assigned to duty with a company or to any staff duty which his regimental commander may impose. A battalion staff officer is subject to any duty which the commanding officer may impose.

247. The regimental noncommissioned staff officers consist of the sergeant-major, the quartermaster-sergeant, commissary-sergeant, and two colour-sergeants, and are appointed by the regimental commander. The battalion noncommissioned staff officers are the battalion sergeants-major, and in engineer troops battalion quartermaster-sergeants. They are appointed by the regimental commander upon the recommendation of the battalion commander. When a battalion is detached and serving at such a distance from regimental headquarters that more than fifteen days are required for exchange of correspondence by mail, the battalion noncommissioned staff officers are appointed by the battalion commander, who will immediately notify the regimental commander. Each noncommissioned staff officer will be furnished with a warrant signed by the officer making the appointment and countersigned by the adjutant. The appointment takes effect on the day upon which it is made, and the warrant may be continued in force upon discharge and reenlistment, if reenlistment be made on the day following discharge; each reenlistment and continuance will be noted on the warrant by the adjutant. Any noncommissioned staff officer may be reduced to the ranks by the sentence of a court-martial, or by order of the commander having authority to appoint such noncommissioned officer. Noncommissioned staff officers will preferably be selected from the noncommissioned officers of the regiment most distinguished for efficiency, gallantry, and soldierly bearing.

248. The public property pertaining to the headquarters of the regiment will be marked "H.Q.," with arm and number of regiment; the equipments in possession of the noncommissioned staff and band will be marked "N.C.S." and "Band," respectively, and with the arm and number of the regiment and the number of the man to whom the articles are issued.

249. The following-named books and papers will be kept in each regiment: An order book, a letters-received book, with index, a letters-sent book, with index, a regimental fund book, and a descriptive book, furnished by The Military Secretary of the Army; all orders, circulars, and instructions from higher authority, copies of the monthly returns, muster rolls of the field, staff, and band, other regimental returns and reports, and all correspondence concerning the regiment or affecting its personnel.

Of the books and papers herein referred to, the books of letters received and letters sent, the muster rolls, the regimental monthly returns and all other returns of the personnel of the regiment, and the general orders and circulars of the War Department will be permanently preserved. Division and department orders, except extracts of special orders, will, when the regiment is relieved from duty in the division and department, be disposed of under instructions of the division and department commanders. The other books and papers will be kept for five years, reckoned from the close of the period of their use in case of books, and from their dates in case of papers, when they will be destroyed under direction of the regimental commander.

250. All orders and circulars from the War Department, or from the headquarters of an army, corps, division, brigade, or territorial division or department in which the regiment may be serving, will be filed in book form, and general orders and circulars indexed as soon as received.

Bands

251. The noncommissioned officers of regimental bands will be appointed by the regimental commanders, upon the recommendation of regimental adjutants, under the same conditions prescribed in paragraph 247 for the noncommissioned staff of the

regiment. The noncommissioned officers of the engineer band will be appointed by the commanding officer of the battalion with which the band is serving; the noncommissioned officers of the artillery bands will be appointed by the artillery district commander, or, if not serving in an artillery district, by the senior artillery officer of the post at which they are stationed....

Article XXX

Troops, Batteries, and Companies

261. Noncommissioned officers will be carefully selected and instructed, and always supported by company commanders in the proper performance of their duties. They will not be detailed for any duty nor permitted to engage in any occupation inconsistent with their rank and position. Officers will be cautious in reproving them in the presence or hearing of private soldiers.

262. Company noncommissioned officers are appointed by regimental commanders, or by battalion commanders under the conditions stated in paragraph 247, on the recommendation of their company commanders; but in no case will any company organization have an excess of noncommissioned officers above that allowed by law. The noncommissioned officers of artillery companies will, upon the recommendation of the company commanders, be appointed by artillery district commanders, or if not serving in an artillery district, by the senior artillery officer of the command.

263. To test the capacity of privates for the duties of noncommissioned officers company commanders may appoint lance corporals, who will be obeyed and respected as corporals, but no company shall have more than one lance corporal at a time, unless there are noncommissioned officers absent by authority, during which absences there may be one for each absentee.

264. The captain will select the first sergeant, quartermaster-sergeant, and stable sergeant from the sergeants of his company, and may return them to the grade of sergeant without reference to higher authority.

265. Each noncommissioned officer will be furnished with a certificate or warrant of his rank, signed by the officer making the appointment, and countersigned by the adjutant; but a separate warrant as first sergeant, quartermaster-sergeant, or stable-sergeant will not be given. A warrant issued to a noncommissioned officer is his personal property. Warrants need not be renewed in cases of reenlistment in the same company, if reenlistment is made the day following the day of discharge, but may remain in force until vacated by promotion or reduction, each reenlistment and continuance to be noted on the warrant by the company commander.

266. Appointments of company noncommissioned officers will take effect on the day of appointment by the authorized commander, and of first sergeants, quartermaster-sergeants, stable-sergeants, cooks, artificers, farriers and blacksmiths, mechanics, saddlers, wagoners, musicians, trumpeters, and first-class privates on the day of appointment by the company commander; but in case of vacancy in a company absent from regimental headquarters, a company commander may make a temporary appointment of a noncommissioned officer, which, if approved by the regimental commander, will carry rank and pay from the date of such appointment.

267. A noncommissioned officer may be reduced to the ranks by sentence of a court-martial, or on the recommendation of the company commander, by the order of the commander having authority to appoint such noncommissioned officer, but a noncommissioned officer will not be reduced because of absence on account of sickness or injury contracted in the line of duty. If reduced to the ranks by sentence of court-martial at a post not the headquarters of his regiment, the company commander will forward a transcript of the order to the regimental commander. The transfer of a noncommissioned officer from one organization to another carries with it reduction to the ranks unless otherwise specified in the order by authority competent to issue a new warrant.

268. When a noncommissioned officer, while in arrest or confinement, is reduced by sentence of a court-martial, the date of the order publishing the sentence is the date of reduction. In all other cases reduction takes

effect on the date of receipt of the order at the soldier's station.

The desertion of a noncommissioned officer vacates his position from the date of his unauthorized absence....

Extract from Army Regulation 245–5, War Department, Washington, 2 June 1942.

Companies—General Provisions

b. Noncommissioned officers.—Noncommissioned officers will be carefully instructed in their duties as such.

c. Privates with view to appointment as noncommissioned officers.—To test the capacity of privates for the duties of noncommissioned officers, company commanders may appoint acting noncommissioned officers, who will be instructed, obeyed, and respected as such; but no company will have more than one acting noncommissioned officer at any time in each grade below the third grade unless there are noncommissioned officers below the third grade absent by authority, during which absences there may be one for each absentee.

4. Squad leaders.—Squad leaders will be held responsible—

a. For the personal cleanliness and appearance of their men.

b. That those who are to go on duty put their arms, equipment, and clothing in the best possible condition previous to the time of entering upon duty.

c. That those coming off duty place their arms and equipments in the designated places.

d. That the bedding, bunks, and all other property issued to or belonging to the men of their squads are kept in a clean and orderly condition.

e. That all Government property issued the members of their squads is properly recorded and charged.

f. That all losses or damages to Government property issued the men of their squads are promptly reported.

g. That the clothing and other effects of deserters, men absent without leave, and men sick in hospital are promptly secured and turned over to the proper agency.

h. That the names of those desiring medical treatment are reported for entry on daily sick book.

i. That those desiring to make deposits present their deposit books at the proper time.

j. That clothing and equipment which is no longer serviceable be turned in for replacement.

5. Inspections.—*a.* Company commanders will hold inspections of the personnel, equipment, and buildings, to include ground contiguous thereto, pertaining to their commands as directed by the commanding officer and at such other times as deemed necessary.

b. No one will be excused from these inspections except the guard, the sick in hospital, and those ordered excused by the commanding officer.

6. Company mess.—*a.* Where companies are not joined in a general mess, the company commander, assisted by the other officers of the company, will supervise the cooking and messing of his men.

b. Where all the companies are joined in a general mess, he will confine his supervision of the mess of his company to observation and to notifying the officer in charge in writing of anything requiring remedy. Should this officer fail to apply proper remedy, report will then be made to the appropriate commander.

c. Kitchens will be placed under the immediate charge of noncommissioned officers, who will be held responsible for their condition and for the proper use of rations.

d. Additional pay for cooks and mess attendants.—See AR 210–50.

8. Miscellaneous.—*a.* When possible the company commander will see that every grave of the men of his company who die or are killed on the battlefield is carefully marked so that future identification can be easily made.

b. Noncommissioned officers will be supported by company commanders in the performance of their duties. They will not be detailed for any duty nor permitted to engage in any occupation inconsistent with their work and position. Officers will be cautious in reproving them in the presence or hearing of privates....

By Order of the Secretary of War:

G.C. Marshall,
Chief of Staff.

Changes
No. 1

WAR DEPARTMENT
Washington25, D.C.,
20 December 1945

AR 245–5, 2 June 1942 is changed as follows:

3. Instruction of personnel.

b. Noncommissioned officers.

(1) Noncommissioned officers will be carefully instructed in their duties as such.

(2) In order that the desired results may be attained, special attention will be given to the following points:

(*a*) The careful initial selection of noncommissioned officer material.

(*b*) The operation of appropriate noncommissioned officer schools.

(*c*) The prompt removal of noncommissioned officers who fail to attain or maintain acceptable standards.

(*d*) The enhancement of the advantages and prestige of the noncommissioned officer grades.

(*e*) The public recognition through new releases, orders, and other appropriate means of the accomplishments and importance of the noncommissioned officers.

(*f*) The delegation to the noncommissioned officers of all authority that is rightfully theirs and the creation of increased opportunity for the noncommissioned officers to exercise command and initiative.

(*g*) The consultation with appropriate noncommissioned officers in planning the implementation of directives.

(*h*) The avoidance of embarrassment of noncommissioned officers in the presence of their subordinates.

(*i*) The thorough indoctrination of every noncommissioned officer with the importance and responsibility of his grade and position.

By Order of the Secretary of War:

DWIGHT D. EISENHOWER,
Chief of Staff

Extract from Army Regulation 600–20, HQ, Department of the Army, Washington, 31 January 1967.

Personnel—General
Army Command Policy and Procedure

Section IV. Enlisted Aspects of Command.

24. General policies. *a.* Except as specifically indicated, all of the policies of this regulation apply equally to all classes of military personnel as listed in paragraph 7. This section is devoted to emphasizing policies of command that are primarily or exclusively related to the enlisted grades. At all echelons of command, commanders and their staffs are charged specifically with the responsibility of insuring equitable delegation of authority and responsibility, as guided by this regulation, to noncommissioned officers by their superiors, whether officer, warrant officer, or other noncommissioned officers.

b. This regulation is applicable to enlisted personnel of all components of the Army. Per-sonnel retired and members of USAR Control Groups prior to 1 July 1955 are exempted from this regulation while in that status.

25. Noncommissioned officers. The guidance in this paragraph is amplified in AR 611–201 which describes in detail the command function of all noncommissioned officer MOS.

a. Sergeant major of the Army. This is the senior sergeant major grade of rank as indicated in paragraph 7. It is also the position title that designates the senior enlisted position of the Army. The sergeant major occupying this position serves as the senior enlisted advisor and consultant to the Chief of Staff of the Army on problems affecting enlisted personnel and their solutions; on professional education, growth and advancement of noncommissioned officers; and on morale, training, pay, promotions and other matters concerning enlisted personnel. He is also available to present the enlisted viewpoint on Department of the Army boards and committees. Other functions of this position include meeting with military and civilian organizations to discuss enlisted personnel affairs, receiving enlisted personnel who visit Headquarters, Department of the Army, and representing all Army enlisted personnel at appropriate ceremonies.

b. Sergeant major. This is the position title that designates the senior enlisted position on the staffs of various commanders. In keeping with the trust, confidence, responsibility, and authority bestowed upon this function, the sergeant major should be considered as a key staff member. As indicated in paragraph 11, it is from the sergeant major of a major unit or installation that the activities of the local NCO channel emanate. This channel functions orally through the sergeant major's and first sergeant's call and does not normally involve written directives.

c. First sergeant. This position title is second to the sergeant major in importance, responsibility, and prestige. In the sense that first sergeants are in direct and daily contact with sizeable numbers of other enlisted men, this position is one requiring outstanding leadership and professional competence. The first sergeant is the senior enlisted assistant to commanders of companies, batteries, and troops. It is normal for company commanders to use the noncommissioned officer channel (para 11) for the conduct of many routine activities, particularly in garrison. Thus, in these activities, the first sergeant occupies an intermediary position between the other enlisted personnel and the officers of the company. He conducts routine company administration and company operations as directed by the company commander. He drafts company orders, reports, and other documents requiring the signature of the company commander. The functions of the first sergeant do not include responsibilities which cannot be delegated by the company commander or which properly belong to the executive officer or platoon leaders.

d. Platoon sergeant. This position title is also one of the key ones in the command structure of the Army. It is normal for platoon sergeants to become vital members of the chain of command under the provisions of paragraph 16. When the officer platoon leader is present, the platoon sergeant is his key assistant and advisor.

e. Section, squad, and team leaders. The importance of these positions stems from the fact that the responsibilities of these echelons of the chain of command (para 11) are habitually exercised by noncommissioned officers. Platoon leaders hold their subordinate leaders responsible—(1) For personal appearance and cleanliness of their soldiers.

(2) That all Government property issued to members of their units is properly maintained and accounted for at all times and that discrepancies are reported promptly.

(3) That, while in a duty status, they be ready at all times to report the location and activity of all individuals of the unit. Thus as the basic reporting unit in formations, the squad is either present, or individuals absent are reported by name and not merely accounted for.

(4) That the unit is prepared to function in its primary mission role.

f. Acting noncommissioned officers. Company, troop, battery, and separate detachment commanders may appoint acting corporals and sergeants in accordance with AR 600–200 for the purpose of filling position vacancies. Additionally, AR 600–200 provides for acting corporals, sergeants, and staff sergeants for casual groups. While so acting they will wear the insignia and have the responsibilities, authority and privileges of the position to which appointed, except that they will not be entitled to the pay and allowances of such higher grades, and such service will not be credited as time in a higher grade for appointment or date of rank purposes.

g. Noncommissioned officer disciplinary policies. The purpose of this subparagraph is to emphasize the important status of noncommissioned officers in the maintenance of discipline in the Army. These policies should be considered together with the provisions of section V and MCM 1951.

(1) NCO authority to apprehend, see paragraph 32, this regulation; article 7(c) UCMJ; and paragraph 19, MCM 1951.

(2) Noncommissioned officers may be authorized by their commanding officers, in accordance with article 9(b), UCMJ, to order enlisted persons into arrest or confinement. Also see paragraph 21a, MCM 1951. This authority is frequently confined by commanding officers to first sergeants, charge of quarters, or other duty positions.

(3) Noncommissioned officers do not have any authority to impose nonjudicial punishment upon other enlisted personnel under article 15, UCMJ. However, the recommendations of noncommissioned officers may be sought and considered by unit commanders.

(4) As enlisted commanders of troops certain noncommissioned officers play an extremely important role in furthering the efficiency of the company, battery, or troops. This function includes the prevention of incidents which, if they occurred, would make it necessary to resort to trial by courts-martial or imposition of nonjudicial punishment. Thus, the NCO is a key assistant to the commander in administering the minor nonpunitive (not to be confused with nonjudicial punishment) disciplinary responsibilities prescribed in paragraph 33, and in paragraph 128c, MCM 1951. See also paragraph 35b, this regulation.

(5) In taking corrective action with regard to subordinates, noncommissioned officers will be guided by, and observe, the principles set forth in paragraph 34e.

(6) For trials of noncommissioned officers by courts-martial whose membership, as provided by article 25(c)(1), UCMJ, includes enlisted persons, the following will apply. When it can be avoided, no member of the court-martial will be junior to the accused in rank or grade. Specialists will not, except under extraordinary circumstances, sit as members of courts-martial of noncommissioned officers. In those cases in which a specialist sits on a court-martial of a noncommissioned officer he should be in a higher pay grade than the accused.

(7) In the case of noncommissioned officers above the fourth enlisted pay grade, summary courts-martial may not adjudge confinement, hard labor without confinement, or reduction except to the next inferior grade.

(8) When nonjudicial punishment (art. 15, UCMJ) is imposed on a noncommissioned officer it may not include correctional custody, confinement on bread and water or diminished rations, or any type of extra duty involving labor or duties not customarily performed by a noncommissioned officer of the grade of the person who is to perform the extra duty.

h. Miscellaneous NCO responsibilities, prerogatives, and privileges. Noncommissioned officers will:

(1) Execute orders on their own initiative and judgment within the authority delegated to them.

(2) Be employed as training instructors to the maximum degree practicable.

(3) Make recommendations relative to unit mission accomplishment and troop welfare. NCO recommendations have traditionally been of immeasurable assistance to their commanding officer on such matters as assignment, reassignment, promotion, privileges, discipline, training, unit funds, community affairs, and supply.

(4) Be utilized only in supervisory roles on fatigue duty, and only as noncommissioned officers of the guard on guard duty, except in temporary situations where other grades are critically short.

(5) Be granted such privileges as organization and installation commanders are capable of granting and consider proper to enhance the prestige of these vital enlisted troop commanders.

(6) Be considered for assignment of quarters (noncommissioned officers with bona fide dependents) by installation commanders upon the basis of several pertinent factors under the provisions of AR 210–14. Determination of the seniority factor of applicants under AR 210–14 will be on the basis of date of rank within pay grade for all enlisted personnel under consideration.

(7) Be afforded pass privileges in accordance with AR 630–20, which provides that

no pass form will be required for staff sergeants and higher.

(8) Be afforded the privilege of establishing and operating noncommissioned officers' open messes as adjuncts of the Army as covered in AR 230–60.

(9) Be afforded separate rooms in barracks areas to the extent feasible under the provisions of AR 210–18.

26. Specialists. *a.* A specialist is a selected enlisted person who has been appointed under the provisions of AR 600–200 for the purpose of discharging duties that require a high degree of special skill. Specialists must have acquired proficiency in the technical or administrative aspects of their MOS field. Specialists, by virtue of their technical skill, are often called upon to exercise leadership with respect to matters related to their specialty. Normally, their duties do not require the exercise of enlisted command of troops. Thus, while leadership proficiency is not a primary prerequisite for advancement to or within the specialist grades, qualities of leadership should be encouraged and recognized.

b. Although the duty positions of specialists are not enlisted command positions, and do not normally require exercise of leadership functions, there are exceptions. In particular, the more senior specialists will occasionally be called upon to assume command under the provisions of paragraphs 16, 17, or 31*a* of this regulation. Additionally, senior specialists are usually soldiers with long service and outstanding ability who contribute in considerable degree to maintenance of the high appearance and conduct standards of enlisted personnel of lesser rank.

c. Specialist Six and Specialist Seven will be exempt from guard and fatigue duty, except in unusual circumstances when their services are required for the proper execution of these duties. In these cases, they will be used only in a supervisory role except in temporary situations where other grades are critically short, but in no case over a noncommissioned officer.

d. Specialist Six and Specialist Seven will be granted, in general, the same type privileges as noncommissioned officers in the organization and installation. A type of exception that might be applied by organization or installation commanders is listed in paragraph 25*h*(9).

e. Specialist Five and Specialist Four may be granted such privileges as the organization and installation commanders consider proper.

f. Under no circumstances will a specialist be granted any prerogatives or privileges that would be detrimental to the prestige of a noncommissioned officer, nor will any specialist be placed in such a position that he would be required to execute orders over a noncommissioned officer in the Army. In connection with joint activities, see paragraph 8*d*.

g. In the case of Specialists above the fourth enlisted pay grade, summary courts-martial may not adjudge confinement, hard labor without confinement, or reduction except to the next inferior pay grade.

h. When nonjudicial punishment (art. 15, UCMJ) is imposed on a Specialist it may not include correctional custody, confinement on bread and water or diminished rations, or any type of extra duty involving labor duties not customarily performed by a Specialist of the grade of the person who is to perform the extra duty.

i. Specialists who show leadership potential should be encouraged to advance toward noncommissioned officer skills in appropriate MOS by undergoing on-the-job training in such duty positions. While in this status, the commander may appoint the specialist as an acting noncommissioned officer.

27. Privates. This class of enlisted men is, as indicated in paragraph 7*d*(3), the basic manpower strength and grade of the Army. While command functions do not normally pertain to privates, they should be indoctrinated in their responsibilities and in their potential for enlisted command duties.

Extract from AR 350–17, Noncommissioned Officer Development Program, HQ, Department of the Army, Washington, 1991.

4.g. *Commanders of battalions, separate companies, and equivalent organizations will—*
(1) Be responsible to develop and implement an effective NCODP.

(2) Ensure the program supports the unit mission and enhances development of noncommissioned officers.

(3) Ensure that the program has stated objectives with measurable and reachable standards.

4.h. *Command sergeant major (CSMs), first sergeants, or senior NCOs of battalions, separate companies, or equivalent organizations will—*

(2) Implement the commander's directives and guidance on the unit's NCODP.

(3) Be responsible for content, pertinence, and implementation of the unit's NCODP.

5.b. As with all leader *training*, the NCODP is a command responsibility. The program reflects command priorities and expectations for leader development, jointly determined by commanders and their senior NCOs.

Extract from AR 600–20, HQ, Department of the Army, Washington, 13 May 2002.

Personnel—General Army Command Policy and Procedure

Chapter 3. Enlisted Aspects of Command

3–1. Delegation of authority

Commanders and their staffs, at all levels of command, are responsible for ensuring proper delegation of authority to NCOs by their seniors. This policy applies whether the senior is an officer, WO, or another NCO.

3–2. Noncommissioned officer support channel

a. The NCO support channel (leadership chain) parallels and complements the chain of command. It is a channel of communication and supervision from the command sergeant major to first sergeant and then to other NCOs and enlisted personnel of the units. Commanders will define responsibilities and authority of their NCOs to their staffs and subordinates. This NCO support channel will assist the chain of command in accomplishing the following—

(1) Transmitting, instilling, and ensuring the efficacy of the professional Army ethic. (See FM 100–1 for an explanation of the professional Army ethic.)

(2) Planning and conducting the day-to-day unit operations within prescribed policies and directives.

(3) Training of enlisted soldiers in their MOS as well as in the basic skills and attributes of a soldier.

(4) Supervising unit physical fitness training and ensuring that unit soldiers comply with the weight and appearance standards of AR 600–9 and AR 670–1.

(5) Teaching soldiers the history of the Army, to include military customs, courtesies, and traditions.

(6) Caring for individual soldiers and their families both on and off duty.

(7) Teaching soldiers the mission of the unit and developing individual training programs to support the mission.

(8) Accounting for and maintaining individual arms and equipment of enlisted soldiers, and unit equipment under their control.

(9) Administering and monitoring the NCO professional development program, and other unit training programs.

(10) Achieving and maintaining courage, candor, competence, commitment, and compassion.

b. AR 611–201 and TC 22–6 contain specific information concerning the responsibilities, command functions, and scope of NCO duties.

(1) Sergeant Major of the Army. This is the senior sergeant major grade and designates the senior enlisted position of the Army. The sergeant major in this position serves as the senior enlisted adviser and consultant to the Chief of Staff, Army.

(2) Command Sergeant Major. This position title designates the senior NCO of the command at battalion or higher levels. He or she carries out policies and standards, and advises the commander on the performance, training, appearance, and conduct of enlisted soldiers. The command sergeant major administers the unit Noncommissioned Officer's Professional Development Program (NCODP).

(3) First Sergeant. The position of first sergeant designates the senior NCO at company level.

The first sergeant of a separate company or equivalent level organization administers the unit NCODP.

(4) Platoon Sergeant. The platoon sergeant is the key assistant and adviser to the platoon leader. In the absence of the platoon leader, the platoon sergeant leads the platoon.

(5) Section, squad, and team leaders. These direct leaders are the NCOs responsible at this level.

c. NCO disciplinary policies are shown below.

(1) NCOs are important to maintaining discipline in the Army. The policies prescribed in this subparagraph should be considered together with the provisions of chapter 4 of this regulation, AR 27–10, and the MCM.

(*a*) NCOs have the authority to apprehend any person subject to trial by court-martial under the MCM (Article 7, UCMJ, and para 302(b), Rules for Courts-Martial (RCM)) and chapter 4 of this regulation.

(*b*) NCOs may be authorized by their commanders to order enlisted soldiers of the commanding officer's command or enlisted soldiers subject to the authority of that commanding officer into arrest or confinement per the MCM (para 304(b), RCM).

(2) NCOs do not have authority to impose nonjudicial punishment on other enlisted soldiers under the MCM (Article 15, UCMJ). However, the commander may authorize an NCO in the grade of sergeant first class or above, provided such person is senior to the soldier being notified, to deliver the DA Form 2627 (Record of Proceedings under Article 15, UCMJ) and inform the soldier of his or her rights. In cases of nonjudicial punishment, the recommendations of NCOs should be sought and considered by the unit commanders.

(3) As enlisted leaders of soldiers, NCOs are essential to furthering the efficiency of the company, battery, or troop. This function includes preventing incidents that make it necessary to resort to trial by courts-martial or to impose nonjudicial punishment. Thus, NCOs are assistants to commanders in administering minor nonpunitive corrective actions as found in AR 27–10 and Part V, paragraph 1g of the MCM. " Nonpunitive measures" are not " nonjudicial punishment."

(4) In taking corrective action with regard to subordinates, NCOs will be guided by and observe the principles listed in chapter 4.

d. NCO prerogatives and privileges are shown below. NCOs will—

(1) Function only in supervisory roles on work details and only as NCOs of the guard on guard duty, except when temporary personnel shortages require the NCO to actively participate in the work detail.

(2) Be granted such privileges as organization and installation commanders are capable of granting and consider proper to enhance the prestige of their enlisted troop leaders.

Professional Status

In carrying out their increasingly important responsibilities, NCOs have earned their professional standing in the U.S. Army. However, broad acceptance of this professional status has been a relatively recent thing. Only during the last century have the Army's leaders come to realize that, for practical reasons as well as to recognize an important job well done, the prestige of NCOs had to be enhanced. They did this by attacking persistent problems in NCO pay, rank, and formal professional development.

Extract from General Regulations for the Army of the United States, 1841.

Article XIII

Non-commissioned Officers

60. It is of essential importance to the service that the station and respectability of the non-commissioned officer be upheld. It is, therefore, earnestly recommended and enjoined upon all officers, to be cautious

in reproving non-commissioned officers in the presence or hearing of privates, lest their authority and respectability be weakened in the eyes of their inferiors; and admonition should, at all times, be conveyed in mild terms, without exposing the individual, whatever be his rank. And it is also directed that non-commissioned officers, in no case, be sent to the guard-room and mixed with privates during confinement, but be considered as placed under arrest, except in aggravated cases, where escape may be anticipated.

61. Non-commissioned officers will be appointed in the manner prescribed by paragraph 45; and when thus appointed and announced, they are not to be removed from their respective places, except by the sentence of a court-martial, or by order of the Colonel, or other permanent commander of the regiment.

62. A non-commissioned officer having been duly appointed, cannot, at his pleasure, resign his place, or relinquish his duties as such, and return to the ranks.

63. Every non-commissioned officer shall be furnished with a certificate of his rank, signed by the Colonel, and countersigned by the Adjutant.

64. Whenever circumstances may make it necessary, Lance-Sergeants may be appointed from the Corporals, and Lance-Corporals from the privates, who, if their conduct be good, and evince capacity for the discharge of such duties, should be promoted to the first vacancies. The appointments will be made in the same manner as that already pointed out for non-commissioned officers.

65. Independent of the particular duties required of non-commissioned officers, (Sergeants and Corporals), when in the ranks, according to the systems of tactical instruction, it is also their duty, at all times, to observe the conduct of the privates, and to report immediately to the proper authority every breach of the general regulations of the service, or of the particular orders of the post....

Article XXII

Non-commissioned Officers' Mess

94. When the circumstances of the service will permit, it is highly desirable, for the maintenance of the respect and authority due the non-commissioned officers, that a separate mess for this class should be organized. Commanders of companies are therefore enjoined to give their attention to this subject.

95. The provisions for the non-commissioned officers will be cooked in the company kitchen, and their meals served at the same hours as those of the company....

Article XXIV

Officers' Waiters or Servants

106. Non-commissioned officers will, in no case, be permitted to act as waiters; nor are they, or private soldiers, not waiters, to be employed in any menial office, or made to perform any service, not military, for the private benefit of any officer, or mess of officers....

General Orders No. 37, Headquarters of the Army, Adjutant General's Office, Washington, 21 October 1852.

I. The following forms of Warrant and Discharge having been adopted by the War Department, are published for the information and government of all concerned:

Form of Warrant for Non-Commissioned Officers.

THE COMMANDING OFFICER OF THE REGIMENT OF Arms of U.S. as established by Resolution of Congress. June 20, 1782, and Act of Sept. 15, 1789, section 3d.

To all who shall see these presents, greeting:

Know ye, That reposing special trust and confidence in the patriotism, valor, fidelity and abilities of   , I do hereby appoint him   in Company   , of the   Regiment of   , in the service of the United States, to rank as such from the   day of   , one thousand eight hundred and   . He is therefore carefully and diligently to discharge the duty of by doing and performing all manner of things thereunto belonging. And I do strictly charge and require all non-commissioned officers and soldiers under his command to be obedient to his orders as . And he is to observe and follow such orders and directions, from time to time, as he shall receive from me, or the future Commanding Officer of the Regiment, or other superior officers and noncommissioned officers set over him, according to the rules and discipline of War. This Warrant to continue in force during the pleasure of the Commanding Officer of the Regiment for the time being.

Given under my hand at the Head Quarters of the Regiment, at , this day of , in the year of our Lord one thousand eight hundred and

By the Commanding Officer: *Commanding the Regiment.*

Adjutant of the Regiment.

Extract from Annual Report of the Secretary of War for the Year 1888.

Non-commissioned Officers

The position of non-commissioned officers is one of ever-increasing importance and responsibility. Noncommissioned officers, properly to perform the duties of their position, require, and should receive, a special education; they should, moreover, be of a higher average class of men, than we have heretofore been able to obtain in the regular service. I recommend that a school for non-commissioned officers of infantry and cavalry be established at Fort Leavenworth, on a plan similar to that now in operation at Fort Monroe for the benefit of the artillery. But it seems useless to expect much improvement in this respect until the pay attaching to these positions is sufficiently increased to offer an inducement for a good class of men to enlist for the purpose of obtaining them. While we have many good noncommissioned officers in the service, it is incontestable that the average of intelligence and efficiency is very far below what it should

be. I therefore most earnestly recommend a material increase in the pay of noncommissioned officers, believing that such a measure would tend greatly to increase the efficiency of the Army.

Pay of Non-commissioned Officers

Fully convinced that the adoption of the recommendation I had the honor to make in my last report would subserve the best interests of the Army, I beg to restate, in brief, the reasons why such a measure should be adopted and urged upon the consideration of Congress.

Much of the efficiency of a company depends on its non-commissioned officers. The very small increase in the pay of this class, totally incommensurate with the responsibility attached to it, is not a sufficient incentive to tempt the best and most reliable soldiers to accept the position, while it is often to the pecuniary advantage of the man to remain in the ranks, as a private on extra duty receives more pay than the sergeant-major or quartermaster-sergeant of a regiment. That this fact is not only wrong but pernicious in its effects, needs no argument. The pay of the lowest non-commissioned officer should not be less than $25, and the pay of the entire class re-adjusted on the suggested pay for the lowest position to $50 or $55 from the highest.

The grade of non-commissioned officer is the intermediary between the lowest in the Army, that of private, and the highest, the commissioned officer. The line of demarkation between these three classes should be as strongly accentuated downward as it is upward, and this is demanded alike by justice to the non-commissioned officers and proper regard for the discipline, efficiency, and morale of the Army.

Extract from Annual Report of the Secretary of War for the Year 1889.

Non-commissioned Officers

The efficiency of the Army, and the welfare and contentment of the enlisted men, depend very largely upon the non-commissioned officers. Hence it is very important that the character and dignity of the latter be elevated as much as possible. The vacancies available for the promotion of enlisted men to the grade of second lieutenant are necessarily very few in number, and the most meritorious non-commissioned officers are too old to commence a career as commissioned officers. Hence each non-commissioned grade should be made a real reward for meritorious service. I respectfully recommend that the pay of non-commissioned officers of infantry, cavalry, and artillery be made the same as that now established by law for like grades in the engineers.

Pay of Non-commissioned Officers

The importance of efficient non-commissioned officers in the line of the Army demands that their pay should bear some proportion to the duties and responsibilities of their respective grade and that it be sufficient to stimulate a soldierly rivalry among the privates to attain even the lowest grade in that class. Rank without adequate pay is robbed of much of its value and is belittled in the eyes of the men whose laudable ambition it should be to obtain it. It must be admitted that the rapid advance made in the art of war requires more study, closer application, and greater capacity on the part of non-commissioned officers than in former years.

The first sergeant of a company may truly be called the hardest worked non-commissioned officer in the Army. He has a direct responsibility for the proper care and use of the arms, equipments, and other property of the company; he is always on duty; must possess tact, sound judgment, superior intelligence, and have a thorough knowledge of all details, orders, and papers pertaining to company administration. A good first sergeant is indispensable to the making of a good company, for without him the best efforts of the captain would be rendered abortive. Exercising a certain supervision over the duties performed by every member of the company, he commands and instructs men in the ranks who receive more compensation than is allowed him, his pay being $6 less than that of a sol-

dier detailed as a mechanic and $1.50 less than is received by the private detailed on duty as laborer. Company sergeants, who are charged with important duties in the internal economy of the company besides commanding guards, escorts, fatigue parties, etc., receive $6.50 less than a soldier teamster in the quartermaster's department; while a private on extra duty receives $8.50 more than the pay of a corporal. These facts sufficiently evidence what little incentive is offered to non-commissioned officers to re-enlist and remain in the service.

The class of non-commissioned officers in the Army occupies the intermediate grade between the private and the commissioned officer, and its duties demand men of good capacity, strict honesty, untiring energy, and possessing high soldierly attributes. Justice to company non-commissioned officers demands that their pay should assimilate to that allowed similar grades in other branches of the service. The sergeant major and the quartermaster sergeant of engineers receive $36 per month; post quartermaster, ordnance, and commissary sergeants, $34; sergeants of ordnance, engineers, and of the Signal Corps, $34; and corporals of those three corps, $20 per month.

I have the honor to submit the following rates of pay which are deemed justly proportioned to the rank and duties of each grade of regimental and company noncommissioned officers: Sergeant major, $36; quartermaster sergeant, $34; chief trumpeter and the principal musician, $30; saddler sergeant, $26; first sergeant, $34; sergeant, $25; and corporal, $20.

The adoption of the above schedule of pay will undoubtedly greatly promote the efficiency of the service, while at the same time doing but simple justice to a meritorious and deserving class of soldiers.

Extract from Annual Report of the Secretary of War for the Year 1891.

School Teachers

To insure that measure of success to the school system in the Army which its importance demands requires school teachers specially trained and fully competent for the duties required of them. In the light of past experience it is not believed that this can be attained by the detail of enlisted men, who, however competent they may be so far as education is concerned, lack in the majority of cases the special and rare qualification necessary to instruct others. In order to secure, therefore, the best results possible, I beg to recommend that legislative authority be asked to enlist for each post a fully qualified school teacher, to be designated as "post school teacher," and to receive the pay and allowances of a hospital steward. Appointments to be made by the Secretary of War after the candidate has passed an examination before a board of officers convened to inquire into the character, special capacity, and aptitude of applicants for these important positions, for which also enlisted men of the Army should be considered eligible. Such a law would be a great inducement to the well-educated enlisted men, and sufficient to insure applications for appointment from well-educated young men in civil life competent as instructors.

While the possession of scholastic attainments necessarily increase the value and efficiency of noncommissioned officers, many cogent reasons exist why mere proficiency in studies should not establish a claim for promotion to that class. Noncommissioned officers are selected because possessing in a high degree courage, honesty, fidelity, force of character, and natural tact and ability in controlling the men. The whole company is often a narrow field for such selections, and serious detriment would result from limiting company commanders to men possessing a certificate of proficiency in studies.

For the benefit of the noncommissioned officer class it is recommended that their instruction be conducted in a post school for noncommissioned officers only, notwithstanding the objection advanced by some officers that such a course would interfere with the duties of company commanders and lessen their authority and responsibilities. The selection and appointment of noncommissioned officers would remain, as now, with captains of companies, but the establishment of a post school for noncommissioned officers would substitute systematic instruction, under an officer selected by reason of his special qualifications, to the present necessarily disconnected method of recitations in tactics, etc., conducted by the captain of each company.

As exemplifying the successful results of a properly conducted school of this class, I beg to submit the following interesting report of the officer charged, for the two past years, with the management and conduct of the school for noncommissioned officers at Fort Myer, Va.:

This school is composed of all the noncommissioned officers at the post, and instruction was given twice a week, on Tuesdays and Thursdays, from 10:45 to 11:45 a.m. The object of the school was to instruct the noncommissioned officers as thoroughly as time and opportunity would permit in their various duties, and to explain the general principles of the drill regulations, minor tactics, especially in hasty sketching and road reconnaissance, Blunt's Small Arms Firing Regulations, anatomy of the horse, shoeing, together with treatment of local injuries.

Owing to the lack of proper text-books, charts, materials, and the shortness of time, the instructor often felt hampered, but this feeling was offset in a great degree by the close attention of the members of the class.

The course may be roughly divided into four parts:

1. Drill regulations.
2. Minor tactics.
3. The horse.
4. Small arms firing regulations.

The method pursued in this part of the course was to assign lessons of definite length and to require recitations in the classroom supplemented by the solution of tactical problems at the blackboard. The schools of the soldier, platoon, and company were studied, likewise the general rules for successive formations in the school of the battalion. Special stress was laid on distances, intervals, and the posts and duties of guides. The general principles of bitting, saddling, and equitation were explained in two lectures, and I might add I think it a mistake that a fuller explanation of these is not contained in the Drill

280

Regulations. When the Drill Regulations had been finished a written examination covering them was given with very satisfactory results, the highest percentage being 96.

The lack of proper text-books adapted to the use of noncommissioned officers rendered it necessary for the instructor to lecture upon the various principles of minor tactics, *e.g.*, advance and rear guards, outposts, hasty sketching, and road reconnaissance. Hasty sketching was exploited at full length and detailed instruction given in the use of various topographical signs, use of instruments, and plotting of a hasty survey. Then the class was divided into parties and sent into the field equipped with box and prismatic compasses, and the road in the vicinity of the post surveyed and plotted. The various maps were then condensed into one large one by two members of the class. I append the originals turned over to me together with specimens of the road reports submitted. The results speak for themselves. In examining this work it should be borne in mind that the majority of the men had never seen a compass, and that in the year previous a few of the class had had but a very limited experience in work of this nature.

In that part of the course pertaining to the horse, lectures were given on the anatomy, the points to be observed in selection, age, shoeing, treatment of injuries with illustration of bandaging, administration of medicines, and stable management. This part of the course was copiously illustrated by enlargements made from the plates in various anatomical works on the subject.…

The modern tendency of individualizing the soldier, together with the adoption of a looser formation in tactical dispositions, have led the French and German authorities to require more from their noncommissioned officers than a mere knowledge of drill regulations; and I doubt that if the general method of instruction of our noncommissioned officers be looked into, they will be found to possess much more than an elementary knowledge of their drill book. The unquestioned necessity of a larger scope in their instruction being admitted, I can see no better way than to unite the noncommissioned officers of each battalion in a class

under a competent instructor and to follow a course prescribed by the War Department. This would necessitate the preparation of a manual which could be very easily compiled from the ample literature on this subject. Such a compilation would possess the advantage of putting the principles before the noncommissioned officers in simple language without that discussion usually found in treatises, and in a way easy of comprehension.

From two years' experience with the class here, I have observed as a result of instruction that each noncommissioned officer takes a greater interest in his duties as he now understands what he is doing; and I think it creates that distinction between the noncommissioned officer and the private which is so desirable. The mere fact that they know more than the men causes them to be looked up to and consequently respected.…

Pay of Noncommissioned Officers

The absolute importance of efficient noncommissioned officers in the line of the Army has been represented in former reports, and especial stress laid upon the unfortunate fact that the inadequacy of the pay of that class not only robs the position of its value, but actually deters suitable men in the ranks from aspiring to promotion.

A bill embodying the recommendations made by this office was introduced in the last Congress, but from reasons not affecting its merits failed to become a law. It is therefore earnestly recommended that the attention of the approaching Congress be called to the eminent justice of the measure. I reiterate the remarks on the subject made in report of 1889, and now again recommend that at least the pay of the first sergeant and of the duty sergeant be increased.

The first sergeant of a company may truly be called the hardest worked noncommissioned officer in the Army. He has a direct responsibility for the proper care and use of the arms, equipments, and other property of the company; he is always on duty; must possess tact, sound judgment, superior intelligence, and have a thorough knowledge of all details, orders, and papers pertaining to company administration. A good first sergeant is indispensable to the making of a good company, for without him the best efforts of the captain would be rendered abortive. Exercising a certain supervision over the duties performed by every member of the company, he commands and instructs men in the ranks who receive more compensation than is allowed him, his pay being $6 less than that of a soldier detailed as a mechanic and $1.50 less than is received by the private detailed on duty as laborer. Company sergeants, who are charged with important duties in the internal economy of the company, besides commanding guards, escorts, fatigue parties, etc., receive $6.50 less than a soldier teamster in the Quartermaster's Department; while a private on extra duty receives $8.50 more than the pay of a corporal. These facts sufficiently evidence what little incentive is offered to noncommissioned officers to re-enlist and remain in the service.

The class of noncommissioned officers in the Army occupies the intermediate grade between the private and the commissioned officer, and its duties demand men of good capacity, strict honesty, untiring energy, and possessing high soldierly attributes. Justice to company noncommissioned officers demands that their pay should assimilate to that allowed similar grades in other branches of the service.

I submit that first sergeants and duty sergeants of companies, troops, and batteries (1,910 in number) should receive the following rates of pay: First sergeants, $34, and sergeants $25 per month.

The increase of pay in these grades is $12 for first sergeants and $8 for duty sergeants, and will increase the annual appropriation by $201,168.

In connection with the foregoing, I beg to say that the highest in rank of the non-commissioned officers of the Army is the regimental sergeant major, whose pay is now only $23 per month. This should be increased to $36, the same pay as is now received by the sergeant major of Engineers. The duties of a sergeant major are most responsible in the correct and safe keeping of the regimental records, and he must be the highest type of the enlisted soldier to fulfill the military duties of his position. In fact he is selected as and he should be the ideal soldier and exemplar to the enlisted men of his regiment and a valuable aid to the regimental commander and his adjutant, and should receive pay commensurate with his rank and important duties. I also beg to recommend that Congress be asked to authorize the appointment of fifty "post sergeant majors," with the same pay as regimental sergeant majors, for assignment to important posts at which there are no regimental headquarters. This grade of noncommissioned officers is greatly needed to aid post commanders and post adjutants in keeping the post records and also in the other duties pertaining to their positions, which have now to be performed by men detailed for the purpose, and are seldom sufficiently well done, due largely to constant changes in troops from one post to another and change in details. This would not be the case were permanent post sergeant majors provided, similar to post quartermaster sergeants, and for the same reason—for the protection of the best interests of the service.

The increase of pay of regimental sergeant majors and the appointment of fifty post sergeant majors will amount to $27,840 per annum.

When the Adjutant-General can state in the posters calling for recruits that there are 2,000 positions of noncommissioned officers in the Army with pay and allowances that make them desirable, the disposition of good men to enlist will surely be greatly stimulated, and it will be economy to secure such men even at the cost of $228,000 per annum....

Extract from Annual Report of the Secretary of War for the Year 1892.

Non-commissioned Officers

With but very few exceptions the intelligence, instruction, character, and efficiency of this class of enlisted men are reported satisfactory for the performance of their duties, and they are required to study and recite in small-arms firing regulations in nearly all infantry and cavalry organizations; in the artillery this duty is exacted in but twenty-one batteries.

The non-commissioned officers have been called the vertebrae of the Army and much thought has been given the subject of improving them. Inquiry into the matter has elicited valuable suggestions from experienced officers, and by far the greater number advocate an increase in pay with a corresponding increase in the requirements as the most feasible steps to accomplish the object desired. Various other suggestions have been made, such as care in selecting recruits, regular and systematic instruction and drill, separate mess and sleeping apartments, competitive examination for appointment and promotion, regular schools for non-commissioned officers, etc. The lot of the non-commissioned officer, with its increased requirements and responsibility, which seem out of proportion to the small increase in his pay, should be made more enviable, and it is an undisputed fact that the extra duty man receives more pay and has less responsibility than the average non-commissioned officer....

Extract from Annual Report of the Secretary of War for the Year 1893.

Non-commissioned Officers

Under recent tactical and other changes in the army the non-commissioned officer has become a more important factor than ever before and much depends upon his efficiency, which in this class of enlisted men is generally very satisfactory, even though some organizations may not report them up to all the modern requirements. The change in requirements has been rather rapid for immediate readjustment, and perhaps we will not be able to get the best men for these positions until their pay is at least equal to that of the extra-duty man, or commensurate with the increased responsibilities and higher duties demanded. The act of Congress approved February 27, 1893, has slightly bettered conditions in this respect by increasing the pay of first sergeants to $25 and that of

sergeants to $18 per month. It should be still more; and our sergeant majors and regimental quartermaster-sergeants, who occupy the highest positions of all enlisted men and receive less pay than first sergeants, deserve speedy consideration.

The reports show that 347 non-commissioned officers hold certificates from service and other schools or have graduated from colleges, and 116 have belonged to the National Guard before they joined the army. These figures indicate to some extent the qualifications and attainments of this class of enlisted men.

In the greater number of organizations the rank of corporal is attained only after one or more years of service, though there are a few in which the average length of service has been reported as less. The greatest average length is reported from the infantry, the greatest in any organization being 11 years. In the cavalry the greatest is 8, and in the artillery 7 years, and in over half of the regiments the average length of service of a private is said to be five or more years before he is promoted.

The instruction of our non-commissioned officers has generally consisted in recitations in Small Arms Firing Regulations, Drill and Army Regulations and Manual of Guard Duty; and a number of company commanders have also instructed them in minor tactics, field service, rapid entrenchments, and kindred subjects. Recitations in Small Arms Firing Regulations have been most active in the infantry and cavalry, and less so in the artillery, though the number of batteries in which they have been held is greater than reported last year, and the extent of the regular instruction of artillerymen was never greater than now in our service. At a few posts the non-commissioned officers have been permitted to attend the lectures at the officers' lyceum, and it is to be hoped that this commendable practice will steadily extend. Inquiry into the subject of improving our non-commissioned officers has elicited about the same suggestions as submitted last year, the greater number of officers advocating an increase of pay; and this seems to be the keynote in our endeavor to secure the best possible material. The discipline and instruction of the service demand specially careful and continuous attention from the officers and non-commissioned officers during this transition period of armament and drill, when so many innovations have been imposed. And the non-commissioned officer was never a more important and responsible individual than now.

Pay of Non-commissioned Officers

Col. P. T. Swaine, Twenty-second Infantry, commanding officer, Fort Keogh, Mont., reports:

It is urgently recommended that the pay of regimental non-commissioned staff officers be apportioned to their rank, as compared with other non-commissioned officers. First sergeants, being of an inferior grade, actually receive more pay, whereas the higher grade should, as in the case of commissioned officers, receive the better compensation.

Col. C. H. Carlton, Eighth Cavalry, commanding officer, Fort Meade, S. Dak., reports:

As the regimental sergeant-majors and regimental quartermaster-sergeants are of higher rank and are selected from and promoted from first sergeants, the regimental sergeant-majors and the regimental quartermaster-sergeants should receive higher pay than the first sergeants; they are now receiving less.

Col. G. S. Poland, Seventeenth Infantry, commanding officer, Fort D. A. Russell, Wyo., reports:

The pay of regimental sergeant-majors and quartermaster-sergeants should be increased to at least $60 per month. They do more work per day (and are liable to perform field service) than many general service clerks and civilians in the employ of the Government who receive $100 per month and upwards.

The pay of each grade of non-commissioned officers should be increased also.

Maj. A. S. B. Keyes, Third Cavalry, commanding officer, Fort Ringgold, Tex., reports:

Greater inducements should be given for re-enlistments, especially to sergeants. First sergeants' pay should be $40 per month, with increase for service, and other sergeants in proportion.

Col. L. L. Langdon, First Artillery, commanding officer, Fort Hamilton, N.Y., reports:

There are many reasons why the pay of sergeant-majors and quartermaster-sergeants should be larger than that of all other non-commissioned officers; but I can imagine none why it should be the reverse, as it is now.

Congress has several times increased the pay of the other non-commissioned staff officers, but the cause, if any, of leaving the regimental non-commissioned staff in *statu quo* each time has, to my recollection, never been explained.

First. Regimental sergeant-majors and quartermaster-sergeants rank all the other non-commissioned officers in this army as well as in every other army; but in others, the English, for instance (if comparisons should be considered), pay goes with rank. The question of rank, which the position itself necessitates, alone is a sufficient reason ipso facto for superiority of pay.

The rates of pay and the rank of the non-commissioned officers are as follows:

1. Sergeant-major. $23.00
2. Quartermaster-sergeant. 23.00
3. Ordnance sergeant 34.00
4. Commissary sergeant 34.00
5. Post quartermaster-sergeant . . 34.00
6. Hospital stewards 45.00
7. Acting hospital stewards 25.00
8. Sergeants of engineers, ordnance, and signal corps. . . 34.00
9. First sergeants. 25.00

(All with the usual increase for continuous service.)

Second. The regimental non-commissioned staff is selected from the best material of a whole regiment on account of the requirements of the position, which are: Good moral character, sobriety, intelligence of a high grade, and the strictest integrity. It is comparatively an easy matter for a well-educated sergeant of the line, possessing common sense and judgment, to fill the positions of ordnance sergeant and first sergeant; but such a man would have to be qualified by nature and education, as well as by special course of study, to make a good sergeant-major.

Third. The duties of sergeant-major comprise the supervision of all the clerical work, post and regimental, the preparation of the numerous and intricate papers relating to regiment and post headquarters, the keeping of all the rosters, the distribution to all the officers and organizations of the orders intended for them, the entering of all communications passing through the offices, the proof-reading from the regimental press, the care of the books, accounts, etc., of the noncommissioned staff and band—in fact all the complicated work, for which the adjutant is responsible to his colonel, passes through the sergeant-major's hands, and he must have at his finger tips all the orders and decisions issued from the army, division, and department headquarters. He must be a man of discretion and tact. In addition, the sergeant-major attends guard mounting every day in the year, and all the battalion parades, inspections and drills.

The duties required of him are more varied and exacting, the hours longer, and an all-day holiday, or even a free Sunday, is an unknown pleasure to him, unless he avails himself of a pass or furlough, which he very seldom does on account of the responsibility for the continued and proper performance of the work intrusted to him.

Fourth. The regimental quartermaster-sergeant has as much as to do daily as a post quartermaster-sergeant, and performs the same duties as the latter if there be none at regimental headquarters, which is very often the case. If not directly, he is morally responsible for a large amount of government property intrusted to his care, as much as any commissary or post quartermaster-sergeant in their departments, who receive larger pay, and as he moves with the regiment whenever it does, or goes into the field, his work doubles, and his responsibility then becomes greater.

Fifth. When a private is on extra duty as a clerk or laborer, teamster or mechanic, his additional pay for this service is from $10 to $15 a month. Thus, a recruit may, and often does, draw more pay than a sergeant-major

or a regimental quartermaster-sergeant. The present sergeant-major of my regiment, prior to his appointment as such was sergeant and school-teacher, and drew $36 a month, but on being promoted to the rank of sergeant-major his pay dropped $8 a month.

Appreciating fully the momentous value of any action by you in such matters, I most earnestly request your attention to the above, with the view of enlisting your interest and endeavor toward the introduction of a separate bill in Congress for better pay to these hard-worked and deserving non-commissioned officers, with the final object to have superiority of pay go hand in hand with rank and responsibility of position, and particularly to offset the oversight of omitting them altogether in the bill passed at the last session of Congress.

A bill increasing the pay of sergeant-major and regimental quartermaster-sergeant to $50 per month, with the usual increase for continuous service in each case, would accomplish the desired result, of which everyone would acknowledge the fairness and justice and no one could complain.

The increased cost to the taxpayers will be slight, as there are only 40 sergeant-majors and 40 regimental quartermaster-sergeants in the whole Army.

Extract from Circular No. 30, War Department, Washington, 1 May 1924.

III—*Issue of old type officers' uniforms to noncommissioned officers of the first, second and third grades.*—The existing stock of officers' breeches, coats and complete uniforms, old type, of the following material:
Serge, 12, 16 and 20/22-ounce,
Melton, 16 and 20-ounce,
Whipcord,
Cotton, olive drab,
Gabardine:
which was manufactured for sale to officers, but which is now obsolete by reason of AR 600–35, as changed by Changes No. 9, AR 600–40, as changed by Changes No. 10, is authorized for issue to noncommissioned officers of the first, second and third grades, until supply is exhausted. The cotton garments will be charged to the clothing

allowance at the price of olive drab cotton issue coats and breeches and the woolen garments at the price of the olive drab woolen issue coats and breeches 20-oz. Braid will be removed from the sleeves of the coat by enlisted men before wearing. Uniform clothing issued under this authority is specifically authorized to be worn at any camp, post or station as long as the clothing is serviceable. (A.G. 421 (3–3–24).)

By order of the Secretary of War:

JOHN J. PERSHING,
*General of the Armies
Chief of Staff.*

Extract from Army Regulation 350–90, HQ, Department of the Army, Washington, 25 June 1957.

Education and Training
Noncommissioned Officer Academies

1. General. These regulations establish a standard pattern for the Noncommissioned Officer Academies in the United States Army. The purpose of Noncommissioned Officer Academies is to broaden the professional knowledge of the noncommissioned officer and instill in him the self-confidence and sense of responsibility required to make him a capable leader of men.

2. Establishment. *a.* Any of the following commanders is authorized, but not required, to establish a Noncommissioned Officer Academy:

(1) Commanding general of a division.

(2) The commander of a major installation, subject to approval of the appropriate Army commander, major oversea commander, or chief of a technical service.

b. Where possible, nondivisional troops will use the Noncommissioned Officer Academy of a nearby division rather than establish a separate facility.

c. Each academy will be designated as "———(division or installation) Noncommissioned Officer Academy" (e.g., 4th Infantry Division Noncommissioned Officer Academy).

d. All academies will conform to the standard pattern prescribed below.

3. Training. *a.* The minimum length of the course of instruction will be 4 weeks.

b. The number of courses conducted annually will be determined by local requirements. Consideration should be given to conducting separate courses for senior noncommissioned officers and for noncommissioned officer candidates. The content of the two courses need not vary appreciably.

c. Exacting selection procedures should be employed to insure the designation of outstanding noncommissioned officer instructors who have completed a course of instruction at a Noncommissioned Officer Academy.

d. Prerequisites for attendance will be determined locally by the commander having jurisdiction of the Academy.

4. Curriculum. *a.* The increased responsibility of noncommissioned officers under the new concepts of atomic warfare will be stressed in all phases of instruction. In all subjects, emphasis will be on how to teach the material presented rather than on the mere presentation of information.

b. No standardized course of instruction is prescribed; however, inclusion of the following subjects is mandatory:

(1) Leadership—minimum of 15 hours.

(2) Drill, Ceremonies and Command—(Drill, Inspection, Fitting and Wearing of the Uniform, Ceremonies, Customs and Courtesies, Conduct of Physical Training Program, etc.)—minimum of 15 hours.

(3) Methods of Instruction—minimum of 30 hours.

(4) Weapons Training—number of hours to be determined by division or installation commander.

(5) Map Reading—minimum of 20 hours.

(6) Tactics—number of hours to be determined by division or installation commander.

(7) Problems of the command and their solution—number of hours to be determined by division or installation commander.

c. An example of a detailed course of instruction which is considered suitable for use by a Noncommissioned Officer Academy is shown in the appendix.

5. Programming, budgeting, and funding. Formal programming is not required. Each command will support its academy from available resources. Use of training aids, furniture, equipment, etc., in support of these academies is authorized.

6. Administration. *a.* In accordance with paragraph 34a, AR 640–203, a notation will be made in paragraph 26 of DA Form 20, Enlisted Qualification Record, for each individual who successfully completes a course at a Noncommissioned Officer Academy as follows, "——(unit or organization) Noncommissioned Officer Academy, 4 weeks, —— (year)." For example, "1st Infantry Division Noncommissioned Officer Academy, 4 weeks, 1957."

b. An individual who has successfully completed a course at a Noncommissioned Officer Academy which meets the criteria established herein will not be permitted to attend another such course.

By Order of *Wilber M. Brucker,* Secretary of the Army:

MAXWELL D. TAYLOR,
General, United States Army,
Chief of Staff.

Extract from Army Circular No. 35–52, HQ, Department of the Army, Washington, 20 May 1958.

Finance and Fiscal Military Pay Act of 1958

1. The Military Pay Act of 1958 has been signed by the President and is P. L. 85–422 dated 20 May 1958. The Act becomes effective on 1 June 1958....

3. The act amends the table "incentive pay for hazardous duty" pertaining to commissioned officers, who perform aerial flights as crew members in accordance with section 204 of the CCA of 1949, as amended, by adding pay grades O–9 and O–10 and by establishing the rate of incentive pay for those grades in the amount of $165 for all categories of years of service. The table for enlisted members, concerning this incentive pay, is amended by adding pay grades E–8 and E–9, and by establishing a rate of $105 for all categories of years of service.

4. The table prescribing special pay for sea and foreign duty contained in section 206 of the CCA of 1949 is amended by adding pay grades E–8 and E–9 and by establishing monthly rates of $22.50 for each of those grades.

5. The act provides that the rates for basic allowance for quarters for pay grades O–9 and O–10 are the same as those prescribed for pay grade O–8, i.e., with dependents $171; without dependents $136.80. Pay grades E–8 and E–9 will receive the same as pay grade E–7, i.e., members on active duty without dependents $51.30; not over two dependents $77.10; over two dependents $96.90. The requirement that a member with dependents in pay grade E–7 have in effect an allotment of $80 per month is equally applicable to pay grades E–8 and E–9. If such enlisted members are on active duty for training, they will receive the same basic allowances for quarters as E–7 on active duty for training. The monthly rate of all other pay and allowances presently authorized for E–7 are for application to E–8 and E–9....

Extract from Army Regulation 600–200, HQ, Department of the Army, Washington, 24 March 1965.

Personnel—General
Enlisted Personnel Management System

Chapter 1

General

1–1. Purpose. *a.* To prescribe policies, responsibilities, and procedures pertaining to career management of Army enlisted personnel.

b. To provide a basis for further consolidation of all Army regulations on enlisted personnel management....

1–3. Applicability. *a.* This regulation is applicable to all enlisted personnel of the—

(1) Active Army.

(2) Army National Guard as indicated:

(a) Soldiers on initial active duty (section VI, chapter 7).

(b) Soldiers on active duty training or full time training duty for 90 days or more (chapter 8).

(3) United States Army Reserve on extended active duty or Initial Active Duty for Training (IADT).

b. The Chief, Army Reserve may issue additional instructions to supplement this regulation.

c. Each chapter in this regulation deals with a specific phase of enlisted career management; however, none of these phases will be used in isolation since they all deal with a system that is totally interrelated.

1–4. Policy. Effective management of Army personnel resources is necessary for successful accomplishment of the Army mission. Consistent with military necessity, the policy of the Department of the Army is to utilize personnel in positions commensurate with their military qualifications and personal attributes and to foster an atmosphere which will motivate all personnel to attain their full potential as soldiers.

1–5. Responsibility. Career management of enlisted personnel is a General Staff responsibility of the Deputy Chief of Staff for Personnel (DCSPER), Headquarters, Department of the Army. Classification, development, and utilization of soldiers within basic policies and procedures prescribed by this regulation are command responsibilities.

a. Except as indicated in b and c below, the Commander, U.S. Army Military Personnel Center is responsible for the conduct and supervision of all enlisted personnel functions and programs prescribed in this regulation.

b. The Surgeon General is responsible for the classification and utilization of inducted physicians, dentists, and veterinarians.

c. Unless otherwise prescribed in this regulation, correspondence pertaining to matters indicated in b above will be addressed to MILPERCEN or the Office of The Surgeon General.

d. The Cdr, MILPERCEN and The Surgeon General are responsible for the preparation and publication of changes to this regulation whenever changes become necessary in matters for which each is the proponent as outlined in b and c above. The Surgeon General will coordinate changes with the Cdr, MILPERCEN to ensure continuity of subject matter and format....

Chapter 3

Personnel Utilization
Section II. Utilization Controls

3–5. Utilization procedures and priorities. Unit commanders and supervisors will utilize soldiers in properly authorized table of organization or table of distribution positions consistent with their MOS qualifications and grades of rank (para 1–7, AR 600–200). Subject to the provisions of section III, the conditions under which soldiers are considered to be properly utilized are listed in a or b below. It is stressed that every effort must be made by the chain of command/supervision to assign and utilize soldiers in their PMOS/CPMOS. This management action affords the soldier necessary professional development protection particularly in the area of PMOS Skill Qualification Test evaluation and proper on-the-job experience credit. The benefits derived impact directly on the individual soldier's career progression in important personnel management purposes such as promotion, reenlistment, QMP, and schooling.

a. Proper utilization. The proper utilization of soldiers must receive the constant personal attention of commanders at all echelons of command. A soldier is considered to be properly utilized when used in a position under one of the following conditions, in the priority listed, or when used in accordance with b below.

(1) In the PMOS at the same grade of rank or two grades higher (provided there are no soldiers available in the proper grade for assignment). Consideration should be given to utilization in the same or higher skill level. Higher skill level will include any other MOS to which the soldier should progress in the normal line of progression in the MOS Career Pattern outlined in AR 611–201. Utilization contrary to this provision for soldiers holding a controlled MOS listed in paragraph 2–18e requires clearance from MILPERCEN, DA (appropriate career branch).

(2) In the Career Progression MOS (CPMOS) (provided skill level is other than "0" (zero)).

(3) In the secondary MOS at the same or higher grade of rank (only when no requirement exists in (1) above).

(4) In an MOS substitute for the PMOS as authorized in AR 611–201 (only when no requirement exists in (1) above).

(5) In an additional MOS at the same or higher grade of rank (only when no requirement exists in (1) above). Consideration must be given to the elapsed time, the change of equipment, functions related to the MOS, and the changes in the grade that have occurred since the soldier last served in the MOS.

(6) In a shortage or balanced MOS, if current PMOS is listed as overstrength in DA Circular 611 series, or otherwise directed by HQDA, in which the soldier is being trained for award of a new MOS.

b. *Authorized exceptions.* Assignments contrary to a above are authorized only when made under the following conditions:

(1) The assignment is under actual combat conditions.

(2) The assignment is to—

(a) Meet an urgent military requirement. Assignments will not exceed 90 days without approval of the appropriate major commander.

(b) Satisfy an exceptional need for a special temporary duty position. Period is limited to 90 days, after which the individual must be returned to perform duties in his/her assigned position for not less than 120 days or for the duration of assignment to the unit.

(3) Major commanders are authorized to extend the utilization period up to 12 months for a soldier on special duty when it has been determined that special training or skills of the soldier are required for total mission accomplishment. This authority may be delegated to the installation commander. Major commanders will establish a system to monitor these specific assignments in excess of 90 days (e.g., Quarterly Reports) to ensure protection of the interest of the individual soldier.

(4) Enlistment Bonus, Selective Reenlistment Bonus, and Variable Reenlistment Bonus recipients must serve in the MOS for which the bonus was awarded, an MOS within normal career progression pattern, or in an MOS designated by HQDA as comparable.

(5) The assignment is for the sole purpose of qualifying the individual for award of a shortage MOS. (See DA Cir 611 series.) The MOS must be at an authorized skill level commensurate with the pay grade.

(6) In support of Reserve summer training.

(7) The assignment is made under special instructions from Headquarters, Department of the Army.

(8) An NCO may be utilized in a specialist position at the same pay grade, provided there are no NCO vacancies available in his/her current pay grade and same or higher skill level.

(9) Soldiers surplus in accordance with AR 614–200, except grade E–9, may be assigned and utilized in their primary MOS in a one-grade lower position to preclude PCS moves and to offset grade or space imbalance between overseas and CONUS. Care will be taken to ensure that soldiers directed to serve in a lower grade position are not penalized through the Enlisted Evaluation System. In instances where the rated soldier is assigned to a position authorized a lower grade, a statement will be included in the narrative portion of the Evaluation Report that the assignment to the lower grade position was authorized by HQDA. The first priority for utilization of NCO's under this exception will be in a lower grade NCO position. Commanders will ensure that soldiers being utilized under this provision are counseled as to the specific reason for such utilization.

c. *Improperly utilized personnel.* A soldier who is not assigned in accordance with a or b above will be considered improperly utilized and will be reported to the next higher echelon of command (para 3–4d). Pending reassignment, the soldier will be utilized in a position which is most commensurate with his/her grade and qualifications. A soldier who is assigned in accordance with *a* or *b* above but who is not utilized in his/her *assigned* position will also be considered improperly utilized. Action will be taken to ensure that the soldier does in fact perform duties in the assigned position.

d. *Other considerations:*

(1) A specialist should not be utilized in an NCO position below his/her pay grade.

(2) In considering a specialist or private for utilization at a higher grade, this sequence should be followed:

(a) Specialist position at the next higher pay grade.

(b) NCO position at present pay grade.

(c) NCO position at a higher pay grade.

(3) Individual assignment limitations recorded on the soldier's Personnel Qualification Record must be considered.

Chapter 4 Section V.

Command Sergeant Major Retention Program

4–19. Purpose. The purpose of the CSM Retention Program is to provide procedures whereby a small number of outstanding CSM may be retained beyond 30 years of active service. This will provide the Army the benefit of their long years of experience, expertise and potential for future continued outstanding service.

4–20. Procedures. *a. Zone of Consideration.* All serving CSM will be considered during their 28th year of active service. Those CSMs in the zone not desiring consideration may submit a letter of declination in accordance with instructions contained in the annual board announcement.

b. Period of Retention. Retention will be authorized up to 35 years of active Federal service or to age 55 whichever occurs first.

c. Retention. The minimum number of CSM to be selected each year will be five. More than five may be selected when the total CSM on active duty beyond 30 years active federal service is less than 25.

d. Selection Proceedings. Selection will be accomplished on an annual basis by a DA Selection Board consisting of five members, one of whom will be the Sergeant Major of the Army, presided over by a major general president. Selection will be based on outstanding performance, demonstrated initiative and significant potential for valuable service in positions of responsibility in accordance with specific guidelines established for the board. Retention beyond 30 years is not to be a reward for past performance but rather based on potential for continued outstanding performance of duty.

e. Board of Recommendations. The board will forward their recommendations to DCSPER, HQDA for approval.

f. Notification Procedures. Commander, MILPERCEN will publish (annually) the LOI and approved recommended list. Commander,

MILPERCEN will personally, through command channels, notify those selected and require their written acceptance within 30 days of receipt. Upon acceptance of retention, authorization for reenlistment will be accomplished by MILPERCEN.

Chapter 7

Section VII. Appointment of Acting Noncommissioned Officers

7–52. Appointment. *a. Units.* Company, troop, battery, and separate detachment commanders may appoint qualified individuals as acting corporals, E–4, and acting sergeants, E–5, to serve in position vacancies existing in their units at their present or higher grade, including those resulting from temporary absences of assigned noncommissioned officers. For appointments to acting corporals, E–4, and acting sergeant, E–5, the individual being appointed may not be more than one grade lower than the grade to which he/she is being appointed. (See para 2–63 for lateral appointments.)

b. Casual groups. Commanders issuing movement orders for casual groups may appoint individuals as acting noncommissioned officers in grades of corporal, E–4, sergeant, E–5, and staff sergeant, E–6, to exercise supervision and control during movements. The number of acting noncommissioned officers will not exceed the following:

(1) One acting corporal to each 12 casuals.

(2) One acting corporal plus one acting sergeant to each 35 casuals.

(3) One acting staff sergeant when appointing two or more acting sergeants for a group.

c. Insignia. Acting noncommissioned officers may wear either the regular insignia of grade permanently affixed to the sleeve or acting noncommissioned officers brassards as described in AR 670–5. Wearing of regular insignia of grade is encouraged in units where experience indicates the acting noncommissioned officer normally will be promoted to the grade in which acting. Acting noncommissioned officers of casual groups and training activities, where frequent personnel changes make regular insignia impracticable, will wear the brassard (AR 670–5).

d. Pay and benefits. Acting noncommissioned officers are not entitled to pay and allowances for such higher grades, and services will not be credited as time in a higher grade for promotion or date-of-rank purposes.

e. Authority. An acting corporal or sergeant, appointed pursuant to the authority contained in this paragraph, has all of the authority of a regular appointed noncommissioned officer of the same grade.

7–53. Orders. *a.* Appointment of acting NCO will be announced in orders using Format 304, appendix A, AR 310–10. Appointment orders will be filed in accordance with AR 640–10 in the action pending portion of MPRJ until such time as termination orders are published.

b. An acting noncommissioned officer's status will be terminated—

(1) At the discretion of the unit commander who made the appointment.

(2) Upon assignment of a regularly promoted noncommissioned officer to the position.

(3) When casual groups reach their destination.

(4) Upon reassignment to another unit.

c. Termination for reasons (1) through (3) above will be accomplished by orders using format 304, appendix A, AR 310–10. Termination due to reassignment will be accomplished in the additional instructions of the order effecting the reassignment (see AR 310–10).

Extract from Army Circular No. 351–42, HQ, Department of the Army, Washington, 23 June 1972.

Schools
Noncommissioned Officer
Education System (NCOES)

1. General. To provide professional development educational opportunities for the Army's noncommissioned officers and specialists, the Noncommissioned Officer Education System (NCOES) was established in 1971. The system provides three levels of career development training (Basic, Advanced, and Senior Levels) to prepare enlisted personnel for the assumption of increasing levels of responsibility. Courses are being implemented at US Army service schools as programs of instruction are developed. All courses will be fully operational in FY 73.

2. Purpose. The purpose of this circular is to provide information concerning the policies and procedures established for the operation of the Noncommissioned Officer Education System (NCOES).

3. Applicability. The NCOES applies to all eligible enlisted personnel of all components of the Army.

4. Concept. The NCOES consists of three progressive levels of instruction (Basic, Advanced, and Senior) designed to prepare enlisted personnel to assume increasing responsibilities compatible with grade progression. Courses are designed to provide training for the full range of noncommissioned officer responsibilities in world-wide assignments. Basic and Advanced Level courses are Career Management Field (CMP) oriented to provide this professional development opportunity for all enlisted personnel, regardless of Military Occupational Specialty (MOS). The Senior Level course is CMP immaterial and provides broad career enhancement training for senior enlisted personnel. NCOES courses are not MOS-producing or ASI/SQI-awarding; rather, they are career (professional development) courses.

5. Objectives. Objectives of NCOES are—

a. To increase the professional quality of the Noncommissioned Officer Corps.

b. To provide enlisted personnel with opportunities for progressive and continuing development.

c. To enhance career attractiveness by providing a system of formal military education.

d. To provide the Army with highly trained and dedicated noncommissioned officers to fill positions of increasing responsibility.

6. Course establishment. Courses will be established by Commanding General, US Continental Army Command, The Surgeon General, and Commanding General, United States Army Security Agency, to provide this educational opportunity to all enlisted personnel in all components of the Army.

7. Course objectives and scope. *a. Basic Noncommissioned Officer courses.*

(1) *Objectives.*

(a) To prepare selected enlisted personnel in grades E4 and E5 and selected E3's from the replacement stream to perform duties appropriate to grades E5, E6, and E7 within their CMP.

(b) To provide training in appropriate supervisory skills.

(c) To develop a willingness to assume responsibilities and the confidence to apply technical knowledge.

(d) To instill a feeling of dignity and a sense of duty and obligation for service.

(2) *Scope of training.*

(a) Training is conducted within the MOS or CMP context to qualify individuals to lead comparatively small groups of enlisted personnel of similar MOS or of the same or associated CMP. Training is oriented toward the 4 skill level.

(b) Emphasis is placed on basic leadership skills and knowledge of military subjects required to effectively lead enlisted personnel at the team, squad, section and comparable levels.

(c) Practical work is stressed throughout the curriculum.

(3) *Course lengths.* Course lengths vary from approximately 8 weeks to 12 weeks depending on the requirements of the MOS or CMP.

b. Advanced Noncommissioned Officer Courses.

(1) *Objectives.*

(a) To prepare selected enlisted personnel in grades E6 and E7 to perform duties appropriate to grades E8 and E9 within their CMP.

(b) To provide training in appropriate supervisory skills.

(c) To increase skills, confidence, and a sense of pride and esprit de corps.

(2) *Scope of training.*

(a) Advanced level training is functional, within the MOS and CMP context, and is oriented toward appropriate MOS qualification above the 4 skill level.

(b) Emphasis is placed on leadership and human relations skills and knowledge of subjects required to effectively perform duty as first sergeant, sergeant major, or comparable noncommissioned officer at the company, battalion, brigade or comparable level of homogeneous units.

(c) Training is oriented on the Army, service, or CMP, as appropriate, to produce competent first sergeants, sergeants major, staff noncommissioned officers, or comparable unit noncommissioned officers.

(d) Emphasis is placed on the philosophy underlying Army objectives and Army systems. Training is directed toward providing a firm comprehension of the noncommissioned officer's role in combat, combat support, and combat service support units.

(3) *Course lengths.* Course lengths vary from approximately 8 weeks to 12 weeks depending on the requirements of the MOS or CMP.

c. Senior Level Course. The Senior Level NCOES course will be conducted at the US Army Sergeants Major Academy (USASMA) at Fort Bliss, Texas.

(1) *Objective.* To prepare selected enlisted personnel in grade E8 to perform duty as command sergeant major with emphasis on leadership, human relations, and training.

(2) *Scope of training.*

(a) Prepare students to assist commanders in the solution of leadership, human relations and training problems.

(b) Instruct students in tactical and administrative operations of divisions.

(c) Update students on contemporary Army problems.

(d) Orient students on national and international affairs.

(e) Improve communication skills.

(f) Develop intellectual depth and analytical ability.

(3) *Course length.* Course length will be approximately 22 weeks.

8. Prerequisites. Following are prerequisites for selection to attend NCOES courses:

a. Basic Noncommissioned Officer Courses.

(1) Grade E4 or E5 (on a test basis RA E3 when selected at the completion of AIT).

(2) MOS evaluation score of 100 or more as this score appears on the Enlisted Evaluation Data Report, in the most recent primary MOS evaluation, except for E3 selected from AIT who are untested. Waiver of MOS test scores is authorized for all personnel who have not been tested, and for those tested whose test results have not been received at the parent unit. Under this waiver authority, it is suggested that a General Technical (GT) score of

100 or higher be used as an alternate discriminator, and that commanders apply the whole-man concept to insure quality selections for course attendance.

(3) Maximum service, as follows:

(a) Personnel in grade E4 must not have completed more than 8 years' service as of the date of entry into the course.

(b) Personnel in grade E5 must not have completed more than 12 years' service as of the date of entry into the course.

(4) Be recommended by unit and/or higher commanders as applicable.

(5) Length of service remaining upon completion of the course must be in accordance with paragraph 10, DA Pamphlet 350–10, except E3 must be on at least a 3-year (Regular Army) enlistment.

(6) Additional requirements, such as physical examinations and security clearances, that pertain to specific courses will also apply.

(7) Waivers of prerequisites will be processed in accordance with paragraph 9, DA Pamphlet 350–10, with the exception of the grade and service remaining prerequisites which are not waiverable.

b. Advanced Noncommissioned Officer courses.

(1) Grade E6 or E7.

(2) Not more than 17 years active service on scheduled report date for the course (may be waived for Reserve component personnel).

(3) MOS evaluation score of 100 or more as it appears on the Enlisted Evaluation Data Report, in the most recent primary MOS evaluation.

(4) Length of service remaining upon completion of course must be in accordance with paragraph 10, DA Pamphlet 350–10.

(5) Additional requirements, such as physical examinations and security clearances, that pertain to specific courses will also apply.

c. Senior Noncommissioned Officer course.

(1) Grade of E8.

(2) Not more than 23 years active service as of 1 September of the fiscal year of attendance (may be waived for Reserve component personnel).

(3) Available to attend, i.e., must be in a CONUS non-stabilized assignment or will have completed 5/6 of a CONUS stabilized or oversea tour on departure from the command to meet school report dates (may be waived with concurrence of the losing command).

(4) MOS evaluation score of 100 or more as it appears on the Enlisted Evaluation Data Report, in the most recent primary MOS evaluation.

(5) Length of service remaining upon completion of the course must be in accordance with paragraph 10, DA Pamphlet 350–10.

(6) Additional requirements, such as physical examinations and security clearances as determined by CG CONARC, will also apply.

General Orders No. 98, HQ, U.S. Continental Army Command, Fort Monroe, Va., 18 July 1972.

TC 001. Following action directed.

United States Army Sergeants Major Academy (5AW3QTAA) Fort Bliss, Texas 79916

Action: UNIT ORGANIZED

Asgd to: Headquarters, United States Continental Army Command (WOGSAAA) Fort Monroe, Virginia 23351

Mission: To provide selected noncommissioned officers a broad and varied, in-depth educational experience designed to qualify them for promotion to Sergeant Major and subsequent service in top level noncommissioned officer positions throughout the United States Army.

Effective date: 1 July 1972

Authorized Strength: 47 Off: 1 WO: 42 EM: 90 AGG: 30 CIV

Required Strength: 47 Off: 1 WO: 42 EM: 90 AGG: 30 CIV

Accounting classification: As appropriate in accordance with AR 37–100.

Files/records: AR 340–18 series applies.

Morning reports: Entry will be made in record of events section of Morning Report prepared for effective date (AR 680–1)

Authority: DA msg DAFD-OTA-CO, 182811Z Jul 72, VOCG confirmed

Special Instructions:

a. TDA 5AW3QTAAOO

b. TPSN 66113

c. Priority Status 20832

d. Equipment section of TDA will be forwarded to DA at a later date.

e. Personnel authorization will be provided from Instructor/School overhead resources. The course will operate as a separate element within the CONARC school system with education and training matters under the jurisdiction of Commanding General, CONARC. Attendance will be by PCS for approximately 22 weeks. The student input of initial class will consist of 160 students and subsequently after DLISW phases out, 200 students per class. Administration and logistical support will be provided by United States Army Air Defense Center and Fort Bliss, Fort Bliss, Texas 79916.

FOR THE COMMANDER:

DONN R. PEPKE
Major General, GS
Chief of Staff

OFFICIAL:
E. THOMAS
Colonel, AGC
Adjutant General

Extract from Army Regulation 350–17, HQ, Department of the Army, Washington, 1 December 1980.

Noncommissioned Officer Development Program (NCODP)

1. Purpose. This regulation prescribes policy, responsibilities, and procedures for the establishment, Army-wide, of the Non-commissioned Officer Development Program (NCODP).

2. Applicability. This regulation applies to the Active Army, Army National Guard (ARNG), and US Army Reserve (USAR).

3. Objectives. a. The objectives of NCODP are the following:

(1) Strengthen and enhance leadership development of the first line NCO supervisor.

(2) Assist and provide guidance in the continuing development of noncommissioned officers.

(3) Increase the confidence of the NCO as a leader.

(4) Realize the full potential of the NCO support channel for the chain of command.

(5) Improve unit effectiveness.

b. NCODP builds upon the contributions of the Army's Enlisted Personnel Management System (EPMS) and the Noncommissioned Officer Education System (NCOES). These two systems provide a valuable foundation for the development of noncommissioned officers; however, it is through the practical application of skills in the individual unit that soldiers achieve their goal of becoming a truly professional noncommissioned officer.

4. Policies. a. The NCODP is a command responsibility.

b. NCODP is a leadership tool to be used at the battalion or equivalent level. It is equally applicable to TDA and TOE structures (see app A).

c. NCO professional development training will be scheduled and reflected on unit/organization master training programs and schedules. Such training will be appropriately structured to the needs of the unit and noncommissioned officer as assessed by the commander. (Suggested topics for NCO professional development programs are at app B.)

d. All soldiers who demonstrate the potential for, or are performing duty in, a leadership position or are designated as an acting noncommissioned officer will participate in NCODP.

e. Separate classes may be conducted for SFC through CSMs.

5. Responsibilities. a. The Deputy Chief of Staff for Operations and Plans (DCSOPS) exercises general staff supervision over policies, regulations, initiatives, and programs relating to NCODP.

b. The Deputy Chief of Staff for Personnel (DCSPER) coordinates all personnel management initiatives and policies which relate to NCODP with the DCSOPS.

c. Sergeant Major of the Army (SMA)—

(1) Acts as the focal point for required DA NCODP actions which do not otherwise define themselves by functional staff responsibility.

(2) Is the focal point for all HQDA agencies and their field operating agencies (FOAs) on decisions which impact on noncommissioned officer development and NCODP policies.

(3) Renders an annual report to the Chief of Staff, US Army (CSA), on the state of the

Army's Noncommissioned Officer Corps. This includes an assessment of the implementation of NCODP in major Army Commands (MACOMs), the ARNG, and the USAR.

d. Chief, National Guard Bureau (CNGB)—

(1) Integrates the NCODP into pertinent directives and programs unique to the ARNG.

(2) Provides advice and assistance to the DCSOPS.

e. Chief, Army Reserve (CAR)—

(1) Integrates the NCODP into pertinent directives and programs unique to the USAR.

(2) Provides advice and assistance to the DCSOPS and the Commanding General, US Army Reserve Component Personnel and Administration Center in the development of NCODP supporting programs for the USAR.

f. The Inspector General (TIG)—

(1) Inquires into the effectiveness of NCODP during scheduled inspections and staff visits.

(2) Provides appropriate feedback to the Army Staff.

g. The Adjutant General (TAG)—

(1) Coordinates with DCSOPS the Quality of Life (QOL) initiatives which impact upon NCODP.

(2) Insures that educational policies, which impact upon noncommissioned officer development, support NCODP.

h. Major Army commands (MACOMs)—

(1) Provide the support and means to promote effective NCODPs in units, organizations, and activities.

(2) Insure that intermediate headquarters assist in supporting battalions and equivalent commands to develop formal NCODPs.

(3) In addition to the above, the Commanding General, US Army Forces Command (FORSCOM) will provide NCODP guidance and assistance to the ARNG and the USAR.

i. The Commanders of battalions and equivalent organizations—

(1) Are responsible for developing NCODPs which are responsive to the needs of their unit and the aspirations and development of their junior leaders.

(2) Insure time and resources are provided for the conduct of unit professional develop-

ment training. This includes formal periods of instruction and timely counseling of NCOs as an integral part of professional development.

(3) Insure that there is, throughout their units, a clear identification of those tasks that are noncommissioned officer business.

(4) Insure that a clear and distinct noncommissioned officer support channel is established. This support channel will not replace the normal supervisory chain of command, but will complement that system.

6. Implementing guidance. *a.* Professional noncommissioned officer training should be programed as integral portions of formal and informal periods of instruction. It should be implemented at the lowest level feasible. This may be company, troop, battery, or separate detachment. (Battalion or equivalent level for more formal type training is appropriate.)

b. Unit programs will complement formal training presented at military and civilian institutions such as that offered by the NCOES and civilian schooling.

c. NCODP professional development training will include instructions applicable to soldiers of all career management fields; it will include familiarization of those tasks common to all career fields. FM 22–600–20 lists specific NCO responsibilities—the broad skeletal structure of a noncommissioned officer's performance. They are as follows:

(1) Train soldiers.

(2) Care for their professional needs.

(3) Account for their status.

(4) Maintain fitness and appearance.

(5) Be concerned about the soldier and his or her family.

(6) Supervise, counsel, motivate, and discipline.

(7) Be loyal.

(8) Plan ahead.

(9) Set the example.

(10) Maintain the unit's equipment and facilities.

d. Portions of the NCODP may be formalized into periods of noncommissioned officer development training which should be institutionalized in all commands. The topics selected should be attuned to the geography, mission, and shortfalls of the unit. They should supplement professional training gained from daily, routine operations.

e. NCO communication links at battalion levels and higher should be established. Their purpose is to consider, but not be limited to, problems and recommendations related to improvements in the development and QOL of all NCOs and enlisted personnel. They also serve to provide recommendations to commanders on topics which affect enlisted personnel.

f. A matrix of NCODP supporting programs and policies is provided at appendix A.

g. A selected list of noncommissioned officer development training subjects is at appendix B.

By Order of the Secretary of the Army:

E. C. Meyer
General, United States Army
Chief of Staff

Specialist Rank

Although the specialists of the two world wars were not combat leaders, and therefore did not receive training in leadership skills, the more senior specialists were often called upon to assume command responsibilities. The distinction between the NCO small-unit leader and specialist became blurred in the post–World War II period as the Army's needs for men and women who combined both technical and leadership skills increased. Today, in the era of the complete, professional soldier, the position of specialist has all but been eliminated from the rank structure. Only the Specialist (formally, Specialist 4th Class) remains.

Extract from Army Circular No. 204, War Department, Washington, 24 June 1942.

IV—Conversion of specialist ratings to technician grades.—1. Section I, Circular No. 264, War Department, 1941, is rescinded.

2. The following enlisted grades are authorized and in appropriate cases will be included in allotments of grades and strengths and in Tables of Organization:

Technician, third, fourth, and fifth grades.

3. *a.* Technicians are noncommissioned officers. They will receive the pay and allowances of the pay grade indicated by their titles. Technicians, third, fourth, and fifth grades will rank among themselves, according to the dates of their warrants, below staff sergeants, sergeants, and corporals, respectively.

b. Technicians are appointed for specific duties of a technical or administrative nature. Warrants should indicate the specialty for which appointed. All appointments during the present war will be temporary and war-

rants issued will so indicate, except that noncommissioned officers holding permanent warrants who are reappointed as technicians as a result of the action prescribed by paragraph 8 will be issued permanent warrants as technicians.

c. All regulations and orders relating to command authority apply to technicians in the same manner as to other noncommissioned officers.

d. The appointment and reduction of technicians is governed by the same regulations applicable to other noncommissioned officers of corresponding grades, except that technicians, fourth and fifth grades, may be reduced upon termination of their assignment to the duties for which they were appointed to the technician grade. The authority to appoint and reduce technicians, fourth and fifth grades, subject to the foregoing provisions, may be delegated by commanders authorized to appoint technicians to company and detachment commanders.

4. *a. Effective June 1, 1942,* all specialist ratings, except air mechanics, are abolished and all enlisted men holding specialist ratings are disrated and reappointed to technician grades as follows:

Old grade and rating	New technician grade
Private, first class, specialist first class	Technician, fourth grade.
Private, specialist first class	Do.
Private, first class, specialist second class	Do.
Private, specialist, second class	Do.
Private, first class, specialist third class	Do.
Private, specialist third class	Technician, fifth grade.

Private, first class,
  specialist fourth class   Do.
Private,
  specialist fourth class   Do.

b. Specialists, fifth and sixth class, are disrated and will be paid according to their rank as privates, first class, and privates.

5. Pending publication of revised Tables of Organization or revised allotments under the technician grade system, grades and ratings now authorized are changed as follows:

a. Substitute technicians, fourth grade, for specialists ratings, first and second classes, and for one-half the number of specialists, third class.

b. Substitute technicians, fifth grade, for one-half of the number of specialists, third class, and for all specialists, fourth class.

c. Eliminate allotments of specialists, fifth and sixth classes.

d. Allotments of privates and privates, first class, will be computed as follows: Subtract from the total number of privates and privates, first class, now shown in Tables of Organization or published allotments, the number of basics (if any) and the total number of technicians determined under the above instructions. One-half of the remainder is the number of privates, first class. The number of privates is the remainder less the number of privates, first class, plus the number of basics authorized.

Extract from Army Circular No. 202, Department of the Army, Washington, 7 July 1948.

II. GRADE STRUCTURE.—4. **Enlisted Grade Structure.**—Effective 1 August 1948—

a. The grade structure for enlisted personnel will consist of seven pay grades with the new titles indicated:

Grade	New titles	Present titles
First	Master sergeant	Master sergeant
		First sergeant
Second	Sergeant, first class	Technical sergeant
Third	Sergeant	Staff sergeant
Fourth	Corporal	Sergeant
Fifth	Private, first class	Corporal
Sixth	Private	Private, first class
Seventh	Recruit	Private

b. The new pay grade titles will replace titles presently in use. Enlisted personnel will be converted to new pay grade titles appropriate to their actual pay grade in accordance with a above.

c. The Noncommissioned Officer Corps will consist of the first four pay grades only.

5. **Conversion of enlisted titles of grade.**—*a.* New warrants (WD AGO Form 58) will be issued for all personnel in grades 2, 3, and 4 in consonance with the pay grade titles above. Warrants will not be issued for personnel below the fourth pay grade....

6. **Technician titles.**—Effective 1 August 1948, technician grade titles prescribed by paragraph 8, AR 615–5, are abolished. Enlisted men who on that date hold appointments as technician fifth grade, technician fourth grade, or technician third grade will be converted to a new pay grade title appropriate to their current pay grade. Appropriate warrants, WD AGO Form 58, indicating new pay grade titles will be issued for personnel in the fourth and third pay grade.

7. *a.* First sergeant title.—The title of first sergeant is not a pay grade title. It remains an occupational title appropriate to a first grade position of such special importance in the Noncommissioned Officer Corps that distinctive insignia of grade is provided.

b. Sergeant major title.—The occupational title of sergeant major will continue to apply to appropriate individuals at regimental and battalion level.

8. **New enlisted insignia of grade.**—*a.* Effective 1 August 1948 two types of enlisted insignia of grade are established, as follows:

(1) Combat insignia worn by combat personnel which will be gold color background with dark blue color chevrons, arcs, and lozenge.

(2) Noncombat insignia worn by noncombat personnel which will be dark blue color background with gold color chevrons, arcs, and lozenge.

b. Both types of grade insignia will be on an embroidered background 2 inches in width forming 1/8-inch edging around the entire insignia and between each chevron and arm.

c. Except for color, combat insignia will be the same as noncombat insignia for the same grade.

d. Listed below are the appropriate insignia for each grade (see fig. 1):

First grade.—Three chevrons above three arcs.

Second grade.—Three chevrons above two arcs.

Third grade.—Three chevrons above one arc.

Fourth grade.—Two chevrons.

Fifth grade.—One chevron.

Sixth grade.—No chevrons.

Seventh grade.—No chevrons.

e. First sergeants will wear the grade insignia of the first grade with the addition of a lozenge between the chevrons and the arcs.

9. Definition of combat personnel.—*a.* Combat personnel are defined, for the purpose of determining entitlement to combat insignia of grade, as all personnel assigned to the designated combat units listed below:

(1) Infantry, armored, and airborne divisions (including 1st Cavalry Division) and component units thereof.

(2) Infantry and armored-cavalry units.

(3) Artillery 75-mm How; 105-mm How or 155-mm How battalions; 8-inch guns, 8-inch How, 155-mm gun, 240-mm gun, and 240-mm How battalions; field artillery observation battalions.

(4) Engineer special brigades and component units thereof.

(5) Engineer combat battalions.

(6) Chemical mortar battalions.

(7) Constabulary brigades, regiments and squadrons, and component units thereof.

b. Action may be initiated by commanders of major commands, to recommend the designation of additional type units other than those defined in a above as combat units. Such action will be forwarded through channels to the Department of the Army for approval.

Extract from Army Regulation 615–15, HQ, Department of the Army, Washington, 2 July 1954.

Separation of Noncommissioned Officers from Specialists

Section I

General

1. Purpose.—These regulations set forth procedures designed to increase the prestige of the noncommissioned officer in the Army by identifying him as an enlisted commander of troops. In order to do so, it is necessary to distinguish the noncommissioned officer from the enlisted technical or administrative specialist. These regulations effect the necessary distinction, and at the same time give full recognition to the importance of the noncommissioned officer and the specialist. While it is the desire of the Department of the Army to restore the noncommissioned officer to his traditional position as the backbone of the Army, it is also of fundamental importance that prestige and respect properly due the specialist be preserved. To accomplish the purpose of these regulations, the following objectives are established:

a. Identify the noncommissioned officer and specialist as separate categories of enlisted personnel.

b. Prescribe Department of the Army policies and procedures governing the conversion of a portion of each present noncommissioned officer grade to specialist grades.

c. Provide for the enhancement of the prestige of the noncommissioned officer.

d. Preserve the respect properly due those persons appointed to specialist grades.

2. Applicability.—These regulations are applicable to enlisted personnel of all components of the Army, except retired personnel.

3. Effective date.—Effective 1 March 1955 conversions to grades and titles outlined in these regulations are hereby effected for enlisted personnel of the Army in accordance with the procedures outlined herein.

4. Definitions.—For the purpose of these regulations, the following definitions apply:

a. Appointment.—Administrative action which effects change from a noncommissioned officer grade to a specialist grade.

b. Noncommissioned officer.—An enlisted person who has been appointed a noncommissioned officer by competent authority for the purpose of exercising leadership over other personnel.

c. Pay grade.—The statutory pay grade established in the Career Compensation Act of 1949, as amended.

d. Promotion.—Administrative action which effects advancement from a noncommissioned officer grade to a higher noncommissioned officer grade, from a specialist grade to a noncommissioned officer grade, from a specialist grade to a higher specialist grade, or from a private grade to a higher grade.

e. Specialist.—An enlisted person who has been appointed or promoted as a specialist by competent authority for the purpose of discharging technical or administrative duties not requiring the exercise of leadership.

f. Title.—The descriptive name by which various categories of enlisted personnel are designated.

Section II

Grade Structure and Titles

5. Scope.—This section establishes the grade structure and titles of grades for all enlisted personnel of the Army.

6. Enlisted grade structure and titles.—a. The grade structure for enlisted personnel consists of seven pay grades with titles as indicated below:

Grade	Noncommissioned officers	Specialists	Privates
E–7	Master sergeant	Master specialist	—
E–6	Sergeant 1st class	Specialist 1st class	—
E–5	Sergeant	Specialist 2d class	—
E–4	Corporal	Specialist 3d class	—
E–3	—	—	Private
E–2	—	—	Private E–2.
E–1	—	—	Private E–1.

b. These titles replace those in use prior to the effective date of these regulations. Conversions to the new titles will be accomplished in accordance with the procedures outlined in paragraphs 10 through 18.

7. Titles of address.—*a.* Noncommissioned officers will be addressed as "Sergeant" or "Corporal" as appropriate.

b. Specialists will be addressed as "Specialist."

c. Personnel in private grades will be addressed as "Private."

Section III

Rank

8. Scope.—This section establishes the order of rank of personnel on and after the effective date established in paragraph 3.

9. Order of rank.—*a.* The noncommissioned officer will rank above all other enlisted personnel regardless of pay grade. The following are the rank of grades in order of precedence:

Order of rank	Pay grade	Grade title
First	E–7	Master sergeant.
Second	E–6	Sergeant 1st class.
Third	E–5	Sergeant.
Fourth	E–4	Corporal.
Fifth	E–7	Master specialist.
Sixth	E–6	Specialist 1st class.
Seventh	E–5	Specialist 2d class.
Eighth	E–4	Specialist 3d class.
Ninth	E–3	Private 1st class.
Tenth	E–2	Private, E–2
Eleventh	E–1	Private, E–1

b. Determination of order of rank among personnel of the same grade will be in accordance with AR 600–15.

Section VI

Responsibility and Authority of the Noncommissioned Officer

24. General.—Noncommissioned officers must be capable leaders. In order to insure that noncommissioned officers are equal to the tasks required of them, commanders of all echelons will give their personal attention to improving the quality and prestige of the noncommissioned officer. The proper assignment of noncommissioned officers, based on MOS, grade, and leadership ability is of utmost importance in the enhancement of the prestige of noncommissioned officers.

25. Enhancement of noncommissioned officers.—In order to instill the desire in the noncommissioned officer to assume added responsibility and to attain the desired results of a competent Noncommissioned Officer Corps, special attention will be given to the following points:

a. Careful selection of noncommissioned officers.

b. Training of noncommissioned officers in their duties and responsibilities.

c. Prompt removal of noncommissioned officers who fail to attain or maintain the acceptable standards of leadership.

26. Authority of the noncommissioned officer.—The position of respect and leadership accorded the noncommissioned officer in the chain of command depends directly on the degree of authority and responsibility that he is allowed to exercise. The delegation of all authority and command prerogatives proper to the position is essential to the development of strong and capable noncommissioned officers. Maximum care must be taken to avoid usurping the authority of the noncommissioned officer as to do so will adversely affect his pride, spirit, ambition, and initiative, and will undermine the prestige upon which his effectiveness is dependent. Thus, in order to cultivate, establish, and maintain the prestige and authority properly due the position of the noncommissioned officer, commissioned officers are specifically charged with requiring of noncommissioned officers the exercise of all responsibility pertaining to their grade. To this end—

a. Noncommissioned officers will be utilized as appropriate in the dissemination of orders to the troops.

b. Noncommissioned officers will be encouraged to execute orders on their own initiative and judgment.

c. Recommendations of noncommissioned officers relative to troop welfare in terms of assignment, reassignment, promotion, privileges, discipline, training, and supply should be sought in order to emphasize the responsibilities of the noncommissioned officer and develop the competency to discharge these responsibilities.

d. Noncommissioned officers will be employed as training instructors to the maximum practicable degree.

e. The correcting and disciplining of noncommissioned officers will be conducted in such a manner as to protect them from degrading embarrassment in the presence of their subordinate.

f. Every noncommissioned officer will be indoctrinated with the importance and responsibility of his rank and position within the command structure of the Army.

g. The successful implementation of this policy is dependent on the extent of leadership exercised by commanders at all echelons of command. Therefore, commanders and their staffs are charged specifically with the responsibility for the development and maintenance of a leadership program which will insure an equitable delegation of authority and responsibility to the noncommissioned officer by his superiors, both officer and enlisted.

Section VII
Prerogatives and Privileges

27. Prerogatives.—a. Noncommissioned officers will be used only in supervisory roles on fatigue duty, and only as noncommissioned officers of the guard on guard duty.

b. Specialists in grades E–7 and E–6 will be exempt from guard and fatigue duty, except in unusual circumstances when their services are required for the proper execution of these duties. In these cases, specialists in grades E–7 and E–6 will be used only in supervisory roles.

28. Privileges.—*a.* Noncommissioned officers will be granted such privileges as the organization and installation commanders are capable of granting and consider proper to enhance the prestige of noncommissioned officers.

b. Specialists in grades E–6 and E–7 will be granted the same privileges as the noncommissioned officers in the organization and installation.

c. Other enlisted personnel may be granted such privileges as the organization and installation commanders consider proper commensurate with their grade. [AG 221 (18 Jun 54) G1]

By order of the Secretary of the Army:

M. B. RIDGWAY,
General, United States Army,
Chief of Staff.

Extract from Message, HQ, Department of the Army, Washington, 28 May 1985, Subject: Elimination of Specialist Ranks.

1. As a result of MACOM Commanders' review of the issue of whether we should have both specialists and noncommissioned officer ranks, the Chief of Staff, Army, has decided that specialist five and specialist six ranks will be eliminated. The specialist four rank will be retained and decisions on whether soldiers in grade E4 are specialists or corporals will continue to be made by commanders in the field based on standards of grade authorizations in AR 611–201. Additionally commanders may laterally appoint specialists four who are serving in SGT positions to corporal in accordance with para 2–43, AR 600–200.

2. Effective date for elimination of SP5 and SP6 is 1 October 1985. In the meantime promotion to E5 and E6 will continue to be made to the appropriate ranks indicated in AR 611–201 as in the past.

3. Implementation instructions for lateral appointment of SP5 and SP6 to SGT and SSG on 1 October 1985 will be announced at a later date in a message to commanders. Affected soldiers will be informed that the cost of changing insignia will be borne by the Army.

4. Request widest dissemination of this information.

APPENDIXES

APPENDIX A

EVOLUTION OF THE NCO INSIGNIA

Since 1775 the Army has set apart its NCOs from other enlisted soldiers by distinctive insignia of grade. Those insignia have evolved over the years, through a variety of shapes, styles, and colors, to today's chevrons. Sometimes changes in uniform style and colors dictated changes in the style and color of chevrons. The history of these insignia is complex and often confusing. In some cases no official records survive to document the use of certain insignia. Many times the vagueness of official records resulted in conflicting interpretations by individual NCOs, leading to a variety of insignia designs for the same official rank. In still other cases, noncommissioned officers wore unauthorized grade insignia, leaving little if any documentation.

At the beginning of the Revolutionary War, the Continental Army did not have consistent uniforms, and the problem of distinguishing rank was often difficult. To solve this problem, in July 1775 General George Washington ordered designations of grade for officers and noncommissioned officers. All sergeants were to be distinguished by a strip of red cloth sewn on the right shoulder; corporals, by one of green.

Epaulettes continued to distinguish NCOs for years to come. In 1779 Washington authorized sergeants to wear two silk epaulettes; corporals would wear one worsted epaulette on the right shoulder. White epaulettes designated infantry NCOs; yellow, the artillery; and blue, the cavalry. The colors of the artillery and infantry epaulettes remained the same until 1798 and 1821, respectively. But the early Army of the fledgling republic changed the type of epaulette worn by the various grades of NCOs when it experienced its first small augmentation in early 1787. The sergeants major, quartermaster sergeants,

and drum and fife majors wore two silk epaulettes; the sergeants, two worsted; and the corporals, one worsted epaulette. Those of the projected cavalry and rifle units, which the Army did not organize until four years later, were to be white. During the quasi-war with France in 1797, the Army prescribed red epaulettes for all NCOs. This break with tradition raised a furor, and only the infantry wore red until 1808, while the artillery managed to keep yellow epaulettes. With the raising of five new infantry regiments in 1808, all infantry NCOs again wore white epaulettes as did the newly organized dragoons. A company of bombardiers, sappers, and miners (engineer enlisted men) came into existence during the War of 1812, and their NCOs wore the same yellow epaulettes as the artillery.

When regulations in 1821 directed the wearing of uniforms with cloth wings, the Army had to find another way to distinguish rank. It adopted a stripe, or chevron, for officers and NCOs to wear on the arm of the uniform, point up. Colors identified the two arms: yellow for artillery and white for infantry. When the Army discontinued the use of wings in 1832, epaulettes and cuff slashflaps replaced chevrons. One year later, however, Congress authorized a regiment of dragoons with a distinctive uniform. Because the dragoon uniforms used metal shoulder scales to protect against saber cuts, the Army authorized yellow chevrons, with points down, to distinguish noncommissioned officer rank. In 1845 one battery of horse artillery received dragoon-type uniforms, with NCOs wearing red chevrons. During the Mexican War, the Army authorized yellow or white chevrons with points up for all branches to wear on fatigue uniforms. In 1851 a new uniform established a system of branch colors, and chevrons reverted to points down. By 1872 eleven grades of NCO existed in the Army, seven with distinctive chevrons.

As the Army became more specialized, it established many new ranks. In 1902, when the Army retained twenty distinctive NCO chevrons, the insignia returned to the point-up position. With the authorization of new specialist grades, the number of new distinctive chevrons increased dramatically. During World War I the Army established temporary branches of service and authorized new chevrons for each pay grade in the new system. Eventually, it instituted over a hundred distinctive chevrons, including ones for the Tank Corps, Aviation Service, and two different transportation services. The cost and confusion became too much, and in 1920 Congress ended the practice of using the chevron to show a specific job or position among enlisted men. The Army consolidated all enlisted ranks into seven pay grades, five of which were for noncommissioned officers. During World War II the Army differentiated between technical and combat grades, although the three technician grades adopted were dropped by the postwar Army.

For a time, the Army reduced the size of its chevrons. To save material, the War Department introduced a smaller, two-inch-wide chevron in 1948. With the smaller size came changes in color to distinguish between combat (blue on a gold background) and noncombat (gold on a blue background) insignia. Another major change in 1948 was the substitution of the staff sergeant's three bars and a rocker for the three-stripe chevron worn by sergeants ever since 1833. At the beginning of the Korean War the Army went back to large chevrons, this time olive drab on a dark blue background. Once again, it authorized seven pay grades,

although the rank titles corresponding to the pay grades changed. In 1955 the Army decided to distinguish between its combat leaders and those soldiers with special skills, splitting the top four enlisted grades into noncommissioned officers and specialists. Once again, it authorized specialists to wear distinctive insignia.

In June 1958 the Army adopted the basic chevron system in use today. The seven pay grades expanded to nine. One new chevron appeared (the three stripes with three rockers and a star for sergeant major), and one chevron returned (the simple three stripes denoting sergeant). The addition of the three-stripe sergeant bumped each chevron up one grade with the result that the ranks of sergeant, staff sergeant, and sergeant first class wore one rocker less. To prevent a morale problem, the Army allowed personnel in those grades to continue to wear their old chevrons until promoted or demoted, when they would wear the proper chevron. This policy continued until 1968, when all personnel had to wear the current appropriate chevron for their grade. In 1958 the Army also adopted larger specialist's chevrons, reserving the smaller versions for female personnel. The Army phased out all but one of the specialist grades during the 1970s and early 1980s, leaving the old "Spec Four" chevron as the insignia for the rank designated "Specialist."

The following plates are an artist's rendition of selected NCO and specialist insignia from 1775 to the present. They do not include all insignia and also exclude metal pin-on insignia, authorized by the Department of the Army in 1967. Dates of individual grade insignia refer to a point in time when NCOs used a particular design, not necessarily the color schemes shown.

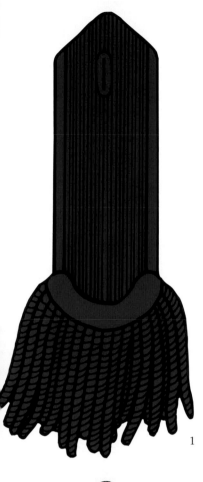

1

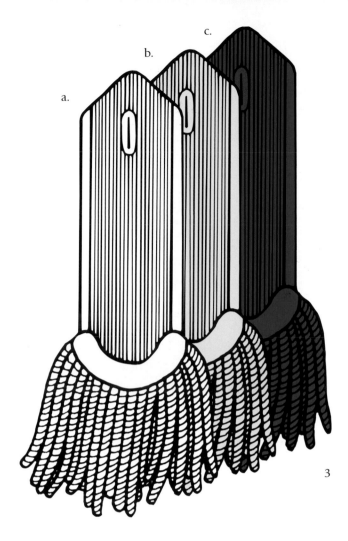

a.

b.

c.

3

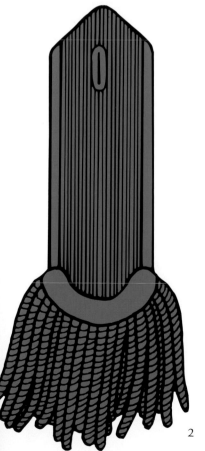

2

NCO Insignia, 1775–1821

1. Sergeant, 1775, worn on right shoulder only.
2. Corporal, 1775, worn on right shoulder only.
3. Sergeant and Corporal, 1779, a. Infantry; b. Artillery;
   c. Cavalry. Corporal's insignia worn on right shoulder
   only.

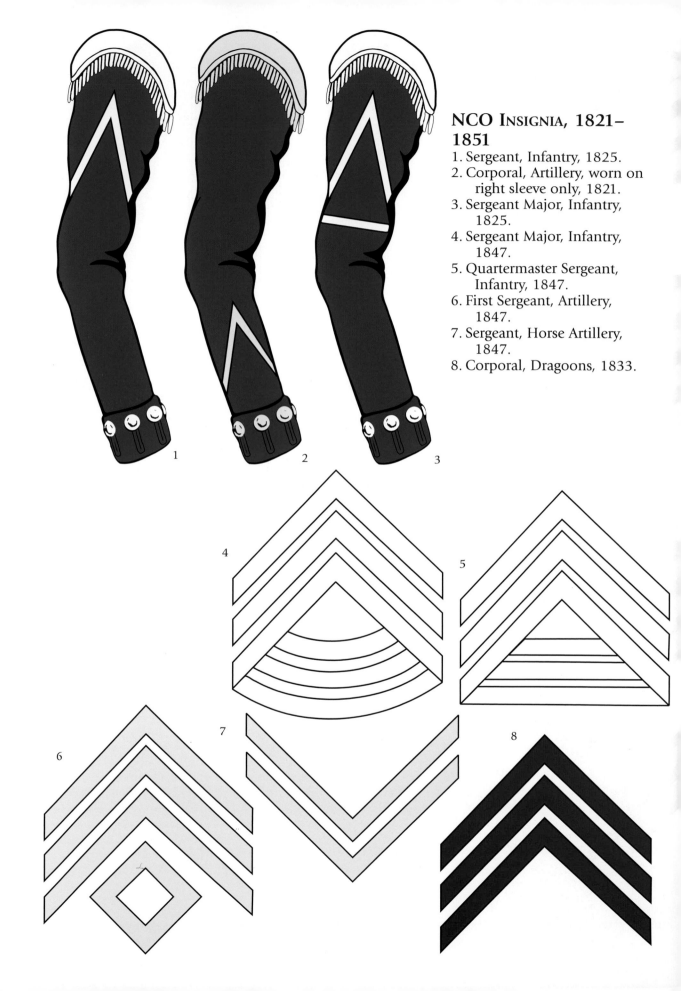

NCO Insignia, 1821–1851

1. Sergeant, Infantry, 1825.
2. Corporal, Artillery, worn on right sleeve only, 1821.
3. Sergeant Major, Infantry, 1825.
4. Sergeant Major, Infantry, 1847.
5. Quartermaster Sergeant, Infantry, 1847.
6. First Sergeant, Artillery, 1847.
7. Sergeant, Horse Artillery, 1847.
8. Corporal, Dragoons, 1833.

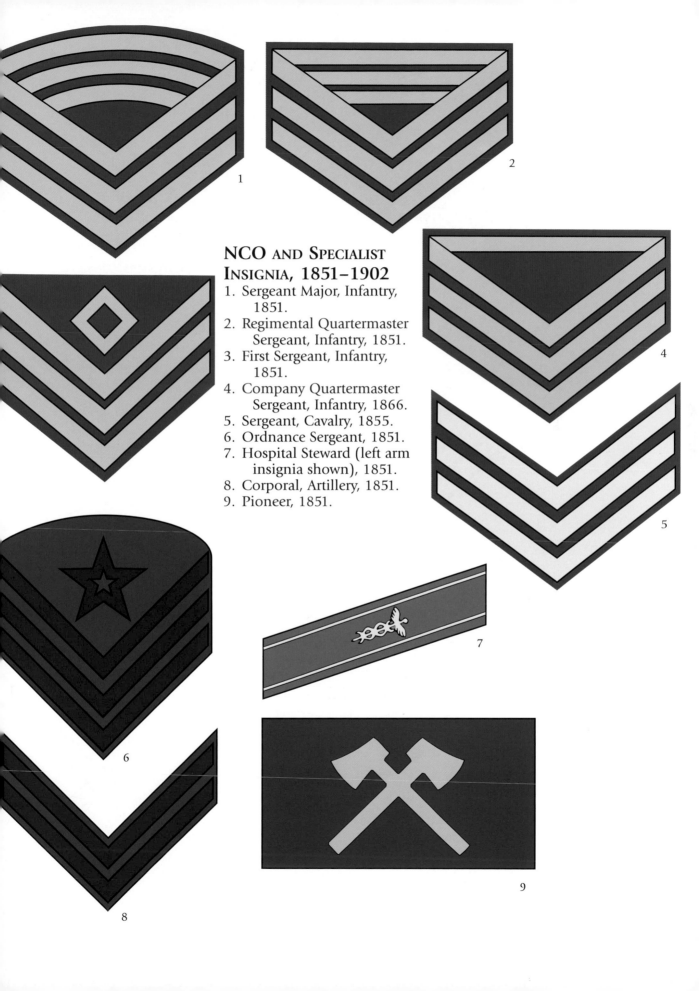

NCO AND SPECIALIST INSIGNIA, 1851–1902

1. Sergeant Major, Infantry, 1851.
2. Regimental Quartermaster Sergeant, Infantry, 1851.
3. First Sergeant, Infantry, 1851.
4. Company Quartermaster Sergeant, Infantry, 1866.
5. Sergeant, Cavalry, 1855.
6. Ordnance Sergeant, 1851.
7. Hospital Steward (left arm insignia shown), 1851.
8. Corporal, Artillery, 1851.
9. Pioneer, 1851.

NCO AND SPECIALIST INSIGNIA, 1873–1902
1. Sergeant First Class of Signal Corps, 1891.
2. Chief Musician, Cavalry, 1899.
3. Color Sergeant, Infantry, 1883.
4. Hospital Steward, 1887.
5. Electrician, 1899.
6. Color Sergeant, Infantry, 1901.
7. Drum Major, Cavalry, 1899.

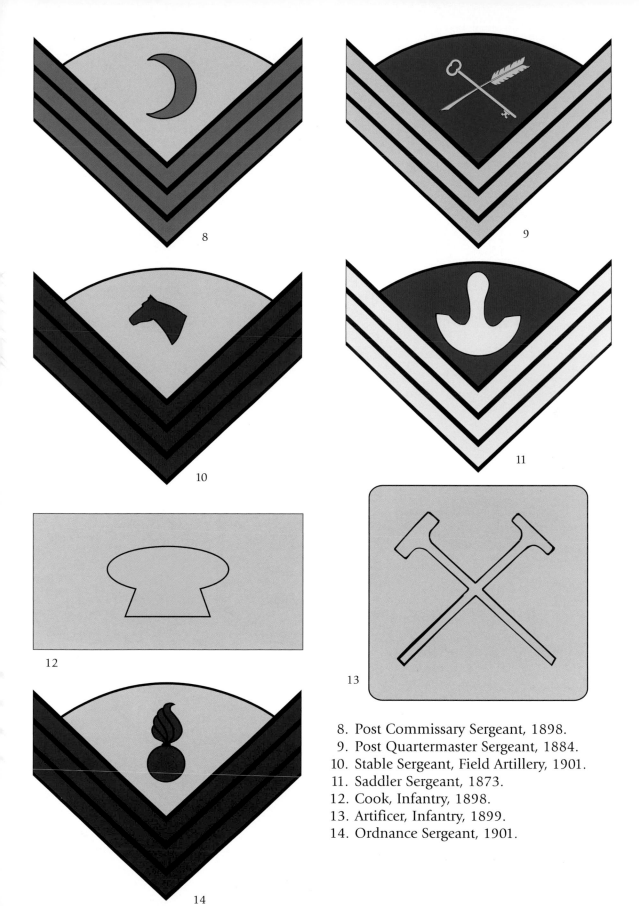

8. Post Commissary Sergeant, 1898.
9. Post Quartermaster Sergeant, 1884.
10. Stable Sergeant, Field Artillery, 1901.
11. Saddler Sergeant, 1873.
12. Cook, Infantry, 1898.
13. Artificer, Infantry, 1899.
14. Ordnance Sergeant, 1901.

NCO Insignia, 1902–1920

NOTE: *Rank insignia authorized for right arm only from May 1918 to March 1921.*

1. Sergeant Major, Senior Grade, Coast Artillery, 1902.
2. Squadron or Battalion Sergeant Major, 1902.
3. Ordnance Sergeant, 1917.
4. Ordnance Sergeant, 1918.
5. Chief Musician, Cavalry, 1902.
6. Color Sergeant, 1902.
7. First Sergeant Engineers, 1902.
8. Sergeant First Class, 1918.

9. Quartermaster Sergeant, 1913.
10. Hospital Steward, 1902.
11. Regimental Quartermaster Sergeant,
    Infantry, 1902.
12. Sergeant, Signal Corps, 1902.
13. Corporal, Infantry, 1902.
14. Lance Corporal, Infantry, 1902.

NCO and Specialist Insignia, 1902–1920

1. Quartermaster Sergeant Senior Grade, 1916.
2. Master Signal Electrician, 1918.
3. Master Engineer Junior Grade, 1916.
4. Master Gunner, 1908.
5. Engineer, Coast Artillery Corps, 1908.
6. Master Signal Electrician, Air Service, 1918.
7. Master Engineer Senior Grade, Tank Corps, 1918.
8. Chief Mechanic, 1907.

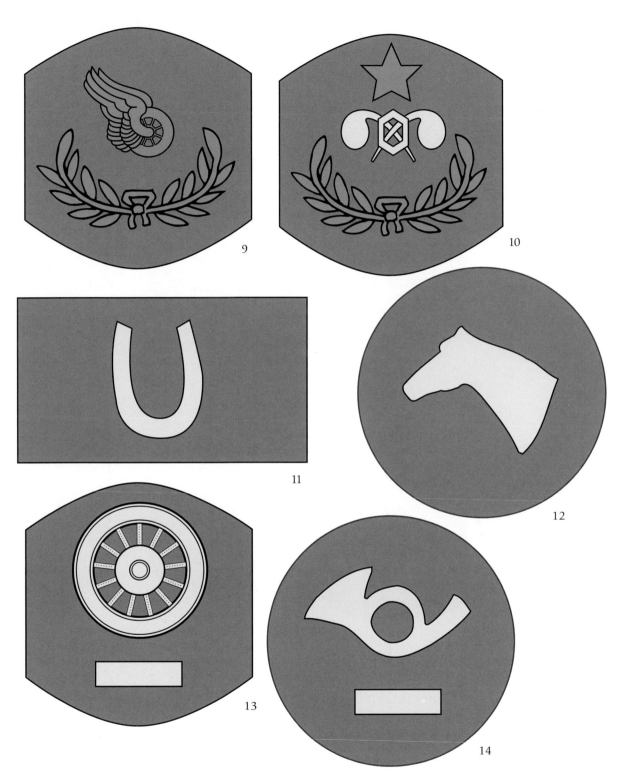

9. Master Engineer Junior Grade, Transportation Corps, 1919.
10. Master Chemical Sergeant, 1918.
11. Farrier, Cavalry, 1902.
12. Farrier, Field Artillery, 1908.
13. Chauffeur, 1918.
14. Bugler First Class, Infantry, 1918.

NCO and Specialist Insignia, 1920–1958

1. Master Sergeant, 1920.
2. First Sergeant, 1920.
3. First Sergeant, 1942.
4. Technical Sergeant, 1920.
5. Technician 3d Grade, 1942.
6. Technician 4th Grade, 1942.
7. Technician 5th Grade, 1942.
8. Master Specialist, 1955.

9

10

11

12

13

14

9. Staff Sergeant, 1920.
10. Sergeant, 1920.
11. Corporal, 1920.
12. Specialist First Class, 1955.
13. Specialist Second Class, 1955.
14. Specialist Third Class, 1955.

NCO Insignia, 1948–1951

Combat chevrons:
1. First Sergeant.
2. Master Sergeant.
3. Sergeant First Class.
4. Sergeant.
5. Corporal.

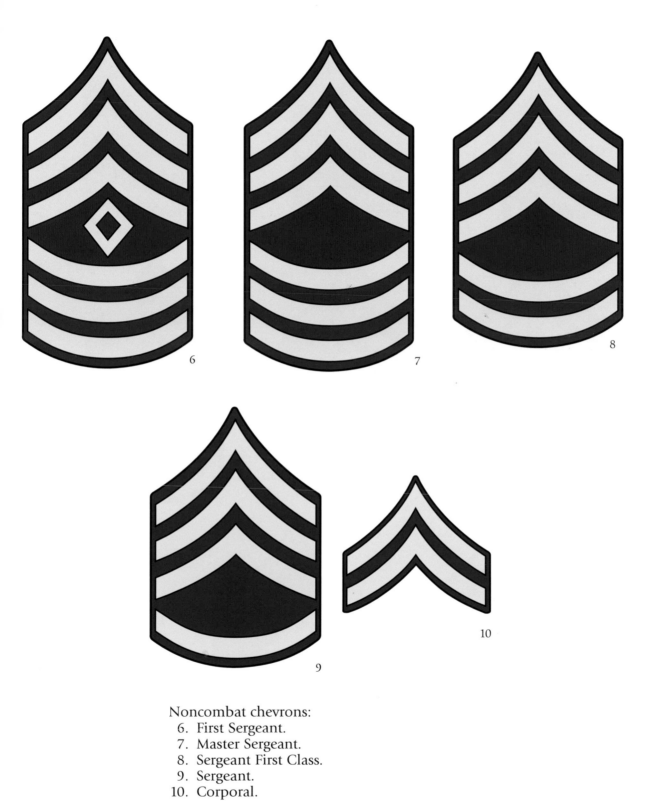

Noncombat chevrons:
6. First Sergeant.
7. Master Sergeant.
8. Sergeant First Class.
9. Sergeant.
10. Corporal.

NCO Insignia Since 1958

1. Sergeant Major of the Army, 2001.
2. Sergeant Major of the Army, 1979.
3. Command Sergeant Major, 1968.
4. Sergeant Major, 1958.
5. First Sergeant, 1958.

6. Master Sergeant, 1958
7. Sergeant First Class, 1958.
8. Staff Sergeant, 1958.
9. Sergeant, subdued, 1966.

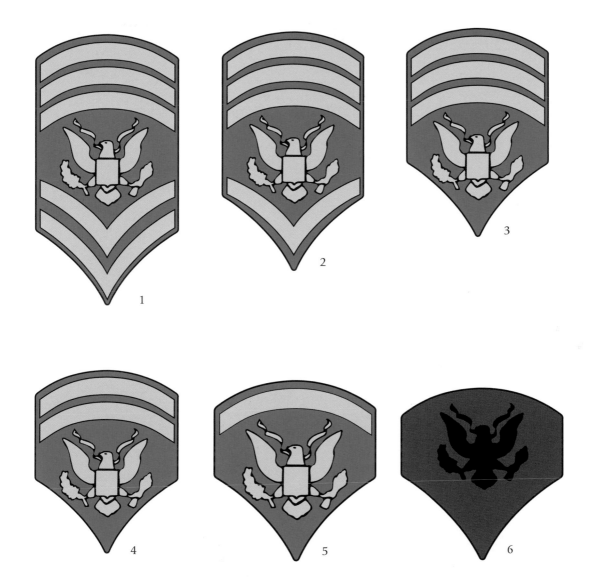

SPECIALIST INSIGNIA SINCE 1959

1. Specialist Nine, 1959.
2. Specialist Eight, 1959.
3. Specialist Seven, 1959.
4. Specialist Six, 1959.
5. Specialist Five, 1959.
6. Specialist Four, subdued, 1966.

Note: Of the specialist insignia, only no. 6 remains in use today, as the insignia for what is now the single grade Specialist.

Newburgh, New York, 3 May 1783, *H. Charles McBarron, 1975. William Brown* (left) *and Elijah Churchill Receiving the First Badges of Merit*

Appendix B

A Gallery of Noncommissioned Officer Heroes

"The sergeants should be brave and prudent…"
—E. Hoyt, *A Treatise on the Military Art*, 1798

The term hero usually refers to individuals who, because of their courage, strength, or skill, stand apart from ordinary men and women. Occasionally, heroism is grim determination or even a matter of timing. But a hero is, most often, an average person who reacts to crisis with quiet professionalism. By virtue of their leadership training, all noncommissioned officers are prepared for those situations from which heroes emerge.

The Army has had its share of heroes, many—if not most—of whom have worn stripes. Throughout the Army's history, its NCO heroes usually were average human beings who responded when circumstances called for exceptional personal effort and sacrifice.

These heroes exemplify Army values. Values are altruistic principles based on moral or traditional standards or codes of conduct. The values that have characterized the deeds of these heroes and the collective personality of the U.S. Army since 1775 include personal courage, loyalty, respect, duty, integrity, honor, and selfless service.

Because the number of recognized heroes is so large, those whose names, portraits, and deeds appear below represent only a tiny fraction of the hundreds upon hundreds who deserve mention. In fact, little information survives on individual heroes from America's early wars. Their portraits and citations were never recorded. Before the Civil War and the widespread use of photography, men of modest incomes—and that included most soldiers—rarely had their portraits painted. For them and countless others through the Army's long history, the record is fragmentary at best. Little is known about them beyond the terse words of their citations for valor.

The American Revolution

William Brown, Sergeant, 5th Connecticut Regiment

On 14 October 1781, during the siege of Yorktown, Sgt. William Brown led the advance party, known in those days as a "forlorn hope," against Redoubt Number 10 in the British defenses. Sergeant Brown declined to wait for sappers to clear the abatis and picket-like fraise that ringed the objective and blocked the way up the slope to the British position. Instead, he led his men over and through these obstructions to enter the redoubt in a surprise assault. Using only their bayonets, the Americans captured the position within ten minutes. Sergeant Brown was among the casualties, with a bayonet wound in the hand. For his bravery during this decisive battle, he received the Badge of Military Merit, the nation's original military decoration, on 3 May 1783 during the same ceremony that recognized Sgt. Elijah Churchill (see below).

John Champe, Sergeant Major, 2d Partisan Corps

Born in Loudoun County, Virginia, Champe entered the Continental Army in

Detail from The Escape of Sergeant Champe, *a Lithograph by Currier and Ives, 1876*

1776 and rose to the rank of sergeant major by 1780. When General Washington sought a volunteer to kidnap the traitor, Benedict Arnold, and return him to face American justice, Lt. Col. Henry Lee selected Champe because of his reputation for daring and patriotism. After a cover story was arranged, the sergeant major "deserted" to the British garrison in New York City in October 1780 and joined Arnold's American Legion. He then made plans to capture Arnold during the general's regular evening walk in the garden and, with the help of two confederates in the city, to spirit the general across the Hudson River to where Colonel Lee would be waiting in Hoboken, New Jersey. Unfortunately, the night before the planned abduction, Arnold and the American Legion began a deployment to Virginia, and Champe could only accompany them. Near Petersburg, he finally managed to desert to the American forces, but without capturing Arnold. Washington, realizing that Champe, if captured, could be hanged as a British deserter, arranged for his honorable discharge. Washington later sought to make Champe a captain in the Army created during the undeclared war with France in 1798, but Champe died before being commissioned. He left future NCOs a singular example of patriotism and selfless dedication to duty.

Elijah Churchill, Sergeant, 2d Legionary Corps

Sergeant Churchill received the Badge of Military Merit for two daring raids in 1781 against Fort St. George and Fort Slongo on Long Island, New York. The first raid took place during a severe November storm and included a hazardous twenty-mile crossing from Fairfield, Connecticut, to Fort St. George in small, open boats over the choppy waters of Long Island Sound. Thrown off course by the gale, the raiding party reached shore and marched several miles behind enemy lines to its objective. Under cover of darkness, Sergeant Churchill led his men in an attack that caught the British by surprise and overwhelmed them. The Americans succeeded in burning a supply schooner anchored off shore and in destroying vast stores of enemy supplies. In this action, as in a later raid against Fort Slongo, Sergeant Churchill did not lose a single man. General George Washington awarded the Badge of Military Merit to Churchill at Continental Army headquarters, Newburgh, New York, on 3 May 1783.

The War of 1812

Thomas Bangs, Sergeant, 22d Infantry

In the winter of 1814 Sergeant Bangs and the other Americans at Fort Niagara faced hostile British forces across the Niagara River in Canada. The weather was bitter cold on 13 February, when five British soldiers, under a flag of truce, attempted to cross the icy river in a small boat with three prisoners of war and three ladies. Frozen and exhausted by their efforts, the British could not reach the American shore before daylight faded. Their boat was quickly swept by the current into Lake Ontario. Sergeant Bangs and two seamen were ordered to the rescue in a small boat. After safely returning to the American shore, Sergeant Bangs and his two companions braved the elements once again to carry the five weary British soldiers back across the Niagara River. They successfully made the trip by moonlight, returning two days later with a letter of thanks from the British commanding officer of Fort George for saving the lives of his men.

The Mexican War

Alexander M. Kenaday, Sergeant, Company G, 3d Dragoons

Alexander Kenaday was living in New Orleans at the outbreak of the Mexican War. With other volunteers, he flocked to the colors for

Alexander M. Kenaday's heroism in the battle of Churubusco formed the centerpiece of this painting by an unknown artist.

a ninety-day enlistment and joined Col. Sam Mark's regiment near Matamoros, Mexico. In August 1846, when his first regiment disbanded, Sergeant Kenaday reenlisted, this time in Company G of the 3d Dragoons. He commanded the detail assigned to guard the headquarters during the battle of Churubusco on 20 August 1847. When a burning ammunition wagon blocked the advancing American troops, Sergeant Kenaday risked his life to climb aboard the wagon and throw the ammunition into a ditch alongside the road. For this valorous action, he was commended by Maj. Gen. Winfield Scott. Kenaday later helped to organize a national veterans association in Washington, D.C.

The Civil War

William H. Carney, Sergeant, Company C, 54th Massachusetts Volunteer Infantry

Born in Virginia, William Carney lived for many years in New Bedford, Massachusetts, before joining one of the first black volunteer regiments raised by the Union. He won the Medal of Honor for heroism on 18 July 1863, when his regiment assaulted Fort Wagner, South Carolina. Seeing the color sergeant felled by enemy fire, Sergeant Carney seized the national flag before it hit the ground. He then carried the Stars and Stripes to the parapet of the fort, where he was wounded in both legs, the chest, and the right arm. Despite the seriousness of his injuries, Carney insisted on carrying the colors as his unit retreated from the fort. With the aid of some of his comrades, Sergeant Carney reached the field hospital, where, still clutching the American flag, he collapsed, saying "The old flag never touched the ground, boys."

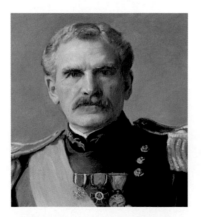

Adna R. Chaffee, *Cedric Baldwin Egeli, 1973. Chaffee later became the second chief of staff of the Army.*

Adna R. Chaffee, First Sergeant, Troop K, 6th Cavalry

A native of Ohio, Adna Chaffee enlisted in the Regular Army's 6th Cavalry in July 1861 and remained with the unit for twenty-seven years. He became first sergeant of Troop K in September 1862, just in time to participate in the bloody battle of Antietam, where he won official recognition for his bravery and leadership skills. Later commissioned a second lieutenant, Chaffee served with the 6th Cavalry during the Indian Wars in the Southwest. Chaffee commanded a brigade in the Santiago campaign during the Spanish-American War. As major general, he served tours in China and the Philippines before becoming Chief of Staff of the U.S. Army in 1904.

Ben Falls, Sergeant, 19th Massachusetts Volunteer Infantry

By 1864 Ben Falls could claim three years of service in the Civil War. His regiment had fought in all the major battles of the Eastern Theater, and Falls had won the Medal of Honor for capturing a Confederate flag at Gettysburg. He and his comrades had every reason to expect to go home at the end of a three-year enlistment. However, the new draftees arriving as replacements clearly did not have the determination of the veterans. Many deserted as soon as they arrived. Sergeant Falls said, "If new men won't finish this job, old men must, and as long as Uncle Sam wants a man, here is Ben Falls." Only thirteen strong, he and his company reenlisted for the duration, knowing that many would never go home. A month later, Sergeant Falls was killed at Spotsylvania Court House. His devotion to duty and country was typical of those who carried the proud distinction, "Veteran Volunteers."

Christian A. Fleetwood, Sergeant Major, 4th United States Colored Troops

Born and raised in Baltimore, Christian Fleetwood enlisted in the Union Army in July 1863 and quickly advanced to the rank of sergeant major. He participated in the 1864 campaign around Richmond, including the battles at Fort Harrison, Chapin's Farm, and New Market Heights. When two color sergeants of his regiment fell at Chapin's Farm, Fleetwood seized the national colors and bore them throughout the engagement. For this courageous act he received the Medal of Honor in April 1865. After leaving the Army in May 1866, he joined the District of Columbia Militia (later National Guard), in which he eventually rose to the rank of major.

William McKinley, Commissary Sergeant, 23d Ohio Volunteer Infantry

William McKinley, *August Penziger, 1897 (Depicted as President of the United States)*

William McKinley enlisted in Col. (later President) Rutherford B. Hayes' 23d Ohio Infantry Regiment in June 1861. During the battle of Antietam, Commissary Sergeant McKinley was in the rear in charge of his unit's supplies. The men had eaten only a scanty breakfast, and McKinley knew that, as the day wore on, they were growing hungry. Gathering some stragglers, McKinley led two mule teams with wagons of rations and hot coffee into the thick of battle. Working his way over rough ground, under fire, McKinley ignored repeated warnings to retreat. He lost one team of mules to enemy fire, but did not return to the rear of the brigade until his fellow soldiers had been properly fed under the most adverse combat conditions. McKinley received a direct commission as a second lieutenant that same month (September 1862), rose to the rank of major by the end of the war, and eventually became President of the United States.

Charles E. Morse, Sergeant, Company I, 62d New York Volunteer Infantry

During the battle of the Wilderness in Virginia on 5 May 1864, Sergeant Morse saw his unit's color sergeant fall mortally wounded. In the close, often confused fighting, Sergeant Morse rushed to his fallen comrade and, though surrounded by the enemy, raised the colors and rallied the men. Soon wounded himself, Sergeant Morse continued to carry the colors for the remainder of the engagement. He subsequently received the Medal of Honor.

The Indian Wars

William C. Bryan, Hospital Steward

Born and raised in Zanesville, Ohio, Bryan enlisted in the Army in St. Louis, Missouri, and became an early member of the medical specialist corps. In March 1876 he was attached to a task force from the 2d and 3d Cavalry engaged in winter operations against hostile Sioux under Chief Crazy Horse. On 17 March the force found the Indian encampment along the Powder River and attacked. During the fierce fighting that followed, Bryan's horse was shot out from under him. Despite heavy fire, he continued to carry out his medical duties on foot and brought two wounded comrades to safety. For his heroism, he was awarded the Medal of Honor.

Richard P. Hanley, Sergeant, Company C, 7th Cavalry

Sergeant Hanley was part of a detail escorting pack mules during the battle of the Little Bighorn on 25 June 1876. During the fighting, one of the mules, loaded with ammunition, stampeded into the Indian lines. Single-handed, Hanley chased the mule, grabbed its bridle, and brought it back to friendly lines. The feat took nearly twenty minutes, during which he was under heavy fire from the Indians and in full view of most of the combatants from both sides. For his courageous act, Sergeant Hanley won the Medal of Honor.

Patrick Leonard, Corporal, Company A, 23d Infantry

Many of the soldiers in the frontier Army were born overseas and immigrated to the United States. Leonard was from Ireland. He was a special soldier, even among Medal of Honor winners, for he won two such medals during the Indian Wars. As a private in the 2d Cavalry, Leonard received his first citation in the summer of 1870 for gallantry in action against hostile Cheyenne. In April 1876 Corporal Leonard, then serving with the 23d Infantry in Nebraska, took part in a skirmish against Sioux warriors in which his sergeant was killed. Because the young lieutenant in charge of the troop was fresh from the East Coast and totally inexperienced in the ways of Indian fighting, it fell to Corporal Leonard and one other corporal to provide leadership in routing the determined enemy.

William McBryar, Sergeant, Company K, 10th Cavalry

Sergeant McBryar, a member of the all-black 10th Cavalry, was one of the last of the celebrated "Buffalo Soldiers" to win a Medal of Honor in the frontier campaigns against the Indians. Sergeant McBryar was cited for bravery and good marksmanship in action against Apache Indians at Salt River, Arizona, in March 1890. Sergeant McBryar's service extended to the Spanish-American War, during which he distinguished himself in Cuba with Company H, 25th Infantry. At the siege of Santiago, he guided the construction of earthworks around the port city, working under fire from the Spanish artillery. He was later commissioned and served as a first lieutenant with the 49th Volunteer Infantry until June 1901. When it became clear that the United States would enter the World War, this devoted old soldier once again volunteered, but was turned down because of his age.

Hampton M. Roach, Corporal, Company F, 5th Cavalry

Corporal Roach received the Medal of Honor for his heroism during an engagement against hostile Indians at Milk River, Colorado, in October 1879. Under fire from a heavily armed foe, Corporal Roach erected breastworks. Over successive nights, he managed to keep his unit supplied with water despite close-range fire from Indians in ambush positions. He was later commissioned as a second lieutenant.

The Spanish-American and Philippine Wars

Anthony J. Carson, Corporal, Company H, 43d Infantry

Anthony Carson was born in Boston and entered the Army from Maiden, Massachusetts. In April 1900 Carson's company deployed to Catubig, Samar, in the Philippine Islands. Attacked by a vastly superior force of insurgents, Corporal Carson's detachment became separated from the rest of the company. Under Carson's leadership, the Americans prepared a defensive position and waited for help to arrive. For more than two days, Corporal Carson demonstrated sound judgment and confidence as he directed his detachment's fire during repeated attacks by the well-armed enemy force. For his exceptional leadership and professionalism under fire, Carson was awarded the Medal of Honor.

Warren J. Shepherd, Corporal, Company D, 17th Infantry

In heavy action against the enemy at El Caney, Cuba, in July 1898, Corporal Shepherd gallantly assisted in the rescue of his wounded colleagues from the front lines. He received the Medal of Honor.

The Boxer Rebellion

Calvin Pearl Titus Receiving the Medal of Honor at the U.S. Military Academy

Calvin Pearl Titus, Corporal (Musician), Company E, 14th Infantry

During an outbreak of violence against foreigners in China during the summer of 1900, American troops joined soldiers from seven other nations to rescue their besieged embassies in the walled city of Beijing. During the assault on 14 August, when his commander asked for a volunteer to scale the east wall of the city without the aid of ropes or ladders, Corporal Titus replied, "I'll try, sir." Under enemy fire Titus successfully climbed the thirty-foot wall by way of jagged holes in its surface. His company followed his lead up the wall, hauling up their rifles and ammunition belts by a rope made with rifle slings. For his daring example, Corporal Titus received an appointment to the U.S. Military Academy at West Point, where he received the Medal of Honor during a review of the Corps of Cadets.

World War I

Michael B. Ellis, Sergeant, Company C, 28th Infantry, 1st Division; War Department General Orders (WD GO) 74, 1919

Sergeant Ellis won a Medal of Honor during an engagement near Exermont, France, on 5 October 1918. Ellis volunteered to go far in advance of his company's attacking wave, single-handedly reducing enemy machine-gun nests. Flanking one position, Sergeant Ellis killed two of the enemy and captured seventeen others. Once he handed off his prisoners to his company, he again advanced alone under heavy fire, capturing ten other machine guns, along with their crews.

James B. Lepley, Sergeant, Company M, 168th Infantry, 42d Division; WD GO 99, 1918

Sergeant Lepley won the Distinguished Service Cross for his actions in July 1918 in Sergy, France. Leading his platoon against a strong enemy position, he personally captured several machine guns and prisoners from a Prussian Guards regiment. Later, near the village of Souain, Sergeant Lepley dashed from his trench under cover of darkness to a nearby woods and, in spite of heavy rifle fire, shrapnel bursts, and lingering poison gas, guided two of his missing men back to safety. His actions demonstrated the best in the tradition of the NCO's looking out for his men.

Patrick Walsh, Sergeant, Company I, 18th Infantry, 1st Division; WD GO 126, 1918

When the United States entered World War I in 1917, Sergeant Walsh already had served for thirty-one years and was eligible to retire. Instead, he elected to remain with his division when it left for France. On 1 March 1918, near Seicheprey, Walsh followed his company commander through a severe barrage to the first line of trenches in preparation for an attack. When his captain was killed, Sergeant Walsh assumed command and initiated an assault that resulted in heavy enemy losses. He was awarded a Distinguished Service Cross for his demonstration of leadership.

Samuel Woodfill, First Sergeant, 60th Infantry, 5th Division; WD GO 16, 1919

A model Regular Army NCO, Sergeant Woodfill was, in the words of General John J. Pershing, "the greatest American soldier of the World War." His more than thirty-three years of service included tours in the Philippines and Alaska, along the Mexican border, and in the Meuse-Argonne sector of France. In France, Woodfill won both the Medal of

Honor and the French Legion of Honor for service under enemy fire and received a battlefield promotion to lieutenant. Discharged from the Army in late October 1919, he reenlisted the following month as a sergeant. Along with Sergeant York, Sergeant Woodfill was one of the pallbearers selected by General Pershing for the burial of the Unknown Soldier in 1921.

Alvin C. York, Sergeant, Company G, 328th Infantry, 82d Division; WD GO 59, 1919

Despite his application to be a conscientious objector, Alvin York went to France with the American Expeditionary Forces and became one of the best known and most decorated heroes of World War I. When his platoon suffered heavy casualties, including three other NCOs, near Chatel-Chehery, France, on 8 October 1918, Sergeant (then Corporal) York assumed command of the seven survivors. Fearlessly, he charged a machine-gun position that was pouring deadly fire on his men. He showed his markmanship with his rifle by killing between 15 and 25 of the enemy (reports differ). The remainder of the now dispirited German unit, consisting of 4 enemy officers and 128 enlisted men with several machine guns, surrendered. Sergeant York won the Medal of Honor for his dramatic action under fire. In 1935, in recognition of his service during the war, the Army placed York on the retired list as a major.

World War II

Jose Calugas, Sergeant, Battery B, 88th Field Artillery, Philippine Scouts; WD GO 10, 24 February 1942

Born in the Philippines, Jose Calugas entered the Army at Fort Stotsenberg in Luzon and later joined the Regular Army's Philippine Scouts. When the Japanese besieged General Douglas MacArthur's American forces in the Bataan Peninsula in early 1942, Calugas was a mess sergeant in Battery B, 88th Field Artillery. On 16 January the Japanese bombed and shelled an American gun position near Culis, knocking out the gun and killing or wounding the entire crew. From his nearby battery, Sergeant Calugas voluntarily raced 1,000 yards across the shell-swept terrain to the position, where he organized a volunteer squad to get the gun back into effective action. For his devotion to duty, Sergeant Calugas received the Medal of Honor.

Edward A. Carter, Jr., Staff Sergeant, Seventh Army Infantry Company 1 (Provisional), 56th Armored Infantry Battalion, 12th Armored Division; WD GO 3, 12 January 1945

Staff Sergeant Carter received the Medal of Honor posthumously in 1997 for his extraordinary heroism in action on 23 March 1945, near Speyer, Germany. His provisional company consisted of black support troops who had volunteered as replacements for the heavy losses the Army sustained in the Battle of the Bulge. When the tank on which he was riding received heavy bazooka and small-arms fire, Sergeant Carter voluntarily attempted to lead a three-man group across an open field. Within a short time, two of his men were killed and the third seriously wounded. Continuing alone, he was wounded five times and finally had to take cover. When eight enemy riflemen attempted to capture him, Sergeant Carter killed six and captured the remaining two. He then crossed the field using his two prisoners as a shield. From the prisoners, he obtained valuable information concerning the disposition of enemy troops.

Marcario Garcia, Staff Sergeant, U.S. Army, Company B, 22d Infantry, 4th Infantry Division; WD GO 74, 1 September 1945

On 27 November 1944, near Grosshau, Germany, Company B, 22d Infantry, encountered intense machine-gun fire and a concentrated artillery and mortar barrage while attacking prepared positions on a wooded hill with only meager cover on its approaches. The acting squad leader, Mexican-born immigrant Private First Class Garcia, single-handedly assaulted two enemy machine-gun emplacements. Although he sustained painful wounds, he refused evacuation. On his own initiative, he crawled forward alone until he reached a position near an enemy emplacement. Hurling grenades, he boldly assaulted the position, destroyed the gun, and with his rifle killed three enemy soldiers who attempted to escape. A short time later when another German machine gun started firing, he single-handedly attacked that position, destroying the gun, killing three German soldiers, capturing four others, and helping to save his company. He fought on with his unit until it took the objective. Only then did he permit himself to be removed for medical care. Staff Sergeant Garcia received his Medal of Honor for his conspicuous heroism, his inspiring, courageous conduct, and his complete disregard for his personal safety.

Jose M. Lopez, Sergeant, U.S. Army, 23d Infantry, 2d Infantry Division; WD GO 47, 18 June 1945

On 17 December 1944, near Krinkelt, Belgium, the 23d Infantry came under heavy attack from advancing German infantry supported by tanks. When the enemy threatened to overrun Company K's left flank, Sergeant Lopez brought over his heavy machine gun from the opposite flank. From a shallow hole that offered no protection above his waist, he cut down thirty-five Germans trying to outflank his position. To his right, he saw a large number of infantry attacking from the front. Although dazed and shaken from enemy shell bursts only a few yards away, he realized that the enemy would soon turn his position. Alone, he carried his machine gun to the right rear of the sector, where he immediately reset his gun and continued his fire. Single-handed, he held off the German advance until he was satisfied his company had withdrawn. Again he loaded his gun on his back and in a hail of small-arms fire ran to a point where some of his comrades were trying to form another line against the onrushing enemy. He fired from this position until he had exhausted his ammunition. Still carrying his gun, he fell back with his small group to Krinkelt. For his gallantry and intrepidity, Sergeant Lopez received the Medal of Honor.

Roy H. Matsumoto, Master Sergeant, 5307th Composite Unit (Provisional), later known as Merrill's Marauders

A native of Los Angeles, California, Roy Matsumoto graduated from middle school in Japan before returning home. From one of the internment centers that the federal government established for Japanese Americans, he volunteered to serve in the Military Intelligence Service Language School and later joined the 5307th Composite Unit (Provisional), the famous Merrill's Marauders. When the Marauder 2d Battalion was trapped at Nhpum Ga, Burma, under cover of darkness, Master Sergeant Matsumoto crawled close to the Japanese lines to secure vital information. One night he returned with word that the Japanese would attempt to cut off a part of the perimeter. After helping to set up an ambush, Sergeant Matsumoto waited with the rest of the Marauders for the attack to start. When the first attack came, the Marauders sprang the trap, mowing down the first wave of attackers. As the second wave stalled in confusion, Sergeant Matsumoto yelled "Charge" in Japanese, causing the second wave to meet the same fate as the first. For his actions at Nhpum Ga, he received the Legion of Merit; on 19 July 1993, he was inducted into the Ranger

Hall of Fame, Fort Benning, Georgia, "for extraordinary courage and service…with Merrill's Marauders."

Audie L. Murphy, Second Lieutenant, (then Staff Sergeant), Company B, 15th Infantry, 3d Infantry Division; WD GO 65, 9 August 1945

From private, Audie Murphy rose to staff sergeant and later received a battlefield commission as a second lieutenant. He was wounded three times, fought in nine major campaigns across the European Theater, and earned thirty-three medals, including the Medal of Honor and every decoration for valor that his country had to offer, some of them more than once. Credited with killing over 240 enemy troops while wounding and capturing many others, he became a legend within the 3d Infantry Division. On 22 September 1944, Staff Sergeant Murphy received the Distinguished Service Cross for extraordinary heroism in action. At 0800 on 15 August he landed near Ramatuelle, France, with the first wave of the assault infantry. Intense machine-gun and small-arms fire from a boulder-covered hill to his front halted the advance. Leaving his men in a covered position, he dashed forty yards through withering fire to a draw. Using this route, he went back toward the beaches, found a light machine-gun squad and, returning up the rocky hill, placed the machine gun in position seventy-five yards in advance of his platoon. In the duel that ensued, Murphy silenced the enemy weapon, killed two of the crew, and wounded a third. As he proceeded farther up the draw, two Germans advanced toward him. Quickly killing both of them, he dashed up the draw alone toward the enemy strongpoint. Closing in, he wounded two Germans with carbine fire, killed two more in a fierce, brief firefight, and forced the remaining five to surrender. His extraordinary heroism resulted in the capture of a fiercely contested enemy-held hill and the annihilation or capture of the entire enemy garrison.

Nicholas Oresko, Master Sergeant, Company C, 302d Infantry, 94th Infantry Division; WD GO 95, 1945

While still a technical sergeant, Oresko was a platoon leader in an attack against strong enemy positions near Tettingen, Germany, on 23 January 1945. Deadly, accurate automatic-weapons fire pinned down his unit shortly after it began its advance. Realizing that a nearby machine gun had to be eliminated, Oresko moved forward alone amid heavy fire until he was close enough to throw a grenade into the German position. He then rushed the bunker and killed the surviving Germans, only to be seriously wounded in the hip at the same time. Although weak from loss of blood, he refused evacuation until assured that his men had taken their objective. While wounded, and in the face of bitter resistance, Sergeant Oresko had killed twelve of the enemy, prevented a delay in the American assault, and enabled Company C to complete its mission with a minimum of casualties. He received the Medal of Honor for his example of heroic personal sacrifice.

Joseph E. Schaefer, Staff Sergeant, Company I, 18th Infantry, 1st Infantry Division; WD GO 71, 1945

On 24 September 1944, Sergeant Schaefer was a squad leader in the second platoon of Company I, holding an important crossroads near Stolberg, Germany. In the early morning hours two enemy companies, supported by machine guns, attacked the key position. The withdrawal of one American squad and the capture of another left Sergeant Schaefer's squad to defend the crossroads alone. Under fire, Schaefer crawled from man to man and ordered a withdrawal to a nearby house for better cover. Sergeant Schaefer's squad successfully repulsed at least three separate assaults, inflicting heavy casualties on the enemy. Once the rest of Company I began a counterattack, Sergeant Schaefer and his men took the lead in regaining their position. Alternately crawling and running in the face of enemy fire, Schaefer overtook the retreating Germans and liberated the squad captured earlier. Single-handed and armed only with his rifle, Sergeant Schaefer killed between fifteen and twenty of the attackers, wounded at least as many more, and took ten prisoners. His courage and determination to hold his position at all costs stopped an enemy breakthrough and won him the Medal of Honor.

Harrison Summers, Staff Sergeant, Company B, 502d Parachute Infantry, 101st Airborne Division; 1st Army GO 31, 1944

Sergeant Summers won the Distinguished Service Cross for his courage during the parachute drops on D-day, 6 June 1944. Because of the widely scattered pattern of the airborne landings, Summers found himself leading only twelve men, none of them from his own unit, in an attack on a concentration of buildings—an objective originally assigned to an entire battalion. As the Americans began to advance, heavy fire drove all but Sergeant Summers to cover. He successfully circled behind the first house, kicked open the door, and killed the enemy soldiers in their firing positions. When a captain from the 82d Airborne Division tried to join Summers, enemy fire brought him down. A lieutenant then attempted to assist Summers, only to meet the same fate. Undaunted, Sergeant Summers worked his way to the back of each building in turn and successfully neutralized the entire German position with his submachine gun.

Hulon B. Whittington, Sergeant, Company I, 41st Armored Infantry, 2d Armored Division; WD GO 32, 1945

On the night of 29 July 1944, near Grimesnil, France, Squad Leader Whittington assumed command of his platoon when the platoon leader and platoon sergeant disappeared during an enemy armored attack. Whittington reorganized the defense and crawled, under fire, between gun positions to organize and rally the men. When an advancing Panzer unit attempted to break through a roadblock, he climbed aboard a tank and directed it into position to fire point-blank at the leading German tank. Its wreckage blocked the entire enemy column of over one hundred vehicles and enabled the American troops to counterattack with hand grenades, bazookas, and tanks. Sergeant Whittington then led a bayonet charge that killed large numbers of the disorganized enemy. When his platoon's medic was hit, Whittington administered first aid to the wounded men. He received the Medal of Honor for his bravery and initiative.

Korean War

Cornelius H. Charlton, Sergeant, Company C, 24th Infantry, 25th Infantry Division; Department of the Army (DA) GO 30, 1952

On 2 June 1951, Charlton's platoon attacked heavily fortified enemy positions on a ridge near Chipo-ri. After the wounding and evacuation of his platoon leader, Sergeant Charlton assumed command, rallied his soldiers, and pressed toward the enemy emplacements on the commanding ground. Eliminating two enemy positions, he continued up the slope until enemy fire pinned down his unit. Regrouping the men, he resumed his advance only to be stopped by enemy grenades. The sergeant was severely wounded, but he refused medical aid and led a third charge, taking the crest of the ridge. Attacking the last enemy position and routing the defenders, he was mortally wounded by another grenade. His gallantry and determination earned him the Medal of Honor posthumously.

Gilbert G. Collier, Corporal, Company F, 223d Infantry, 40th Infantry Division; DA GO 3, 1955

Corporal Collier was point man of a combat patrol seeking contact with the enemy near Tutayon, Korea, on the night of 19–20 July 1953. In the darkness, Collier and his patrol leader slipped and fell from a steep, sixty-foot cliff. Incapacitated by a badly sprained ankle, the officer ordered the patrol to return to the American lines. Although he had suffered a painful back injury, Corporal Collier elected to remain with his leader. As they made their way toward the American lines under the cover of darkness, they ran into an ambush. In the ensuing firefight, Collier killed two enemy soldiers but was seriously wounded and became separated from his officer. His ammunition gone, Collier met four more attackers with his bayonet, killing or wounding them. With his last bit of strength, Collier made an effort to reach and help his leader, but fell victim to his many wounds. His courage earned him the nation's highest award, the Medal of Honor.

Jerry K. Crump, Corporal, Company L, 7th Infantry, 3d Infantry Division; DA GO 68, 1952

During the night of 6–7 September 1951, a numerically superior enemy force launched an assault against Corporal Crump's platoon on Hill 284, near Ch'orwon, Korea. Crump repeatedly exposed himself to danger in order to deliver effective fire into the enemy ranks. He inflicted numerous casualties among the Communist attackers. Seeing two enemy soldiers about to capture an American machine gun, Corporal Crump charged, killing both with his bayonet and recovering the gun. As he returned to his foxhole, now occupied by four wounded members of his squad, a grenade landed among them. Crump instantly threw himself upon it, absorbing the blast with his body. His selfless disregard for his own safety earned a Medal of Honor.

John Essebagger, Jr., Corporal, Company A, 7th Infantry, 3d Infantry Division; DA GO 61, 1952

Corporal Essebagger was part of a two-squad force protecting the right flank of an American withdrawal near Popsu-dong, Korea, on 25 April 1951. Essebagger's unit repulsed several attacks by an enemy far superior in numbers. When his covering force itself had to retreat, Corporal

Essebagger chose to remain in position to cover the withdrawal. He killed or wounded several of the foe, but in enabling the American squads to reach safety, he was mortally wounded. He earned a posthumous Medal of Honor.

Charles L. Gilliland, Corporal, Company I, 7th Infantry, 3d Infantry Division; DA GO 2, 1955

On 25 April 1951, near Tongmang-ni, Korea, a numerically superior enemy force launched a determined attack against the defensive perimeter of Gilliland's company. The enemy forces pushed up a defile, killing many of the American soldiers around him. Gilliland poured a steady stream of fire into the attackers and held his position, despite a serious head wound. When the position became indefensible, his unit received orders to fall back to new defensive positions. Corporal Gilliland volunteered to remain behind to cover the withdrawal. He lost his life making certain that his comrades made good their escape. He received the Medal of Honor posthumously for demonstrating that leadership not only means "follow me," but sometimes demands the ultimate sacrifice.

Carolyn H. James, Master Sergeant, Eighth U.S. Army Headquarters, Seoul, Korea, 1952

When Carolyn James enlisted in 1945, women represented a distinct minority of the Army, and indeed the status of the Women's Army Corps (WAC) in the postwar forces was in doubt. But General Eisenhower, like General Marshall, recognized the value of capable women in freeing men from administrative jobs so that they could be available for combat. James was one of the first two WACs to serve in the theater during the Korean War, when she worked as a stenographer at Eighth Army headquarters in Seoul. While serving with the U.S. Army Air Defense Command in 1960, she became the Army's first female sergeant major.

Benito Martinez, Corporal, Company A, 27th Infantry, 25th Infantry Division; DA GO 96, 29 December 1953

Corporal Benito Martinez, a machine gunner with Company A, 27th Infantry, distinguished himself on 6 September 1952, in Satae-ri, Korea. While manning a listening post forward of the main line of resistance, his position was attacked by a hostile force of reinforced company strength. In the bitter fighting that ensued, the enemy infiltrated the defense perimeter. Corporal Martinez realized that encirclement was imminent and elected to remain at his

Detail of Benito Martinez from Sandbag Castle, *Matt Hall, c. 2001*

post to stem the onslaught. He raked the attacking troops with crippling fire, inflicting numerous casualties, and refused any attempts to rescue him because of the danger involved. Soon thereafter, the hostile forces rushed the emplacement, forcing him to withdraw with only an automatic rifle and pistol to defend himself. After a courageous six-hour stand, he called in for the last time, stating that the enemy was advancing on his position. His magnificent stand enabled friendly elements to reorganize, attack, and regain key terrain. Corporal Martinez received the Medal of Honor for his conspicuous gallantry and outstanding courage above and beyond the call of duty.

Hiroshi H. Miyamura, Corporal, Company H, 7th Infantry, 3d Infantry Division; DA GO 85, 4 November 1953

Corporal Miyamura received the Medal of Honor for his conspicuous gallantry and intrepidity above and beyond the call of duty in action against the enemy. On the night of 24 April 1951, near Taejon-ni, Korea, an enemy attack threatened to overrun Company H's position. Corporal Miyamura, a machine-gun squad leader, was aware of the imminent danger to his men and unhesitatingly engaged the enemy with a bayonet, killing approximately ten in close hand-to-hand combat. Returning to his position, he administered first aid to the wounded and directed their evacuation. As another savage assault hit the line, he manned his machine gun and delivered withering fire until he was out of ammunition. He

Corporal Hiroshi H. Miyamura, George Akimoto, 1977

ordered the squad to withdraw while he stayed behind to render the gun inoperable. Then he bayoneted his way through infiltrated enemy soldiers to a second gun emplacement and assisted in its operation. When the intensity of the attack necessitated the withdrawal of the company, Corporal Miyamura ordered his men to fall back while he remained to cover their movement. He killed more than fifty of the enemy before his ammunition ran out and he was severely wounded. He maintained his magnificent stand despite his painful wounds, continuing to repel the attack until the enemy overran his position. When last seen he was fighting ferociously against an overwhelming number of enemy soldiers.

Mitchell Red Cloud, Jr., Corporal, Company E, 19th Infantry, 24th Infantry Division; DA GO 26, 25 April 1951

On 5 November 1950, Corporal Red Cloud was in position on the point of a ridge near Ch'onghyon, Korea, immediately in front of the company command post. He gave the alarm as Chinese Communist troops charged from a brush-covered area less than a hundred feet from him. Springing to his feet, he delivered devastating point-blank automatic rifle fire into the advancing enemy. His accurate and intense fire checked this assault and gained time for the company to consolidate its defense. With utter fearlessness he maintained his firing position until severely wounded by enemy fire. Refusing assistance, he pulled himself to his feet, wrapped his arm around a tree, and continued his deadly fire again, until he was fatally wounded. His heroic act stopped the enemy from overrunning his company's position and gained time for reorganization and evacuation of the wounded. Corporal Red Cloud's mother received his posthumous Medal of Honor on 4 April 1951 from the Chairman of the Joint Chiefs of Staff, General Omar N. Bradley.

Vietnam Era

Webster Anderson, Sergeant First Class, Battery A, 2d Battalion, 320th Artillery, 101st Airborne Division; DA GO 80, 1969

Webster Anderson, then a staff sergeant, was serving as Chief of Section in Battery A near Tam Ky on 15 October 1967. During the early morning hours a determined North Vietnamese infantry unit, supported by heavy mortar, recoilless rifle, rocket-propelled grenade, and automatic-weapons fire, attacked his battery. When the initial enemy assault breached the defensive perimeter, Anderson climbed the exposed parapet to lead the defense. He directed effective howitzer fire against the attackers and personally killed a number attempting to overrun his position. During the action Sergeant Anderson was severely wounded by grenades. Unable to stand, he propped himself against the parapet and continued to direct fire and to encourage his men. When an enemy grenade landed within the gun pit near a wounded member of his crew, Anderson, heedless of his own safety, crawled to the grenade and tried to throw it. It exploded in midair, grievously wounding him. Although now only partially conscious, he refused medical attention and continued to rally his men in the defense of their position. Sergeant Anderson's actions earned him the Medal of Honor.

Roy P. Benavidez, Staff Sergeant, Detachment B–56, 5th Special Forces Group (Airborne), 1st Special Forces; DA GO 8, 1981

A Texas native of Mexican–Yaqui Indian descent, Staff Sergeant Benavidez received word on 2 May 1968 that a twelve-man insertion team was in trouble west of Loch Ninh, near the Cambodian border. Three helicopters had already attempted to extract the men but could not penetrate heavy enemy fire. Benavidez volunteered to join a second rescue attempt. When his helicopter arrived at the scene, he jumped out alone and ran seventy-five meters under intense fire to reach the location of the surviving team members. Wounded several times, he nevertheless managed to organize survivors and direct defensive fire while the rescue helicopter landed in the perimeter. Through a withering hail of bullets, he dragged several team members to the aircraft. He then ran back to the dead team leader's body to recover top secret documents before they fell into enemy hands, only to be wounded again, this time in the abdomen and back. Moments later, the rescue helicopter, riddled by enemy bullets, shuddered and crashed to the ground. Although critically wounded himself, Benavidez made his way to the crashed helicopter, pulled out the survivors, and organized a new defensive perimeter. He kept up the spirits of his wounded comrades, distributing water and first aid while running back and forth under intense fire. After a second helicopter arrived, he dragged several men to the aircraft; when a Communist soldier broke into the perimeter Benavidez killed the man in hand-to-hand combat. After one final trip to the perimeter, making sure that all classified materials were accounted for, he returned to the helicopter and collapsed on the deck. For his heroic efforts Staff Sergeant Benavidez received a Distinguished Service Cross, which the Army upgraded to a Medal of Honor in 1981.

Glenn H. English, Jr., Staff Sergeant, Company E, 3d Battalion, 3d Infantry, 173d Airborne Brigade; DA GO 39, 1974

On 7 September 1970, in Phu My District, Vietnam, Staff Sergeant English was riding in the lead armored personnel carrier in a four-vehicle column when an enemy mine exploded in front of his vehicle. As the vehicle swerved, a concealed enemy force opened fire with automatic weapons and antitank grenades, striking the vehicle several times and setting it on fire. English escaped the disabled vehicle and then led his unit in a vigorous assault on the entrenched enemy position. This prompt and courageous action routed the enemy and saved his unit from destruction. After the assault, he heard the cries of three men still trapped inside the vehicle. Paying no heed to warn-

ings that the ammunition and fuel in the burning personnel carrier might explode at any time, English raced to the vehicle and climbed inside to rescue his wounded comrades. As he was lifting one of the men to safety, the vehicle exploded, mortally wounding him and the man he was attempting to save. Staff Sergeant English's conspicuous gallantry and intrepidity in action at the cost of his life were an inspiration to his comrades. He received a posthumous Medal of Honor.

Mildred C. Kelly, Command Sergeant Major, Aberdeen Proving Ground, Maryland, 1974

Mildred C. Kelly, a former high school teacher from Tennessee, enlisted in the Women's Army Corps in 1950 at a time when black women could find few opportunities in American society. Having completed her basic and advanced training at Fort Lee, Virginia, she served tours of duty as a personnel administrator at Fort Knox, Fort Benjamin Harrison, Fort McClellan, Fort Hood, and the U.S. Army Ordnance Center at Aberdeen Proving Ground, as well as a two-year deployment to Japan. In 1971 she and five male first sergeants advised Army Chief of Staff William C. Westmoreland on proposed guidelines for non-commissioned officers in the emerging all-volunteer Army. When she became command sergeant major at the Aberdeen Proving Ground in June 1974, she became the first woman to hold the highest-ranking enlisted job at any major Army installation with a predominantly male population. She also became the first black woman to earn the rank of command sergeant major. During her distinguished career, she earned the Army's Meritorious Service Medal, two Army Commendation Medals, the National Defense Service Medal with oak leaf cluster, and the Good Conduct Medal with eight awards.

Paul Ronald Lambers, Sergeant, Company A, 2d Battalion, 27th Infantry, 25th Infantry Division; DA GO 79, 1969

Sergeant Lambers' unit, 3d Platoon, Company A, had just established a night defensive position astride a suspected enemy infiltration route on 20 August 1968, when it came under attack by a battalion of Viet Cong. When his platoon leader fell seriously wounded, Lambers assumed command and, disregarding intense enemy fire, abandoned the safety of his position to secure a radio and direct the defense. Running through a hail of bullets, he reached the 90-mm. recoilless rifle crew whose weapon was malfunctioning. He assisted in its repair and then directed canister fire at point-blank range against enemy troops who had breached the defensive wire. When the enemy charged the position, knocking out the recoilless rifle, Lambers single-handedly drove them off with Claymore mines and grenades. He then moved from position to position, providing assistance where the pressure was heaviest and inspiring the men to do their utmost. During the operation he continued to direct artillery and helicopter gunship fire, sometimes to within five meters of his own position. For his brave leadership, Sergeant Lambers was awarded the Medal of Honor.

Clarence Eugene Sasser, Specialist Fifth Class, Headquarters and Headquarters Company, 3d Battalion, 60th Infantry, 9th Infantry Division; DA GO 26, 1969

Sasser, then a private first class, won the Medal of Honor for his actions in Dinh Tuong Province, Vietnam, on 10 January 1968. An aidman serving with Company A, Sasser participated in an airmobile assault that came under heavy fire from fortified enemy positions on three sides of the landing zone. Over thirty men became casualties within a few minutes of landing. Sasser repeatedly ran across an open paddy through a hail of fire to locate and assist the wounded. Despite wounds to one shoulder and both legs, he refused medical attention for himself and continued to search for additional casualties. In all, Sasser spent five hours wounded in the mud, actively caring for his fellow soldiers before they were finally evacuated.

Fred William Zabitosky, Staff Sergeant, 5th Special Forces Group (Airborne), 1st Special Forces; DA GO 27, 1969

On 19 February 1968, Sergeant Zabitosky was an assistant team leader on a nine-man Special Forces long-range reconnaissance patrol deep in enemy-controlled territory in South Vietnam. Suddenly, a numerically superior force of North Vietnamese soldiers attacked his patrol. Exposing himself to a hail of enemy bullets, Zabitosky organized his team into a perimeter and directed their defensive fire. Realizing the gravity of the situation, he ordered his patrol to move to a landing zone for helicopter extraction while he covered their withdrawal with rifle fire and grenades. Rejoining the patrol, he then supervised the positioning of each man to meet the increasing enemy pressure. Heartened by his leadership, the team held the enemy at bay until the arrival of tactical air support and a helicopter extraction team. As his comrades began to board the helicopters, Zabitosky remained behind to adjust helicopter gunship strikes. After boarding one of the rescue helicopters, he positioned himself in the door, delivering fire on the enemy as the ship took off. Engulfed in a hail of bullets, the helicopter spun out of control and crashed, knocking Zabitosky unconscious. Recovering consciousness, he ignored his extremely painful injuries and, heedless of the danger of exploding ordnance and fuel, pulled the severely wounded pilot from the blazing wreckage. He made repeated attempts to rescue his patrol members but was driven back by the intense heat. Despite his serious burns and crushed ribs, he carried and dragged the unconscious pilot through a curtain of enemy fire to within ten feet of a hovering rescue helicopter before collapsing. For his courage and devotion to duty Staff Sergeant Zabitosky received the Medal of Honor.

Somalia

Gary I. Gordon, Master Sergeant, U.S. Army Special Operations Command; DA GO 14, 1994

On 3 October 1993, Master Sergeant Gordon was serving as Sniper Team leader, U.S. Army Special Operations Command with Task Force Ranger in Mogadishu, Somalia. His sniper team provided precision fires from the lead helicopter during an assault and at two helicopter crash sites, despite intense enemy automatic weapons and rocket-propelled grenade fires. When Master Sergeant Gordon learned that ground forces were not immediately available to secure the second crash site, he and another sniper unhesitatingly volunteered for insertion to protect four critically wounded personnel there, despite being well aware that large numbers of enemy were converging on the site. After his third request for insertion, Gordon received permission to perform this volunteer mission. Forced to land one hundred meters south of the crash site, Gordon and his fellow sniper, armed only with sniper rifles and pistols, fought their way through a dense maze of shanties and shacks to reach the critically injured crew. After pulling the wounded men from the wreckage, Gordon and his team member established a perimeter around the downed aircraft. Gordon then used his long-range rifle and sidearm to kill an undetermined number of attackers until he depleted his ammunition. Gordon recovered more ammunition from the downed helicopter and, after giving some of it to the dazed pilot, returned to the perimeter to fend off the approaching enemy personnel. After his team member was fatally wounded and his own rifle ammunition exhausted, Master Sergeant Gordon returned to the wreckage, recovered a rifle with the last five rounds of ammunition, and gave it to the pilot with the words, "Good luck." Then, armed only with a pistol, Gordon continued to fight until he was fatally wounded. His extraordinary heroism and devotion to duty saved the pilot's life. For his remarkable display of courage Gordon posthumously received the Medal of Honor.

Randall D. Shughart, Sergeant First Class, U.S. Army Special Operations Command; DA GO 14, 1994

On 3 October 1993, while serving as a Sniper Team member of the U.S. Army Special Operations Command with Task Force RANGER in Mogadishu, Somalia, Sergeant First Class Shughart joined Master Sergeant Gordon in providing precision fires from the lead helicopter during an assault and at two helicopter crash sites despite intense automatic-weapons and rocket-propelled grenade fire. While providing suppressive fires at the second crash site, Shughart and his team leader learned that ground forces were not immediately available to secure the site. They unhesitatingly volunteered for insertion to protect the four critically wounded personnel despite the growing number of enemy personnel closing in on the site. After their third request, Shughart and his team leader received permission. Forced to land one hundred meters south of the crash site, Shughart and his team leader, armed only with sniper rifles and pistols, fought their way through a dense maze of shanties and shacks to reach the critically injured crew. After pulling the pilot and the other wounded men from the wreckage, Shughart and his fellow sniper established a perimeter around the downed aircraft. Shughart then used his long-range rifle and sidearm to kill an undetermined number of attackers. Sergeant First Class Shughart continued his protective fire until he depleted his ammunition and was fatally wounded. His extraordinary heroism and devotion to duty saved the pilot's life. For his remarkable display of courage Sergeant First Class Shughart posthumously received the Medal of Honor.

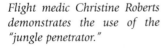
Flight medic Christine Roberts demonstrates the use of the "jungle penetrator."

Kosovo

Christine Roberts, Sergeant, 50th Medical Company, Task Force Falcon, 2001

Sergeant Roberts, a flight medic, was stationed with Task Force Falcon in Kosovo when she received word on 28 June 2001 that a pair of American soldiers from the 1st Cavalry Brigade Reconnaissance Troop had triggered a land mine while on patrol. From a UH–60 helicopter, Roberts used a jungle penetrator to lower herself 200 feet through thick trees to reach the two men on a steep mountain slope. Carrying 100 pounds of emergency medical equipment and weapons, she made her way through the undergrowth, using a stick to probe for mines as she walked. Upon reaching the two, she discovered that one soldier, Sergeant Richard P. Casini, had stepped on an antipersonnel mine and had lost most of his right foot. Despite having rigged a tourniquet to stanch the bleeding, Casini was only minutes from going into shock. Roberts improved the tourniquet and then helped Casini limp to the harness on the jungle penetrator, which then lifted the wounded man to safety. Careful not to detonate any mines, Roberts extracted the second soldier and then herself. The UH–60 raced for home, and minutes later Sergeant Casini was undergoing treatment in the Camp Bondsteel hospital. Surgeons were unable to save his foot, but due to the extraordinary effort of Sergeant Roberts he did not lose his life. For her bravery and coolness in a demanding situation, Roberts received the Soldier's Medal, the highest peacetime decoration a soldier can receive.

Pentagon

Christopher D. Braman, Staff Sergeant, Office of the Administrative Assistant to the Secretary of the Army, 2001

Braman received the Soldier's Medal for heroism above and beyond the call of duty on 11 September 2001, when terrorists used a hijacked airliner, with over thirty thousand pounds of jet fuel to attack the Pentagon. Upon impact a thunderous explosion and a horrific fire killed scores of military and civilian personnel, injured hundreds of others, and left others in a state of shock. Staff Sergeant Braman rushed toward the hole in the building caused by the plane's impact with a fire extinguisher and called out for survivors. He entered the impact area and without regard for his personal safety helped rescue numerous people from the smoke and fire. In one instance, through fire and smoke that almost completely blocked visibility, he heard a woman calling for help. Risking death by smoke inhalation, he continued forward, finally found the woman, and ensured that she reached safety. His unyielding devotion to his fellow soldiers and civilians undoubtedly saved lives and showed America's resolve to overcome acts of terrorism.

The examples above extol two kinds of heroism. The solitary NCO, acting in the frenzy of the moment, reveals a rash courage that sometimes defies logic, inspires awe, and often serves as the catalyst that carries a stalled attack to success even at the cost of his own life.

Equally celebrated, however, is the brave small-unit leader who, with cool determination, directs his men through deadly fire in the heat of battle to gain the objective against all odds and with a minimum of casualties. The first is the act of a brave individual soldier; the second, no less brave, demonstrates the NCO's sense of unit cohesion and teamwork, the aim of professional training. The Army and the nation have been well served by both kinds of heroes.

APPENDIX C

SUGGESTIONS FOR FURTHER READING

Military history is essential for the serving professional, whether for recreation or serious study. In either case, such reading enhances professional development by providing a greater understanding of the development of the Army's roles, traditions, and capabilities. Even for the casual reader, these accounts of NCO experiences in peace and war offer valuable practical lessons. The editors of this volume highly recommend the following books, including two works of fiction. Not only do they provide an accurate account of NCO life throughout the history of the Army, but they are well written, accessible, and interesting. Many other titles could be added, but these offer a good starting point.

Ambrose, Stephen E. *Band of Brothers: E Company, 506th Regiment, 101st Airborne from Normandy to Hitler's Eagle's Nest.* New York: Simon and Schuster, 1992. Famous account by the well-known World War II historian of one company's experience during that war.

Armstrong, William H. *Major McKinley: William McKinley and the Civil War.* Kent, Ohio: Kent State University Press, 2000. Civil War experiences of a quartermaster sergeant who became President of the United States.

Atkinson, Rick. *Crusade: The Untold Story of the Persian Gulf War.* Boston: Houghton Mifflin, 1993. Comprehensive account, covering political as well as military perspective.

Bainbridge, William G. *Top Sergeant: The Life and Times of Sergeant Major of the Army William G. Bainbridge.* New York: Fawcett Columbine, 1995. Autobiography of the fifth Sergeant Major of the Army, covering his experiences in World War II, role in restructuring NCOES, and service as SMA.

Beaudot, William J. K., and Lance J. Herdegen. *An Irishman in the Iron Brigade: The Civil War Memoirs of James P. Sullivan, Sergt., Company K, 6th Wisconsin Volunteers.* New York: Fordham University Press, 1993. Previously serialized in 1880s; covers entire war.

Benavidez, Roy P. *The Three Wars of Roy Benavidez.* San Antonio, Tex.: Corona Publishing Co., 1986. Memoir by the Medal of Honor winner.

Bill, Alfred H. *Valley Forge: The Making of an Army.* New York: Harper, 1952. An account of daily life at Valley Forge during the winter of 1777–1778.

Bolton, Charles K. *The Private Soldier Under Washington.* Williamstown, Mass.: Corner House, 1976. A discussion of life in the ranks during the American Revolution.

Bowden, Mark. *Black Hawk Down: A Story of Modern War.* New York: Atlantic Monthly Press, 1999. The battle in Mogadishu from the soldier's perspective; based on numerous interviews and now the subject of a major motion picture.

Cash, John A., John N. Albright, and Allan W. Sandstrum. *Seven Firefights in Vietnam.* Washington, D.C.: Government Printing Office, 1970. A classic account of small-unit actions in the Vietnam War.

Charlton, John B., and Robert G. Carter. *The Old Sergeant's Story: Fighting Indians & Bad Men in Texas in 1870 to 1876.* Mattituck, N.Y.: J. M. Carroll & Co., 1982. A personal narrative of a cavalry sergeant during the period of the Indian wars.

Coffman, Edward M. *The Old Army: A Portrait of the American Army in Peacetime, 1784–1898.* New York: Oxford University Press, 1986. The U.S. Army during its first century, including recruitment, composition, training, and other aspects.

Cornish, Dudley T. *The Sable Arm: Negro Troops in the Union Army, 1861–1865.* New York: Norton & Co., 1966. The role of the black soldier in the Civil War.

Crane, Stephen. *The Red Badge of Courage*. New York: Penguin, 1995. The classic novel of an infantryman in Civil War combat. Crane himself did not serve, but he talked to many who did, giving his account an uncommon realism for a Civil War battle piece.

Dobak, William A., and Thomas D. Phillips. *The Black Regulars, 1866–1898*. Norman: University of Oklahoma Press, 2001. Covers daily details of Army existence, reasons for enlisting, previous service, relations among troops and civilians, reasons for getting out, and post-Army lives.

Fehrenbach, T. R. *This Kind of War: A Study in Unpreparedness*. Washington, D.C.: Center of Military History, 1990. One man's impassioned view of the consequences of unpreparedness during the Korean War; written from small-unit perspective and regarded by many as best study of the conflict.

Fisher, Ernest F., Jr. *Guardians of the Republic: A History of the Noncommissioned Officer Corps of the U.S. Army*. New York: Ballantine Books, 1994. Chronicles the rise of the NCO Corps from colonial times to the present; especially good on personnel policies.

Gillespie, Mark F., et al. *The Sergeants Major of the Army*. Washington, D.C.: Center of Military History, 1995. A new edition will appear shortly.

Gugeler, Russell A. *Combat Actions in Korea*. Washington, D.C.: Government Printing Office, 1970. A series of vignettes focusing on the role of platoon- and company-level fighting in Korea.

Hogan, David W., Jr. *225 Years of Service: The U.S. Army, 1775–2000*. Washington, D.C.: Center of Military History, 2000. Brief history of the contributions the Army has made to the nation throughout its history.

Holm, Jeanne. *Women in the Military: An Unfinished Revolution*, rev. ed. San Rafael, Calif.: Presidio Press, 1982. History and role of women in armed forces. Latest edition goes through Persian Gulf War.

Infantry in Battle. Washington, D.C.: Infantry Journal, Inc., 1934. A series of vignettes concerning infantry actions during World War I.

Jones, James. *The Thin Red Line*. New York: Charles Scribner's Sons, 1962. Another classic novel of combat in the jungles of Guadalcanal during World War II by a former NCO.

Keegan, John. *The Face of Battle*. New York: Vintage Books, 1977. Classic account of combat at the enlisted-soldier level in the battles of Agincourt, Waterloo, and the Somme.

Lee, David D. *Sergeant York: An American Hero*. Lexington: University Press of Kentucky, 1985. Biography of a hero of World War I.

Linderman, Gerald F. *Embattled Courage: The Experience of Combat in the American Civil War*. New York: Free Press, 1987. Uses personal accounts to show centrality and meaning of courage in the ethos of the Civil War soldier.

Lowe, Percival G. *Five Years a Dragoon ('49 to '54) and Other Adventures on the Great Plains*. Norman: University of Oklahoma Press, 1965. A personal narrative by an NCO in the period after the Mexican War.

MacDonald, Charles B., and Sidney T. Mathews. *Three Battles: Arnaville, Altuzzo, and Schmidt. U.S. Army in World War II*. Washington, D.C.: Government Printing Office, 1952. A classic study of small-unit actions in Germany and Italy during 1944.

Mauldin, Bill. *Up Front*. New York: Henry Holt, 1945. An insightful look at the average soldier in World War II.

Moore, Harold G., and Joseph L. Galloway. *We Were Soldiers Once, and Young…* New York: Random House, 1992. Detailed, personal view of a unit going into combat in Vietnam for the first time; subject of a popular motion picture.

Moskos, Charles C., Jr. *The American Enlisted Man: The Rank and File in Today's Military*. New York: Russell Sage Foundation, 1970. The classic examination of the social, economic, and educational changes in American enlisted personnel in the post–World War II era.

Murphy, Audie. *To Hell and Back*. New York: Henry Holt, 1949. The memoir of the most decorated soldier of World War II.

Nalty, Bernard. *Strength for the Fight: A History of Black Americans in the Military*. New York: The Free Press, 1986. An authoritative survey of race relations in the U.S. armed forces since the Revolution.

Rickey, Don, Jr. *Forty Miles a Day on Beans and Hay: The Enlisted Soldier Fighting the Indian Wars.* Norman: University of Oklahoma Press, 1963. The classic story of the enlisted man in the Indian wars.

Smith, George W., and Charles Judah, eds. *Chronicles of the Gringos: The U.S. Army in the Mexican War, 1846–1848: Accounts of Eyewitnesses and Combatants.* Albuquerque: University of New Mexico Press, 1968. The Mexican War as described by soldiers who fought it.

Stallings, Lawrence. *The Doughboys: The Story of the AEF, 1917–1918.* New York: Harper, 1963. Traces the enlisted man of World War I from training camp to battlefield.

Terry, Wallace, ed. *Bloods: An Oral History of the Vietnam War.* New York: Random House, 1984. Personal, down-to-earth accounts by twenty black soldiers who served during the Vietnam War.

Westover, John G. *Combat Support in Korea.* Washington, D.C.: Government Printing Office, 1986. A series of vignettes on the role of combat support and combat service support soldiers in Korea.

Wiley, Bell I. *The Life of Billy Yank: The Common Soldier of the Union.* Indianapolis, Ind.: Bobbs-Merrill, 1952. The classic description of the common soldier in the Civil War armies based on letters, diaries, and private journals.

———. *The Life of Johnny Reb: The Common Soldier of the Confederacy.* Indianapolis, Ind.: Bobbs-Merrill, 1943.